**POWER AND GOVERNMENTS
AN INTRODUCTION TO POLITICS**

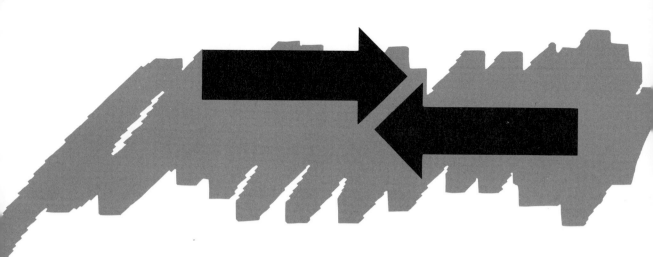

POWER AND GOVERNMENTS
AN INTRODUCTION TO POLITICS

FRED H. WILLHOITE

Coe College

with the assistance of Margaret I. Haupt

Coe College

Brooks/Cole Publishing Company
Pacific Grove, California

Brooks/Cole Publishing Company
A Division of Wadsworth, Inc.

© 1988 by Wadsworth, Inc., Belmont, California 94002.

All rights reserved. No part of this book may be reproduced, stored in a retrieval system, or transcribed, in any form or by any means—electronic, mechanical, photocopying, recording, or otherwise—without the prior written permission of the publisher, Brooks/Cole Publishing Company, Pacific Grove, California 93950, a division of Wadsworth, Inc.

Printed in the United States of America
10 9 8 7 6 5 4 3 2

Library of Congress Cataloging-in-Publication Data
Willhoite, Fred H.
   Power and governments : an introduction to politics / Fred H. Willhoite, with the assistance of Margaret I. Haupt.
      p.   cm.
   Includes index.
   ISBN 0-534-08442-7 :
   1. Power (Social sciences)   2. Political science.   I. Haupt, Margaret I.   II. Title.
JC330.W55 1987
306'.2—dc19

Sponsoring Editor: Cynthia C. Stormer   *Project Development Editors:* John Bergez, Stephanie Mischak   *Editorial Assistants:* Linda Loba, Mary Ann Zuzow   *Production Editor:* Phyllis Larimore   *Manuscript Editor:* Meredy Amyx   *Permissions Editor:* Carline Haga   *Interior and Cover Design:* Katherine Minerva   *Art Coordinator:* Sue C. Howard   *Interior Illustration:* Accurate Art, Inc.   *Photo Researcher:* Marquita Flemming   *Typesetting:* Graphic Composition, Inc., Athens, Georgia   *Cover Printing:* Phoenix Color Corp., Long Island City, New York   *Printing and Binding:* Maple-Vail Book Mfg. Group, Binghamton, New York

Photo Credits
Page 20, The Oriental Institute, University of Chicago; **36,** A. Degean/Sygma; **76,** UPI/Bettman Newsphotos; **89,** J-P Laffont/Sygma; **123,** Roger Malloch/Magnum Photos, Inc.; **149,** Peter Souza—The White House; **162,** UPI/Bettman Newsphotos; **210,** Henri Cartier-Bresson/Magnum Photos, Inc.; **231,** National Archives; **267,** Reuters/Bettman Newsphotos; **289,** Tennenbaum/Sygma; **316,** Reuters/Bettman Newsphotos; **328,** Marc Ribaud/Magnum Photos, Inc.; **345,** Philip Jones Griffiths/Magnum Photos, Inc.; **355,** The Metropolitan Museum of Art; **359,** J-P Laffont/Sygma

To Lois, a truly *benign* power

PREFACE

The title of this book describes as accurately as possible its coverage and contents. The dual focus is on political power—its origins, nature, forms, pursuit, and uses—and on how the major types of present-day governments organize and exercise power in relations with their citizens and with other sovereign states.

Among political scientists, how to introduce students to the study of politics remains a contentious issue on which no consensus is likely to emerge. This book aims at avoiding two approaches that I find unsatisfactory: either a semiencyclopedic collection of political and governmental facts with no clear connections among major topics, or the kind of thematic treatment that seems designed mainly to convert readers to a particular normative-ideological view of politics.

In contrast to the encyclopedic approach, this book does have a strong theme. All of its explanations and analyses of both domestic and international politics are grounded in a single explicit premise: because of their nature and social circumstances, human beings persistently seek to gain and retain power, defined as the capacity to produce intended and foreseen effects on other people. Consistent use of the power-competition theme ties together and places within a comprehensible context the multitude of subjects, details, and historical and contemporary examples included in the text.

Unlike some "thematic" texts, however, this book is not intended as an exercise in partisan or ideological persuasion. Its main objective is to help curious readers acquire basic knowledge and understanding of the complex and confusing phenomena of politics and government. It deals with many controversial topics, such as political ideologies, revolution, and the causes of war, but with the conscious aim of analyzing them in terms of empirical evidence and logical argument. I'm sure we all wish that the political world were other than it is, at least in some ways, but students need first of all to confront its defining traits and features. Focusing on realistic explanation and analysis provides a valid and important way of helping students begin to make some sense of the booming, buzzing confusion of political life.

Organization

The five parts of this book are arranged so as to clarify and emphasize the central theme and to enable students to use a growing inventory of political terms, concepts, and information. In addition to defining some basic terms and briefly describing the scope of political science, the first chapter suggests three lines of argument supporting the fundamental premise of the book. Some of the material, especially the attempted reconstruction of the origins and cultural evolution of government and the state, is somewhat out of the ordinary for political science texts. However, most of the great political theorists, from Plato to Marx, have speculated on the origins of social and political structures, and questions in that vein occur spontaneously to inquisitive beginning students. This empirically based but necessarily speculative discussion also provides important support for the central premise and related emphases in the text. The other chapters in Part One attempt to make the power concept useful for analysis by sorting out basic types of political power and strategies of competing for it and by explaining significant links between power and political ideas. The resulting types and categories are consistently and persistently employed in the analysis of all major topics.

Part Two is the explanatory core of the book, focusing on the three major types of governmental systems in the contemporary world: constitutional democracy, authoritarianism, and totalitarianism. The chapters in this part describe the principal ways in which each variety of government organizes and employs the types of power, and strategies of competing for power, described in Part One.

In Part Three the analysis extends to the international arena. It focuses mainly on the development of the international state system, the meanings and significance of the balance of power among states, and the nature of international conflict and cooperation.

A distinctive feature of this text is its relatively extended analysis of revolution, comprising the two chapters of Part Four. The scope of this treatment reflects the momentous and continuing impact of revolutionary phenomena on the politics of the twentieth century. Revolution is also a topic that is inherently intriguing to students. In addition, it has probably generated more mythical and wishful thinking about politics in the modern era than any other subject and seems especially to require an analysis that focuses on actual methods of struggling for and using power in revolutionary and postrevolutionary situations.

The brief concluding Part Five is overtly normative. It is closely linked, however, to the preceding empirical, analytical chapters. Its purpose is not to tell students what they should or must believe and feel about politics but to encourage them to think hard and long about developing personal responses to the knowledge and understanding of political life that they have begun to acquire.

Audience and Features

This book is designed primarily for college students in introductory political science courses. It should also be useful for upperclass political science majors trying to gain an overview of disciplinary subject matter and to develop analytical and critical skills.

It is *not* intended only or even mainly for potential political scientists; its ideal reader is anyone who really wants to become that too-often mythical but indispensable person, the informed citizen. For that reason, the book makes considerable use of terminology and ideas that frequently appear in political journalism—with an emphasis on making them as precise as possible and rejecting some common usages as shallow, misleading, or both. Terminology doesn't need to be esoteric to promote thinking that goes well beyond the surface appearances conveyed by daily news reports. As the chapter notes make clear, I am deeply indebted to the research of many political and social scientists, as well as that of scholars in several other academic disciplines.

Two features of the text are especially designed to help students master its most important concepts and information. Key terms are printed in boldface type, usually when they first appear, and are listed for review at the end of each chapter. Comprehending those terms in context should amount to understanding the chapter in which they appear.

The second study aid is an extensive, alphabetically organized glossary at the end of the book. It fully defines frequently used vocabulary that is important for political analysis and comprehension.

In a general introductory course, an important advantage of using a text that deals with large, fundamental, and controversial questions is the endless opportunities it provides for assigning a variety of supplementary readings, ranging from classic thinkers such as Plato and Hobbes to polemical and professional articles on current political topics. Relevant films and videotapes also abound and will inevitably multiply. With all supplementary materials it should be possible, more or less subtly, to make connections between the enduring categories, problems, and issues considered in the text and their exemplification in present-day political dilemmas and debates.

Preface

Acknowledgments

At this point acknowledgments are in order. First and foremost, credit must go to my close and treasured colleague Margaret Haupt. She was my prime consultant on each chapter as the manuscript slowly grew, and hers was the major role in producing materials and ideas on international politics, especially for chapters 10 and 11.

I am grateful to Hiram Caton, of Griffith University in Australia, and to John Strate, of Wayne State University, for carefully reading chapters 1 through 9 and offering a number of helpful criticisms, corrections, and suggestions. I would also like to thank my former colleague in the Coe foreign language department, Alexy Almasov, for his critical but appreciative reading of chapters 8 and 9. A number of conscientious reviewers for Brooks/Cole contributed immeasurably to the process of slowly transforming this project from a basic conception of politics into full-blown analysis and detailed explanation. Their perceptive comments persuaded me on many points, large and small, that their judgment and information were superior to mine. I am truly grateful for their indispensable contributions.

Erika Linden Smith, Coe '86, showed great industry and ingenuity in finding answers to many factual questions. Time after time, Mrs. Diane Howard, of the Coe support staff, patiently, perceptively, and efficiently turned my heavily marked manuscripts into beautifully typed new or revised chapters. Mrs. Mary Miskimen's skill with the word processor was extremely helpful in putting most of the package together for the first time. Reviewers of the text were: Roger Anderson, Bowling Green State University; Douglas Brown, Arizona Western College; Jerry Bursey, Northeastern University; Kristina Cline, Riverside City College; John Culver, California State Polytechnic University; Charles Cutter, San Diego State University; Larry Elowitz, Georgia College; Herbert Levine, University of Southwestern Louisiana (emeritus); Marvin Rogers, University of Missouri, Columbia; Brian Wallace, Capital University; Truman Wood, Mankato State University; and David Woodard, Clemson University. My editors at Brooks/Cole, and most especially John Bergez, offered invaluable detailed suggestions for improving the understandability and attractiveness of the book. Other indispensable Brooks/Cole helpers with this project were Cindy Stormer, Phyllis Larimore, Stephanie Mischak, Meredy Amyx, Linda Loba, Mary Ann Zuzow, Sue Howard, Katherine Minerva, and, not least, Marquita Flemming, who first decided that it was worth doing. I'm extremely grateful to all these talented people.

In a broader perspective, I would like to express my appreciation to Peter Corning, of Palo Alto, California, and Roger Masters, of Dartmouth College, for many years of stimulation, conversations, and correspondence concerning the nature of evolutionary theory and its relevance to our understanding of human nature and politics. Only small fragments of those concerns can be reflected in a text intended mainly for introductory students, but the influence of these distant professional colleagues has been substantial. I know that they have some important disagreements with my ideas about human nature, cultural evolution, and politics. They have long inspired me, though, by their tremendous scholarly energy and dedication to reformulating the study of politics as a genuine life science. My intellectual debt is beyond payment; shortcomings and errors in understanding, interpretation, and presentation are entirely my own.

Fred H. Willhoite

CONTENTS

PART ONE   POLITICAL POWER   1

ONE   POWER AND THE ORIGINS OF POLITICS   3

Two Kinds of Politics   4
Power Defined   5
Governing and Governments   6
A Power-Oriented Perspective on Politics   7
Political Science: The Study of Power   9
    Subfields of Political Science   10
    Related Disciplines   11
Why the Pursuit of Political Power?   12
    The Lessons of Experience   13
    Political Theorists on Human Nature and Power   15
    The Evolution of Political Power   17
Summary   22
Review List of Key Terms   23
Notes   24

TWO   COMPETING FOR POWER   25

Types of Political Power   27
    Coercion   27
    Inducement   29
    Persuasion   31
    Authority   33
    Combinations of Types of Power   38
Strategies of Competition for Power   39
    Cooperation   39
    Toleration   42
    Domination   43
    Elimination   45

Summary 48
Review List of Key Terms 50
Notes 50

THREE   POWER AND POLITICAL IDEAS 52

The Nature of Ideology 54
Ideology and Interests 56
    Reductionist Views of Ideology 56
    Ideology as Personal Conviction 57
    A Modified View 58
Functions of Worldview Ideologies 59
    Orientation 59
    Legitimation 60
    Delegitimation 60
Worldview Ideologies: Some Basic Categories 62
Ideology and Power: The Case of Nationalism 64
    Origins and Effects of European Nationalism 65
    The Spread of Nationalism 67
    Nationalism and Political Power 71
    Ethnonationalism and Political Conflict 74
Summary 76
Review List of Key Terms 78
Notes 78

PART TWO   POWER AND GOVERNMENTAL SYSTEMS 81

FOUR   FUNCTIONS AND TYPES OF GOVERNMENT 83

Basic Functions of Government: Essential Similarities 84
    External Protection 84
    Enforcing Law and Order 86
    Self-Protection 87
    Economic Management 88
    Cultural Reinforcement 90
Bureaucracy and Governmental Functions 92
Basic Types of Government: Important Differences 95
    Methods of Classification 95
    Basic Categories 97
Summary 101
Review List of Key Terms 102
Notes 103

FIVE CONSTITUTIONAL DEMOCRACY: DEVELOPMENT, PRECONDITIONS, ELEMENTS 104

Development of Democracy   106
    Ancient Democracy   106
    English Constitutionalism   107
    Constitutionalism and Modern Democracy   109
Preconditions of Democracy   111
    Patterns of Historical Development   112
    Socioeconomic Pluralism   114
    Level of Economic Development   115
    Conflict among Communities   116
    Beliefs and Commitments of Political Activists   117
Universal Elements of Democracy   118
    An Effective Constitution   118
    Representative and Accountable Government   120
    Qualified Majority Rule   121
    Multiple Political Parties   123
    Organized Interest Groups   124
Summary   126
Review List of Key Terms   128
Notes   128

SIX CONSTITUTIONAL DEMOCRACY: TYPES, PROBLEMS, STRENGTHS 130

Types of Constitutional Democracy   131
    Structures of Central Government   131
    Territorial Organization   142
Problems of Democracy: Factions and the Economy   145
    Critics of the Market Economy   146
    Advocates of the Market Economy   146
Strengths of Democracy   148
    Personal Freedom and Autonomy   148
    Governmental Responsiveness   149
    Absence of Mass Coercion   150
    Peaceful Change   150
Summary   151
Review List of Key Terms   153
Notes   154

SEVEN AUTHORITARIANISM 155

Classification   156
    The Third World   158

Why Authoritarianism?   159
    Hobbes and the State-of-Nature Problem   160
    The "Political Lag" Explanation   161
Types of Authoritarian Government   163
    Traditional Authoritarianism   165
    Personal-Rule Authoritarianism   168
    Corporate-Rule Authoritarianism   173
    Party-Rule Authoritarianism   178
Problems of Legitimacy   180
Summary   182
Review List of Key Terms   183
Notes   184

EIGHT   TOTALITARIANISM: IDEOLOGICAL DOMINATION   186

The "Totalitarianism" Controversy   188
Two Phases of Totalitarian Development   191
    Revolutionizing Totalitarianism   191
    Institutionalized Totalitarianism   192
Why Totalitarianism?   193
Domination   195
    Winning Supreme Power   195
    Coercion   197
    Ideological Monopoly   199
    Indoctrination   209
Summary   215
Review List of Key Terms   217
Notes   218

NINE   TOTALITARIANISM: ORGANIZATION AND PROBLEMS   221

Cooperation: Party and State   222
    Party Membership   222
    Party Structures   223
    The Nomenklatura   226
Toleration   228
Elimination   229
Problems of Legitimacy   232
    Science and Soviet Ideology   232
    An Ideological Power Elite   233
    Legitimacy and Nonelites   235
    Problems of Legitimacy and Soviet Foreign Policy   237
Summary   240

Review List of Key Terms   242
Notes   242

PART THREE   POWER AND INTERNATIONAL POLITICS   245

TEN   INTERNATIONAL POLITICS: SOVEREIGN STATES AND SECURITY   247

The Sovereign State in International Politics   248
    Expansion of the Modern State System   250
    Continuing State-Centeredness of International Relations   252
    International Anarchy and the Primacy of Security   254
Power Resources and Effective Power   256
Great Powers in International Politics   257
International Anarchy and International Law   260
    Main Traits of International Law   260
    Criticisms of International Law   262
Security through International Organization?   263
    Origins of Modern International Organization   263
    The League of Nations   264
    The United Nations   265
    UN and Other "Peacekeeping" Efforts   266
Summary   269
Review List of Key Terms   272
Notes   272

ELEVEN   INTERNATIONAL POLITICS: STATECRAFT AND THE BALANCE OF POWER   274

Difficulties of International Power Wielding   275
Instruments and Techniques of Statecraft   277
    Propaganda   277
    Diplomacy   277
    Economic Statecraft   278
    Military Statecraft   279
Balancing Power among States   283
    Balance-of-Power Politics   283
    Status Quo and Revisionist States   284
    War   285
    Benefits of Balance of Power   285
The Bipolar Balance and International Stability   287
    Sources of Instability   287
    Nuclear Deterrence and Stability   291
Summary   293

Contents

    Review List of Key Terms 295
    Notes 296

PART FOUR   POWER AND REVOLUTIONARY CHANGE 297

TWELVE   REVOLUTION: CONCEPTS AND CAUSES 298

Problems in Defining Revolution 299
    The Progressive Bias 299
    Revolution and Coups d'État 300
    Political, Social, and "Great" Revolutions 301
Why Revolutions? 302
    Background Causes 303
    Conditions Favoring Revolution 305
    Revolutionary Detonators 310
    Organizing for Revolution 313
Summary 319
Review List of Key Terms 322
Notes 322

THIRTEEN   REVOLUTION: SEQUENCES AND CONSEQUENCES 324

Sequences of Revolutionary Developments 325
    Rule of the Moderates, or Coalition Government 325
    Rise and Rule of the Radicals 330
    Thermidor? 335
Revolutionary Consequences 336
    Two Revolutionary Traditions 337
    Political Outcomes 339
    Revolutions and Development 341
Summary 346
Review List of Key Terms 348
Notes 348

PART FIVE   POWER AND VALUES 351

FOURTEEN   EVALUATING AND CIVILIZING POLITICAL POWER 353

How Should Government and Politics Be Evaluated? 354
    Absolute versus Contextual Standards 354
    Absolute Ends or Standards versus Experience 360

How Can Political Power Be Civilized?   363
    Flaws and Problems of Democracy   365
    Human Nature and the Permanent Problems of Power   367
What Can We Do about Governments and Power?   369
Summary   370
Review List of Key Terms   373
Notes   373

Glossary   375
Index   383

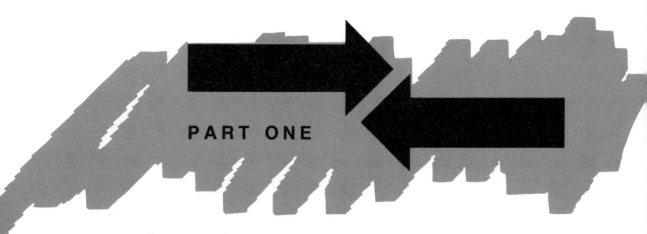

PART ONE

POLITICAL POWER

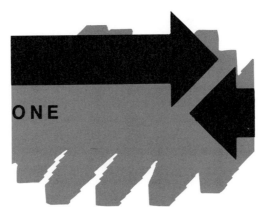

Power and the Origins of Politics

Since power enables us to realize more of our desires than would otherwise be possible, and since it secures deference from others, it is natural to desire power except in so far as timidity interferes.
Bertrand Russell, Power: A New Social Analysis

Two Kinds of Politics

In Shakespeare's *Julius Caesar*, senators join in a successful plot to assassinate Caesar, but Mark Antony's stirring speech delivered over the victim's corpse turns the Roman crowd against the assassins.

Mark Twain's Tom Sawyer tricks his friends into whitewashing a fence by pretending reluctance to let them join in the "fun" of his boring job.

Responding to a surprise Japanese attack on Pearl Harbor, the U.S. Congress enthusiastically declares war on Japan. Nearly four years later the war effort succeeds, as the Japanese government surrenders unconditionally.

A friend of yours is arrested for selling a marijuana cigarette, but his father, a state senator, uses extralegal influence to get his son's police record erased.

What do these situations have in common? Mainly **politics,** in the sense of efforts, both successful and unsuccessful, by some people to gain and exercise power over others. Some people may think that they are totally uninvolved in politics and not even much interested in the subject, but in the broad sense in which we are defining it no one can totally avoid political relationships—except, maybe, a lifelong hermit.

So that you won't jump to the conclusion that this is actually a book on winning friends and influencing people or on succeeding through intimidation, we hasten to make a simple distinction between *personal* and *public* politics. **Personal politics** involves people's seeking and using power to advance their self-defined interests within family, workplace, and other nonofficial social settings. **Public politics** refers to power-related efforts to influence, regulate, or control activities or policies that concern the larger community and its governance.

Emphasis on competition for power is also central to social scientist Max Weber's very similar definition of politics as "striving to share power or striving to influence the distribution of power, either among states or among groups within a state."[1] Our definition is somewhat broader, since it applies to political systems that are not full-fledged "states."

In practice, private and public politics are often closely linked. For example, a corporate employee may try to get promoted by impressing the boss (personal politics) with an effective defense of the company's interests before a government regulatory agency (public politics). Or a president's wife may use her personal relationship to influence his decisions about official appointments and policies. As we will explain, public politics developed originally out of personal, face-to-face politics involving relations within and between families and small kinship-based societies. Since public politics is the central subject matter of political science, this book will consider the private variety only as it intersects with public politics.

Power Defined

At this point it is important to say what we mean by **power,** a term we have already used freely and one that is the organizing concept of this book. This deceptively simple word has been defined, redefined, analyzed, argued over, and discussed at sometimes exhausting length by political philosophers, sociologists, and political scientists. Although numerous definitions of power have been proposed, many differ more in wording than in substance. The most important real disagreement concerns how broadly and generally or how narrowly and specifically we should formulate our basic concept of power.

Without getting into the complex details of this long-running debate, we can illustrate the contrast between broad and narrow definitions. Two famous English philosophers, for example, come down firmly on the side of breadth. Thomas Hobbes (1588–1679) asserts: "The power of a man, to take it universally, is his present means, to obtain some future apparent good. . . ." Bertrand Russell (1872–1970) suggests: "Power may be defined as the production of intended effects."[2] For our purposes these definitions seem not so much incorrect as impractically broad, since they would include people's relations with inanimate things and animals. Our only concern will be power relationships among *people,* not power over nature or technological power in itself.

Typical of narrowly focused definitions are those proposed by two American social scientists. Sociologist Daniel Bell proposes: "Power is the ability to command which is backed up, either implicitly or explicitly, by force." Political scientist Robert Dahl essentially agrees: "Influence of this kind, when compliance is attained by creating the prospect of severe sanctions for non-compliance, is often called power."[3]

We would not deny the reality or the central importance for public politics of coercive force and other "severe sanctions"—far from it, as the following chapters will make clear. But we prefer to call this kind of phenomenon *coercion* and to classify it as only one variety of a much broader type of social relationship for which we will use the label *power* rather than, for example, Dahl's umbrella term, *influence*.

The definition of power that works best for our approach to describing and analyzing politics has been proposed by political sociologist Dennis Wrong. It was inspired by Hobbes and Russell but is clearly and exclusively social: "Power is the capacity of some persons to produce intended and foreseen effects on others."[4] We will interpret this definition as including the coercion that Bell and Dahl emphasize, as well as three other basic categories of power—persuasion, inducement, and authority.

No single definition of such a broad and ambiguous term as *power* can be claimed as clearly correct while all others are inaccurate. We agree with Dahl's remark about the numerous attempts to define and analyze power: "In the abstract it is impossible to say why one classification system should be preferred over another."[5] Definitions and categories, unless they are far removed from all normal uses of a term or concept, should be selected mainly for their helpfulness in analyzing and explaining things in the real world.

The definition of power that we have endorsed and adopted is so broad that its author can justifiably assert: "Power is inherent in all social interaction, which consists of actors reciprocally producing effects on one another."[6] We strongly favor Dennis Wrong's definition because we believe that patterns and structures of public political power evolved originally out of personalized, small-scale social relationships. Also, as we suggested earlier, personal and public politics have remained continuously intertwined in human experience. Any narrower definition would not do justice to our conviction that trying to affect intentionally the actions of other people is a fundamental and universal feature of social existence.

Governing and Governments

Public politics is dominated in almost every society today by the phenomenon of **government.** For this reason, most of the contents of this book will concern the nature, activities, policies, and fates of governments and relationships among them. So we complete our brief preliminary exercise in basic definitions by turning to *government*.

Formal institutions of government have not always existed; they originated in the course of human cultural evolution. But processes of *governing* have been present in every society, small and large, prehistoric and contemporary. **Governing** means using power to handle conflicts within a society and to cope with problems common to the entire society. For example, there are no formal laws or government officials in African hunting-gathering bands. Instead their members use persuasive arguments by kinsmen, such as warnings about the potentially self-destructive risks of violence, in efforts to settle disputes peacefully. Order, safety, and cooperative relationships among bands are vital concerns for all members of these tiny societies.

Only in much larger and more complex societies do political roles, or **offices,** develop—positions that different people may fill at different times. Here we refer to the positions of chiefs, kings, emperors, royal ministers, generals, bureaucrats, presidents, legislators, first secretaries, and so on. Even your sorority, fraternity, or academic club has offices and officers and therefore its own government. But because these kinds of organizations fall within the sphere of personal politics, as defined earlier, we would call their official structures **private governments.**

How are **public governments** distinctive? First, their field of operations and responsibility is considerably broader than those that typify nearly all private governments. Second, public governments have a distinctive means of exercising power, described very precisely by Robert Dahl: *"The Government is any government that successfully upholds a claim to the exclusive regulation of the legitimate use of physical force in enforcing its rules within a given territorial area."* [7]

This definition does not mean that a public government *only* decrees laws and ensures obedience to them by means of physical force. Governments obviously do many other kinds of things, but they are the only institution in complex societies that claims the right to have the final word on how physical force may be lawfully used to enforce society-wide rules. Governments may, of course, allow certain forms of private violence—boxing, football, spanking—but only within legal boundaries maintained by the threat of official force.

A Power-Oriented Perspective on Politics

There are other legitimate and useful ways to think and learn about politics besides focusing on power. Aristotle (384–322 B.C.), the renowned Greek philosopher, conceived of politics as the highest form of ethics. He taught that students of politics should seek knowledge of how to shape the laws and institutions of the community so as to promote the physical, moral, and intellectual "good life" for its citizens. This approach in no way prevented Aristotle from being a realistic and perceptive observer of the varied pursuits and uses of political power in the ancient world.

Similarly, some present-day political scientists would endorse the following definition of politics: "An activity which expresses the wills of individuals in the ordering of their public affairs. The term is derived from the Greek word polis (or city state). The objective of politics (or man's political activities) is policy, i.e., a certain conduct in public affairs."[8] We have no quarrel with this definition or with related conceptions of politics as creative social problem solving or as the means by which societies make and implement basic value choices. These are valid ways of thinking about public politics, focusing mainly on the stakes and outcomes of the struggle for power.

We have chosen political power as *our* central organizing concept because it is comprehensive enough to include everything political. In addition, we believe that paying primary attention to the various forms and uses of power can best help you to begin developing a realistic understanding of the complex and confusing world of politics. That is our primary goal in this book. We do not aim to convert you to a liberal, conservative, Marxist, fascist, Catholic, Protestant, Jewish, humanist, Zen Buddhist, vegetarian, or any other doctrinal view of what politics *ought* to be or become. We are most concerned with trying to make some factual sense of what it *is*.

Our purpose does not mean that we have no moral concerns or commitments or consider them unimportant. We believe deeply in the value of trying to learn and to communicate honestly about politics. Furthermore, learning about the means and ends involved in competing for and using public power forces us to confront important and difficult problems of personal and social ethics: Who has the right to rule? Do I have an obligation to obey, and what are its moral limits? In what circumstances, if ever, is killing justified? dishonesty? betrayal? We do not intend to prescribe how you should answer questions like these, though we will deal very explicitly with issues of political evaluation in the concluding chapter of this book. Mainly we hope that you will gain some insight into the kinds of knowledge you need to acquire and consider when you try to make your own political decisions, either in the abstract or under the pressure of real-life choices.

Our approach to the study and analysis of politics also does not mean that we consider all politics to be about *nothing but* power. In actuality, politics has been and is "about" almost anything in which people have an interest—sex and marriage, kinship, hunting territories, quarrels and revenge, who works and for whom, ritual, religion, education, art and music, economic opportunity and security, ethnic identity, military forces and weapons.

The specific kinds of interests and ends that people try to realize through politics often change over time and from place to place. Ancient Egyptian pharaohs built pyramids as massive ceremonial tombs for themselves, but there is no interest in pyramid building today. Present-day autocrats are more likely to construct official sports palaces and stadiums, meeting halls, ministry headquarters, and huge international airports. In many primitive societies people believe in fighting against witchcraft, which they consider the cause of illness and death, by exiling or killing suspected witches. In modern secular societies, social action against illness takes such public forms as compulsory health insurance and governmental subsidies for hospitals and medical research. No matter how much public goals and interests may change over time or vary among societies, power must be mobilized and used in efforts to realize them. It is the necessary means to all public ends.

Power is the ever-present, inescapable common feature of all political systems, tiny and enormous, prehistoric and present-day, primitive and sophisticated, simple and complex. Dennis Wrong, whose definition of power we have adopted, cautions that it is misleading to define all politics as a "struggle for power." Some people may seek to limit or abolish certain types of power: "Politics includes both a struggle *for* power and a struggle to limit, resist and escape *from* power."[9] That is certainly true, and we have defined politics as including efforts not only to gain, or "struggle for," power but also to *exercise* it. In some circumstances it may be exercised in order to abolish or limit specific uses of power, such as arbitrary arrest and imprisonment, censorship, or torture. However, that kind of effort *requires* power in order to succeed. In practical terms, it aims at a new distribution of effective power by removing some or all of it from people or institutions that have exercised power arbitrarily.

Political Science: The Study of Power

More than specialists in any other academic field, political scientists focus on the ways that political power is won, organized, used, maintained, destroyed, transferred, explained, justified, and criticized. In the broadest sense, **political science** is the disciplined, scholarly study of ideas, behavior, institutions, and policies related to public politics and government.

Political science is an extremely diverse discipline, and there is much disagreement about what it should include, as well as its methods and purposes. Most political scientists, however, agree that the *empirical* study of politics and government is extremely important, whether or not they do it themselves. **Empirical evidence** is based on observation or experience; it is what we loosely refer to as "facts." Of necessity, much evidence consists of written or oral reports of observations originally made by someone other than the researcher and of numbers based on many different observations, such as census reports.

In the last several decades, empirically oriented political scientists have made increasing use of **survey research**—analyzing responses to questionnaires designed to obtain information from voters, citizens, and government officials. Public opinion polling, such as the Gallup Poll, is the best-known form of survey research. Political scientists try to use survey and other interview data to discover the main causes of various kinds of political behavior, such as voting in elections, communicating with public officials, voting in legislative bodies, and executive decision making. This kind of data requires careful evaluation and sophisticated analysis because it consists of people's reports *about* their behavior and not the actual political activities that the researchers are trying to understand.

Political science, like the other social sciences, has become considerably more quantitative in recent decades. Election and census statistics have long been available and much used by political scientists, but there is a tendency now to assign and manipulate numbers in dealing with almost any kind of political subject. For example, one study counts and categorizes incidents of political violence within a given set of countries over a particular period of time and attempts to show how the totals relate to the number of organized political parties in each country.[10] Knowledge of statistics and competence in computer analysis of data have increasingly become essential tools for political researchers.

By no means are all political scientists engaged in quantitative research, and various kinds of qualitative assessments and comparisons remain very important within every major area of the discipline. A very brief description of the principal subfields of political science as currently organized in the United States can at least highlight its great diversity of subject matter and approaches.

Subfields of Political Science

The subfields of political science are political theory, comparative politics, American government and politics, and international politics. Nearly all political scientists fit—some not too comfortably—into one or more of these academic pigeonholes.

Political theory includes the history of political ideas, usually starting with the ancient Greeks and extending to present-day political thinkers; political philosophy, the careful analysis and evaluative criticism of political theories; and empirical theory, the formulation of hypotheses about political relationships that are tested against data drawn from empirical research. Constructing and testing empirical theories is not restricted to scholars who call themselves political theorists. It is the basic approach used by nearly all empirical researchers in every subfield of political science.

Comparative politics refers to the study of government and politics in countries other than the researcher's native land. Sometimes academic courses and research focus on a geographical bloc of states, such as those of Western or Eastern Europe or Southeast Asia or West Africa. Concentrating on particular types of government, such as democratic, communist, or military, is also common. Part Two of this book draws heavily upon a variety of research and publications in comparative politics.

The study of **American government and politics** is most common, of course, in the United States and deals with every conceivable aspect of its political life—parties, interest groups, elections, institutions of government, public opinion, and many others. We would include within this gigantic subfield certain areas of study that are sometimes described as distinct subfields in themselves: public law, public administration, state and local government, and public policy. Public law deals mainly with interpretations of the U.S. Constitution by the Supreme Court but also includes studies of judicial politics and behavior. Public administration focuses on the structure, organization, procedures, and behavior of the administrative departments and agencies of government, the "bureaucracy." Most courses in public administration concentrate on the federal government of the United States, although "comparative bureaucracy" designates a specialization within comparative politics. The field of state and local government includes the study of urban, rural, suburban, and regional politics and governmental institutions. Public policy has mushroomed as a focus of study and research in recent years, as increasing numbers of political scientists have tried to determine the actual effects of governmental policies, both on target populations and on the political process itself.

International politics deals with such topics as diplomacy and rivalry, cooperation, and warfare among sovereign states, as well as with foreign and national security policies of particular states. It also includes the study of international law and international organizations, especially the United Nations. In an age of instant communications, economic interdependence, conflicting ideologies, and nuclear weapons, the study of international power relationships attracts at least some attention from many political scientists who specialize in other subfields.

Related Disciplines

Political scientists do not have a monopoly on the study of political power and public governments, much less on significant research, ideas, and insights about them. History provides an essential foundation for all political study and understanding. Some journalists and other nonacademic writers are very adept at digging out hard-to-find information from informants or obscure documents or at interpreting political trends or events in ways that stand up well over time.

To some extent, scholars from other social science disciplines also deal with government and politics. Economists are frequently concerned with the nature of government taxing, spending, monetary and trade policies, and with determining their actual or potential effects on production levels, inflation, and employment.

Sociology includes the study of ethnic and racial groups, sex roles, social class, and many other subjects of great relevance to the shaping of public opinion and official policies. Political sociology is a distinct subfield of that discipline. It overlaps considerably with the kind of empirical political science that attempts to discover significant relationships between social categories such as religion, ethnicity, educational experience, and class on the one hand, and political attitudes and behavior, on the other.

Psychology may or may not be considered a social science, since it tends to focus mainly on the causes of individual behavior or on the structures and processes typical of human mental processes. But political psychology is a budding interdisciplinary field. It would include, for instance, attempts to explain political leaders' actions in terms of their supposedly formative childhood experiences. Social psychology has long had an impact on political science studies of, for example, small groups of decision makers such as governmental committees and cabinets.

Political scientists often use research and concepts drawn from economics, sociology, and psychology. However, with a few exceptions, they have largely ignored anthropology. Political scientists are usually interested in recent and contemporary governments and political developments within large-scale, complexly organized societies. Most anthropological research and writings have been based on participant observation of very small preliterate societies historically remote from major world civilizations.

Some anthropologists also deal with archeological materials, trying to discover from ancient and fragmentary evidence how our ancestors may have lived before the existence of written records. In a part of the following section we will use some anthropological and archeological research and ideas to suggest how and why the nature and scope of political power came to be radically transformed in the course of prehistoric human experience.

Why the Pursuit of Political Power?

There is no universally accepted answer to the basic question of why people seek political power. In our judgment, though, there are various good reasons to believe that power seeking and power wielding are inevitable and inescapable features of human societies. We mean power not only in the generally approved form of rational persuasion but also as manipulation and coercion. Lying and forcing people to act in certain ways are not morally attractive kinds of behavior, but they are part and parcel of the human social condition. We will briefly present three lines of argument that converge in support of that conclusion. We consider first the lessons of historical and contemporary experience, next the dominant viewpoint on human nature and power in Western political thought, and finally a scientific perspective on the same problem.

The Lessons of Experience

It is always risky and possibly foolish to make sweeping generalizations about history, but we feel confident in declaring that there is no record of any organized society or historical period totally free of the harsher forms of political power. Warfare features as prominently in the fragmentary records of ancient Mesopotamia and Egypt as in the newspapers of our blood-soaked twentieth century. Riots, rebellions, revolts, assassinations, civil wars, fierce government suppression of "enemies"—all are the stuff of real historical melodrama, ancient and modern, East and West. In addition, we know of no government that has ever renounced all coercive threats and punishments as essential means for enforcing law and order.

No one is likely to quarrel with this characterization of human political experience, past and present. In isolation, though, it doesn't take us very far toward understanding the universality of the struggle to gain and use political power. To advance down that road, we need to think about two common features of our own experience—disagreement and scarcity—and try to relate them to political life.

Have you ever disagreed with your parents, brother, or sister about something you wanted to do or get for yourself? Who hasn't? In political language, what's involved is a **conflict of interests.** For instance, you have a strong interest in using a family car for the big homecoming dance, while your sister is just as determined to drive it the same night to visit her out-of-town boyfriend. If that's the only car available, you are caught in a condition of severe **scarcity** so that if your interest is satisfied your sister's is completely denied, and vice versa. As most of us know from painful experience, that kind of situation sometimes leads to quarrels and hard feelings. Your parents may simply lay down the law to settle the conflict, even if their assertion of authority makes either or both of you very unhappy.

Fortunately, most conflicts of interests within families are not as irreconcilable as our example, and compromises can generally be worked out. Part of growing up is learning to get by on half a loaf, recognizing that we can't have everything we want because of scarcity and the needs and desires of other people. Another part is learning to lose sometimes without destroying relations with the people we love and respect.

In some ways the broader society is similar to your family—though the differences are at least equally important. Suppose there is an unused school building in your hometown, and a businessman offers to lease it for a sizeable fee. It would be cheaper for him than other buildings, and the school board is pleased to cut its losses. However, people in the neighborhood of the building oppose leasing it to a business; they are afraid that commercialization will decrease the value of their expensive houses. Local governments have to deal with this kind of disagreement all the time, and there is often no way they can please everyone. Whatever they decide, someone—the businessman, the school board representing taxpayers, or neighborhood homeowners—is going to be worse off than with the opposite decision.

Scarcity doesn't always take material forms. It can simply mean that in some conflicts over policy only a single interest can win, while all others lose. Take, for example, the longstanding controversy about abortion laws in the United States. Some people declare that abortion is an absolute moral evil and want to outlaw it completely. Others believe with equal sincerity that each woman has an absolute moral right to choose abortion for herself. Still others would prefer to place some legal restrictions on abortion but not to prohibit it in all cases.

If the totally antiabortion group succeeds in getting its position written into law, the other groups lose completely, but the same is true if the right-to-abortion position prevails. A compromise outcome of partial prohibition means total loss for both absolutist groups. This kind of situation is bound to inspire efforts on all sides to mobilize and organize in order to enhance interested groups' effective power, their capacity to influence public policy. Even if members of a group feel no strong personal desire for public political power, they are compelled to seek it or risk being steamrollered by opponents whose policy views they regard as intolerable. To put it more generally, the high stakes of politics force individuals and groups who feel threatened by opposing political interests to engage in **self-defensive power seeking**—at the very least.

Broadening the perspective of this discussion, we turn to sociologist Gerhard Lenski's four basic "postulates about man and society" based on broad knowledge of historical and social science research:

1. People need society for psychological and economic reasons.

2. Human beings are self-interested; as a rule, we can be expected to protect and advance our own interests as we understand them. Even cooperation usually aims at personal gain for the cooperators, may involve some antagonism between them, and can deteriorate into conflict. We are most likely to help other people when the costs and risks to ourselves are relatively low.

3. Most things that people strive for are in short supply—affected by the condition of scarcity. We can readily develop unlimited appetites for goods and services, since they can have status value as well as practical uses. Desire plus scarcity produces struggles for rewards in every society.

4. Individuals "are unequally endowed by nature with the attributes necessary to carry on these struggles." Natural differences in abilities are

an important basis of social inequalities but not their most important cause.[11]

Political Theorists on Human Nature and Power

Support for the view that self-interested power-seeking tendencies are deeply rooted in human nature and social circumstances is easy to find in the tradition of Western political thought. In briefly highlighting a few theorists' ideas, we are not trying to appeal to them as final authorities. We simply suggest that it is significant to find basic agreement across many centuries among theorists who differ in other important respects and who are generally considered the keenest observers and interpreters of political life.

All the classic political thinkers recognize the existence and importance of self-interested power seeking, and most of them also consider it unavoidable. We mention as representative examples the views of Aristotle, St. Augustine, Thomas Hobbes, and James Madison.

Aristotle, writing in the fourth century B.C., was the most systematic of the ancient Greek philosophers; he has been among the most influential of all political theorists. Commenting on a plan to do away with social conflict by legislating material equality, he declares: "None of these evils [lawsuits, perjury, flattery of the rich] . . . is due to the absence of communism. They all arise from the wickedness of human nature." Aristotle also asserts that self-interested desire tends to bias and warp political judgment: "He who commands that a man [rather than the law] should rule adds the character of the beast. Appetite has that character; and high spirit, too, perverts the holders of office, even when they are the best of men."[12]

Six centuries later St. Augustine (A.D. 354–430) used the Christian concept of **original sin** to characterize human nature. He meant disobeying God and pridefully asserting human desire instead, as represented in Adam and Eve's yielding to the serpent's temptation in the Garden of Eden. All human beings are children of Adam, and except for the few upon whom God has bestowed his divine grace, they are selfish and willful and persistently ignore divine law. Among the results of human sinfulness are "quarrels, law-suits, wars, treasons, angers, hatreds, deceit, flattery, fraud, theft, robbery, perfidy, pride, ambition, envy, . . . ferocity, wickedness, . . . perjuries, oppression of the innocent, . . . plots, . . . unrighteous judgments, violent deeds, plunderings, and innumerable other crimes. . . ."[13]

St. Augustine declares that this world is inescapably marred by sinful human striving and that God has ordained harsh and punitive government as a partial remedy for its effects. Both government and slavery stem from men's sinful desires to conquer and exploit other people. By creating some degree of enforceable order, though, they fulfill the divine purpose of modifying the destructive consequences of sin. More than a thousand years later the most influential Protestant Reformers, Martin Luther and John Calvin, thoroughly endorsed Augustine's emphasis upon self-centered power seeking as an inevitable expression of man's sinful lust and pride. It is a belief with deep roots in the Western Christian tradition.

Writing in the seventeenth century, the secular political philosopher Thomas Hobbes was as emphatic as the theologians about human self-centeredness. This trait was not an effect of sin, though, but simply the nature of the human creature. In Hobbes's view, each person is driven by a basic urge to preserve his or her life as long as possible. This natural urge gives rise to needs and desires that we must fulfill as means to **self-preservation.** Because we can anticipate future needs and desires, we must try to assure ourselves of the means of fulfilling them both now and in the future. That means is power, the capacity to get what we want from nature and from other people. Therefore: "I put for a general inclination of all mankind a perpetual and restless desire of power after power that ceases only in death."[14]

Hobbes believed that human beings' natural, competitive striving for power and its benefits would lead to general anarchy, insecurity, and social misery in the absence of strong, even absolute, government able to enforce its version of law and order. That was not the political conclusion of James Madison (1751–1836), although he agreed with Hobbes on the inevitability of **self-centered power seeking.** Madison expressed his ideas most memorably as one of the three authors of *The Federalist*. This is a collection of essays written in 1787–1788, originally to win support for the newly proposed U.S. Constitution but soon recognized as the classic statement of American constitutionalist theory.

Madison emphasizes the fallibility and self-centered bias of human reason: "As long as the connection subsists between [man's] reason and his self-love, his opinions and passions will have reciprocal influence on each other; and the former will be objects to which the latter will attach themselves." Elsewhere he declares that we cannot count on those in politics to act as benevolent "angels" toward other people. If we want to prevent governmental oppression and exploitation, we had better assume that political actors are ambitious for power and structure the government so that the ambition of some can check the ambition of others: "This policy of supplying, by opposite and rival interests, the defect of better motives, might be traced through the whole system of human affairs, private as well as public."[15]

In our judgment, these four theorists represent both moderate and extreme versions of the predominant view in the Western political tradition: that self-centered power seeking is a central tendency in human behavior.

A contrasting perspective did begin to gain prominence in the eighteenth century and has played a large role in modern revolutionary ideology, especially Marxism, as explained in chapter 8. It is the essentially utopian view that self-centered competition for power and its rewards has resulted solely from social circumstances of scarcity and inequality. Modern science and technology and revolutionary politics make it possible to abolish material scarcity and all inequalities of condition, leading to a society of perfect cooperation, altruism, and harmony. To understate drastically a case that will be explored extensively in later chapters, the track record for this utopian prediction of the end of coercive power and self-centeredness has been very poor. Movements whose leaders claim to believe in it have produced more coercive and far more murderous regimes than those they destroyed and replaced.

The Evolution of Political Power

A third line of argument about power seeking assumes an evolutionary perspective on human life and societies.

■ Biological Evolution

In the most basic biological terms, we are the heirs of thousands of generations of creatures who competed most successfully for survival and reproduction. Tendencies to be totally passive and uncompetitive in the face of threats and opportunities would have been highly unadaptive and could never have become prominent among our behavioral motivations.

This perspective does not imply that we are *only* competitive, or always nastily so, nor that we are mere puppets controlled by our genes. High intelligence and behavioral flexibility are very important inherited traits of our species, and the more we learn, the greater our capacity to decide consciously how to respond to whatever behavioral tendencies are typically human.

We would propose that one of our most basic motivations as social animals is a desire "to produce intended and foreseen effects on others"[16]—in short, to wield power. *All* that we mean is a commonly felt need or desire to get our own way when our wishes or purposes clash with other people's. The way you feel when you and your sister both desperately want to use the same car at the same time exemplifies the most basic level of the desire for power. Individuals with none of this elementary motivation could never have survived the dangers and challenges of evolutionary competition.

We would suggest that the level of power motivation differs significantly among individuals, as do their opportunities for gratifying it. Obviously, most people cannot or do not try to seek power in the arena of public politics. That pursuit often has high costs such as significant personal risks or even dangers, can involve unpleasant burdens, and may have little chance of success. Of course, there is seldom a shortage of competitors for governmental power, especially for the most important decision-making positions. It is obvious from everyday experience, though, that even people who avoid public politics do try to exercise power within the private settings of family, neighborhood, club, school, and workplace.

To suggest a significant impact of biological evolution on human behavior is still controversial, although we think there is good evidence for it.[17] We present our brief speculations on this subject as nothing more than suggestive support for the basic premise of this entire book:

> because of their nature and their social condition, human beings seek to gain and use power.

■ Cultural Evolution

There is considerable evidence that competition for power and its rewards—territory, natural resources, marital alliances, slaves, tribute—played a critical part in the cultural evolution of political systems and institutions. These have changed in fundamental ways over time. Anthropologists and prehistorians generally agree that there were no society-wide systems of command by a few and obedience by the many until they began to appear in the ancient Near East seven to eight thousand years ago.

For at least two million years our ancestors lived in societies numbered in the dozens of individuals, with everyone related by marriage, blood ties, or both. Until about twelve thousand years ago, these tiny, independent societies were nomadic, living off wild animals and plants. Possibly because of overcrowding in certain regions abundant in vital food resources, some groups began to plant and cultivate crops, necessarily settling down for long periods of time.

Studies of surviving preliterate societies, whether nomads or village dwellers, strongly suggest that there was no true political authority in these small prehistoric societies. Some individuals would have unusual influence with their neighbors because of attractive personalities or outstanding abilities in hunting, fighting, or other survival skills. No one could be compelled to follow them, though, much less to obey their commands. The political order was literally **anarchy**—the absence of rule or government. In larger villages some skillful "big men" might organize lineage (kin-group) alliances and gain extra rewards for their members, but those men still had to work mainly through persuasion, not by giving orders. Our ancient ancestors were almost certainly unwilling to give up their personal and family power by voluntarily recognizing anyone else's power to make decisions for the whole society.

Chiefdoms How was it possible, then, for government and the state to arise? We think that the most likely answer to this question has been proposed by anthropologist Robert Carneiro.[18] He points out that warfare between independent village societies is very common but by itself does not lead to conquest and enlarged social systems. If useable land is available and reachable, the survivors of a defeated village flee the victors and reestablish their independence in a new site. What might happen, though, if the vanquished were unable to survive by running away?

The **Carneiro theory** proposes that this was the case with prehistoric village peoples who lived in highly populated fertile regions sharply limited by natural barriers such as mountain ranges, oceans, and deserts, or by the social barrier of strong and hostile neighboring peoples. Under such restrictive conditions, defeated communities could either submit to political domination by the victors and work harder to pay taxes and tributes to them—or face extinction. Thus were born **chiefdoms,** the first multicommunity political systems and the first to feature ongoing relations of superiors and inferiors.

Chiefdoms were still organized by kin groups, but some of the lineages were now ranked higher than others in dignity and privileges. The highest-ranking lineage supplied the hereditary chief. His ruling authority and the special rights of "noble" lineages were justified and sanctified by teachings of the official religious cult, which the chief often served as high priest. The gods—usually deified ancestors—always commanded obedience and respect for rank. Chiefs did not maintain general law-enforcement systems, but they could use coercion—hereditary executioners, rituals of human sacrifice—to impress everyone with their supernatural authority and the religious duty of recognizing and submitting to it.

States Continued warfare among chiefdoms within sharply bounded regions such as the Tigris-Euphrates "Fertile Crescent," the Nile Valley of Egypt, and coastal Peru enlarged the scope of conquests until kin-group organization was left behind and victorious political leaders organized populations on the basis of territory. These new and larger political units were full-fledged **states,** with centralized governments able to "collect taxes, draft men for work or war, and decree and enforce laws."[19]

Victorious chiefs became kings whose priests proclaimed them as divine beings or at least the favorites of the gods. Palaces, rituals, costumes, elaborate tombs, and retinues set them apart from the common herd. Monarchs and their noble allies used their supreme power to build up fortunes, acquire additional wives and concubines, and ensure the hereditary transmission of their authority and riches.

Coalitions of kings and their helpers and supporters—priests, advisers, generals, tax collectors, nobles—shared the spoils of war and the regular taxes and tributes extracted from peasant and craftsman commoners.

Ancient kings claimed direct authority from the gods. Here, King Darius of Persia, backed by his priests and chief ministers, receives tributes that his power and majesty enabled him to extract from Persian subjects.

Common people had to work harder to pay their overlords and still try to sustain their own families. The ruling few exploited their concentrated power to become enormously wealthier than the great bulk of the population.

In many cases commoners did receive one important benefit from their states: protection, both through official legal systems that decreased the dangers of private feuding and from governmental defense against bandits, nomadic raiders, or even more ruthless and predatory rulers. For most people, the only alternative to state protection was vulnerability to plunder, rape, and violent death. It isn't surprising, then, that commoners tended to develop and teach their children sincere belief in the king's divine right to their loyal support and obedience.

In addition, subjects' obedience was essential for protection against their own overlords. Early states, and most later ones, have featured substantial differences between rulers and ruled in their abilities to mobilize and use coercive force. Most governments haven't hesitated to use cruel punishments against rebels and dissidents.[20]

The cultural evolution of government and the state (see figure 1-1) is not a very pleasant story, but it does have a positive side. The establishment in sizeable territories of peace and security, although based on law enforcement that strongly favored the rich and powerful, made possible increases in production, trade, and wealth, and so the growth of cities. Urban life stimulated the great developments in the arts, literature, religion, philosophy, and science that we justifiably label the emergence of high civilization.

The most important change in the course of cultural-political evolution was the development of ever-larger **imbalances of power** between and within societies. Competition for resources and power continued at an

1 Power and the Origins of Politics

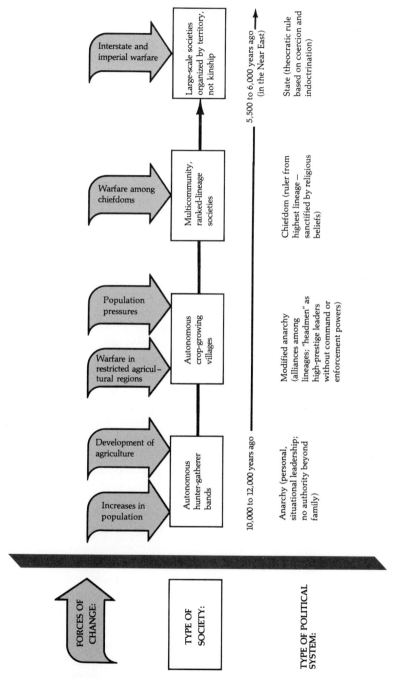

Figure 1-1 Schematic diagram of social-political evolution

accelerated rate within the new conditions created by settled agricultural life. Coercion and official indoctrination rather than kin ties and mutual aid became the most important means of holding together much larger and more complex societies. Those that didn't succeed in establishing effective institutions to mobilize and exercise political power were absorbed by societies that did. It long ago became obvious that societies with large and diverse populations absolutely require institutionalized government to function at all.

Today nearly everyone lives within the jurisdiction of a fully functioning state, a political system usually defined as combining four basic features: "(1) people; (2) territory; (3) government, i.e., the agency through which the policies of the state are formulated and carried out; (4) sovereignty, i.e., supreme power, both internal and external, including the authority to make final legal decisions and the physical power to enforce them."[21] The governmental power of the state is an unavoidable solution to collective problems but also a more or less terrible problem for every people on earth.

We have described how three arguments converge in support of our premise that self-centered power seeking is a constant in human nature and societies. This assertion can never be "proved" in the definitive sense in which Galileo demonstrated the rotation of the planets around the sun. However, we certainly can't see any convincing reasons to doubt that the competitive quest for power fundamentally conditions human relations within and between societies.

Serious students of politics try their best to understand what forms that competition takes in the public arena, how and why political institutions and processes have developed, and how they affect and are shaped by people who play various roles in the ongoing dramas of political life—rulers, bureaucrats, military commanders, revolutionaries, candidates, subjects, and citizens.

Summary

In the broadest sense, politics involves people's efforts to gain and exercise power—the ability to produce intended and foreseen effects on other people. We are concerned mainly with attempts to influence, control, or change public governments—distinctive sets of institutions and offices that seek to regulate conflict within society and deal with its other common problems as well. Public governments successfully uphold a claim to have the final word on the lawful use of physical force in the enforcement of their rules. Politics and government involve many aims and activities other than competing for and using power, but power is the essential means to all political ends and so provides a useful focus for efforts to develop a realistic understanding of politics.

Political science is the academic discipline that concentrates most on how people compete for and use public governmental power. Empirical and quantitative methods have become increasingly important in political science. However, qualitative and evaluative approaches remain significant within all major subfields of the discipline. In the United States, these include political theory, comparative politics, American government and politics, and international politics. Scholars in other academic fields—especially history, economics, sociology, psychology, and anthropology—have also contributed a great deal to the disciplined study of politics.

As a preliminary to the study of power and governments, we consider and endorse the premise that human beings have a strong tendency to act as self-interested power seekers in every kind of society and political system. The lessons both of history and of common experience indicate that scarcity of valued goods and disagreement about policies inevitably promote competition for power and its rewards. Most classic political theorists, such as Aristotle, St. Augustine, Hobbes, and Madison, contend that power seeking is a central human tendency and must be assumed in the construction and operation of governments.

Finally, human beings evolved as successful competitors for resources and are therefore likely to try to get their own way in cases of serious disagreement or conflict. The cultural evolution of political systems in prehistory was propelled in part by competition for scarce resources, including power held by some people over others. Political development featured a growth of imbalances of power based originally on conquest and consolidated in early states by the use of systematic coercion and religious indoctrination.

Three lines of argument converge, then, to support the premise that because of their nature and social circumstances human beings can be counted on to compete for power. The next chapter describes the stakes of and major strategies used in that competition in the public arena.

Review List of Key Terms

politics
personal politics
public politics
power
government
governing
office
private government

public government
political science
empirical evidence
survey research
political theory
comparative politics
American government and politics

international politics
conflict of interests
scarcity
self-defensive power seeking
original sin
self-preservation

self-centered power seeking
anarchy
Carneiro theory
chiefdom
state
imbalances of power

Notes

1. Max Weber, "Politics as a Vocation," in *From Max Weber: Essays in Sociology*, ed. Hans Gerth and C. Wright Mills (New York: Oxford University Press, 1946), p. 78. Weber (1864–1920), a German scholar, was perhaps the most influential social scientist of the twentieth century.
2. Thomas Hobbes, *Leviathan*, Parts 1 and 2 (Indianapolis: Bobbs-Merrill, 1958), p. 56; Bertrand Russell, *Power: A New Social Analysis* (New York: Norton, 1938), p. 35.
3. Daniel Bell, *The Coming of Post-Industrial Society* (New York: Basic Books, 1973), p. 453; Robert A. Dahl, *Modern Political Analysis*, 3rd ed. (Englewood Cliffs, N.J.: Prentice-Hall, 1976), p. 47.
4. Dennis H. Wrong, *Power: Its Forms, Bases, and Uses* (New York: Harper & Row, 1979), p. 2.
5. Robert A. Dahl, "Power," in *International Encyclopedia of the Social Sciences*, ed. David L. Sills (New York: Macmillan and Free Press, 1968), vol. 23, p. 412.
6. Wrong, *Power*, p. 253.
7. Dahl, *Modern Political Analysis*, p. 10. (Italics in original.)
8. Joseph Dunner, ed., *Dictionary of Political Science* (Totowa, N.J.: Littlefield, Adams, 1970), p. 418. Reprinted by permission.
9. Wrong, *Power*, p. 13.
10. See G. Bingham Powell, *Contemporary Democracies: Participation, Stability, and Violence* (Cambridge, Mass.: Harvard University Press, 1982).
11. Gerhard E. Lenski, *Power and Privilege: A Theory of Social Stratification* (New York: McGraw-Hill, 1966), pp. 29–32.
12. Ernest Barker, ed. and trans., *The Politics of Aristotle* (New York: Oxford University Press, 1958), pp. 51, 146.
13. Henry Paolucci, ed., *The Political Writings of St. Augustine* (Chicago: Regnery, 1962), p. 2.
14. Hobbes, *Leviathan*, p. 86.
15. James Madison, *The Federalist*, nos. 10 and 51, in *The Federalist Papers*, ed. Clinton Rossiter (New York: New American Library, 1961), pp. 78, 322.
16. You should recognize here the operative part of Dennis Wrong's definition of power, cited earlier in this chapter.
17. See, for instance, Richard D. Alexander, *Darwinism and Human Affairs* (Seattle: University of Washington Press, 1979); Napoleon A. Chagnon and William Irons, eds., *Evolutionary Biology and Human Social Behavior* (No. Scituate, Mass.: Duxbury, 1979); and Elliott White, ed., *Sociobiology and Human Politics* (Lexington, Mass.: Lexington Books, D. C. Heath, 1981).
18. See his articles: Robert Carneiro, "A Theory of the Origins of the State," *Science*, 169 (August 21, 1970): 733–738; idem, "The Chiefdom: Precursor of the State," in *The Transition to Statehood in the New World*, ed. Grant D. Jones and Robert R. Kautz (New York: Cambridge University Press, 1981), pp. 37–79.
19. Carneiro, "Theory," p. 738.
20. For citations of the research on which this version of the evolution of politics is based, as well as an argument linking biological and cultural evolution in the emergence of governmental systems, see Fred H. Willhoite, Jr., "Political Evolution and Legitimacy: The Biocultural Origins of Hierarchical Organizations," in *Biology and Bureaucracy: Public Administration and Public Policy from the Perspective of Evolutionary, Genetic and Neurobiological Theory*, ed. Elliott White and Joseph Losco (Lanham, Md.: University Press of America, 1986), pp. 193–231.
21. Dunner, *Dictionary of Political Science*, p. 498.

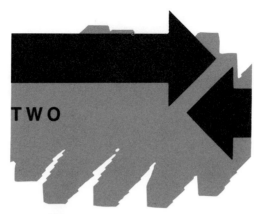

TWO

Competing for Power

> *Many men have imagined republics and principalities that never really existed at all. Yet the way men live is so far removed from the way they ought to live that anyone who abandons what is for what should be pursues his downfall rather than his preservation. . . .*
> **Niccolò Machiavelli, The Prince**

Machiavelli (1469–1527) was a government official and writer who lived in Renaissance Florence. The works published after his death—including *The Prince*—have made him one of the most famous, notorious, and controversial of all political thinkers. No one has ever observed more closely or written more memorably about political power seeking or pointed out more starkly its moral dilemmas.

One of his examples illustrating ambition combined with ruthlessness was Oliverotto da Fermo, who wanted to seize control of his native city. Backed by a band of armed followers, Oliverotto plotted with some dissatisfied citizens to overthrow the city government. He then invited all the leading citizens to an elaborate banquet. After dinner, Oliverotto began a political discussion and suggested that everyone retire with him to a more private room:

> But they were scarcely seated when soldiers rushed out from certain hiding places and slew Giovanni [Oliverotto's uncle] and all who were with him.
>
> After the slaughter, Oliverotto mounted his horse, rode through the city and laid siege to the palace of the chief magistrates, who were constrained by fear to obey him, and set up a government at the head of which he placed himself.[1]

Nearly five centuries later, refreshments preceded another political ambush. Early in 1986, while tea was being served at a meeting in Southern Yemen of the ruling party's executive body, President Hassani's guards began firing their machine guns at some of his colleagues. The president was not present at the meeting, having planned and ordered the massacre. He did not have Oliverotto da Fermo's success, however. The targeted politburo members were armed and accompanied by their own armed guards, and a wild gunfight broke out. It continued in the streets of the capital city of Aden and spread to outlying areas, resulting in unknown thousands of deaths. The president's opponents won the battle, and he fled into exile.[2]

Turning a feast or a routine meeting into an occasion for ambush and slaughter seems a filthy trick, but competition for power and its rewards has inspired many deeds that far surpass these occasions in destruction and nastiness. Nevertheless, most competition for political power does not involve dramatic and bloody events such as ambushes, wars, revolutions, and reigns of terror. This chapter will focus initially on classifying and explaining the stakes of that competition—the major types of political power. Then we will analyze and illustrate the strategies pursued by competitors for power.

Types of Political Power

There are many complex systems of classifying and analyzing forms of power, and we have no quarrel with any of them. Ours is a relatively short and simplified classification scheme, mainly because it is restricted to public political power. We believe that it is a comprehensive and useful set of categories, broad enough to include every relevant kind of political power relationship and applicable to both domestic and international politics.

Our categories of political power are *coercion, inducement, persuasion,* and *authority.* Although we will analyze them separately, we will also illustrate briefly how they interact with each other in actual political situations.

Coercion

Coercion refers to the use or threat of severe sanctions by power wielders against those whose actions they seek to control. You must obey or else something bad will happen to you, or something awful is being done to you *because* you disobeyed.

■ Use of Force

The "something awful" may be psychological force or pressure. For instance, Trobriand Islands chiefs employed court sorcerers to cast spells on people who had offended chiefly rights or dignity.[3] Medieval popes could sometimes affect secular rulers' decisions by threatening them with excommunication. If people truly believe in the magical powers of sorcerers or in "no salvation outside the church," they are vulnerable to the use or threat of psychic force by the supposed controllers of supernatural sanctions.

Psychic pressure is no mere relic of an unenlightened past. Brainwashing techniques have often been used by contemporary dictatorships against both political and military prisoners to break their morale and extort fraudulent, propagandistic confessions from them. This was the fate of many U.S. prisoners of war both in Korea and in North Vietnam. In Arthur Koestler's brilliant novel *Darkness at Noon,* psychological torture helps to manipulate the thoughts and words of a character modeled on the "old Bolsheviks" who gave false confessions at Stalin's staged purge trials in the 1930s.

Public humiliation and screamed accusations were frequently directed against disfavored officials and teachers during the Chinese "Great Proletarian Cultural Revolution" in the late 1960s. Techniques of this kind also helped the Rev. Jim Jones control his wretched Guyana jungle community, which he led to annihilation by mass suicide in 1978. Psychic force should not be underrated as an instrument of political coercion.

It is most potent, however, in combination with actual or threatened *physical* force. Prisoners are physically held captive in the first place, and the Jonestown suicides were helped along by fanatical armed guards who made escape nearly impossible. It would be difficult, unfortunately, to overestimate the political significance of physical force. The frequency of its use strongly supports a famous philosopher's assertion that history is a "slaughter-bench."[4] Read any daily newspaper and try to refute him!

Various factors, such as economic resources, prestige, and religious beliefs, interact to determine the balance of power between states or among groups within a state. Generally speaking, though, the capacity for using physical force is most critical. One example should suffice, since you can easily think of many others. For about a thousand years the Hawaiian Islands were inhabited by Polynesian people who were organized into half a dozen paramount chiefdoms. Wars among them were frequent, but no single chief could ever gain a decisive military edge—until Europeans and North Americans began arriving in 1778. Within four decades one chief had acquired firearms and mercenary soldiers, decisively upsetting the ancient balance of power and enabling him to establish a kingdom in all of Hawaii.

■ Threat of Force

The most efficient kind of coercive power is the **credible threat** of force rather than its actual use. If you can get your subjects to obey solely because they are afraid not to or get a rival state to give up something without fighting, you have saved human and material resources and not been compelled to take the risks that the use of force always involves. But force that remains a mere threat or is not used successfully cannot be relied upon to assure obedience.

Power wielders' belief that they must sometimes use force decisively in order to make their threats credible is illustrated in a famous chapter of *The Peloponnesian War,* written by an Athenian soldier and historian, Thucydides, in the fifth century B.C. This war was fought between coalitions of Greek city-states—one dominated by Athens and the other by Sparta. The bitterness of this twenty-seven-year conflict was exemplified in a confrontation between the Athenians and a Spartan ally, the island city of Melos.

Athenian envoys pointed out to the Melians that since they faced a greatly superior military force, it would be sensible for them to surrender without a fight and submit to Athenian rule. When the Melians refused, the Athenians declared that if they allowed Melos to remain independent and neutral, Athenian allies and subject states would consider it a sign of weakness and try to break away from Athenian control. Such efforts could spell disaster for the empire of Athens and for her prospects in the war. Still the Melians refused to give up, and the Athenians laid siege to the city. When surrender finally came, they executed all men of military age and sold the women and children into slavery.[5]

This probably strikes you as a brutal and terrifying instance of "teaching a lesson" through the use of destructive force. It is also possible that such tactics cost the Athenians more support than they gained, since Athens eventually lost the war.

Sometimes, though, *failure* to back up threats with effective force can also have horrendous consequences. The classic modern example is the French and British policy in the 1930s of threatening to retaliate against Hitler's violations of treaties and of Austrian and Czechoslovak sovereignty, followed by inaction and acceptance of his promises not to do it again. This policy of threats and **appeasement** encouraged Hitler to move boldly even when he believed his military capabilities to be inferior to his adversaries'. The terrible consequence was the Second World War.

Coercive power is always dangerous; if it weren't it would be pointless. But it is also essential to the working of systems of law and order within any sizeable and complex society. On the whole, the centralization of coercive enforcement power in the state has made life somewhat more physically secure for most people most of the time than it was in prestate societies. Where kinship is the primary basis of social organization and there is no effective society-wide system of law enforcement, "the individual case always holds the threat of a little civil war. . . ."[6] Feuds, revenge raids, and ambushes make violent death a much more likely threat than it usually is for most citizens even of arbitrarily governed states.

We will make clear in later chapters, however, that states differ significantly in the organization and control of coercive force. As we all must be painfully aware, the capacity of modern states to employ destructive physical force against both external and internal enemies surpasses the wildest dreams of the most power-mad primitive king or feudal baron.

Inducement

If coercion is the "whip" of power, **inducements** are the "carrots." They are *rewards* that are promised and bestowed in efforts to control or at least influence the recipients' actions. Inducements are more varied than the forms of coercion. Medals for heroism, a king's praise of a faithful minister, grants of land to military supporters, bribes of "cooperative" officials, campaign funds and votes for candidates favorable to organized interest groups, public policies favoring the policy makers' backers and voters—all are inducements, limited in variety only by resources and ingenuity.

Autocratic rulers have often confiscated opponents' land and redistributed some of it to allies, firming up vital support for their regimes. Notable examples include England's King Henry VIII, whose break with the Roman Catholic church in the sixteenth century enabled him to confiscate vast ecclesiastical estates; Tsar Ivan the Terrible, who used this technique to undermine the independence of the old nobility in sixteenth-century Russia; and the Tokugawa shogun in seventeenth-century Japan, who seized and redistributed to his allies the estates of nobles who were reluctant to recognize his position as the ruling power behind the "divine" emperor.[7]

Inducements are commonly used also in relations between sovereign states. In return for a cash payment, the French government ceded title to the vast Louisiana Territory to the United States in 1803. Most foreign economic and military aid since the Second World War has been intended to enhance the donor's influence with the receiving government, whatever the positive or negative effects on economic development. By promising to return all of the occupied Sinai desert—and doing so in 1982—the Israeli government induced the largest Arab state, Egypt, to make peace and grant official recognition to the state of Israel.

If inducements are such a frequently used kind of power, and if the positive reinforcement of rewards is at least as effective in shaping behavior as the negative reinforcement of punishments, why don't power seekers and governments use rewards exclusively to get what they want? Why take the risks and incur the costs—including the dangers of revenge, rebellion, or defeat—that coercion often involves? We suggest two broad answers to these questions.

First, inducements cannot work when there is an irreconcilable conflict of interests between competitors for power. If you are a militarily powerful autocrat who longs to conquer, subjugate, and exploit another people, their interest in avoiding that fate will require that you use coercion to get your way. If you are a militant revolutionary who passionately desires to create a new kind of social order controlled by a new elite, you must expect the current government to resist your efforts violently. Both sides in such total conflicts inevitably use coercive tactics. It is impossible to imagine what "rewards" could induce people to become slaves or serfs or to give up all privileges and power, and probably their lives.

Second, resources for use as inducements are always relatively scarce. A poor man may have no money to bribe a public official, even if that is the only way to get a favorable decision from him. Even a monarch can run short of useable wealth. Machiavelli long ago warned princes not to be generous with their own resources, since recipients could bleed them dry.

He suggested that they rely mainly on plunder from conquered peoples to reward faithful allies and lieutenants. This policy has been followed as second nature by most conquerors, but aggressive war always risks life, limb, fortune, and power. Plunder has its costs.

Offices with some power and privileges attached may also be used as inducements. But, as a harried U.S. president, John Adams, once observed, every appointment under a spoils system creates one ingrate and ten enemies. The demand for office always exceeds the supply.

A constant problem for all large-scale states and empires has been to assure that officeholders—tax collectors, provincial governors and military commanders, royal ministers—will not use their delegated power to pursue their own interests in conflict with policies of the central government. To combat this tendency many autocratic rulers have appointed individuals of low social status—slaves, eunuchs, members of lowly ethnic groups—as top advisers and officials. They wanted to assure that subordinates would be totally dependent upon the ruler's favor and therefore more reliable than nobles with large estates, family prestige, and armed retainers.

In general, the effectiveness of delegating power as an inducement is always limited by the risk of undermining the inducer's *own* power position. Every military takeover of a government by an officer who has earlier been rewarded with promotion illustrates this principle.

Persuasion

To influence someone's actions by means of argument or information is the exercise of power as **persuasion.** We will distinguish three main types of political persuasion: rational, manipulative, and indoctrinational.

■ Types of Persuasion

Rational persuasion means attempting to influence someone's decision with information that the persuader believes to be true and advice that he or she thinks it would be in the subject's best interests to follow. President Harry Truman once remarked: "I sit here all day trying to persuade people to do the things they ought to have sense enough to do without my persuading them. . . . That's all the powers of the President amount to."[8] A U.S. president, despite his high authority, is not a dictator. Officials who are subject to congressional and interest-group pressures, as well as independently elected members of Congress, often have some choice about whether to comply with the president's wishes.

Rational persuasion is very commonly used within the private deliberations of governments and political organizations. In that setting, decision makers' interests are often similar enough that they all want to find a successful course of action. Also, despite all the popular cynicism about political rhetoric and advertising in democratic countries, political parties and candidates often succeed in accurately informing voters about the general policy line and major interests that they intend to represent.[9]

Manipulative persuasion involves using lies and deception, distorting and withholding relevant information. Consider a few examples: Hitler's claim that Poland had attacked Germany on September 1, 1939, was a lie that fooled no one for very long but was intended to camouflage his own brutal invasion of Polish territory. The political ambushes described at the beginning of this chapter were made possible by deceiving some of the people present on those occasions. The Soviet Union claimed that U.S. forces were using "germ warfare" during the Korean War, an untruth that had little impact on Western opinion.

Manipulative persuasion can raise difficult ethical and philosophical problems that we cannot explore in this context. It has surely been used at times by every government, however noble or praiseworthy we might generally consider its methods and objectives. We are wise to be suspicious of such techniques, however, because they are used so frequently to harm rather than protect the interests of the manipulated. We must also recognize that some governments use lies and deception much more than others, mainly because governments differ greatly in their ability to prevent people from challenging official lies.

Indoctrinational persuasion works over a much longer period of time than do specific efforts at rational or manipulative persuasion. Indoctrination involves attempts to shape people's beliefs, attitudes, and biases so that they will react in predictable ways to political events, messages, and symbols. This is a process that begins in childhood, as parents teach their children basic cultural norms and beliefs about authority, settlement of disputes, friends and enemies, rights and responsibilities. It continues in such settings as hunting and gathering expeditions, schools, apprenticeships, workplaces, ceremonial feasts and dances, church services, lodge and union meetings, and ideological study groups.

Indoctrination, whether deliberate or inadvertent, centrally directed or decentralized, aims at producing a kind of conditioned response in its subjects. Racial and ethnic prejudices are all-too-familiar examples that have enormous political importance. But attitudes that most of us claim to admire, such as hatred of tyranny, cruelty, and gross human misery, can also be promoted by indoctrination. Actually there are no foolproof methods of indoctrination. It simply does not "take," at least not completely, with many people. Learning from experience and exposure to conflicting attitudes and perceptions help to reduce its effectiveness. Nevertheless, indoctrination has always been and will undoubtedly remain an important form of persuasive power.

■ Means of Persuasion

Political persuaders tend to rely mainly on certain kinds of resources. One that has often proved effective is personal rhetorical skill, the ability to speak and argue impressively. In many primitive chiefdoms there was an official court "speaker," who earned and held his office with oratorical skills. In ancient Athens professional teachers of rhetoric, the "sophists," offered to instruct well-to-do young men in methods of speaking persuasively in popular courts and assemblies. An obscure Nebraska politician, William Jennings Bryan, so electrified the 1896 Democratic Party nominating convention with his "Cross of Gold" speech that he became the youngest man in U.S. history ever to win a major party presidential nomination. Tragically, the most persuasive political orator of the twentieth century was ex-corporal Adolf Hitler. Rhetorical talent—especially an effective television style—can still matter in politics, though it is by no means essential for gaining or exercising power.

In modern societies, much more important resources for political persuasion are the mass media of communications and mass formal education. The best evidence for the importance of persuasion as political power is the very small number of governments that have ever permitted anything approaching a free and diverse "marketplace of ideas." Censorship, harsh punishment for intellectual and religious "dissidents," maximum secrecy about the operations of government—these have been the historical norm.

The development of more effective techniques of mass communication, from Gutenberg's printing press to television and computer networks, has not been sufficient to change that normal state of affairs. It may be that modern communications technologies have actually increased the capacities for manipulative and indoctrinational persuasion by regimes that dictate the entire content of the media and of formal education. As chapter 8 will explain, this is an essential defining feature of totalitarian regimes. Historical experience has clearly shown that only multiple and unofficial sources of information and interpretation can check and limit governmental persuasive power.

Authority

Political **authority** is usually defined as *legitimate* power, the right to give commands that people have a moral obligation to obey. No government can long function without some degree of authority in this sense, any more than it can operate without effective means of coercion. In practice these two types of political power tend to vary inversely: the more people believe in the legitimacy of their government, the less they will need to be compelled to obey it. A low level of legitimacy requires that a government use much more coercive force to secure obedience.

Edmund Burke (1729–1797), a renowned British politician and writer, put this point memorably in his criticism of Enlightenment thinkers who wanted to base the authority of government solely upon appeals to individual reason and self-interest:

> On the scheme of this barbarous philosophy . . . laws are to be supported only by their own terrors and by the concern which each individual may find in them from his own private speculations or can spare to them from his own private interests. In the groves of *their* academy, at the end of every vista, you see nothing but the gallows. Nothing is left which engages the affections on the part of the commonwealth.[10]

Burke was claiming that any government that does not inspire in its subjects an emotional faith in its legitimacy and seeks to rely completely on coercion and inducements will be compelled increasingly to depend upon the punishment "gallows." His opponents retorted that the French monarchy had never so "engaged the affections" of its subjects that it could get along without frequent resort to the gallows, sometimes even for petty crimes. These critics of the old regime charged it with incompetence, oppressiveness, and unyielding defense of aristocratic privilege. Its claims to authority no longer deserved the French people's belief.

Both parties in this controversy made valid points. We can interpret their arguments as pointing up the subtle connections that can usually be found between governments' appeals to their people's self-interests and to some "higher good"—the safety of the state, protection of the "true faith," preserving the constitution. These objectives, of course, may require people to sacrifice personal interests, sometimes even their lives.

■ Divine Right

The French monarchy that Burke defended was one of the last important Western examples of an ancient type of political authority—**divine-right absolutism.** As we pointed out in chapter 1, rulers and priests in chiefdoms typically claimed that the chiefly lineage was descended from divine ancestors whose authority on earth is embodied in the living ruler. In one of the earliest large states, Old Kingdom Egypt of the third millennium B.C., religious leaders taught that the king (pharaoh) was the divine protector of cosmic and earthly order. He was often portrayed as Horus, the falcon god whose outstretched wings guarded the country and whose fierce eyes were the sun and the moon. In the premodern African kingdom of Dahomey, even ministers of state had to grovel and throw dirt on their heads in the divine king's presence. His awesome powers were displayed in the daily sacrifice of two slaves, dispatched as messengers to the king's ancestors in the spirit world.[11]

The teaching and practice of divine-right monarchy never took such extreme forms in medieval Europe, mainly because religious authority was monopolized by a church that could rival most secular monarchs in political power. The centralizing monarchies in early modern Europe—Britain, France, and Spain—revived autocratic divine-right claims but without long-term success. The beginning of the end for that type of legitimacy was symbolized in the trial and execution by antimonarchical revolutionaries of two reigning kings, Charles I of England in 1649 and Louis XVI of France in 1793. Among the notable twentieth-century graveyards of divine-right monarchy are China (1911), Russia (1917), and Iran (1979).

■ Popular Authority

The regime that replaced the deposed shah of Iran actually claimed a kind of divine legitimacy as implementer of the revealed truth of Islam. Its leaders labeled it an Islamic *republic*, which roughly means a government founded on "the people." In the contemporary world the only basis for legitimacy that *anyone* ever claims in public is that government must be "of the people."[12] Nearly universal agreement at this general level on the basic principle of governmental legitimacy has not produced a worldwide ideology of authority, much less similar regimes everywhere. Important differences in ideologies and regimes will be considered at length in Part Two of this book.

■ Types of Authority

The most influential attempt to categorize the major types of political legitimacy was proposed by Max Weber: he identified *charismatic, traditionalist,* and *legal* forms of authority.[13] First, **charismatic authority** refers to people's following a leader because they believe that he or she has extraordinary personal qualities that command their obedience, such as magical gifts, access to divinely revealed truth, or heroic military abilities. This is an intensified form of the "personal" authority that typifies the smallest and least complex of human societies. Charismatic authority lasts only as long as the followers' faith remains strong; it is by nature extremely unstable but can have enormous political impact.

As a rule charismatic leaders emerge only in times of social and political crisis. When things seem to be falling apart, many people strongly desire a political "savior." Not every crisis *does* produce charismatic leadership, though, and its appearance is always a surprise. Who would have believed before 1979 that an obscure Islamic leader in exile, the Ayatollah Khomeini, could inspire a massive and successful rebellion against the heavily armed, U.S.-backed Iranian monarchy? Or that an unknown shipyard

Charismatic leadership can play a critical role in the rapid emergence of political movements. Here, Lech Walesa, himself a manual worker, is cheered by thousands of his fellow Polish workers as they join in proclaiming the birth of the unofficial Solidarity trade union in 1980.

worker, Lech Walesa, could lead a spontaneous mass movement of workers' protests and unauthorized organizing against the communist regime of Poland in 1980? Yet these unexpected eruptions of charismatic authority did occur in recent years, with significant political consequences.

Weber's second category is **traditional authority;** it is based on the development and persistence of habits of obedience over many generations. People often assume that the political norms and institutions with which they grew up are the only ones conceivable and therefore obviously "right." Most societies in which people believe in the divine legitimacy of the regime exemplify traditional authority. The gods themselves are often deified ancestral rulers.

Even in relatively secularized societies, longevity of political beliefs, rituals, and institutions can contribute very significantly to their effective authority. By all accounts this is true of modern Britain. Its actual "constitution" consists not of any single written document but largely of centuries-old parliamentary and legal traditions that have changed gradually over time.

Third, **legal authority** is based upon acceptance of publicly articulated, society-wide rules and regulations issued by duly authorized public officials. Obedience is commanded not by custom or tradition but by "the law," understood as a rationally ordered and administered structure of explicit rules. A modern governmental bureaucracy best exemplifies legal authority. This concept does not specify any single ultimate source of law; it may be an elected parliament or a self-selected political elite. But "legal" authority does tend to enhance the importance of "official processes" and the necessity of going through "proper channels" rather than governing according to the personal whims of top leaders.

Weber emphasized that no governmental system ever represents a pure type of any one of these three kinds of authority, although the legal variety has become more pervasive in modern societies. The proliferation of regulations and the bureaucracies that administer them is an obvious characteristic of nearly all governments in the twentieth century.

■ Authority and Performance

Whatever the specific features of any government's system of authority, the practical effectiveness of its claims to legitimacy depends heavily upon governmental *performance*. An ancient Chinese emperor who proved unable to fend off attacks from barbarians or remedy the disastrous effects of floods or famine could be accused of having lost the "Mandate of Heaven," the supernatural sanction for his supreme authority. Sometimes the result was disobedience or even rebellion.

The German Weimar Republic (1919–1933) is an important twentieth-century example of a regime whose legitimacy was destroyed in large measure by its inability to cope with serious problems. Established in the aftermath of the defeat and downfall of the German Empire in the First World War, the republic was considered illegitimate from the outset by most supporters of the former monarchy. Its authority was further eroded by hyperinflation in the 1920s; the temporary worthlessness of the currency panicked a large proportion of the German people. Ultranationalist parties, including Hitler's Nazis and a strong communist party, were implacable enemies of the republic. Though represented in parliament, they also organized private paramilitary forces and brawling street gangs whom the government could not effectively control.

Mainly, though, the Weimar Republic died because of the impact on Germany of the Great Depression in the early 1930s. Widespread unemployment and poverty inspired mass protests and increased voting for extremist parties of right and left. The fatal step was the appointment of Adolf Hitler as chancellor (prime minister) of a right-wing coalition government. He used his control of official and unofficial means of coercion to ride roughshod and illegally over parliamentary opposition, securing an "Enabling Act" that made him the supreme dictator of Germany. In part he succeeded because the republican government had so little remaining legitimacy or support that no one was willing to risk its defense.

In contrast, the deeply rooted and nearly universal belief in the legitimacy of their constitutional systems within British and American societies enabled their regimes to survive the Great Depression without serious challenges. No government, though, is completely immune to an erosion of legitimacy caused by dissatisfaction with its performance. Ideological criticisms of "the system" are much more likely to find a receptive audience in times of economic crisis, widespread social disorder, or drawn-out and costly warfare.

■ International Authority?

A final question about authority: Does this type of power function in relations *between* independent states? It is easy to grasp how coercion, inducements, and persuasion (for instance, international propaganda efforts) operate among as well as within societies, but the case of authority is not so clear-cut or obvious. International law and the United Nations (discussed more fully in chapter 10) might be cited as types of international authority, but only in a feeble sense.

International law consists of treaties and conventions (such as the Geneva Convention on the laws of war) and of certain longstanding customary practices. But in a pinch, governments always deny that they are bound by any rules to which they have not specifically agreed in writing, and almost always they interpret those rules in accord with their national interests. In 1945 the United Nations Charter created a Security Council with authority to enforce sanctions against "aggressor" states. Yet deep conflicts of views and interests among the world's major powers have prevented this mechanism from dealing with most serious international conflicts.

At the end of the Second World War the major victors—the United States, the Soviet Union, and Great Britain—set up an international tribunal in Nuremberg, Germany, to try the top Nazi leaders for "crimes against humanity." Most of them were convicted and punished. The Nuremberg trials did not start a trend, however; governments have committed many more "crimes against humanity" in the decades since without inspiring the creation of similar tribunals. It is very hard to say whether there is some kind of dawning international political morality. If so, it has little *effective* authority, and there is seldom any way of enforcing it, even against the bloodiest tyrants. International authority possesses, at most, a feeble degree of legitimacy.

Combinations of Types of Power

We conclude this discussion of the major forms of political power (see table 2-1) by emphasizing their interrelatedness in political practice. For example, the Athenians tried to *persuade* the Melians to surrender by threatening them with superior *coercive* power and offering the *inducement* of sparing their lives and city. Athenian spokesmen also refused to recognize the *authority* of a divine morality that condemned their treatment of Melos.

Table 2-1 Types and subtypes of political power

Type	Definition	Examples
Coercion	Use or threat of sanctions	
Psychic pressure		"Brainwashing"
Physical force		Athenians on Melos
Inducements	Rewards for compliance or support	Israel's return of Sinai to Egypt
Persuasion	Influencing with argument or information	
Rational		Cabinet discussions
Manipulative		Hitler's claim of attack by Poland
Indoctrinational		School lessons in patriotism
Authority	Legitimate power, right to command	
Charismatic	Following extraordinary leader	Khomeini, Walesa
Traditional	Long-term persistence of norms and habits	"Conventions" of British constitution
Legal	Public laws and rules	U.S. government

The mix of these forms differs significantly across societies and circumstances. Stable sacred chiefdoms and constitutional democracies rely much more on consensual authority—general belief in their legitimacy—and much less on coercion than do newly established conqueror-states, military juntas, or totalitarian dictatorships. In times of foreign crisis a democratic government will probably rely on coercion—the draft—to raise armed forces, whereas a volunteer force recruited by financial inducements may seem adequate in peacetime. Throughout this book we will emphasize that one of the most informative ways of comparing governments is to focus on their structures and techniques for exercising power, both over their own populations and in relations with other states.

Strategies of Competition for Power

There are four main strategies that political power seekers adopt toward their competitors: *cooperation, toleration, domination,* and *elimination.* Like the forms of power, two or more of these strategies are often used in combination under specific political circumstances.

Cooperation

At first glance it may seem self-contradictory to list **cooperation** as a *competitive* strategy, but, as we pointed out in chapter 1, cooperative alliances of chiefs, warriors, and priests played a critical role in the cultural evolution of government and the state. **Coalitions**—groups whose members

share certain purposes and work together to realize them—have always been and remain a central structural feature of all politics.

Members of a coalition cooperate with each other in order to compete more effectively with other coalitions and individuals for valuable resources, including power. Cooperators may not receive equal benefits, though; their distribution depends largely upon the power relationships among coalition members. The Cabinet is the coalitional grouping that heads the British government; the prime minister is one of its members but is always considered "first among equals." The prime minister's status means, for example, that he or she is likely to have more effective power over British foreign policy than any of his or her colleagues or the Cabinet as a whole.

Cooperative groups that have an ongoing existence are often referred to as **organizations.** They are usually structured as a formal **hierarchy,** with multiple levels of authority. Officials at lower levels are answerable to their superiors, on up to the top level. Organizations feature a division of labor and responsibilities among their officials and employees and operate by more or less stable rules and procedures. A governmental ministry of health or a manufacturers' lobbying group would be an example of a political organization.

Historically, many large organizations have relied heavily upon coercion to carry on a cooperative enterprise from which the rewards were highly unequal. The slave laborers who built the ancient Egyptian pyramids and Stalin's political prisoners who constructed the White Sea–Baltic canal are typical examples.[14] An army staffed by draftees also exemplifies an organization highly dependent upon coercion. But in other kinds of organizations coercion is minimal or absent, and it is mainly inducements that keep their cooperative efforts going. These may be as minimal as a bureaucratic employee's salary and fringe benefits or as maximal as the hope of gaining supreme power, which can sometimes inspire dedicated revolutionaries to follow orders blindly.

Coalitions and organizations must continually cope with certain kinds of threats to their effectiveness and sometimes even to their existence. In a coalition it is always possible that some members will decide that they can do better for themselves by **desertion** of their partners, and they may even turn against them. For instance, a struggle for leadership took place within the Communist Party of the Soviet Union after Lenin's death in 1924. The main contenders were Joseph Stalin and Leon Trotsky.

Stalin proved more skillful as a coalition builder, exploiting his position as first secretary of the party. Not only did he appoint his men to subordinate party positions but he persuaded other top leaders such as Lev Kamenev and Gregory Zinoviev to provide him with crucial support within the inner councils. After this coalition had defeated Trotsky and forced him into exile, Stalin's personal power rapidly eclipsed his partners'. Within a few years these former top leaders and partners of Stalin were convicted on outrageously false charges of treason and executed. Teaming up with the wrong coalition partner can be hazardous to your health.

More recently, the Arab states' de facto coalition opposing official recognition of Israel was broken by Egyptian President Sadat. He decided that the national interests of his country could be better served by making a unilateral peace agreement with the Israeli government. The results were the Camp David Agreement in 1978, the temporary political isolation of Egypt within the Arab world, the return to Egypt of all its territory, and the assassination of President Sadat by opponents of his peace policy. Peacemaking can also be a dangerous occupation.

Just as the deserter is a constant hazard for small coalitions, many large-scale organizations must struggle constantly with the problem of **free riders:** people who benefit from an organization but do not contribute as they should to its functioning. Some civil servants protected by legal tenure and complex removal procedures may decide not to work very hard. Any particular free-rider employee's poor performance will have little effect on the total department, but if free riding spreads very widely, it can produce considerable frustration for departmental clients. A factory worker may benefit from high wages and short hours negotiated by a union, whether or not he or she joins the union and pays its dues. This possibility persuades some people to support laws that allow the "union shop"—compulsory union membership.[15]

Some political organizations, especially large political parties and interest groups, try to combat the free-rider problem by offering inducements to members that go beyond the supposed main purpose of the organization. The French Communist party, for example, sponsors leisure-time and recreational programs for members and their families in an effort to keep rank-and-file members. The American Farm Bureau Federation provides discount insurance and other financial aids to members as tangible personal benefits for supporting what is mainly a lobbying organization. Inducements can pay off.

Toleration

A second competitive strategy is to accept the right of one's competitors to exist and to seek power within a framework of general rules that permit only peaceful methods of competition. **Toleration** can range from grudging and suspicious acceptance of competitors as a necessary evil to a deep-seated consensus on the full legitimacy and permanence of political opposition. Complete, institutionalized political toleration is evident, for example, in official recognition of the "Leader of Her Majesty's Opposition" in the British House of Commons. As a competitive strategy, toleration involves representatives of rival groups in constantly trying to maximize their gains from unavoidable compromises.

General toleration of political competitors is a distinctive product of cultural evolution within a small proportion of complex human societies. Broadly speaking, the emergence of politically tolerant systems depends a great deal upon a particular kind of power balance within a society: *"The likelihood that a government will tolerate an opposition increases as the expected costs of suppression increase."*[16] "Costs" include political damage, organizational problems, and risks of severe and even successful resistance, in addition to economic difficulties.

Political toleration has tended to develop mainly in societies where effective power resources were so dispersed, or decentralized, that it was impossible to prevent organized opposition. The formation of the United States by voluntary and limited agreement among previously independent states is one classic example. If such a system persists for very long, deep-seated value commitments, emotional attachments, and vested interests develop in defense of its constitutional framework of political toleration.

Richard Nixon, the only U.S. president to resign his office, learned the hard way that a constitutional consensus on political toleration can set limits even to a head of state's using dirty tricks against political opponents.

Where these kinds of constitutional values and practices do not establish deep and broad roots within a society, basic institutions such as competitive elections, politically neutral courts, and legal criticism may be extremely precarious. Serious divisions between hostile political forces may then produce violent conflict rather than toleration and compromise. Bloodshed and a new, intolerant regime become highly probable. Examples include the fate of the Weimar Republic; the breakdown of the Spanish Republic in a civil war, ending with the victory of Franco's authoritarian regime in 1939; and the 1973 military coup in Chile, which overthrew the elected socialist president, concluding several decades of elective democracy and producing a harshly punitive government. Political toleration cannot be created at will, nor are there any guarantees that it will long survive.

On the international scene, toleration applies best to relatively stable and long-lasting "balance-of-power" systems that have occasionally emerged among similar states within particular regions of the world. Examples are the competing city-states of ancient Sumeria and, later, of ancient Greece, and the European state system from about the sixteenth century until the First World War. This kind of international system features rivalry for commercial, territorial, and sometimes colonial advantage among states. Their competition typically involves patterns of shifting alliances that reflect each government's vital interest in preventing the rise of a dominant conquering power. Because of the relatively even and changeable balance of effective power, campaigns of conquest and subjugation are uncommon. In effect each state recognizes the right to continued existence even of its bitterest enemies—so long as the balance is not decisively upset.

The principle of mutual and universal toleration among sovereign states is currently embodied in the United Nations Charter: "All members shall refrain in their international relations from the threat or use of force against the territorial integrity or political independence of any state. . . ." (Article 2). International politics since the adoption of this charter in 1945 surely illustrates one of the oldest laws (predictable regularities) of political life: legal principles are almost never self-enforcing.

Domination

Using the strategy of **domination,** some individuals and coalitions gain and keep positions of superior power and privilege by coercive means, mainly armed force and intimidation. As we explained in chapter 1, the domination strategy could not be used so long as people lived exclusively in small, independent, kin-based societies. Only in relatively crowded, highly restricted regions did conquest and domination become possible. Where people could not flee their militarily stronger would-be overlords, the first institutionalized patterns of public political inequality—chiefdoms, then states—emerged and flourished.

Political domination always requires cooperation. The most absolute monarch or total dictator can never rule without loyal and effective helpers. However, a relatively small group can function as a ruling elite, dominating the subject mass of the population, when the rulers control a near-monopoly of coercive force. Effective force is the indispensable foundation for rule that also relies upon indoctrinational persuasion, minimal inducement ("protection"), and an official ideology of authority.

Historically, agrarian societies, based upon large-scale peasant agriculture, exemplified most clearly that kind of regime. The Akkadian Empire of ancient Sumer, the ancient Egyptian monarchy, the Roman Empire, Imperial China, the monarchies of India, and most states of Europe until the nineteenth century all exhibited the basic political structure of a subject mass ruled by a tiny elite.

The **governing class**[17] never exceeded 2 percent of the population in any agrarian society; the French nobility in the late eighteenth century represented only 0.6 percent and the nineteenth-century Russian nobility 1.25 percent of their populations. Most high officials were members of the nobility, although rulers also recruited talented commoners, who were sometimes rewarded with hereditary titles and estates for their families.

Whatever their disputes among themselves—and they were frequent—members of the governing class cooperated in their domination and exploitation of peasants and artisans, who were wholly excluded from politics. Squeezing the agricultural surplus from commoners through taxes, tributes, forced labor, tolls, bribes, the sale of offices, rents, and royalties, the small governing class obtained half or more of all social income. To say the least, their level of material security, comfort, and luxury was much higher than the peasants'. The strategy of domination paid off handsomely for the ruling elite.

Since organized cooperation can greatly increase the power of the cooperators, regimes based largely on domination normally try to prevent or at least closely regulate all nonelite coalitions and organizations. In medieval Europe, heretical religious groups were ruthlessly suppressed as potential threats to the established ecclesiastical-political order. Twentieth-century totalitarian regimes demonstrate a similar intolerance toward all organizations that they do not originate, sponsor, and control. Political history clearly implies that the only practical means of preventing political domination is broad dispersion of organizational power. That kind of social arrangement requires considerable freedom of association, though, which has been historically rare.

As an international political strategy, domination has frequently been tried, often successfully. The history of conquests and incorporation of conquered territory into the victor's domain is clear evidence. One example should suffice: the United States seized and annexed a large section of Mexican territory—the present states of California, Arizona, and New Mexico—by winning the 1848 war between the two countries. Without going that far, militarily superior states may allow subject states some degree of internal autonomy but control their foreign relations and main economic policies, as did the nineteenth-century British empire. Or a militarily dominant state may allow weaker states to claim full formal sovereignty, while it seeks to make dutiful satellites of them by ensuring that their leadership and policies fit into its political-ideological mold. This pattern is exemplified by the post–World War II relationship between the Soviet Union and such Eastern European states as Hungary, Czechoslovakia, and Poland.

No doubt it seems a tragedy of politics that the strategy of domination has so frequently worked and shows no signs of disappearing. It is also important to note that it does not *always* succeed: the Greeks prevented Persian conquest; Napoleon's marauding armies were halted and reversed; Britain was not invaded by the Nazis; Franco's Spanish authoritarianism was succeeded by constitutional democracy.

Domination is not risk-free for a governing class. People really don't enjoy getting pushed around and exploited. Banditry, peasant revolts, urban riots, slave uprisings, rebellions, and revolution have sometimes disrupted the lives of ruling elites. Even when these violent protests fail, as most of them have, a few grudging concessions may be wrung from frightened rulers. Unfortunately, there is no guarantee that successful efforts to destroy an oppressive regime will actually decrease the amount of political domination within the society. That kind of change in the governmental system depends on much more than the ideological claims and promises of victorious revolutionaries (see chapter 13).

Elimination

In a political context, **elimination** has two very different meanings. First, it refers merely to ending competitors' effective political power. Within systems based on political toleration, that is the normal outcome of parliamentary votes or competitive elections that are lost by the party in power. Both victory and defeat are temporary, however, and current winners are willing to accept defeat should they lose official power in the future.

Within nontolerant political systems, rivals' official power may be eliminated by competing members of the political elite. In 1964, Nikita Khrushchev was forced by his Soviet Politburo colleagues to retire from his post of top leadership, and he died a natural death in obscure private circumstances. In 1967, a coalition of colonels seized control of the Greek government from civilian politicians but allowed them either to go into exile or to live out of the public eye.

In a second sense, *elimination* means the use of physical force to imprison or kill competitors, opponents, and enemies, real or imagined. Most people find political imprisonment, torture, and killing to be the grimmest and most depressing features of politics. They have been and remain such common practices, though, that realistic understanding is impossible without confronting them.

Pursuing a strategy of political domination always involves selective eliminations, as did Oliverotto da Fermo's treacherous murder of civic leaders. Critics, dissidents, and rebels are also likely targets for imprisonment or execution. Where the dominant elite desires to exploit the labor of its subjects, it will have no interest in eliminating any sizeable portion of them unless it feels desperately threatened. Peasant uprisings are savagely suppressed, but mass extermination of peasants is rare.

When invaders of occupied lands are mainly trying to gain that territory for their own use, extensive killing becomes a real possibility. Prehistorians are still debating whether our direct ancestors, early *Homo sapiens sapiens*, exterminated the Neanderthal subspecies of humans who lived in Western Europe until about 35,000 years ago. What does seem clear is that the Neanderthals disappeared about 5,000 years after modern-type humans began to migrate from the east into the west of Europe. It is difficult to believe that Neanderthals peacefully gave up their rich hunting lands and voluntarily starved.

One anthropologist suggests that the Western Neanderthals were "culturally swamped" by modern humans, who brought with them a much more sophisticated technology for producing stone tools—and weapons.[18] He proposes an analogy with the fate of Native Americans who confronted the superior military capabilities and political organization of European immigrants and their descendants. Massive, forced, and often lethal exiles and massacres of Native Americans in one-sided wars were common features of that conflict of peoples and cultures for the use and control of land.

In the conduct of warfare, selective mass killing is sometimes used to terrify and intimidate potential enemies. The Athenian destruction of Melos; the Romans' slaughter of the citizens of their long-time rival, Carthage, after which they plowed up the ground and sowed it with salt; the Nazi annihilation of the Czech village of Lidice in the Second World War—these are only a few famous examples from a possible catalogue of thousands.

Inside a state, elimination may be used as a strategy in competing for power, either unofficially, officially, or both. Unofficial efforts include assassination of public officials. Julius Caesar, Russian Tsar Alexander II, U.S.

Presidents Lincoln, Garfield, McKinley, and Kennedy, President Park of South Korea, President Sadat of Egypt, and Prime Minister Gandhi of India all exemplify the ever-present threat of a leader's violent elimination. Assassinations alone do not usually change governments and regimes very much, although the 1914 assassination of the heir to the Austro-Hungarian throne was an important exception to that rule. It triggered the First World War, an enormously destructive conflict that set off far-reaching political changes throughout the world.

Organized terrorism usually involves not only assassination attempts but also bombings of innocent civilians, hijackings, kidnapping, and extortion. Most terrorists claim to act in the name of a political cause, usually some variety of frustrated nationalism. Oppositional terrorism alone cannot bring down a regime. A terrorist group succeeds only when it develops into a full-scale revolutionary movement that attains sufficient military power to defeat the government's forces. For example, the Sandinista movement, which led in the armed campaign that defeated the Somoza regime and took power in Nicaragua in 1979, originally exploited political hostage taking to get publicity and money.

It is *official* policies of eliminating certain kinds of people that have proved most destructive, primarily because a government has all the coercive, organizational, and technological resources of the state at its command. Leaders of some governments have deliberately and ruthlessly carried out policies of mass extermination against those whom they defined as dangerous enemies. We will mention only three horrendous examples from recent history.

Adolf Hitler, the dictator of Nazi Germany, made no secret of his sincere belief that the Jewish people were the most dangerous and treacherous enemy of mankind, and especially of the "Master Race" he championed. Hitler used the power and resources of the German state to attempt the systematic extermination of all the European Jews. He was finally stopped, but only after the murder of six million innocent men, women, and children.

By 1929 Joseph Stalin had become the supreme ruler of the Soviet Union. Before his death in 1953, Stalin had engineered the deaths of tens of millions of innocent citizens of the USSR; details of his campaigns for eliminating "enemies of the people" are discussed in chapter 9. With his quarter-century reign of terror, Stalin holds the all-time numerical record among tyrants for turning their own subjects into corpses.

In percentage terms, however, he may have been surpassed in this grisly competition by the Cambodian Khmer Rouge regime of Pol Pot in the mid-1970s. These fanatical Marxist-Leninists drove all city dwellers into the countryside without food or shelter, executed tens of thousands who had had any connection with the former regime or its U.S. allies, and killed most people who had any formal education. Possibly 30 to 40 percent of the Cambodian population were killed by Khmer Rouge actions before Pol Pot and his helpers fled the invading Vietnamese in 1978.

These mass-murdering regimes differed somewhat in the nature of their victims and, to a lesser extent, in their ideologies. What they had in common, though, was a structure of unrestrained, highly concentrated, and monopolistically organized coercive power. It enabled them to carry to nightmarish extremes official policies of eliminating "enemies" and political competitors.

In concluding this sometimes depressing subject of competing for power, we note that the strategy of *cooperation* is a universal of politics. It is essential for successfully *dominating* or *eliminating* competitors, as we have explained, but it is also inseparable from a strategy of political *toleration*. Cooperative associations such as political parties and interest groups compete and compromise with each other inside a constitutional framework that limits their techniques of striving for power and its rewards.

Summary

In public politics, power assumes four primary forms: coercion, inducement, persuasion, and authority.

Coercion is the use or threat of severe sanctions by some people against others whose actions the power wielders seek to control. It includes both psychological pressure and the use or credible threat of physical force. Coercive force is always dangerous, but sometimes it is essential for deterring destructive aggressors, and it is always necessary for preserving law and order in complex societies.

Inducements are rewards either given or promised for acting as the reward-providers desire. Inducements are many and diverse, both in domestic and in international politics. They are not effective, however, when competitors for power have irreconcilable interests. Resources for use as inducements are never unlimited, and rewarding people with offices doesn't guarantee that they will faithfully protect their patron's interests rather than their own.

Persuasion as power involves using arguments and information to get people to act as the persuader desires. Persuasion is rational when it communicates only what the persuader believes to be true and in the subject's best interests. Manipulative persuasion uses lies and deception to influence its targets. Long-term indoctrinational persuasion starts in childhood and aims at producing emotional responses and biases relevant to politics and public policy.

Authority is legitimate power, the right to give commands that people have a moral obligation to obey. No government can function for long without minimal authority, though its amount and basis differ greatly among governments. The less authority a government has, the more it must rely on coercion, and vice versa. Social scientists often refer to three types of authority, as categorized by Max Weber: charismatic, based on belief in the extraordinary, possibly supernatural, qualities of a leader; traditional, the persistence of habits of obedience over many generations; and legal, deriving from public and duly authorized rules and regulations. The authority of any government tends to be diminished or sustained by people's experience of its actual performance.

In practice, the primary forms of political power interact in many complex combinations. Structures and processes for exercising power are an important focus of comparisons among governments.

Competitors for political power pursue, singly or in varied combinations, four main strategies: cooperation, toleration, domination, and elimination. These are summarized in table 2-2.

People cooperate by forming coalitions and organizations to advance their political and governmental interests. Benefits gained from cooperation tend to be distributed according to power relationships among the cooperators. Coalitions are always vulnerable to desertion by one or more members. Large organizations often confront the problem of free riders who receive organizational benefits but contribute little to producing them.

Toleration is a strategy mainly of governmental systems in which peaceful organized opposition is accepted as legitimate. Competition operates within rules that prohibit efforts to cripple or destroy any organized political competitor respectful of those rules. Such governments have been historically rare and may not survive very intense political conflict. They include, however, all functioning political democracies.

Domination involves gaining and keeping superior power and privilege by coercive means. It always requires cooperation within a ruling elite or governmental class and has been the main strategy of most governments throughout history. Efforts by states to dominate other states—through

Table 2-2 Strategies of competition for power

Type	Definition	Examples
Cooperation	Working together for common goals	Coalitions, organizations
Toleration	Accepting political diversity	Democracy
Domination	Control through coercion	Imperial rule
Elimination	Getting rid of competitors or enemies	Losing elections, assassination, genocide

conquest and absorption of territory, coercive control of basic policies, or the creation of satellite regimes—have often succeeded.

Elimination can refer to deprivation of power through an election or through forced removal from office. But it also means the physical destruction of competitors, whether for positions of rule or for control of territory. The most extreme type of elimination involves annihilating entire categories of people whom absolute rulers classify as threats to their ideological cause.

Whatever the power strategies that competitors pursue in any time and place, they always produce or inspire ideas intended to explain and justify their actions and policies. Human beings are the supremely symbolizing, linguistic, idea-generating species. We shall next consider how those traits are expressed in the endless quest to gain and exercise political power.

Review List of Key Terms

coercion
psychic pressure
credible threat
appeasement
inducement
persuasion
rational persuasion

manipulative persuasion
indoctrinational persuasion
authority
divine-right absolutism

charismatic authority
traditional authority
legal authority
cooperation
coalition
organization
hierarchy

desertion
free rider
toleration
domination
governing class
elimination

Notes

1. Niccolò Machiavelli, *The Prince*, in *The Prince and Selected Discourses*, ed. and trans. Daniel Donno (New York: Bantam Books, 1966), p. 37.
2. See John Kifner, "Massacre over Tea: Southern Yemen Conflict," *New York Times*, February 9, 1986, pp. 1, 9.
3. E. Adamson Hoebel, *The Law of Primitive Man* (New York: Atheneum, 1979 [1954]), pp. 187–188.
4. G. W. F. Hegel, *Reason in History*, ed. and trans. Robert S. Hartman (Indianapolis: Bobbs-Merrill, 1953), p. 27.
5. See Thucydides, *The Peloponnesian War* (New York: Random House Modern Library, 1951), pp. 330–337.
6. Hoebel, *Law*, p. 280.
7. See Gerhard E. Lenski, *Power and Privilege: A Theory of Social Stratification* (New York: McGraw-Hill, 1966), pp. 218–219.
8. Quoted in Richard E. Neustadt, *Presidential Power: The Politics of Leadership* (New York: Wiley, 1960), pp. 9–10.
9. In fact, studies of U.S. presidential elections have found that voters learn more about candidates' issue positions from paid political commercials than from television news. See Thomas E. Patterson and Robert D. McClure, *The Unseeing Eye: The Myth of Television Power in National Elections* (New York: Putnam, 1976), pp. 125–128; Thomas E. Patterson, *The Mass Media Election: How Americans Choose Their President* (New York: Praeger, 1980), pp. 169, 192.

10. Thomas H. D. Mahoney, ed., *Reflections on the Revolution in France* (Indianapolis: Bobbs-Merrill, 1955), pp. 87–88.
11. Jac. J. Janssen, "The Early State in Ancient Egypt," in *The Early State*, ed. Henry J. M. Claessen and Peter Skalnik (The Hague: Mouton, 1978), pp. 218–220; Lenski, *Power and Privilege*, pp. 153–155.
12. See Reinhard Bendix, *Kings or People: Power and the Mandate to Rule* (Berkeley: University of California Press, 1978).
13. This discussion is based on *From Max Weber: Essays in Sociology*, ed. Hans Gerth and C. Wright Mills (New York: Oxford University Press, 1946), pp. 295–301.
14. Dennis H. Wrong, *Power: Its Forms, Bases, and Uses* (New York: Harper & Row, 1979), pp. 139–140.
15. See Mancur Olson, *The Logic of Collective Action* (Cambridge, Mass.: Harvard University Press, 1965).
16. Robert A. Dahl, *Polyarchy: Participation and Opposition* (New Haven: Yale University Press, 1971), p. 15. (Italics in original.)
17. This is Gerhard Lenski's term. Our discussion of agrarian societies is based mainly on his *Power and Privilege*, pp. 219–230.
18. See Bernard G. Campbell, *Humankind Emerging*, 3rd ed. (Boston: Little, Brown, 1982), pp. 419–420.

THREE

Power and Political Ideas

And indeed the most coldly calculating people do not have half the success in life that comes to those rightly blended personalities who are capable of feeling a really deep attachment to such persons and conditions as will advance their own interest.
Robert Musil, The Man Without Qualities

A great deal of intelligence can be invested in ignorance when the need for illusion is deep.
Saul Bellow, To Jerusalem and Back

If you were a high school student who desperately wanted a part-time job but couldn't find one, you might readily agree with arguments against minimum wage laws. It would make sense to you that employers would hire more inexperienced workers if they could pay them less than the law now requires. But if you were a high school graduate trying to make it on your own with a minimum-wage job at a restaurant, you would probably believe that minimum-wage laws are essential to prevent ruthless exploitation of unorganized workers.

This example illustrates two important points: first, it is usually possible to make a persuasive-sounding argument for either side of most public-policy controversies; second, most people tend to agree with the position that favors their self-interest. This does not mean that all arguments are equally valid, factually or logically. Neither does it mean that self-interest and opinions always coincide—but that is a real and politically significant tendency.

Ideas and beliefs are an extremely important feature of politics; they both affect and are strongly affected by competition for power in every society. What we believe and how we think are determined by much more than the ways our physical senses perceive the world around us. Emotional needs and drives and habitual thought patterns all contribute to **selective perception**—a tendency to notice and attend seriously only to certain types of observations, usually those that seem to confirm what we already think. Strongly partisan Democrats, for example, tend not to pay careful attention to Republican messages.

We also tend to leap to conclusions based on very little information. Studies of how people most often think about other people reveal, for instance, that we are much more likely to remember and draw sweeping inferences from vividly and personally communicated information than from masses of abstract data. Actually seeing someone use food stamps at a supermarket checkout and then get into an expensive car in the parking lot may lead an observer to conclude that all food stamp recipients cheat.

He or she will tend, quite illogically, to take this single observation as representative of a huge population and simply refuse to believe valid surveys showing that nearly all food stamp users are truly needy.[1] It may require considerable training and self-discipline to overcome this deep-seated pattern of thinking. Also, of course, it is much easier to spot this tendency in other people than in ourselves. How well beliefs work for us, practically and psychologically, powerfully affects what ideas we take seriously and accept as true.

We all learn from experience that it is extremely hard to think clearly, calmly, and objectively about ourselves. Take, for example, students who copy other students' term papers and turn them in as their own work. The cheaters may tell themselves that their assignments were unreasonable and pointless, justifying a failure to spend time doing them. These students may truly persuade themselves that they acted from perfectly defensible motives and indignantly reject any suggestion that they are dishonest. **Self-deception** can influence much of our thinking—but especially how we rationalize our efforts to gain and use power.

The Nature of Ideology

Serious explorations of the plentiful and complicated connections between ideas and political power are usually classified as the study of **ideology.** This has become one of the most ambiguous words in politics, journalism, and political science—fields with no shortage of terms that are difficult to define clearly or use objectively. But because the word is used so commonly, it is impossible to avoid, and the phenomena to which it most often refers are undoubtedly important.

The term *ideology* was first suggested by French writer Antoine Destutt de Tracy at the beginning of the nineteenth century. He used it to label a proposed "science of ideas" that would attempt to discover the precise causal connections between people's sense experiences and their thoughts.[2] The first really influential concept of ideology, though, was formulated by Karl Marx (1818–1883), the most important intellectual founder of revolutionary communism.

Marx asserted that the economic structure of any society—land, technology, markets, the property system—fundamentally shapes all other institutions and relationships, as well as people's thoughts and beliefs: "It is not the consciousness of men that determines their existence, but, on the contrary, their social existence [i.e., economic situation] determines their consciousness."[3] At any given time, the prevailing ideas in a society justify and rationalize the power and privileges of the economically dominant class. They are the people who control the means of production, whether land under feudalism or factories in industrial societies.

Let's consider two examples: The prevailing religion in a peasant society may teach that all true believers will receive a glorious reward after death, more than making up for the great inequality of rewards in this life. That belief would work to the advantage of the rich and powerful by persuading poor people to accept their earthly condition rather than rebelling against it. Business executives are likely to believe strongly that private enterprise is the best possible economic system, since it provides them with freedom to try to maximize their own profits.

Marx's concept of ideology did not imply a conscious, deliberate plot by the dominant class. Its members may sincerely believe in the religious or philosophical doctrines that justify their position in society. Ideologies always take the form of principles claimed to be good for society as a whole, not merely a single class or segment.

This concept of ideology has a good deal of validity and usefulness. We would broaden the category of "interests" to which ideas and beliefs become attached to include not only economic benefit but also gaining or keeping power, for whatever reasons. We will classify as **rationalization ideology** all ideas that attempt to justify or legitimize anyone's material or power interests.

In the twentieth century a broader conception of ideology has developed, reflecting historical trends and changing uses of the term. In practice, ideology now involves more than rationalization; it implies some kind of distinctive political "worldview." From this perspective, self-conscious and systematic political ideologies, such as liberalism, conservatism, socialism, and communism, are largely a modern phenomenon.

These systems of ideas began to emerge in Western European societies in the seventeenth and eighteenth centuries and have spread throughout the world, as traditional societies began to undergo rapid economic, political, and cultural alterations. Ancient religious beliefs and customary patterns have been challenged by secular doctrines that both reflect changes in the distribution of power and help to bring them about.[4]

We will define a **worldview ideology,** then, as a set of ideas that are intended to interpret society and politics, justify a particular kind of political and social order, and encourage action on their behalf.[5] Such an ideology provides a picture of the social and political world within the framework of a particular interpretation of history. That is, it specifies what is "wrong" with the world and why. If it is an official ideology, it explains how it has provided the "cure" for previously existing evils and what new ones must be combated.

In addition, a worldview ideology claims to provide the best possible solutions for all social and political problems. Finally, it calls for commitment to the ideological cause, including action to bring to power those who profess it or to defend it against real or supposed enemies. A worldview ideology is closely linked to political action and so to political power.

How are rationalization ideology and worldview ideology related? In truth, *all* worldview ideologies function as rationalization ideologies, because one of their essential purposes is to justify and legitimize the power of particular kinds of political groups and leaders.

Cultural beliefs and values not linked to any specific worldview ideology can also be used to rationalize positions on public issues. For example, a deep suspicion of governmental power has been embedded in the political culture of the United States since colonial times. It has been appealed to by such diverse groups as opponents of progressive income taxes, foes of censorship, supporters of religious schools, and proponents of legalized marijuana. Essentially nonpolitical ideas and beliefs can function in some circumstances as rationalization ideologies—otherworldly religious teachings, for example.

The most influential broad types of worldview political ideologies in the contemporary world are nationalism, democratic capitalism, democratic socialism, and Marxism-Leninism (revolutionary socialism or communism). There are also subcategories of these major types; for instance, both liberalism and conservatism in the United States fit mainly under the umbrella of democratic capitalism. Some ideologies combine more than one major type—for example, nationalist communism.

German National Socialism (nazism) and Italian fascism were politically important ideological movements before the end of the Second World War but now have few followers. However, fascist-like ways of thinking and organizing are far from extinct in military and collectivist dictatorships.

Ideology and Interests

In a broad sense, how does ideology relate to competing for and using political power? That is, what is the connection between ideas and interests—especially material benefits and power—in politics? On this question there are two extreme positions that we consider exaggerated and inadequate.

Reductionist Views of Ideology

First, there is the claim that ideology is always nothing but rationalization for the interests of those who profess and promote it. Sociologist Pierre van den Berghe, for instance, asserts: "Ideology is a sophisticated belief system the purpose of which is to facilitate the transmission of credible, self-serving lies."[6] Since he also refers to ideology as a form of "collective self-deceit," Professor van den Berghe clearly implies that people whose interests are protected by ideological "lies" almost always believe in their truth and are not deliberate, scheming liars.

Two classic versions of this reduction of all ideas and beliefs to rationalizations for individual and group self-interest are the theories of Marx (in one interpretation, at least) and of Friedrich Nietzsche (1844–1900), an influential German philosopher.

Marx declared that "the mode of production in material life determines the general character of the social, political, and spiritual process of life."[7] He apparently meant that the ideas prevalent in any society are solely a distorted, self-serving rationalization of the interests of the dominant class—people who own and control productive wealth.

Nietzsche asserted: "Above all, a living thing wants to *discharge* its energy: life as such is will to power." It follows that any system of thought "always creates the world in its own image; it cannot do otherwise, for philosophy *is* this tyrannical desire; it is the most spiritual will to power, to 'creation of the world'. . . ."[8]

There is a fatal flaw in theories that reduce all ideas to rationalizations, whether of economic interest or of personal power drives. These theories are themselves ideas, and if they were correct, then they could be nothing but rationalizations and could logically make no claim to truth independent of the class interests or power drives of their authors. Marx's theory, then, would reflect only the impact upon one mind of the class system of his society, and Nietzsche's would represent nothing more than his will to be more powerfully influential than other philosophers. Since Marx and Nietzsche believed that they were communicating truth about ideas, they could not have meant that *their* ideas were merely rationalizations.

Ideology as Personal Conviction

A second view of the relationships between ideas and interests is hard to connect with particular thinkers, but it is often implied by most of us, as well as by theorists and ideologists. This view denies any element of rationalization in one's own beliefs and might be expressed in these terms: "I hold to *my* political principles because they are objectively true and, if practiced, will promote the good of the whole society or even of all humanity. Ideally, everyone should rise above self-interest in deciding on ideological commitments and rely solely on genuine knowledge and moral insight. People are capable of acting consistently with their moral principles, even against their own interests. In all modesty, if I always favor the public interest over self-interest, why can't everyone else?"

This view at least has the merit of claiming some kind of objective truth. Unfortunately, it has the defect of claiming infallibility and total unselfishness—rare qualities at best. Furthermore, if a person who holds this view resists having his or her claims to truth tested or even denies obvious facts that conflict with them, as often occurs, we are rightfully suspicious that important interests lurk in the background. If we notice that businesspeople almost always oppose higher corporate taxes and that ruling Communists always argue against freedom of the press, we have good reason to suspect that something more than sincere commitment to ideological principles accounts for their views.

A Modified View

In our judgment, there is overwhelming evidence for a carefully qualified version of Marx's and Nietzsche's views of the links between ideas and interests. The material and power interests of individuals and social groups strongly *condition*, *color*, and *bias* their political perspectives, the ideas about politics and policy to which they are attracted and become attached. For instance, consider a study of the political views of leaders of self-styled "public interest" consumer groups in the United States. When asked what degree of influence various leadership groups, such as business, unions, the media, and feminists, should have in American society, they give a strong first-place ranking to "consumer groups"—themselves.[9]

The close links between ideas and interests become especially obvious when an ideology is changed or "reinterpreted" in line with its interpreters' vital interests. For example, white Southern politicians helped lead the struggle for American independence from Britain in the 1770s and endorsed the claim of the Declaration of Independence that "all men are created equal." The conflict between that belief and the institution of slavery seems absolute. What happened? Logically, slaveowners could either free their slaves or give up the belief in basic human equality. But most did neither: they simply incorporated into their ideology a belief that black people are not fully human and so are not covered by the language of the Declaration.

A more recent example was Adolf Hitler's classifying his Japanese military allies as "honorary Aryans." "Aryans" were the pseudoracial group of highest value in Hitler's racist ideology, which labeled Asian peoples in general as grossly inferior to Nordic Europeans. Surely the slaveowners' and Hitler's ideological flexibility was inspired by strongly felt needs to protect their economic and political interests. The examples could be multiplied endlessly, and they could be drawn from every single type of political ideology.

In contrast, there do seem to be numerous cases in which actions and policies inspired by ideological commitment are carried through even when they do not serve the interests of the political actors. For instance, most Republican members of the U.S. Congress supported the Voting Rights Act of 1965, which first provided effective protection for black voters in the Deep South. It was entirely predictable that most of those new voters would not vote Republican, but the ideological commitment of those members of Congress to the enforcement of constitutional rights significantly influenced their positions.

A very different example of the impact of ideology on policy was Hitler's treatment of European peoples whom his racist doctrine classified as inferior or harmful. Instead of trying to win over the peoples of Eastern Europe where his armies were temporarily successful, he treated the supposedly inferior Slavs with brutality and contempt. He also devoted enormous industrial and military resource to his mad but systematic policy of exterminating the Jews. Fanatical belief in his own ideology led in both cases to policies that weakened German power.

In brief: interests and political ideas tend to coincide; when they don't, ideas tend to change; but strong belief in political ideas—ideologies—can sometimes inspire policies that do not support or may even undercut the material or power interests of the policy maker.

Functions of Worldview Ideologies

Of the major types of political power, persuasion and authority are most closely related to ideology. We will emphasize these categories of power in describing briefly what we consider the three main functions of political ideologies: **orientation, legitimation,** and **delegitimation.**

Orientation

A worldview ideology provides its believers with a sense of understanding history and society and with cues about what kinds of things they should pay attention to or ignore. In the United States, for example, many ideological liberals tend to regard history as a progressive march toward greater economic and social equality and liberation from the authority of "outworn" traditional values and institutions. A high proportion of American conservatives, however, believe that economic progress has been produced by free enterprise and unequal rewards and feel strongly attached to traditional patriotic and religious values and institutions.

These ideological orientations have consequences. In discussing human rights in the contemporary world, for instance, liberal writers and editors will tend to devote most of their attention to political oppression and persecution in countries with traditionalist or "right-wing" governments. Conservative publications will cover most thoroughly human rights abuses in communist-controlled countries. These tendencies certainly do not mean that liberals favor communism or that conservatives approve of military tyranny. Rather, their ideological biases lead them to perceive different types of regimes as the major threats to the human rights that each type of ideologist values most highly. If their readers can be persuaded that a particular policy accords with their ideological bias, they are much more likely to support it than they would be otherwise.

Legitimation

A central function of ideology is "to define a particular program of social action as legitimate and worthy of support."[10] We would add: to define a political system, regime, or government as legitimate and worthy of obedience. Legitimacy reinforces authority, a fundamental form of political power.

People who believe strongly in the moral validity of a movement or regime may be readily persuaded to act even in risky ways on its behalf. A few British and United States diplomats, for example, betrayed official secrets to the Soviet Union in the 1930s and 1940s mainly out of ideological conviction that Soviet communism represented the progressive "wave of the future." Large numbers of untrained Iranians were mobilized to fight against Iraqi troops in the 1980s, persuaded by the leaders of the "Islamic republic" that their lives were a necessary price to pay for a sacred cause.

Strong ideological belief among political elites, whether of a movement seeking governmental power or of a regime that has it, greatly reinforces their self-confidence and sense of commitment. Elites who are thoroughly persuaded of their own ideological legitimacy are best able to persuade and mobilize followers; movements or regimes that they lead are formidable competitors for power.

Delegitimation

Every political ideology is to some degree a "fighting faith." Its advocates will often work to discredit and undercut the legitimacy of rival ideological movements and regimes. For example, Soviet leaders since the late 1950s have persistently declared that "peaceful coexistence" with the West does not extend to ideological combat. In fact they devote enormous organizational effort and resources to propaganda broadcasts, publications, efforts to manipulate information in non-Soviet media, and training and indoctrination of political activists from all over the world. These efforts combine in an endless campaign to undermine the legitimacy of pro-Western political groups and governments. In a less organized and consistent fashion, the United States government has responded with similar efforts aimed at communist movements and regimes.

In some cases, events can contradict the claims of a reigning ideology so obviously as to weaken the legitimacy of a regime whose leaders profess that ideology. In his influential 1944 book, *An American Dilemma*, Swedish social scientist Gunnar Myrdal emphasized the contradiction between the

American ideology of equal rights and the extensive system of racial segregation that then existed in the southern and borderline southern states of the United States. The commitment of many Americans to democracy and human dignity led them also to deny the legitimacy of legalized segregation. Their efforts and attitudes finally led to the abolition of official discrimination.

The leaders of ruling Marxist-Leninist parties always claim to represent the true historic interests of the working masses of the population. In Poland, for instance, this claim is symbolized in the official name of the ruling communist party: the Polish United Workers Party. That is why the spontaneous and massive effort in 1980 to organize Solidarity, a trade union independent of the ruling party and government, was seen as a profound threat to the legitimacy and stability of their regimes by the communist leaders of Poland and of the Soviet Union. If the toiling masses actually reject the self-proclaimed party of the workers, who is in error, the workers or the ruling party? Ideology, then, can sometimes function as a double-edged sword.

A final comment on the functions of ideology: despite claims and pretenses, ideologists do not really seek to provide objective, factual descriptions of society and politics: "No great ideology has ever regarded the disciplined pursuit of truth—by scientific procedures and in the mood characteristic of modern science—as part of its obligations."[11] In this important sense, ideology differs from scholarship or science, even though it may sometimes use and influence their methods and findings.

This difference does not mean that objectivity about politics is easy; scholars are always affected, at least unconsciously, by their biases, including ideological beliefs. In principle, though, however difficult and imperfect the practice, the interpretations and conclusions of scholars and scientists are open to correction and disproof by relevant evidence.

The mindset that tends to go with total commitment to an ideology can result in ignoring, denying, or trying to explain away evidence that threatens the basic assumptions and values of the ideologist. Because of an ideological opposition to governmental regulation of business, for example, a conservative economist may try to minimize scientific evidence about the health effects of toxic wastes. Similarly, ideological hostility to private business may inspire a liberal environmentalist to portray the most fragmentary data about toxic wastes as evidence of a chemically induced mass plague.

Students of politics need to learn about contemporary ideologies and to become aware of the varied and often subtle ideological biases of political activists, leaders, journalists, scholars, scientists, editors, professors, clergymen, book reviewers, and anyone else who says or writes anything publicly about politics. But total cynicism about sources of information and comment can be self-defeating. Ideologically motivated statements and studies can sometimes be wholly or partially true; bias does not always lead to falsehood. The world cannot be neatly divided into political truth tellers and ax-grinding ideologists. The quest for a broad understanding of politics requires that we learn to compare and critically sift through information that comes from ideologically diverse sources. It is an endless and demanding task.

Worldview Ideologies: Some Basic Categories

There are many systems of classifying and comparing ideologies, but we suggest that a simple fourfold set of categories, presented in figure 3-1, can point up some important differences among worldview political ideologies.

Limited ideology and **comprehensive ideology** refer to the breadth of concerns addressed by a political worldview. **Critical ideology** and **supportive ideology** simply call attention to whether ideas are being used to attack or to defend and legitimize a particular regime.

A comprehensive ideology includes doctrinal views of almost everything that interests or concerns human beings: human nature and motivation, ultimate reality and religion, the meaning of history, and the proper roles of art and literature in society, as well as the nature and functions of government and political processes. The most influential modern ideology of this type has been Marxism—not that all Marxists have the same views on all those subjects; far from it. Most Marxian ideologists do agree, however, that Marxism ought to have something definitive to say about all of them; certainly Marx believed that he did.

The Iranian Ayatollah Khomeini's version of Islam seems to fit within the "comprehensive" category. It was used to attack the government of the shah of Iran before 1979, and since the rise to power of Khomeini's radical clerics it has legitimized the revolutionary Islamic regime (see chapters 12 and 13). This religiously based ideology pronounces not only on government and religion and their relationships but on art, music, popular culture, education, relations between the sexes, and clothing styles. It aims at enforcing and implementing through the concentrated power of government a particular religious worldview for the whole society.

In contrast, democratic socialists seldom if ever insist that there is a single correct ideological interpretation of such subjects as human nature, religion, history, or the arts. They generally restrict their party ideologies to criticisms of capitalism and proposals for reshaping the economy and government. As democrats they favor allowing a great deal of personal autonomy and not dictating official religious, philosophical, or cultural standards for society as a whole. This ideology in some form is professed

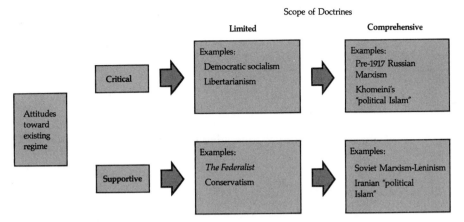

Figure 3-1 Categories of worldview ideologies

by a number of major European parties such as British Labor, the French Socialists, and the West German Social Democrats.

Socialism, whether democratic or autocratic, is strongly opposed by libertarians, who fervently believe that all individuals should be allowed to lead their own lives as they see fit, including their economic lives. Understandably, then, libertarians strongly oppose almost all governmental intervention in the economy; they favor a much smaller and less active government than any that has ever existed in a modern state. Obviously, their basic principle is completely incompatible with any attempts to impose on society uniform doctrines or detailed codes of behavior.

Strictly speaking, *The Federalist* did not support an existing regime. As we noted in chapter 1, it was written in 1787–1788 as part of a successful propaganda campaign for the newly proposed U.S. Constitution. However, this work has long been considered the classic analysis and defense of a plan of government that has endured for two centuries. Although it does state a view of certain tendencies in human nature, it otherwise deals almost exclusively with governmental and economic issues.

Present-day conservatism in countries such as Britain and the United States staunchly defends limited government, the rule of law, private property, and the market economy. There is enormous religious and philosophical variation among conservatives, however, ranging from Christian fundamentalism to atheism and scientific skepticism. Conservative ideologists are equally diverse in their cultural tastes and standards. There is no uniform conservative ideological "line" that all or even very many philosophical conservatives seek to impose on most areas of human activity.

The comprehensive-supportive type of ideology emerged in 1917 with the seizure of power by the revolutionary Marxist Bolsheviks in Russia. Hitler's Nazi doctrine and Mussolini's Italian Fascism were also important twentieth-century examples. The official South African Nationalist ideology of *apartheid* ("separate development," in practice meaning racial segregation, discrimination, and white supremacy) also fits reasonably well within this category.[12]

The leaders of regimes with comprehensive-supportive ideologies tend to insist upon ideological conformity in most spheres of social life. They also monopolize the right to pronounce on the current meaning and implications of the ideology. No matter how much these leaders may revise or even contradict their ideology in practice, they persistently deny that any ideological change has occurred or will ever be permitted. Starting in the early 1960s, Chinese Marxist-Leninist leaders charged Soviet Marxist-Leninist leaders with the ideological crime of "revisionism," an accusation that the Soviets hotly denied.

Emphasizing ideological continuity and uniformity in no way restricts the tactical flexibility of the ruling elites. It does provide them, though, with an important mechanism of indoctrinational persuasion, an all-encompassing framework within which to interpret events to the general population, and a measuring rod for testing people's overt loyalty to the regime.

Ideology, then, combines ideas, feelings, and practice: its ideas provide both context and content for political persuasion and aim at creating and sustaining authority. Both as rationalization and as worldview, ideology remains a critically important component of politics in the modern age.

In order to illustrate more concretely some of the important uses and effects of ideology in politics, we turn to an extended case study of a particular ideology—**nationalism.** Devoting considerable attention to it seems justifiable also for its own sake, for nationalism has been the most broadly appealing political ideology in the nineteenth and twentieth centuries. As historian Anthony D. S. Smith declares, "Of the visions and faiths that compete for men's loyalties in the modern world, the most widespread and persistent is the national ideal."[13]

Ideology and Power: The Case of Nationalism

As summarized by political scientist Elie Kedourie, nationalist "doctrine holds that humanity is naturally divided into nations, that nations are known by certain characteristics which can be ascertained, and that the only legitimate type of government is national self-government."[14] The key term here is *nation*, the Latin root of which refers to "birth." *Nation* implies, then, a collection of people who belong together because of common traits that they were born with or acquired from family and culture while growing up.

In some cases the most important trait that nationalists single out is common genetic heritage, or "race," but this is inevitably combined with cultural characteristics, especially language, religion, literature, folk arts, customs, and traditions. Where race is not involved, selected cultural traits alone serve as the focus of national identity. National consciousness may also develop out of people's sharing a common territory, historical experience, or political institutions over an extended period of time.

Nation is a very slippery word, quite susceptible to manipulative interpretations. In a practical sense, it tends to be defined subjectively, through people's beliefs and actions: "Although objective factors are of great importance for the formation of nationalities, the most essential element is a living and active corporate will."[15]

Another term often used in connection with *nation* is **ethnic group,** which in its most general sense refers to "a basic human category . . . characterized by unity of race and culture."[16] In practice, *nation* is so elastic that its meaning is not restricted to "a self-conscious ethnic group."[17] That definition would apply reasonably well to some nations, such as the French and the Japanese, but it would not apply at all to multiethnic nations such as the American, Mexican, or Indonesian.

In political terms, either a "nation" has its own government or, if not, dissatisfied nationalists may claim to represent its true political interests. Their goal is to achieve national self-government, or at least some kind of special political status within a larger governmental framework. For example, French-speaking Canadians, most of whom live in the province of Quebec, have traditionally been considered a distinctive ethnic group within the Canadian nation. In recent decades, though, a Quebec nationalist movement has emerged, claiming the right to nationhood—including some kind of political autonomy—for the French-speaking majority in the province.

Origins and Effects of European Nationalism

Ethnic grouping is ancient, as is **patriotism,** the love of one's homeland, but the ideology of nationalism is distinctively modern. It appeared considerably later than the emergence of the first European nation-states—France and Britain. They began to take shape in the Middle Ages through the military, diplomatic, and political successes of a series of monarchs who worked at centralizing governmental authority in royal hands. Those rulers managed to overcome the prevailing pattern of medieval politics in which effective power to govern was mainly held by hundreds of noble and churchly feudal lords ruling small territorial units. By the seventeenth century a widespread sense of nationhood within clearly defined state boundaries seems to have developed among the French and English people.[18]

■ Rise in France

As an ideology, nationalism emerged from the explosive mixture of ideas and events that swept across Europe from 1789 until 1815. This turbulent period began with the French Revolution and encompassed both Napoleon's imperial conquests and his final defeat by the anti-French European powers. Ideologically, the revolutionary regime repudiated all traditional claims to political authority, such as divine right, inheritance, and conquest. In the words of the Declaration of the Rights of Man and the Citizen, adopted by the National Assembly in 1789, "The principle of sovereignty resides essentially in the Nation; no body of men, no individual, can exercise authority that does not emanate expressly from it."[19] The practical meaning of this claim was powerfully symbolized by the public execution in 1793 of the reigning French king, Louis XVI.

When the outraged and frightened monarchs of Europe, led initially by the Austrian Hapsburgs, threatened the revolutionary regime, its leaders called for national unity and total self-sacrifice by its massive citizen-armies. Louis de Saint-Just, a prominent radical revolutionary, declared: "There is something terrible . . . in the sacred love of the fatherland; it is so exclusive as to sacrifice everything to the public interest, without pity, without fear, without respect for humanity."[20]

The French armed forces succeeded not only in defending their country but in conquering large areas of Europe, spreading the doctrines of popular sovereignty and liberation from traditional religious and political authorities. Under the military rule of Napoleon Bonaparte, however, the French came to be seen by many Spaniards, Italians, Prussians, Austrians, and Russians as foreign oppressors to be resisted and driven out. Ironically, the French stirred up and intensified national feeling in other European countries, and traditional rulers exploited it to mobilize their populations against Napoleon's forces. Although the victors tried to restore the old order after 1815, they could not long contain the new forces of nationalist ideology and movements.

For example, much of Italy was included within the Austrian Hapsburg Empire, and Italian nationalist movements seeking expulsion of all foreign overlords and a unified Italian state were active by the 1830s. The most notable ideologist of Italian nationalism, Giuseppe Mazzini (1805–1872), founded Young Italy, a revolutionary organization committed to achieving a united and independent Italian republic.

■ Italian Nationalism

Mazzini claimed to be seeking above all the good of humanity. Because the human population is so enormous, however, he declared that individuals can relate directly to others only through the nations into which God has divided mankind. In Europe, selfish kings had ignored such natural boundaries as great rivers and mountain ranges that God had intended to mark the limits of specific nations—"today there is perhaps no nation except England and France whose confines correspond to this design."[21]

Mazzini urged the many peoples of Europe to become aware of their unity and destiny, throw off alien monarchies, create their own free governments, and work in harmony with one another to realize God's purpose of leading humanity to a new age of happiness and fulfillment. The people whom God had chosen to initiate the age of armed "national liberation" struggles and ultimate political salvation for humanity were the Italians. They had suffered much at the hands of foreign conquerors but had a glorious Roman past to inspire them. Mazzini called upon Italians to reject all forms of individualism, to submerge themselves, even to the point of complete self-sacrifice, in the great nationalist movement that would ultimately lead all nations to greatness.

Mazzini's ideology exemplified messianic nationalism, the national cause as a form of political salvation for its devout believers. Similar ideologies were articulated by Germans, Poles, Russians, and Serbians and by self-proclaimed spokesmen for nearly every ethnic group in nineteenth-century Europe—especially those still incorporated into the multiethnic Hapsburg and Ottoman (Turkish) Empires.

Mazzini was typical of messianic nationalist ideologists in his disappointment with the political results of nationalist efforts. A unified independent Italian state did come into being by 1861, thanks largely to the political skills of Camillo de Cavour, chief minister in the northwestern Italian monarchy of Savoy, and to armed assistance against the Austrians from French Emperor Louis Napoleon. Mazzini felt that the nationalist fervor that he had done so much to stir up had been exploited by scheming, power-seeking politicians.

The Spread of Nationalism

In fact, practical-minded and opportunistic political leaders did make the most of the climate of opinion created by nationalist propaganda and organizations. By 1870 a unified German state had also emerged through a combination of military success and political shrewdness orchestrated by the chancellor of Prussia, Otto von Bismarck. "Pan-German" nationalists, who sought a state that would unite all German speakers, were especially frustrated by Bismarck's decision not to include in the new German Empire the ethnic German portions of the Hapsburg Empire.

By the end of the nineteenth century, the map of Europe had been significantly changed by new nation-states (see figures 3-2, 3-3, and 3-4). That kind of territorial unit had come to seem the natural and inevitable form of political organization. Nationalist movements and agitation in the Balkans and elsewhere in Eastern Europe, sponsored or opposed by rival great powers, helped lead to the First World War (1914–1918).

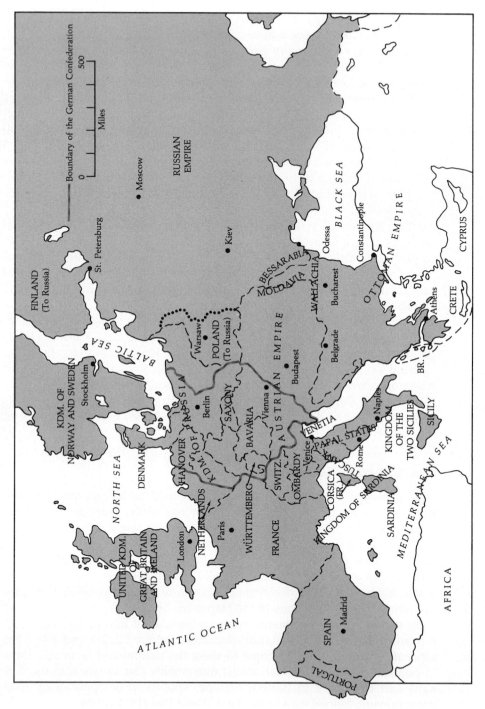

Figure 3-2 Europe in 1815

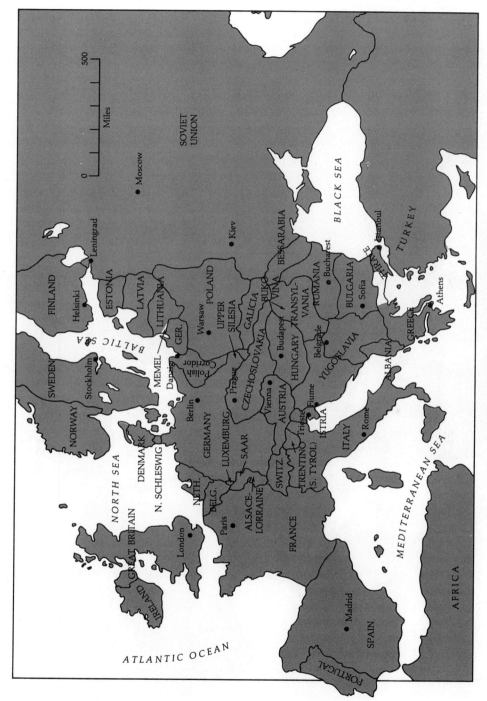

Figure 3-3 European nation-states after the First World War

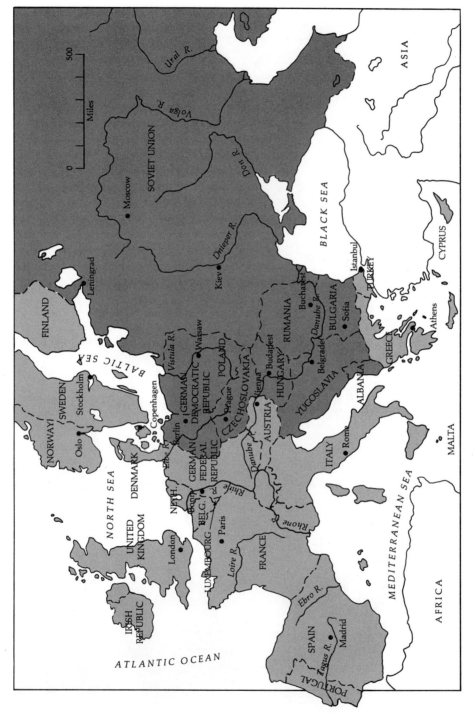

Figure 3-4 European states after the Second World War

During that war, U.S. President Woodrow Wilson declared: "'Self-Determination' is not a mere phrase. It is an imperative principle of action. . . . This war had its roots in the disregard of the rights of small nations and of nationalities which lacked the union and the force to make good their claim to determine their own allegiances and their own form of political life."[22]

Although Wilson intended the right of **national self-determination** to apply only to Europe, the concept and nationalist ideology that justified it were taken up by leaders of anticolonial movements within the overseas European empires. After the First World War, nationalist movements were organized among members of the educated elites in countries as varied as British India, French Indochina, and the Dutch East Indies.

As a rule, non-Western nationalists asserted their resentment not only against alien rule but against the radically different culture introduced into their lands by Europeans. Typical was Gandhi's assertion that the "tendency of Indian civilization is to elevate the moral being, that of the Western civilization is to propagate immorality."[23] Recently, that same point of view has been even more vehemently expressed and much more rigidly enforced in the Ayatollah Khomeini's revolutionary-Islamic Iran.

The Western cultural invention of nationalism proved extremely useful to anticolonial politicians for articulating demands and organizing political movements. Nationalist efforts helped lead Britain, France, the Netherlands, Belgium, and Portugal either to give up control of or to be driven out of their overseas territories in the post–World War II period.

A kind of international legitimacy was bestowed upon nationalist ideology by the United Nations Charter, adopted in 1945, in its pledge of "respect for the principle of equal rights and self-determination of peoples" (Article I, paragraph 2). Disputes, often violent, continue in many parts of the world over who constitutes a "people" or nation with a right to political self-determination.

Nationalism and Political Power

The many different political uses of nationalism have made it an extraordinarily flexible and ambiguous ideology. As clearly summarized by political scientist A. W. Orridge:

> Nationalism is not a set and defined ideology or kind of political movement that can be exactly described and that is transferred whole from place to place. Rather it is a few simple ideas about the relationship between states and cultures that first emerged as a response to the prestige of countries such as France and Britain. It is adopted and adapted by

> political leaders in a wide range of situations who emphasize very different elements of the original models. In this way the different kinds of nationalism multiply and each in turn can become the model for other kinds of nationalism, which in their turn also borrow and modify the idea.
>
> The idea that separate cultures deserve some political recognition can be used in the defense of an immense range of interests.[24]

It is very clear, then, that nationalism has served not only as a political worldview but as a rationalization ideology connected to a wide variety of political and economic interests. In different times and places nationalism has been linked closely not only with "national liberation" from foreign rules but also with ideologies and movements of imperialism, racism, fascism, nazism, socialism, and communism.[25] One specific example: even Mazzini, the ideologist of independent nations in the service of humanity, urged Italy to extend its "civilizing mission" to the presumably less civilized peoples of Asia.[26] He apparently decided that some nations *are* justified in dominating others—so long as it was his nation that was the master and not the victim.

Throughout its history nationalist ideology has been intimately connected with the ambitions of would-be political elites and the political needs of elites who have newly risen to power. According to Kedourie's analysis of nationalism,[27] for instance, the originators of German nationalism in the late eighteenth century were young intellectuals from humble families. They were frustrated by exclusion from important positions in government, which were generally reserved for sons of the aristocracy. In addition, these socially marginal young men resented and envied the influence of French language, literature, ideas, and intellectuals in German lands, especially at the Prussian court of Frederick the Great.

In reaction, they exalted and idealized the German language and called for an ideal culture-community within which they would play a leading role. "The Scholar," wrote Johann Gottlieb Fichte (1762–1814), the most influential ideologist of early German nationalism, "sees not merely the present—he sees also the future: he sees not merely the point which humanity now occupies but also that to which it must next advance. . . . In this respect, the Scholar is the *Guide* of the human race."[28]

Nationalism as support for new governing elites is clearly evident in most of the states that have emerged from former European colonial empires since the Second World War. When those countries had originally been brought under European control, they were not nation-states. In nineteenth-century sub-Saharan Africa, for example, there were about six thousand distinct cultural-linguistic groups, organized politically into bands, chiefdoms, principalities, and empires. In competing for African colonies late in that century, European governments set off their territorial

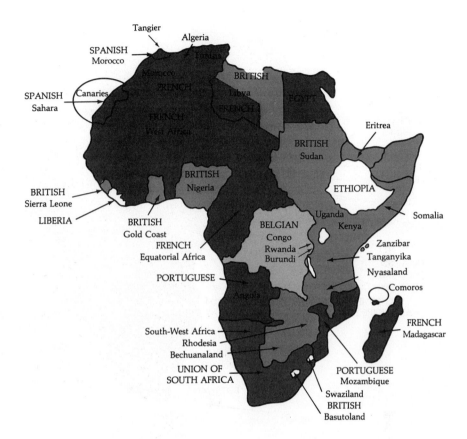

Figure 3-5 Late colonial Africa (about 1950)

claims with arbitrarily drawn boundaries. These colonial administrative units often incorporated deadly ethnic enemies and divided members of the same linguistic-ethnic groups.[29]

When leaders of anticolonial nationalist movements gained independence for these European-created countries and became their new governing elites, they always insisted that the colonial boundaries be respected as the territorial borders of their new states (see figures 3-5 and 3-6 for comparisons of colonial and post-colonial Africa). Having used nationalist ideology to inspire and lead independence movements, they hoped that it would also create a sense of common nationhood among their diverse peoples. Sékou Touré, the leader of the West African state of Guinea, confidently predicted as he took power from the French: "In three or four years, no one will remember the tribal, ethnic, or religious rivalries which,

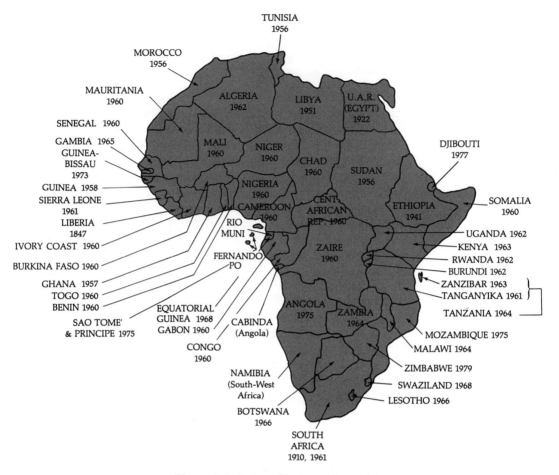

Figure 3-6 States of independent Africa

in the recent past, caused so much damage to our country and its population."[30]

That expectation proved to be far off the mark, not only in Africa but in much of the Third World. Political scientist Crawford Young does believe, however, that policies and nationalist ideology have combined with some effectiveness in a few countries, such as Indonesia, Nigeria, Cameroon, and Kenya, so that some degree of national consciousness has developed.[31]

Ethnonationalism and Political Conflict

The issue of ethnic diversity leads to our final main point about nationalism. It illustrates the earlier observation that an ideology can sometimes be used as a political weapon against others who claim devotion to it. We refer specifically to the worldwide phenomenon of **ethnonationalism**.[32]

The marriage between ethnicity and nationalism goes back to the origins of that ideology, as seen in the emphases on the distinctiveness of the German language and of historic Italian culture. But there are thousands of ethnic groups in the contemporary world and only about 160 sovereign states. It is not surprising that nationalism should be an important ideological weapon in competitive struggles among ethnic groups for power and resources.

In the Middle East an ethnonationalist struggle for control of the same territory has continued for decades. The Palestine Liberation Organization claims to represent a nation deprived of its homeland and determined to retrieve its own country. Militantly opposing that claim, the Israelis believe their state to be the legitimate homeland of the long-exiled Jewish people and deny the distinctive "nationhood" of the Palestinian Arabs.

French-Canadian Quebec nationalism has developed along with a sizeable new intellectual community of French-speaking Canadians. Even the old British nation has been challenged by resurgent Scottish and Welsh nationalism since the 1970s, mainly in the service of movements protesting the economic decline of Scotland and Wales.

Ethnonationalism—the claim that an ethnic group is a nation with its own right to political self-determination—has been most troublesome for Third World countries. Ethnonational conflict, sometimes severe and violent, has wracked a majority of them at some point in the past few decades.[33] Rulers of these states uniformly reject ethnonationalist claims to self-determination and identify the true "nation" with the boundaries of their states, despite the absence in most of them of very much national consciousness or awareness.

The outcomes of ethnonationalist struggles are not determined by showing up the self-contradictions of nationalist leaders who oppose other people's efforts at self-determination. What counts is the effective balance of power between ethnonationalists and their adversaries. Military capabilities and aid from other countries are generally more important in determining that balance than is the power of ideological persuasion.

For example, from 1967 to 1970, the large Ibo ethnic group attempted to secede from Nigeria and establish the independent state of Biafra in which it would be numerically dominant. This effort was opposed not only by the Nigerian government but by both the Soviet Union and the major Western powers. The Nigerian army had no trouble getting military aid, while the Biafrans ran short of all supplies. After a ferocious civil war, Biafran secession was defeated.

By contrast, in 1971 Bengali leaders in East Pakistan declared its separation from West Pakistan as the new sovereign state of Bangladesh. In part because of its longstanding policy of checking Pakistani military power, the government of India sent in its much larger army to defend Bangla-

For many of his fellow Poles, Pope John Paul II embodies a combination of charismatic, religious, and nationalist authority. Here, he bestows a blessing on an enormous throng during his visit to Poland in 1983.

desh. The balance of power strongly favored the new state, and it survived. It remains, however, the sole example in the Third World of successful ethnonationalist "self-determination" in the postcolonial period.

Nationalism in a variety of forms seems likely to remain a feature of the political world indefinitely. It can still provide an emotionally powerful focus for grievances and resentments against foreign domination, as does the strongly nationalist Catholicism that flourishes among the anti-Russian Polish people. So long as there are ethnically defined groups whose members feel resentful and deprived and would-be political elites to articulate an ideology that appeals to their distinctiveness, nationalism will persist. As is true of all other important political ideologies, its precise shape in any particular time and place will continue to depend upon the strategies and fate of those who use or oppose it in the struggle for power.

Summary

Study of the connections between ideas and political power focuses mainly on *ideology*, a term with various meanings. Marx defined it as ideas that rationalize and justify the position of the economically dominant class—those who own and control the means of production. The term can be usefully broadened to include power interests and relabeled *rationalization ideology*—ideas that attempt to justify or legitimize anyone's material or power interests.

Modern worldview ideologies are more or less systematic sets of ideas intended to interpret society and politics, justify a particular kind of politics and social order, and encourage action on their behalf. All worldview ideologies function as rationalization ideologies for political groups and organizations. The most influential present-day worldview ideologies are nationalism, democratic capitalism, democratic socialism, and Marxism-Leninism.

Reductionist interpretations of ideas in politics—arguing that they are *nothing but* rationalizations for material or power interests—cannot be supported, but neither can the view that interests and ideas have no special connections. As a rule, interests and ideas tend to coincide, and when they don't, ideas tend to change. However, strong ideological beliefs can sometimes inspire policies that do not support, or may even undermine, the material or power interests of the policy makers.

Worldview ideologies have three main functions: to orient people's attention and concerns within a framework of beliefs and values; to legitimize regimes, programs, and policies; and to delegitimize ideological opponents. Intense commitment to a political ideology often leads to ignoring or distorting facts inconsistent with the believer's worldview.

Worldview ideologies differ significantly in the scope of their doctrines and in their attitudes toward the political status quo. Some ideologies are comprehensive, incorporating doctrinal views on almost every kind of human activity or concern, whereas others are limited mainly to government and public policy issues. Both comprehensive and limited ideologies can be used either to support or to criticize and attack existing governmental and social systems. Political ideologies combine ideas, feelings, and action in efforts to reinforce political persuasion and to create and sustain distinctive types of authority.

Nationalism provides an important example of modern political ideology. It emphasizes the alleged common traits of particular peoples and claims for them a right of national self-rule. In practice, *nation* usually means what nationalists say it does. They may emphasize common race, religion, or language, living together in a common territory, or simply a shared history.

Nationalism has been coupled with a great variety of other ideologies and movements and exploited by political leaders whose purposes differed immensely. It has been used not only to legitimize struggles against alien rule but also in efforts by some nations to impose their rule on others. In recent decades, nationalist leaders in new states have used ideology, with minimal success, in attempts to create a sense of nationhood among their diverse peoples.

Many states, old and new, confront claims by ethnonationalists—people who claim that their ethnic group is a distinctive people who deserve political self-determination. Government leaders strongly resist efforts by ethnonationalist movements to break up existing states. Nationalism in varied forms is destined to remain an important component of the struggle for power within and among states. Its precise character and role depend on the interests and strategies of those who make or resist nationalist claims.

Review List of Key Terms

selective perception
self-deception
ideology
rationalization ideology

worldview ideology
orientation
legitimation
delegitimation
limited ideology

comprehensive ideology
critical ideology
supportive ideology
nationalism

ethnic group
patriotism
national self-determination
ethnonationalism

Notes

1. See Richard Nisbett and Lee Ross, *Human Inference: Strategies and Shortcomings of Social Judgment* (Englewood Cliffs, N.J.: Prentice-Hall, 1980), pp. 43–62.
2. Hans Barth, *Truth and Ideology*, trans. Frederic Lilge (Berkeley: University of California Press, 1976), p. 2.
3. Karl Marx, *A Contribution to the Critique of Political Economy,* reprinted in *Marx and Engels: Basic Writings on Politics and Philosophy,* ed. Lewis Feuer (Garden City, N.Y.: Doubleday/Anchor Books, 1959), p. 43.
4. See Willard A. Mullins, "On the Concept of Ideology in Political Science," *American Political Science Review* 66 (June 1972): 498–510.
5. This is a simpler statement of the main elements in Mullins's definition (ibid., p. 510); for similar definitions, see Thomas R. Dye, *Power and Society: An Introduction to the Social Sciences,* 4th ed. (Monterey, Calif.: Brooks/Cole, 1987), p. 228; and Reo M. Christenson et al., *Ideologies and Modern Politics,* 3rd ed. (New York: Harper & Row, 1981), p. 4.
6. Pierre L. van den Berghe, *The Ethnic Phenomenon* (New York: Elsevier, 1981), p. 9.
7. Marx, *Critique of Political Economy,* p. 43.
8. Friedrich Nietzsche, *Beyond Good and Evil,* trans. Marianne Cowan (Chicago: Regnery Gateway, 1955), pp. 15, 9.
9. S. Robert Lichter and Stanley Rothman, "What Interests the Public and What Interests the Public Interests," *Public Opinion* 6(2) (April/May 1983): 48.
10. Harry Johnson, "Ideology and the Social System," in *International Encyclopedia of the Social Sciences,* vol. 7, ed. David L. Sills (New York: Macmillan and Free Press, 1968), p. 81.
11. Edward Shils, "The Concept and Function of Ideology," in *International Encyclopedia of the Social Sciences,* vol. 7, ed. David L. Sills (New York: Macmillan and Free Press, 1968), p. 73.
12. See A. James Gregor, *Contemporary Radical Ideologies: Totalitarian Thought in the Twentieth Century* (New York: Random House, 1968), pp. 221–276.
13. Anthony D. S. Smith, *Nationalism in the Twentieth Century* (New York: New York University Press, 1979), p. 1.
14. Elie Kedourie, *Nationalism* (New York: Praeger, 1961), p. 9.
15. Hans Kohn, *Nationalism: Its Meaning and*

History (Princeton: D. Van Nostrand, 1955), p. 10.
16. Walker Connor, "The Politics of Ethnonationalism," *Journal of International Affairs* 27(1) (1973): 2 fn.
17. Ibid., p. 3.
18. Hugh Seton-Watson, *Nations and States: An Enquiry into the Origins of Nations and the Politics of Nationalism* (Boulder, Colo.: Westview, 1977), p. 17.
19. Quoted in Kedourie, *Nationalism*, p. 12.
20. Quoted in Kedourie, *Nationalism*, p. 18.
21. Guiseppe Mazzini, *The Duties of Man and Other Essays*, ed. T. Jones (London: Dent, 1907), p. 52; quoted in Dante Germino, *Modern Western Political Thought* (Chicago: Rand McNally, 1972), p. 313.
22. Woodrow Wilson, Statement of February 11, 1918; reprinted in *Modern Political Ideologies*, ed. Alan P. Grimes and Robert H. Horwitz (New York: Oxford University Press, 1959), pp. 501–502.
23. Mohandas K. Gandhi, *Indian Home Rule* (Ahmedabad: Navajivan Trust, 1946 [1909]); reprinted in *The Ideologies of the Developing Nations*, rev. ed., ed. Paul E. Sigmund (New York: Praeger, 1967), p. 105.
24. A. W. Orridge, "Varieties of Nationalism," in *The Nation-State: The Formation of Modern Politics*, ed. Leonard Tivey (New York: St. Martin's Press, 1981), pp. 51–53.
25. For a careful analysis of these relationships, see Smith, *Nationalism*, esp. pp. 43–149.
26. Germino, *Modern Western Political Thought*, pp. 317–318.
27. Kedourie, *Nationalism*, pp. 43–49.
28. Fichte, *The Vocation of the Scholar* (1794); quoted in Kedourie, *Nationalism*, p. 50.
29. Arnold Hughes, "The Nation-State in Black Africa," in *The Nation-State: The Formation of Modern Politics*, ed. Leonard Tivey (New York: St. Martin's Press, 1981), pp. 123–124.
30. Sékou Touré, *Toward Full Reafricanization* (Paris: Présence Africaine, 1959), p. 18; quoted in Crawford Young, "Nationalizing the Third-World State: Categorical Imperative or Mission Impossible?", *Polity* 15(2) (Winter 1982): 163.
31. Young, "Nationalizing the Third-World State," p. 176.
32. See Connor, "The Politics of Ethnonationalism."
33. Connor, "The Politics of Ethnonationalism," p. 2.

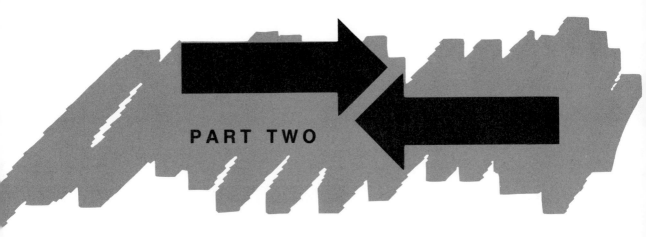

PART TWO

POWER AND GOVERNMENTAL SYSTEMS

FOUR

Functions and Types of Government

But what is government itself, but the greatest of all reflections on human nature?
***James Madison,** The Federalist, No. 51*

Governments are clearly the main focus of power in the modern world. Individuals, coalitions, and organizations strive as best they can to influence, control, use, resist, overthrow, change, and replace them. What governments do makes a big difference to all of us, whether we pay attention to them or not.

Many present-day governments are massive complexes of interlocking institutions that seem designed to frustrate attempts to understand how they operate and what they do or do not accomplish. In this chapter we will start trying to make some sense of this confusion, first by describing the main functions common to all governments. Second, we will focus on bureaucracy, the departments charged with carrying out most of those functions. Finally, we will propose a classification of contemporary governments that emphasizes important differences among them.

Basic Functions of Government: Essential Similarities

At an extremely abstract level, political scientists Gabriel Almond and G. Bingham Powell assert that all governments use their authority, backed by a credible threat of force, to make, apply, and pass judgment on conformity to "rules" for society as a whole.[1] But it is possible to be much more specific if we consider only the governments of sovereign states. All of them have been and continue to be involved with five functions: external protection, law enforcement, self-protection, economic management, and cultural reinforcement. In considering each of these functions we will also discuss briefly the kinds of institutions and organizations that are usually involved in performing them.

External Protection

Governments try to protect the state not only against military invasion and conquest but against any lesser encroachments upon its territory or sovereignty by the governments of other states. Our discussion of the origins of the state in chapter 1 strongly implies that **external protection** has always been the most basic function of politically independent societies. Those that could not effectively defend themselves were eliminated or incorporated into larger political units.

Almost always protection requires armed forces, either a state's own or those of its close allies. Raising and financing armies has been a problem for most governments. Their solutions have included conscription, hiring professional soldiers (mercenaries), rallying civilian volunteers to defend the homeland, and maintaining a standing professional military establishment.

From the perspective of civilian political leaders, the military can be a problem not only because of its expense but because its activities may extend well beyond preventing or defeating external attacks. Numerous Roman emperors, Napoleon Bonaparte in revolutionary France, and the many African military rulers since the 1960s all represent the historically common phenomenon of military leaders' using the forces they command to seize control of the entire government. The kinds of regimes that can result will be considered in chapter 7.

Governments of all kinds also use **diplomacy** to deal with foreign governments. Diplomats try to negotiate agreements that provide some benefits to their own government and usually to the other parties, such as mutual military assistance or guarantees of nonaggression. For example, foreign ministers Molotov of the Soviet Union and Ribbentrop of nazi Germany, acting on instructions from Stalin and Hitler, startled the world in 1939 by signing a nonaggression treaty between governments that had previously treated each other as bitter ideological enemies (see figure 4-1). This pact secured Hitler against attack from the east, enabling him to wage successful war for two years in Poland and in Western Europe. A secret treaty clause gave Hitler's approval to Soviet moves into the Baltic states and parts of Poland.

This example demonstrates that rulers sometimes interpret external "protection" as requiring invasion and conquest of other states. Such moves may intimidate potential enemy states, protect the ideological cause that a supreme leader seeks above all to advance (such as Hitler's fanatical racism), or create a larger buffer zone between the expansionist state and a potential enemy. Aggressive imperialists most often try to cloak their motives with the rhetoric of "essential security."

The supervision of military policy and diplomacy has always been a primary responsibility of executive leaders and institutions, and no government can possibly do without them. The **executive** is the part of government that is always on the job, unlike parliamentary bodies, which may be either out of session, powerless, or both. The executive, whether one person such as a president or a small group such as a military junta, is the most active part of the government and has many functions in addition to

Figure 4-1 David Low's classic response to the Hitler-Stalin Pact

external protection. It is always possible that executives will need to act quickly and decisively in response to emergencies. Executive power evolved originally from the pressures of military competition, and it retains something of the authority that must accompany responsibility for coping with threats and dangers.

Enforcing Law and Order

Glaucon, a character in *The Republic*, the most famous dialogue written by the Greek philosopher Plato (427?–347 B.C.), proposes an explanation of why people usually obey the law. He suggests that each of us would like to do as we desire, even harm other people if we could get away with it. We are afraid, though, that if everyone had that much freedom, nothing could stop others from harming us. So we enter into an implied agreement with everyone else that we will not harm others so long as no one hurts us. The only way to enforce that bargain is to establish general laws with penalties for breaking them. It is actually fear of getting caught and punished that usually keeps us from breaking the law and harming others in our own interest. If we think we will not be caught, we are easily tempted to violate the law for our own benefit.

Glaucon's theory is certainly not an adequate explanation for law-abiding behavior. Childhood indoctrination in the moral duty of obeying the law, civic pride and honor, habit, rational belief that it is in everyone's interest to have a lawful society—all play some part in reinforcing tendencies to respect the law. But threats of coercion are never entirely absent in any state: always some officials, whether called sheriffs, royal guards, constables, police, or something else, are authorized to arrest and hold lawbreakers. Nearly always—most contemporary British police being the main exception—these officials are armed and may use force on those who try to resist or escape from them.

Courts of some kind have the responsibility of trying accused lawbreakers, although sometimes prisoners do not live long enough in custody to reach trial. Enormous numbers of political prisoners in Stalin's Soviet Union were executed without trials. The same fate has also befallen some political activists in South African jails—though these regimes by no means invented or monopolize the practice.

Persons found guilty of lawbreaking are subject to punishment: fines, confiscation of property, exile, torture, imprisonment, death. The kinds, severity, and frequency of punishments have varied enormously among historical periods and societies, but even the mildest have featured very unpleasant sanctions. Fear of punishment has always been considered a necessary, if not a sufficient, motive for ensuring generalized observance of the law.

Laws and courts also provide a regularized and peaceful method of settling disputes among individuals and groups within a society. Lawsuits may drag on interminably; they may often benefit mainly the lawyers on both sides; they may sometimes produce peculiar verdicts. Most people, though, probably prefer an established legal system to dispute "settlement" by means of revenge and blood feuds, which are extremely common in prestate societies. **Law and order** sometimes becomes an ideological slogan to veil the policies of an oppressive elite, as it was in the segregation-era U.S. South or in martial-law Poland after 1981. However, genuine fear of lawlessness and disorder are powerful motives for obedience most of the time, even for people who have no voice in making the laws that rule their lives.

Self-Protection

Every government attempts—not always successfully—to protect itself against internal enemies. *Government* here is ambiguous. Sometimes the objective is mainly to preserve the existing regime or form of government, such as monarchy or democracy. In other cases the threat is not to the system of government but to its current leaders: for instance, a military coup directed against a military government. Most antiregime movements, of course, also seek to replace the existing rulers: Russian revolutionaries in 1917 wanted both to depose Tsar Nicholas II and to destroy the tsarist autocracy.

Laws against attempting to overthrow a government exist in every state, and most governments even severely restrict or outlaw peaceful criticism and opposition. Absolutist rulers are especially inclined to use extremely harsh methods of combating internal threats to their power. Unspeakable torture, drawing and quartering, agonizingly painful methods of execution, slaughter of huge groups of innocent people, and large and deadly concentration camps have typified the techniques of ancient and modern despots all over the world.

In addition, surveillance by secret police, the use of informers, and requiring official permission to travel or relocate are methods of internal security typical of many states throughout history. The most liberty-respecting states outlaw conspiracies that aim at the violent overthrow of the government, but these regimes do legitimize efforts at peaceful political change through democratic procedures.

Threats of violent subversion of a regime tend to inspire not only harsh responses but particularly vicious and violent conflict if official suppression proves inadequate. Civil wars and revolutions are notorious for indiscriminate violence. The stakes for participants can be extremely high: either total power or total powerlessness and possibly death.

Most governments seek to gain support by a variety of means, featuring persuasion and inducements, but all consider official coercion to be a legitimate means of **governmental self-protection**. In some states military forces are used much more frequently against domestic opponents than against the armed forces of other states—an historic tendency in Latin America. In addition to enforcing laws against nonpolitical criminals, some police forces, such as the U.S. Federal Bureau of Investigation, also attempt to act against terrorist and other "subversive" groups.

Economic Management

All governments are deeply involved in the economic life of their societies, although the range of variation among them is great. The folk wisdom about the inevitability of death and taxes points up one policy of every government: the compulsory extraction of wealth from members of the society to support official policies and personnel. No government ever gets by on voluntary contributions. For instance, one of the fatal flaws of the United States Articles of Confederation (1781–1788) was dependence of the national government on state governments' willingness to provide its operating funds.

Taxation is also a kind of **economic management**: it can encourage some kinds of activity and discourage others. Governments have always regulated the economy in a variety of other ways as well: encouraging, limiting,

One of the distinctive features of modern governments is that they provide a large variety of social programs. One of the more important is unemployment insurance, as represented by this local office of the U.S. jobs service program jointly sponsored by the federal and state governments.

or controlling foreign trade; granting or withholding licenses or monopolies; coining money and regulating banking and investment; establishing and enforcing laws concerning property and labor, and so on.

Governments have also undertaken economically important public works. In ancient India and China rulers built and managed large and complex irrigation systems, reinforcing the highly concentrated power of their governments.[2] Public roads as promoters of commerce and tax collecting interested the Roman government two thousand years ago as much as they do the U.S. government, which began constructing the massive interstate highway system in the 1950s. These kinds of public works, as well as such facilities as water systems, sewers, bridges, and public utilities, make up the **infrastructure** of the economy, its essential foundation.

An increasingly important kind of official economic activity in the twentieth century consists of **social programs**—welfare payments of various kinds, old-age pensions, medical assistance, unemployment compensation, and nutritional programs, to name the most obvious categories. The biblical Hebrew character Joseph helped an Egyptian ruler establish a program of food storage and redistribution to cope with famines, and Elizabethan England had "poor law" authorities who gave meager charity to the destitute. General policies of providing subsidies and services to broad categories of the population were not common prior to the twentieth century, however. Industrialization, urbanization, the decline of extended family support systems, and the spread of democracy are usually considered to be major causes of this important development. Both democratic and nondemocratic governments usually support at least some of these kinds of programs today.

Aside from defense against external threats, probably no function bears more upon the long-term fate of a government than its perceived economic performance. Increasingly, people blame their governments and not the gods for inflation, unemployment, hunger, waste, and poverty.

Cultural Reinforcement

No government has ever been completely indifferent to the shape and direction of its society's culture, in the broad sense of symbols and activities that express significant beliefs and are intended to persuade others to share them. In this context, efforts at **cultural reinforcement** have mainly involved religion, education, literature, and the arts. As we explained in chapter 1, the oldest political ideologies were religious in form, emphasizing that the earthly hierarchy reflected the heavenly pattern of the gods. In some societies religious conformity has been enforced by coercive state power, such as that of the sixteenth-century Spanish Inquisition. In other countries, most notably the Soviet Union, the regime has mobilized official coercion to discourage and penalize religious belief and practice.

During the past century, many scholars have contended that the modern age has developed a predominantly secular orientation, so that religion has become a much less significant force in shaping governments and their policies. That viewpoint may well be an overstatement. The 1979 Iranian Revolution was carried out in the name of a fervent Islamic faith, which seemed to provide an inspirational ideology for large portions of the population. Perhaps the most devotedly Catholic country in the world is Poland, where the church has served as a haven for critics of and dropouts from official communism. In a variety of ways, most contemporary governments continue to concern themselves with religious groups and activities.

In the great majority of countries, education has become an important official concern only since the nineteenth century. An exception was the Aztec society of fifteenth-century Mexico, in which the government maintained separate and unequal school systems for sons of nobles and of commoners. The former were taught how to lead and command and the latter how to serve and obey.[3] In most societies of the past only the wealthy and wellborn received much formal instruction, often from private tutors.

Modern industrial, technological societies require mass education, however, and Thomas Jefferson asserted two centuries ago that the fate of democratic government depends upon it as well. Nondemocratic governments today also take education very seriously. They may attempt to offset its potentially unsettling effects by incorporating huge doses of ideological indoctrination into the curriculum at every level, and they commonly try to prevent the teaching of "subversive" ideas.

Mass education, and especially mass higher education as practiced in the United States, is an historically recent development and does not yet exist in most societies. Its effects on societies and governments are not yet entirely clear, but it has seemed to enlarge considerably the number of groups and individuals competing to influence public policy in democratically governed countries. It has probably led also to considerably sharper and more frequent criticisms of governments in those societies. The huge college-educated population may be less likely to defer to the alleged superior knowledge and competence of elected leaders. There is no reason, though, to believe that Jefferson was wrong and that ignorance would more effectively promote stable and effective democratic government.

Governments have often functioned both as promoters and as censors of literature and the arts; complete official indifference to these elements of culture has been extremely rare. Almost all the great artistic monuments of the past, from the Sphinx in ancient Egypt, the Parthenon in democratic Athens, the Taj Mahal in India, and the royal palace at Versailles to the Statue of Liberty in New York harbor, were government-sponsored projects. So were thousands of hideous buildings and monuments.

Some regimes have taken the arts so seriously that they have imprisoned and executed painters, sculptors, composers, poets, and novelists whose works criticized or simply did not conform to the ideological requirements of the regime. Hitler's nazi Germany and Stalin's Soviet Union provide prime examples of that kind of seriousness. In 1974 the post-Stalin Soviet government forcibly exiled the Nobel Prize-winning Russian writer Alexander Solzhenitsyn. His worldwide fame probably saved him from returning to the forced-labor camps that had provided him with memorable settings for his works.

In considering the basic functions and institutions of government, we may seem to have overlooked one prominent type of governmental body: the **legislative branch**—congress or parliament. But it is not really appropriate to consider legislative institutions in a discussion of what governments have in common; that kind of body has not functioned as the actual source of law for most governments, past or present. Executives—absolute monarchs in earlier eras, military juntas, revolutionary committees, or ruling party committees—are much more likely to make laws than are freely elected legislative bodies. Even where legislatures do decide on laws, the elected executive tends to have a more or less decisive part in shaping them.

All the basic functions of government discussed in this chapter are not new, although they have certainly taken on different forms over the centuries. These kinds of activities can be traced back to the earliest states; they seem to be functional necessities for any state that survives for any length of time. Problems of defending against other states in balance-of-power competition and of coping with inevitable conflicts of interest within society require external defense, internal law enforcement, and protection against internal enemies. Those functions in turn require that eco-

Table 4-1 Functions of governments

Function	Typical Methods and Institutions
External protection	Armed forces, diplomacy, executive
Law enforcement	Police, courts, prisons, executions, indoctrination
Self-protection	Antisubversion laws, informers, spies, secret police, army
Economic management	Taxation, regulation, public works, social programs, bureaucracy
Cultural reinforcement	Official religion, education, censorship or control of literature and the arts

nomic resources be produced, procured, and mobilized to support the apparatus of government and that cultural trends not erode all support for the regime. All these functions, then, summarized in table 4-1, are essential for maintaining complex, interdependent societies in a world of sovereign states.

Bureaucracy and Governmental Functions

In the twentieth century, the expansion of social services and economic regulation, of governmental ownership of industry in many countries, and of technologically advanced military establishments, have combined to produce significant growth in a very important governmental institution—**bureaucracy.** This term refers primarily to the appointees and employees of the executive departments of government, though some modern legislative bodies such as the U.S. Congress have extensive bureaucracies. In addition, in countries such as France the judiciary is organized as a bureaucratic career service. "The term bureaucracy also is often used in a negative sense with suggestions of officialism, rigidity, delay, and lack of imagination."[4] We are using it in a purely descriptive way, however.

Bureaucracy is as old as formal government: chiefly or royal advisers, executioners, military commanders, and tax collectors served as indispensable executive assistants in early chiefdoms, and states. In premodern governments public employees were relatively few, and their appointment and tenure in office depended entirely on the desires and whims of reigning monarchs. Competence could be important, but family connections and unswerving loyalty to the monarch's cause were often more so. In some elected governments, as in eighteenth-century Britain and in the United States during most of the nineteenth century, government offices were either sold to the highest bidder or filled with political supporters of the victorious party (the **spoils system**). On the Continent, however, professional bureaucracies were established in seventeenth-century Prussia and in early nineteenth-century Napoleonic France.

Some kind of **merit system** of administrative employment is supposedly maintained by nearly all contemporary governments. Typically, it covers employees below the top layers of political appointees who head ministries and departments and are directly accountable to the highest executive authority—president, prime minister, presidium, or whatever.

According to Max Weber's influential formulation, modern bureaucracies usually possess these formal characteristics:

- impersonally defined rights and duties for each employee
- arrangement of offices in a definite hierarchy of command (top down) and responsibility (bottom up)
- selection of personnel on the basis of previously defined qualifications, usually demonstrated through competitive examinations
- fixed salaries and pension rights and termination only by retirement or under carefully defined circumstances (guaranteed tenure)
- administrative work as a full-time occupation
- promotion in a career structure based on seniority or merit
- employee as occupant and not owner of his position.[5]

A typical bureaucracy is illustrated in figure 4-2.

These structural traits characterize bureaucracies in present-day constitutional democracies more fully than in Third World authoritarian states, where spoils systems of public employment are very much alive. In totalitarian states on the Soviet model, demonstrated loyalty to the ruling party can be more important than technical competence. However, hierarchical organization, job-related qualifications, fixed duties and responsibilities, full-time work, fixed salaries, possibility of promotion, and nonownership of positions by employees generally do typify the bureaucracies even of nondemocratic governments.

Bureaucracies are usually intended by their founders to serve as organizational tools for use as the top political authorities see fit.[6] Bureaucratic organizations always become significant political factors in themselves, though, and their formal organizational charts never describe with complete accuracy relationships within and among bureaucratic agencies.

In part these tendencies appear because bureaucrats cannot avoid influencing policy decisions. The laws and decrees that they are obligated to implement are often framed in broad and general terms that require more precise rules or leave room for different interpretations in varied circumstances. This **administrative discretion** gives some bureaucrats decision-making power that they cannot help exercising. Even when they are simply functioning as advisers to politically appointed superiors, long experience can enable them to affect the direction of policy: knowledge can become persuasive power.

Making the assumption that bureaucrats engage in competition for power in order to protect and advance their self-interest provides some

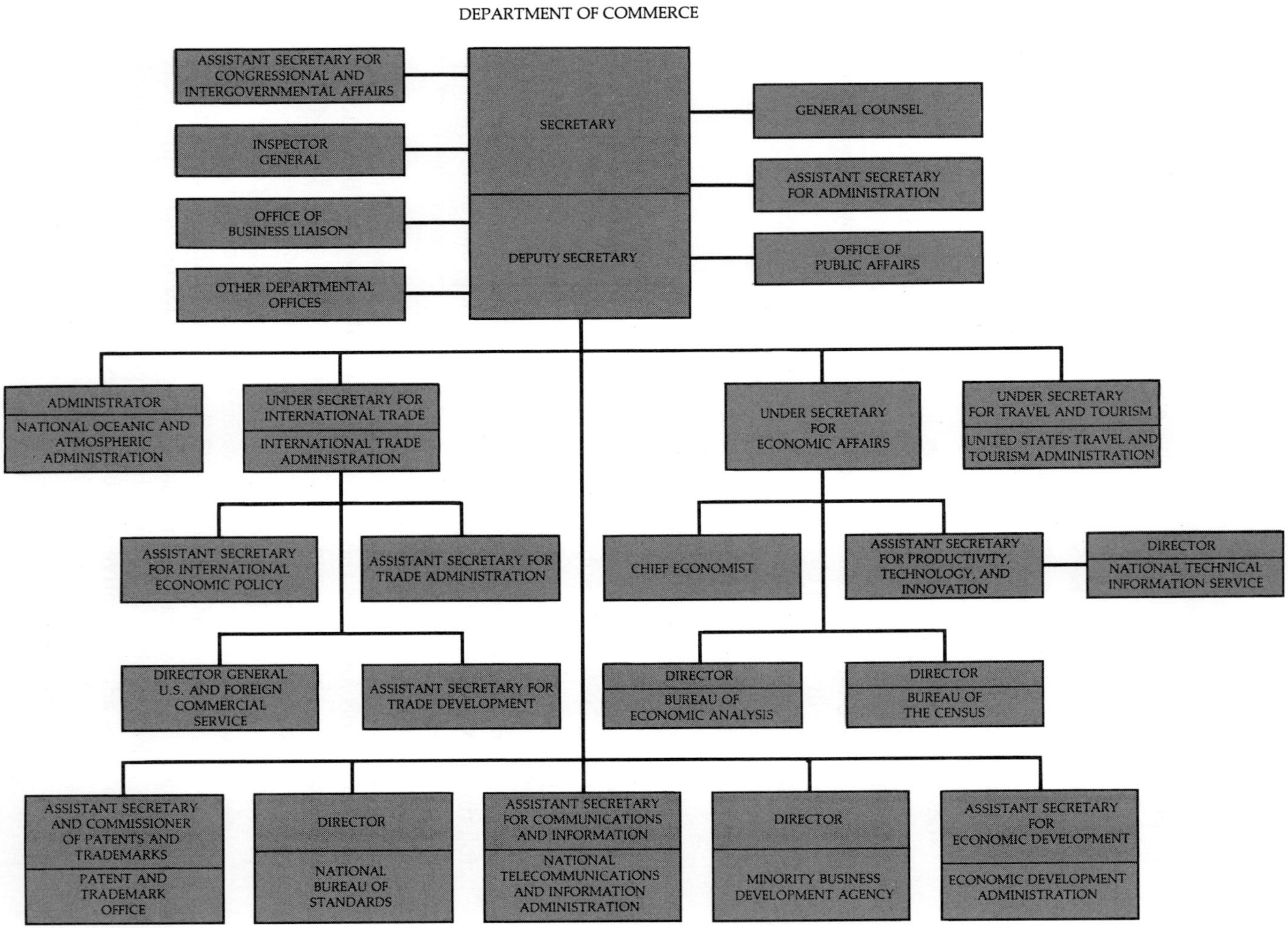

Figure 4-2 A typical bureaucratic organization: Structural diagram of a U.S. government department shows complex hierarchy common to nearly all modern bureaucracies (Source: *United States Government Manual 1986/87*)

insight into the operations and tendencies of bureaucracies. Examples include the premium that officials place on the survival and autonomy of their own bureaus, their efforts to promote the growth of their organization when the result will be more power, income, and prestige for themselves, and the strong tendency of bureaus to engage in fierce rivalry over programs that overlap their areas of functional responsibility.[7] In general: "Organizational behavior can be explained as well—if not better—by changes in power in organizations as by conscious attempts to achieve goals. . . ."[8]

None of these tendencies means that bureaucracy is inherently evil or even undesirable, much less avoidable. They do suggest, however, that a power-oriented interpretation of behavior can provide us with realistic understanding of officialdom and that we will overlook much that is important about modern politics unless we pay attention to bureaucracy. Further, if we compare professional bureaucracies not with some ideal of pure public service but with traditional tax collectors working on a commission system and ignorant officials elevated by birth or favoritism, we may feel more charitable toward the huge organizations that try to cope with the mushrooming business of government.

Basic Types of Government: Important Differences

Although they have essential functions in common, governments are by no means all the same, as we well know. In ways that mattered most to people subject to their power, Hitler's regime differed radically from the Weimar Republic it replaced. Pol Pot's murderous Cambodian regime was also quite different from the military government that it overthrew in 1975.

Methods of Classification

Attempts to understand governments better by classifying them according to important dissimilarities are an ancient feature of Western political thought. The most influential classification has been Aristotle's, devised in the fourth century B.C. He used two criteria: the location of ultimate decision-making power in the state and the main purposes for which that power is used. Aristotle asked, is ruling power actually exercised by one person, a few, or many? Does the government operate in the common interest of society, or does it seek mainly to further the personal interests of the rulers? These two standards combine to produce six main types of political regimes,[9] as indicated in figure 4-3.

For Aristotle, monarchy and aristocracy are purely ideal forms of government. They would require rulers to be so virtuous that they would always put the good of the community first and never exploit their power for personal ends. Such men would be gods rather than human; rightly

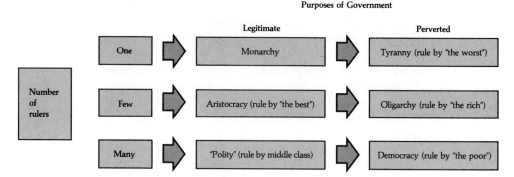

Figure 4-3 Aristotle's classification of governments

constituted laws, and not the will of any individual or group, should be sovereign.

Aristotle contends that pure democracy, in the sense of rule by the mass of the poor, passes quickly into tyranny: a demagogue gains high office by appealing to popular passions and then seizes full control of the government in order to gratify his own desires. Only oligarchy (rule by the wealthy minority), tyranny, and "polity" seem to be realistic political possibilities. "Polity," in Aristotle's classification, is a regime dominated by the middle class, which must be numerous and strong enough to outweigh both the rich and the poor in the social balance of power.

Aristotle's classification of governments may seem long outmoded. It was originally designed to apply only to the ancient Greek *polis*, or city-state, a relatively small community subject to frequent political changes. Certainly the Persian and Egyptian kings in Aristotle's time believed that they were presiding over monarchies, but Aristotle does not even consider such huge states. He was at least as much interested in evaluating regimes as in classifying them accurately.

The city-state that Aristotle idealized is one of a half dozen kinds of political systems that now belong almost entirely to the past. Other historical types, according to political sociologist S. N. Eisenstadt, include primitive political systems (for example, bands, tribes, chiefdoms), patrimonial empires (for example, Charlemagne's early medieval domain), nomadic or conquest empires (for example, the Mongols in medieval Russia), feudal systems (such as those in most of medieval Europe), and centralized bureaucratic empires (for example, the Roman Empire).[10] If regimes like these are nearly extinct, we are left with the problem of categorizing the governments of approximately 167 present-day sovereign states.[11]

Aristotle may still be a helpful guide in that effort if we try to get beyond his terminology and limited sample of governments and focus on the basic questions implied in his criteria of classification: How is power distributed or structured? What standards guide or govern the uses of official power?

On the structuring of public political power: Is it concentrated in a self-authorized, self-directing, self-perpetuating elite? Or is it divided, fragmented, balanced, restrained in regularized and reliable ways?

On standards of governance: Does the government make up its own rules and change or ignore them as it sees fit? Or is it guided and restrained by preestablished laws that apply to public officials as well as to everyone else?

Basic Categories

■ Constitutionalism

If the answer to the second question for each of these two alternatives is yes, we may classify the government in question as *constitutional*, because it complies with the basic meaning of **constitutionalism:**

> A determinate, stable legal order which prevents the arbitrary exercise of political power and subjects both the governed and the governors to "one law for all men." Constitutionalism is not identical with constitutions, which at times are rather meaningless paper documents, incongruous with existing political organization and processes. An effective constitution, "written" or "unwritten," is, however, an essential ingredient of the legal order which may be called constitutionalism.[12]

Constitutionalism complies with Aristotle's insistence that enforceable laws rather than human will should be the ultimate authority in the state.

Historically, constitutional government has not always been democratic, in the sense of allowing widespread participation in the exercise of public political power. Governmental authority could be divided between a monarch and an aristocracy, or between secular rulers and church authorities, as often occurred in medieval Europe.

Today, however, the only effective form of constitutionalism is **constitutional democracy.** It is a government in which freely expressed public opinion and free elections provide both the basis of governmental authority and the fundamental institutionalized restraints on governmental power. Constitutional democracy, then, is one of our two basic categories of contemporary governments; countries such as Sweden, Japan, Canada, France, Britain, Venezuela, and the United States fit comfortably within it.

■ Autocracy

What if governmental power *is* concentrated in a self-authorized, self-directing, self-perpetuating elite? And what if that ruling elite can make up its own rules and change or ignore them as it sees fit? A government that fits this description is obviously not a constitutional democracy.

What term best covers the wide variety of nondemocratic governments that rule more than three-fifths of present-day sovereign states? The main candidates are *tyranny, despotism, absolutism, dictatorship,* and *autocracy.* We have no objections to the first three terms, but they have fallen out of fashion in the twentieth century and are most often used to label governments of the more or less distant past.

Dictatorship is a term that originated in the ancient Roman Republic, where *dictator* referred to an official temporarily invested with absolute power in order to cope with a serious threat to the state. In the twentieth century, it has come to mean a "regime of unchallenged privilege for leader or leadership group. . . . Dictator's will is frequently law; rule by decree in police state."[13] The term is reasonably appropriate but perhaps has taken on such harsh and negative connotations that it is s not the best choice for descriptive purposes.[14]

That leaves **autocracy,** which literally means "self-authorized rule." It is often used to refer to absolute one-person rule (the "tsarist autocracy" in Russia) but has been usefully broadened by political scientists Carl J. Friedrich and Zbigniew K. Brzezinski: "An autocracy is any political system in which the rulers are insufficiently, or not at all, subject to antecedent and enforceable rules of law—enforceable, that is, by other authorities who share the government and who have sufficient power to compel the lawbreaking rulers to submit to the law."[15] *Autocracy* in this sense will serve as our category that includes all contemporary nondemocratic governments; Ethiopia, Cuba, Chile, Zaire, Poland, and the Soviet Union are varied examples that fit the basic definition.

The fundamental differences between constitutional democracies (which he calls simply *democracy*) and autocracies are clearly summarized by political scientist Giovanni Sartori:

> In democracy no one can choose himself, no one can invest himself with the power to rule, and therefore no one can arrogate to himself unconditional and unlimited power. The difference between democracy and its opposite lies in the fact that in a democracy power is scattered, limited, controlled, and exercised in rotation; whereas in an autocracy power is concentrated, uncontrolled, indefinite, and unlimited.[16]

Autocracies are so diverse, though, that it seems necessary and justifiable to distinguish between two subtypes. We do this by suggesting another specific line of questioning about the standards that guide any government's performance: How comprehensive and thoroughgoing are its efforts to regulate and control the activities of individuals and groups within the society? Does its official ideology justify leaving them little or no autonomy? To what extent is that ideology reflected in practice?

Constitutional democracies almost always allow a much greater degree of autonomy, through protections for individual liberty and freedom of association for groups, than does any autocracy. But very significant differences in this respect can be found among contemporary autocratic regimes.

Authoritarianism Not very long after his forced exile from the Soviet Union, Alexander Solzhenitsyn was visiting in Spain. Its long-time autocratic ruler, General Francisco Franco, had recently died. Solzhenitsyn wanted to photocopy some pages, and his hosts escorted him to a public coin-operated copying machine. He asked if that kind of machine had been generally available when Franco was alive. When the answer was yes, he declared: "You don't know what a real dictatorship is!" All photocopying machines in the Soviet Union are restricted to closely supervised official uses.

This example illustrates that autocratic regimes differ significantly in the breadth and depth of their control over society. Those with less extensive controls, such as General Franco's regime, exemplify **authoritarianism.** An authoritarian political system is defined and described by sociologist Robert Nisbet as

> one in which governmental repressiveness is habitual, the role of the military is commonly great, and use is made of such practices as torture, imprisonment without due process, and summary, anonymous execution. But at the same time, government in authoritarian as opposed to totalitarian societies is naturally checked in its power by the continued existence of largely free institutions—family, clan and kindred, church, social class, village and town, cooperative and confederation, all claiming and in large measure receiving corporate rights of autonomy. The values of tradition tend to be very strong in authoritarian societies, particularly the values of kinship, religion, and regional culture. Spain under Franco [1939–1975], Portugal under Salazar [1933–1968], Argentina under Peron [1946–1955], and Saudi Arabia are all examples of authoritarian states in the twentieth century.[17]

Nisbet probably overstates the degree to which more recent authoritarian autocracies have felt guided or restrained by tradition, but he correctly emphasizes that these regimes do allow a significant amount of independent activity within society. In general, people can act, speak, and write as they see fit so long as they are not perceived by the rulers as threatening the policies or the power of the government. There may be, for example, much religious freedom, so long as religious teaching and churches are not used to oppose the government. When they are, religious freedom is limited or suppressed.

Totalitarianism The term *totalitarian* was first popularized by Italian dictator Benito Mussolini, who used it to describe the all-encompassing state that his fascist movement aspired to create.[18] In the 1930s some commentators and political scientists began speaking of **totalitarianism** as applying to three specific regimes: fascist Italy, nazi Germany, and communist Russia. Despite the great differences among them, the leaders in these countries seemed strongly motivated by "totalist" objectives. Political scientist Bernard Crick contends that totalitarian rule represents

> the attempt to solve the basic problem of the adjustment of order to diversity by creating a completely new society such that conflict would no longer arise: it attempts to do this by means of the guidance and enforcement of a revolutionary ideology which claims to be scientific, thus comprehensive and necessary, both for knowledge and allegiance.[19]

The "attempt" at total control and direction of society may be mainly bluff, as was Mussolini's, or it may be extremely ruthless and thorough, as was the case with Hitler and Stalin. Also, the Ayatollah Khomeini's Iran, as mentioned in chapter 3 and discussed in chapters 12 and 13, demonstrates that champions of a totalist ideology may claim for it a religious rather than a scientific foundation.

"Totalist" points up the basic ideological, and often practical, contrast between the two varieties of autocracy: "Whereas in authoritarian society everything is permitted that is not explicitly forbidden, nothing is permitted in totalitarian society that is not explicitly authorized."[20]

■ Comparisons

Three basic categories—constitutional democracy, authoritarian autocracy, and totalitarian autocracy—seem to us most useful in pointing up the fundamental distinctions among present-day governments. In figure 4-4 all states above the line are constitutional democracies; those below are autocratic. The diagram also places examples of states on a continuum, ranging from the most restricted to the most comprehensive scope of governmental control over society. It suggests that democracies differ somewhat in the extent of governmental activity, mainly in the degree of official intervention in the economy and the size of the public sector in comparison with the private.

The diagram also shows that autocratic regimes can be differentiated by their closeness either to constitutional democracy or to the totalitarian ex-

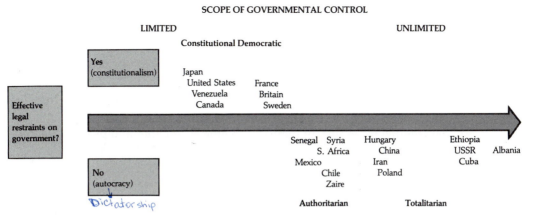

Figure 4-4 Types of contemporary government as of 1987

treme. Mexico, for example, combines in a distinctive way elements of democratic and authoritarian rule, as we explain in chapter 7. Both the Chinese and Hungarian governments retain officially totalist ideologies, but in practice they may now permit their citizens enough autonomy to be appropriately placed on the borderline with authoritarianism.

Finally, it is worth repeating that we intend these terms to be understood descriptively, which is why we have devoted so much attention to defining them. We use these three categories mainly because they can help us to explain fundamental differences among governments in the structures and uses of official power.

Summary

All governments necessarily try to perform five functions. First, they must provide external protection for their population and territory. Armed forces and diplomacy serve this purpose, as directed and supervised by executive officials.

Second, all governments attempt to enforce internal law and order, using police, courts, prisons, punishments, and indoctrination to preserve some kind of social peace.

Third, every government tries to protect itself against attack and possible overthrow. Penalties for unsuccessful rebels are usually severe. Many regimes use secret police, informers, and sometimes units of the armed forces to prevent or ward off threats to their existence.

Fourth, governments are involved, to very different degrees, in managing the economic life of their societies. Taxing, licensing, regulating, issuing currency, controlling credit, and building public works are all common ways that governments affect economies. Increasingly they have also implemented welfare and other social programs to cope with problems stemming from rapid changes in industrial societies.

Finally, all governments are involved to a greater or lesser degree in transmitting and reinforcing certain cultural values. They may do so directly through official religious and educational establishments or indirectly by censoring or sponsoring literary and artistic production.

Changes in the ways that governments perform these functions have contributed to significant increases in official activities and programs in the twentieth century. This growth has led to an enlarged role for bureaucracy, the part of a government that implements public policies. Modern bureaucracies, especially in constitutionalist regimes, recruit most civil servants through competitive examinations and guarantee their tenure and status to protect them against partisan pressures and dismissal.

Bureaucrats inevitably influence the content of policy. They must frequently apply generally worded laws to specific circumstances, determining what the law means in practice. Bureaucrats engage in political rivalry and conflict and are never simply passive and neutral tools of top officials. However, their expertise and general respect for rules and laws make them an indispensable component of modern governments, whatever the problems created by bureaucratic organization.

Although all governments perform common functions and maintain bureaucracies, they are by no means alike. Significant differences involve the extent to which governments are bound by duly established laws and the breadth of governmental control of society. Constitutional democratic governments are effectively limited by laws and free elections, whereas autocratic governments are not. Constitutional democracies also allow the most autonomy to individuals and groups within society, and authoritarian autocracies permit considerably more than do totalitarian regimes.

Some governments seem to combine features of two or more types and are difficult to categorize. However, very important distinctions among contemporary regimes can be clarified and highlighted by using a simple threefold scheme of classification: constitutional democracy, authoritarianism, and totalitarianism.

Review List of Key Terms

external protection
diplomacy
the executive
law and order
governmental self-
   protection
economic manage-
   ment

infrastructure
social programs
cultural reinforce-
   ment
legislative branch
bureaucracy
spoils system

merit system
administrative discre-
   tion
constitutionalism
constitutional democ-
   racy
dictatorship

autocracy
authoritarianism
totalitarianism

Notes

1. Gabriel Almond and G. Bingham Powell, *Comparative Politics: A Developmental Approach* (Boston: Little, Brown, 1966), pp. 128–163.
2. See Karl A. Wittfogel, *Oriental Despotism: A Comparative Study of Total Power* (New Haven: Yale University Press, 1957).
3. Donald V. Kurtz, "The Legitimation of the Aztec State," in *The Early State*, ed. Henri J. M. Claessen and Peter Skalnik (The Hague: Mouton, 1978), pp. 182–183.
4. Joseph Dunner (ed.), *Dictionary of Political Science* (Totowa, N.J.: Littlefield, Adams, 1970), p. 70.
5. Based on Martin Albrow, *Bureaucracy* (New York: Praeger, 1970), pp. 44–45; and on Reinhard Bendix, "Bureaucracy," in *International Encyclopedia of the Social Sciences*, vol. 2, ed. David L. Sills (New York: Macmillan and Free Press, 1968), p. 206.
6. Victor A. Thompson, *The Development of Modern Bureaucracy: Tools out of People*, University Programs Modular Series (Morristown, N.J.: General Learning Press, 1974), p. 1.
7. Anthony Downs, *Inside Bureaucracy* (Boston: Little, Brown, 1967), pp. 8, 17, 211–222.
8. Dennis J. Palumbo, "Organization Theory and Political Science," in *Handbook of Political Science*, vol. 2, *Micropolitical Theory*, ed. Fred I. Greenstein and Nelson W. Polsby (Reading, Mass.: Addison-Wesley, 1975), p. 361.
9. Ernest Barker, ed. and trans., *The Politics of Aristotle* (New York: Oxford University Press, 1946), pp. 110–116.
10. S. N. Eisenstadt, *The Political Systems of Empires* (Glencoe, Ill.: Free Press, 1963), p. 10.
11. This number is based on the listing of states in Raymond D. Gastil, "The Comparative Survey of Freedom 1986," *Freedom at Issue*, January/February 1986, 8–9.
12. Dunner, *Dictionary of Political Science*, p. 120.
13. Ibid., p. 145.
14. See Juan J. Linz, "Totalitarian and Authoritarian Regimes," in *Handbook of Political Science*, vol. 3, *Macropolitical Theory*, ed. Fred I. Greenstein and Nelson W. Polsby (Reading, Mass.: Addison-Wesley, 1975), p. 185.
15. Carl J. Friedrich and Zbigniew K. Brzezinski, *Totalitarian Dictatorship and Autocracy* (New York: Praeger, 1961), p. 4.
16. Giovanni Sartori, *Democratic Theory* (New York: Praeger, 1965), pp. 151–152.
17. Robert Nisbet, *Prejudices: A Philosophical Dictionary* (Cambridge: Harvard University Press, 1982), p. 18.
18. E.g.: "Fascism is totalitarian, and the Fascist State, the synthesis and unity of all values, interprets, develops and gives strength to the whole life of the people" (Benito Mussolini, "The Doctrine of Fascism" [1932]; reprinted in *Modern Political Ideologies*, ed. Alan P. Grimes and Robert H. Horwitz [New York: Oxford University Press, 1959], p. 412.)
19. Bernard Crick, "The Elementary Types of Government," *Government and Opposition* 3 (Winter 1969): 9.
20. Nisbet, *Prejudices*, p. 19.

Constitutional Democracy: Development, Preconditions, Elements

You may cover whole skins of parchment with limitations, but power alone can limit power.
***John Randolph,** in W C. Bruce,*
John Randolph of Roanoke

Democracy is one of the truly magical words of twentieth-century politics. Along with *peace, freedom, equality,* and *justice*, it arouses people's positive feelings almost universally. But that reaction makes these words extremely useful for manipulative persuaders, and no political term has been more shamelessly abused than *democracy.*

Military juntas who use force to put an end to democratic regimes, as in Chile in 1973 and Nigeria in 1983, always declare their intent to establish law and order and prepare the way for restoring democratic government on a sounder basis. Unfortunately, these self-styled guardians of democracy claim, the only way to save it for an indefinite long run is to kill it here and now.

At least military rulers are usually not shameless enough to call their authoritarian regimes "democratic." This is the practice, though, of the elites who control totalitarian communist regimes: the single-party autocracy in East Germany calls itself the "German Democratic Republic," and a similar governmental system in China is officially labeled a "People's Republic." The head of another **"people's republic"** clarified the meaning of communist "democracy" soon after being installed in office by Soviet tanks that had crushed the Hungarian rebellion of 1956:

> The task of the leaders is not to put into effect the wishes and will of the masses. . . . The task of the leaders is to accomplish the interests of the masses. Why do I differentiate between the will and the interests of the masses? In the recent past we have encountered the phenomenon of certain categories of workers acting against their interests.[1]

There is nothing new about autocrats claiming to rule in the "true interests" of their subjects while coercively preventing the open expression and organization of those interests. What is unique to the twentieth century is the claim that such regimes are truly democratic. This usage points up both the enormous importance of persuasive power in contemporary politics and the universal popularity and appeal of democracy.

That popularity has developed only within the past century or so. Many champions of constitutional—effectively limited—government in the nineteenth century were afraid of or even opposed to the granting of full political rights to the mass of the population. They feared that government would become foolishly shortsighted or even an oppressive "tyranny of the majority." Debates about these and other possible problems of democracy continue, but in the twentieth century democracy has taken on a clear and definite political meaning, both in theory and in practice.

After discussing the emergence of constitutional democracy, we will consider conditions that favor this form of government and attempt to describe realistically the kinds of institutions, organizations, and processes that function in all contemporary democratic systems.

Development of Democracy

Constitutional democracy is a distinctively modern form of government, a political outcome mainly of Western European and American developments since the seventeenth century. But the idea of self-rule is very ancient. The absence of formal government in tiny hunter-gatherer societies means, as a member of one of the few surviving examples of this most ancient form of human society told an inquiring anthropologist, "'Each of us is headman over himself!'"[2] That kind of anarchy was almost certainly the most ancient and longest-lasting type of political system.

As we explained in chapter 1, there are very good reasons to believe that individuals and societies gave up their relative autonomy only when compelled to do so in the course of the cultural evolution of politics. Although the development of states mainly featured more effective domination, enthusiastic and unresisting acceptance of it by dominated populations has been extremely rare.

Ancient Democracy

Fragmentary records from the early Sumerian city-states that flourished four to five thousand years ago suggest the presence of some popular elements in governments that came to be controlled mainly by priests and warriors. There is clear and abundant historical evidence for the existence of a type of self-rule—**direct democracy**—in a number of the small states of classical Greece (especially in the fifth and fourth centuries B.C.).

The largest, best-known, and most influential of these states was Athens. The supreme authority in democratic Athens was an assembly in which all citizens were entitled to participate. Only native-born men could be citizens, so the majority of the population—women, resident aliens, and slaves—were excluded from the assembly. Even so, participation in government was still much broader than in the monarchies that were the normal governments of the ancient world. In Athens, most administrative offices were filled by drawing lots, and terms were very short. Only generals were elected by the assembly. Important trials were conducted by juries made up of hundreds of citizens and without professional lawyers or judges.

In its prime, in the fifth century B.C., democracy was held in high esteem by most Athenians: Athens headed a coalition of Greek states that defeated efforts at conquest by the mighty Persian Empire; encouraged and sponsored some of the most glorious public drama, sculpture, and architecture ever created; and provided an environment that stimulated the development of wide-ranging rational inquiry in the forms of philosophy, science, and mathematics.

Greek democracies also tended to be turbulent and mostly short-lived, because they were afflicted with serious factional conflict. At least that is the impression conveyed by the most influential of the philosophers, Plato and Aristotle. Plato's hostility to democracy probably originated in the trial and condemnation by a popular Athenian jury of his great teacher, Socrates (470?–399 B.C.), and Aristotle was Plato's most important pupil.

The influence of their political writings, combined with the destruction of the ancient Roman Republic by fierce factional strife in the first century B.C., contributed to the low esteem in which democracy was held by most educated people for nearly two thousand years. Until the nineteenth century, democracy meant direct citizen rule on the Athenian model, possible only in a relatively small and compact city and inclined to perish from internal conflict. In a few medieval cities, especially in northern Italy, republics functioned occasionally. The democratic element in those states tended to decline as wealthy merchant families rose to prominence and established oligarchic rule.

English Constitutionalism

These scattered instances of ancient and medieval popular governments had very slight influence on the rise of modern constitutional democracy. To oversimplify drastically a long and complex story, constitutionalism and representation came early and democratization of governments much later. In medieval Europe, political power was mainly decentralized and fragmented among numerous feudal lords, monarchs, and officials of the Church. Ambitious kings usually tried to gain more effective control over lands that they ruled officially, while dukes, barons, and other nobles were militarily strong enough to get away with ignoring royal edicts most of the time. For many centuries there was no real French, English, Spanish, German, or Italian "state" that could collect taxes and enforce its laws as rulers saw fit.

A number of medieval monarchs sometimes convened councils in which nobles, the higher clergy, and, occasionally, well-off commoners were represented, primarily as a means of securing tax funds and soldiers for royal war making. It was only in England that this kind of institution evolved into a fundamental and enduring element of constitutionalism. The British parliament is usually traced to King John's instructing the commoner "knights of the shires" to elect delegates to a Great Council from which he expected to gain approval of an expanded tax in 1213.

Two years later a coalition of nobles forced the king to sign the **Magna Charta,** a charter recognizing their feudal rights and liberties. It is considered the fundamental document of British constitutionalism because it declares definite limits upon the king's authority. In one specific provision we can even detect a guarantee similar to the modern constitutional concept of "due process of law": "No freeman shall be taken, or imprisoned, or disseized, or outlawed, or banished, or anyways destroyed, nor will we pass upon him, nor will we send upon him, unless by the lawful judgment of his peers, or by the law of the land."[3]

Complex struggles for power continued for the next four centuries in Britain, among rivals for the throne, their noble supporters and opponents, kings and church officials. They culminated in the seventeenth century in religious, legal, and political battles between the king's party and a majority of members of the House of Commons. The Commons had risen from its lowly beginnings to become a body that claimed the right to approve all taxing and spending bills. King Charles I refused to summon parliament from 1629 until 1640, and a civil war broke out. Parliamentary forces won the military struggle, executed the king in 1649, and established a commonwealth under the leadership of Oliver Cromwell, the leader of the victorious army. When he died the regime fell apart, and the monarchy was restored in 1660.

The power struggle between parliament and crown had not ended. King James II, who assumed the throne in 1685, was strongly suspected of desiring to restore Catholicism as the established church, although few Catholics remained in England, and he was not inclined to defer to parliamentary judgment in running the government. In 1688 parliamentary leaders invited James's Protestant daughter Mary and her Dutch husband William of Orange jointly to take over the English throne. King James had no means of effective resistance, and this **Glorious Revolution** succeeded. It settled the longstanding contest between parliament and monarch in favor of the representative, collective body: "Thus at a time when continental European feudal kingdoms were turning into absolute monarchies, feudal limitations on the royal prerogative in England were developing into parliamentary restrictions on the exercise of Crown power. . . . Since 1689 no monarch has challenged the **supremacy of Parliament.**"[4]

Constitutionalism and Modern Democracy

Out of this critical seventeenth-century period came the first important modern theory of constitutional government, formulated by English philosopher John Locke (1632–1704). In 1690, Locke declared that God had created human beings as rational and social creatures to live in harmony with one another in a "state of nature" in which each person was free and, outside the family, no one had authority over others. God had also decreed a **law of nature** that human reason could discover and that binds everyone not "to harm another in his life, health, liberty, or possessions. . . ."[5]

In the state of nature each person is both judge and enforcer of the law of nature, but since people tend to be biased toward their own interests, conflicts can too easily lead to violence. Life becomes dangerous and insecure, inspiring people to agree among themselves to establish a government authorized to make and enforce laws in order to establish secure peace and justice within the community.

The fundamental purpose of government remains the protection of everyone's natural rights to life, liberty, and property (interpreted as an extension of each individual's person). The government may take no property without the owner's consent, given either in person or through elected representatives. The legislative body (parliament) represents the interests of the people and attempts to oversee the executive (who may be a monarch) to prevent abuses of power.

When either the executive or the legislative body, or both, consistently and extensively violates the people's natural rights, popular rebellion against such tyranny is legitimate and inevitable. Its purpose is to get rid of the abusers of power and establish a new government that will faithfully protect people's fundamental rights.

■ The Extended Republic

Even if you have never heard of John Locke, his ideas may seem familiar: they were essentially incorporated into the Declaration of Independence in 1776 and have remained the root ideas of American political life ever since.[6] That "all men are created equal," that legitimate government must be based upon "the consent of the governed," that the people have a right to rise up and overthrow a government that persistently violates their **unalienable rights**—all these Lockean themes had become "self-evident" truths to the American colonists.

Accustomed for a century and a half to a large measure of locally elected self-government, they resented and resisted efforts by the British government to assert a larger degree of control over the American portion of its empire. It might be difficult to make a case that British rule in any way resembled the tyranny that Locke had denounced, but the movement for independence proved unstoppable. The enduring result of the American Revolution (1775–1783) was a new sovereign state, the United States of America, which in 1789 began operating a new kind of government—an **extended republic.**

This term was used by James Madison, whose ideas on human nature were briefly considered in chapter 1, to describe the newly proposed United States Constitution of 1787. He boldly argued (in *The Federalist*, Nos. 10 and 51) that popular government would work better in a large country than in the small city-states where it had been tried in ancient and medieval times. Conflict among factions had been the fatal disease of small republics. Factions—self-seeking organized political groups—are inevitable in any state that allows political freedom, but their effects could be controlled and limited by the size and diversity of a big country, as well as by specific constitutional devices.

The larger and more varied the population, the greater the number of factions, and the more they will check and limit each other. Any majority would have to include so many different interests that the compromises holding it together would rule out any single-minded program of oppressing and exploiting the minority. It would also be extremely difficult for any majority faction to gain control of most individual state governments, the presidency, and both houses of Congress at the same time. These various levels and institutions of government would usually respond to somewhat different political pressures and check and balance each other. A populous "extended" republic, then, would keep conflict peaceful by sustaining a many-sided and constantly shifting social and political balance of power.

■ Democratic Governments

Originally, the representative republic of the United States was "democratic" only in a relative sense. In late eighteenth-century Britain about 3 percent of the population could vote in House of Commons elections, and the powerful House of Lords was hereditary and appointive in membership. The electorate was proportionately much larger in the United States, although voting qualifications varied among the states. Vermont had universal manhood suffrage, which was used also by Connecticut and New York in elections for state conventions that considered the proposed federal constitution in 1788. Most states, however, required voters not only to be free and male but also to own a modest amount of property and pay taxes.

In the nineteenth century popular bases of government were greatly enlarged in both the United States and Britain. Most property restrictions on voting by white males were removed by U.S. state governments in the

1820s and 1830s, but it required a bloody Civil War to extend the vote to nonwhites. Except for a few years in the 1870s, this constitutional guarantee remained a dead letter for most of the black population in the South until the mid-twentieth century. It took the **Voting Rights Act of 1965** to provide at last a protected right to vote for blacks in much of the Deep South. Women were guaranteed voting rights in 1920.

In Britain a series of parliamentary acts, in 1832, 1867, and 1884, progressively expanded the right to vote, although British women were not made voters on the same terms as men until 1928. The legal powers of the House of Lords were not reduced significantly until 1911. Only in the twentieth century, then, did the United States and Britain become fully inclusive constitutional democracies.

On the European Continent democratic government was born of violent and long-continued social conflict. The French Revolution of 1789 created a short-lived republic, but the French people experienced two Napoleonic empires, two monarchies, and another short-lived republic (1848–1852) before constitutional democracy was definitively established in the 1870s.

In West Germany and Italy, what seem to be relatively secure democratic governments were created only in the aftermath of defeat in the Second World War. By the mid-1970s, with the demise of authoritarian regimes in Portugal and Spain, the government of every Western European country was a constitutional democracy. Most governments in the world, however, were not.

Preconditions of Democracy

Why not? Why, as of 1987, were only about one-third of the world's sovereign states constitutional democracies—especially in light of the universal popularity and appeal of the word *democracy*? No one can give a definitive answer to that important question, but a great deal of research has been aimed at understanding what kinds of historical, economic, and social conditions are favorable or hostile to the emergence and flourishing of democratic government.[7]

As Robert Dahl makes clear, full-fledged constitutional democracy combines two fundamental and historically unusual features: (1) effective rights to criticize publicly, to oppose, and even to replace the officeholders in government by nonviolent means; (2) effective rights to peaceful political participation, especially the right to a free and secret ballot, for nearly all adults.

In our terminology, the strategy of toleration must characterize competition for political power within the society. For that condition to develop and continue, the balance of power among political groups and social forces must prevent any group or coalition from gaining its ends by domination and the permanent political elimination of its rivals. Historically, that kind of power balance has been rare, and most states have been dominated exclusively by ruling elites. As we have seen, efforts at royal domination were successfully resisted in England, and the political system was opened up increasingly to participation by diverse segments of the population.

Once a system of political toleration has come into existence, most participating political groups develop a vested interest in preserving the system that allows them to operate and influence public policy. As Dahl emphasizes, these political competitors need to maintain a **fundamental trust** in each other. They must believe that if their opponents control the government they will not use its power to destroy their critics and competitors or replace toleration with domination. Bitter historical experience suggests that that kind of trust cannot be granted automatically. Two examples: through success at the polls, the Nazis became the largest (though not a majority) party in the German parliament in 1933; when their leader became head of a coalition government, he proceeded to outlaw all other political parties. In 1948 the Czech Communist Party, the largest in the parliament (though also not a majority), used its control of critical levers of government to destroy the democratic regime and replace it with single-party domination (backed by "friendly" nearby Soviet armed forces).

What conditions, then, are most favorable to the development and continuation within a society of basic trust among political competitors and so to the prospects for democratic government? Five circumstances seem best to fill this bill:

- mainly peaceful changes in political institutions and processes over a considerable period of time
- socioeconomic pluralism
- a relatively advanced level of economic development and modernization
- little conflict among ethnic or other distinct communities
- strong commitments to constitutional democracy on the part of most political activists.

As the following discussion points out, democratic government *can* emerge and survive in a society in the absence of one or more of these favoring conditions. It usually takes longer, and the regime is likely to be less stable and secure than where most or all of the favorable circumstances are present. We are considering *probabilities*, not any ironclad "laws" of democratic development and survival.

Patterns of Historical Development

Which is more favorable to the prospects of democracy, violent revolution or peaceful evolution? The historical evidence strongly favors evolution over revolution,[8] but that short answer is inadequate. More precisely, it has proved nearly impossible to establish a stable, long-lived constitutional democracy after widespread violent turmoil has brought down or followed the collapse of an autocratic regime. The Civil War in seventeenth-century Britain put an end to royal absolutism but did not replace it with democracy. Rather, it produced a constitutionalist system controlled by a narrow range of social and economic elites. Constitutional democracy evolved peacefully in Britain as the franchise was gradually broadened in the nineteenth century.

Understandably, revolutionary violence intensifies hostility and distrust among competing groups and interests. The more intense the fighting, the more desperate and extreme the tactics—torture, massacres, mass executions—are likely to become. Extensive violent conflict also favors the rise of the most ruthless and uncompromising types of revolutionary and antirevolutionary leaders, as we explain in chapter 13. Violence and terror leave a legacy of bitterness, fear, and distrust that makes the winners reluctant to allow the losers to participate in postrevolutionary politics, for fear that they might gain enough power to avenge their previous losses.

The classic case here is France after 1789. The society was deeply divided along religious and political lines until very recent times, despite the overthrow of the divine-right monarchy in the early 1790s. Relatively secure constitutional democracy was finally established in 1870, mainly by default. In the aftermath of Emperor Louis Napoleon's defeat by the Prussian army and his flight from the country, a constituent assembly met. It was dominated by monarchists, but they were divided among several claimants to the throne and had to compromise on a parliamentary republic. Even then, many royalists and ultraconservative Catholics remained hostile to the Third Republic until its destruction by conquering German forces in 1940. Elemental political trust did not flourish in France, in part because the revolutionary origins of democracy alienated important groups from the start.

The enormous helpfulness to a democratic regime of a nonviolent birth was pointed up by the reemergence of popular government in Spain after the death of long-time dictator Francisco Franco in 1975. Franco had overthrown a turbulent and short-lived republican government by winning a three-year civil war in 1939; he then established a military-dominated authoritarian regime. In practice, the regime became somewhat less oppressive in Franco's later years. Illegal but tolerated labor unions and political parties began to organize and make plans for the future, operating at first in exile but increasingly inside Spain.

In the political transition after Franco's death, King Juan Carlos, whom Franco had groomed with the hope of restoring a traditionalist monarchy, and several Franco-era officials played critical roles. These leaders apparently believed that only parliamentary democracy could save Spain from renewed political violence with an unpredictable outcome. Important also was the repeated declaration by the leader of the Spanish Communist Party that he absolutely rejected revolutionary violence and was dedicated to preserving democratic political freedoms. His statements made it difficult for military authoritarians to persuade people that the Communists would seek power by revolutionary tactics, as they had in the Civil War period. In addition, the Catholic Church, whose leaders had opposed the secular republic of the 1930s, was no longer hostile to inclusive democracy.

These favorable circumstances made possible free elections for a constituent assembly, which designed a new democratic constitution for Spain. In 1981, a Francoist national guard colonel and a few of his troops invaded parliament and held its members hostage for eighteen hours. He called for a military overthrow of the new government but drew almost no favorable response from armed forces commanders, and he was placed under arrest. By 1983, the democratic Socialist Workers' Party had been elected to a parliamentary majority and controlled the reins of government—tolerated both by their antisocialist opponents and by military leaders. The peaceful, broadly based transition to democracy had apparently laid a foundation for the growth of mutual trust among leaders of major competing political forces in Spanish politics. The free and fair reelection of the socialist government in 1986 strongly reinforced that impression.

Socioeconomic Pluralism

To what extent are economic, informational, and organizational resources centrally controlled or broadly distributed within the society? This is an extremely important consideration, because resources like these often function as essential bases of political power. We have already noted, for example, how English kings' need for tax revenues led to representation of various interests within the government and eventually to effective restraints upon the monarchy. Within contemporary democracies, groups without access to funds are severely handicapped in competing for political influence.

Even groups with little money, though, can often find ways to bring their cause or grievance to public attention, because the communications media are not monopolistically owned and controlled. Or individuals with similar views can get together and form new organizations in an effort to influence the government, as civil rights, environmentalist, and antiabortion groups have done in recent years in the United States. That kind of effort would be impossible if the right and capacity to organize were monopolized by the government.

Historically, constitutional democracy has developed only in countries in which most property was privately owned and the economy was mainly market oriented rather than government controlled. This relationship continues to hold, despite the great expansion of governmental economic programs and regulation in all democratic states during this century. If newspapers could buy their newsprint only from the government, if critics of the party in power had only the government to turn to for employment, how secure would freedom of peaceful opposition be, and for how long?

Nearly all contemporary theorists of democracy agree that totally centralized control of economic resources would undercut the vital rights to oppose and criticize the government. They do not agree, however, on whether a private-enterprise, market-based economy is necessary to assure **socioeconomic pluralism**.[9] Democratic socialists, for example, favor extensive governmental controls and redistribution of wealth to remedy large economic inequalities, which they claim produce massive inequalities of political influence among citizens.

Level of Economic Development

What are the relationships between the degree of industrialization and wealth of a country and its political system? In general: "The higher the socioeconomic level of a country, the more likely it is to have a competitive [democratic] political regime. The more competitive a country's political regime, the more likely the country is at a relatively high level of **socioeconomic development**."[10]

By themselves these relationships don't tell us *how* economic development and democracy are connected. It seems plausible that a productive and growing economy can favor peaceful compromise as the principal method of settling conflicts. If the size of the economic pie is relatively small and fixed, one group's economic gains mean somebody else's losses. **Zero-sum conflicts** (those in which the winner's pluses and the loser's minuses add up to zero—whatever you win I lose, and vice versa) have a notorious tendency to produce hard feelings and even violence.

If the economic pie is relatively large and growing, gains can go to some groups (for example, old-age pensioners, welfare recipients) without producing actual losses for others (for example, taxpayers). Of course, relative gains and losses still inspire much disagreement within wealthy societies, but violent political-economic conflicts are more likely where majorities live in marginal circumstances.

It is also plausible that constitutionalist governments helped promote the economic growth and prosperity of the world's richest countries. The rule of law, security for private property and investments, and eventually freedom of labor union organization, almost certainly made vital contributions to the development of contemporary high mass-consumption economies.

As table 5-1 clearly shows, there is no perfect correspondence between

Table 5-1 Economic development and democracy

	Number of Countries	Number Democratic
High-income	24	18 (75.0%)
Middle-income	60	14 (6.6%)
Low-income	36	2 (5.5%)

Data source: Samuel P. Huntington, "Will More Countries Become Democratic?", *Political Science Quarterly* 99 (Summer 1984): 199 (income categories based on 1981 data).

democracy and economic level. On the one hand, the Soviet Union has a relatively advanced industrial economy. As chapter 9 explains, however, its political elites have fiercely and successfully resisted any movement toward restraints upon governmental power, much less democratization. On the other hand, a few very poor countries have established democratic governments: Sri Lanka and India are prime examples.

In both of these countries there has been a good deal of violent political conflict, both economic and ethnic, and constitutional freedoms have been suspended on occasion. Prime Minister Indira Gandhi of India declared a state of emergency and ruled by decree from 1975 to 1977, jailing a number of opposition politicians. When she did allow elections to take place, her opponents won and took control of the government for three years.

A wealthy and productive economy, then, is not an absolute requirement for democratic government, but it certainly helps to promote governmental stability and security. Since the Second World War, constitutional democracy has not collapsed in any of the most advanced industrial countries. It did end, at least temporarily, in countries with much less developed economies, such as Nigeria, Chile, Uruguay, Turkey, and the Philippines.

Conflict among Communities

Is a country divided among distinct racial, religious, language, or other ethnic communities? If so, there will probably be great difficulty in establishing and maintaining basic trust among political groups. Each cultural group will be reluctant to entrust the fate of its religion, language, or traditions to other groups that may form a political majority in the country as a whole.

Even before India was granted full independence by Britain in 1947, Muslim leaders insisted upon dividing the country to prevent the Hindu majority from dominating the Islamic minority. As a result, Pakistan was created, accompanied by hundreds of thousands of deaths in Hindu–Muslim rioting and by the forced removal of twenty million people from regions newly made exclusive for each religious group.[11]

India has continually been plagued by language-group rioting, but no single group approaches a majority. Although one northern language, Hindi, is the official language of India, it is not rigidly imposed upon the entire country. In fact, the language of most official communications and of the educated elites is English, a legacy from the former imperial overlord.

Cultural and **ethnic group conflicts** create serious problems in any society. They are especially troublesome for democratic governments, which cannot readily coerce sizeable groups of people who have full political rights. The long history of exploitation and discrimination suffered by black people in the United States and the continuance of racial grievances and unrest provide a telling example. It is clear, though, that blacks are much less vulnerable to gross abuse since they have acquired enforceable political rights than when their constitutional right to vote was frequently denied.

In some countries specific public policies and even constitutional provisions have been designed to assure various cultural groups that their vital interests will be protected: for example, designating two official languages, as Canada has done with English and French; guaranteeing regional control of educational and cultural policies, as in Switzerland; realigning federal structures so that regional governmental boundaries coincide better with ethnic group geography, as in India. Such provisions will be considered more fully in the discussion of types of democratic government in the next chapter.

In general, ethnic and cultural uniformity, as in the Scandinavian countries, probably make peaceful, democratic procedures easier to maintain than they are in countries where significant group differences make it harder to create mutual trust. As much experience demonstrates, though, it is certainly not impossible, and most democracies are multicultural and multiethnic countries.

Beliefs and Commitments of Political Activists

Robert Dahl argues persuasively that the existence of democracy in some countries and its absence in others cannot be fully explained by the kinds of social and economic factors that we have been considering.[12] The **beliefs of political activists** and elites about the legitimacy and necessity of democratic government in their countries has some independent effect both on whether it will be tried and on its chances of success.

Argentina and Venezuela are both Latin American countries with valuable natural resources and relatively large numbers of educated people. Whereas Venezuela has maintained a vigorously competitive democratic system since the fall of a military autocracy in 1958, Argentina has alternated between inept elected governments and increasingly brutal military regimes. In Dahl's view, this difference can be partially explained by the failure of both elites and nonelites in Argentina to develop deep-seated belief in constitutional democracy. Instead, "a somewhat cynical but not overly exaggerated formulation of a basic norm of Argentine politics would be this: I believe in elections as long as I can be sure that my opponents will not win."[13]

Contrasts between democratic Jamaica and totalitarian Cuba, both in the Caribbean, and between the Asian giants, democratic India and communist China, reinforce the same point. Both Jamaica and India were longtime British colonies, and elites in both those countries were strongly influenced by education in the constitutional and democratic traditions of Britain. They tended to identify democracy with civilized government, a fact that helps explain why, against difficult odds, they established and have tried to sustain the basic institutions and procedures of constitutional democracy.

A summary of the conditions favorable to development of constitutional democracy is presented in table 5-2.

Universal Elements of Democracy

Constitutional democracies differ in important ways, but this section will focus on the features that they all share and that are essential to the functioning of legal opposition and of equal rights to political participation. These elements are an effective constitution, representative and accountable government, qualified majority rule, multiple political parties, and organized interest groups.

An Effective Constitution

We do not mean simply or necessarily written documents such as the Constitution of the United States or the Constitution of the French Fifth Republic. Some documents called "constitutions" place no effective limits on the powers of governments because they were not designed to do so and provide no real protection for individual rights. Others provide protection only on paper and are either ignored or "temporarily" suspended.

An **effective constitution** is a reasonable, though never sufficient, guide to official practice. It specifies how governmental institutions are to be structured and offices filled, what basic rules of procedure government officials will follow, and how far official authority extends.

Certain **basic political rights** must be protected for the democratic process to function: freedom from arbitrary arrest and punishment, freedom of public expression (speech and press), freedoms of association and assembly. If governments can throw their opponents in jail simply to remove

Table 5-2 Conditions favoring constitutional democracy

Circumstances	Importance	Examples
Nonviolent birth	Fosters basic trust	Spain after Franco
Socioeconomic pluralism	Economic, media, and organizational resources basic to political power	Private property, free labor unions
High level of economic development	Dampens conflict, facilitates compromise	Western European "welfare states"
Ethnic homogeneity	Avoids common type of severe conflict	Sweden, Denmark
Strong commitment to democracy by elites and activists	Enables system to survive serious conflicts and crises	india, Venezuela

them from the political scene, censor or prohibit critical political speeches or publications, or outlaw peaceful public meetings of their opponents, democratic government cannot exist. In addition, people must be allowed to cast their ballots freely and secretly, and votes must be counted accurately and honestly. To the extent that these requirements are violated, a government is not democratic.

In most democratic systems, basic rights and procedures are spelled out in a fundamental document usually called the *constitution* (in West Germany, the "Basic Law"). Commonly, methods of enforcing constitutional provisions are stated or implied, such as dividing authority between executive and legislative institutions and authorizing independent courts to protect individual rights and the integrity of constitutional processes. In some countries, such as the United States, Australia, West Germany, and India, high courts even exercise authority to strike down as unconstitutional official acts of government.

How is it possible, then, that Britain can be considered the oldest constitutional government in the world, since there is no basic document called *the* Constitution of the United Kingdom of Great Britain and Northern Ireland? The short answer is that any British Government is effectively restrained by **basic political conventions** (traditions and customs) in which the British people, and especially the politically active elites, deeply believe.[14]

Even though official acts of parliament are supreme law and cannot be challenged in the courts, "the recognition of the [parliamentary] opposition as an essential part of that [political] order 'divides' the power and protects the individual."[15] Opposition members of parliament cannot prevent the majority-backed Government (administration) from enacting its budget and legislation, but they can and do constantly criticize the party in power and publicize alternatives to its policies. These activities provide the minority party with a real chance to become the majority and replace the governing party by winning the next election. Elections must be held at least every five years and usually occur more frequently; they are the ultimate popular check on the government.

In theory, any British Government could use its parliamentary majority to outlaw opposition and abolish people's political rights. But in Britain, belief in constitutional democracy is so general and so profound that its essential rights and procedures seem unshakably secure. That kind of bedrock opinion is more important to the continued operation of democratic institutions than are written guarantees and procedures—in any country.

Representative and Accountable Government

The most basic difference between ancient and modern democracies is **representation:** in modern systems citizens elect the individuals who govern, whereas in ancient Athens citizens participated directly in most governmental activities. Contemporary democracy is "a political system in which the people exercise power to the extent that they are able to change their governors, but not to the extent of governing themselves."[16] That right and ability of people to "change their governors" is the essential meaning of democratic government's accountability to the governed.

There are many reasons why modern democracy must be almost entirely representative rather than direct, but two can be mentioned briefly. First, the scale of modern states is enormously greater than the direct democracies of antiquity, as is the percentage of the population who are citizens with full political rights. Even the few million adult citizens of small countries like Belgium and Portugal could not possibly assemble and deliberate as did the few thousand who attended the Athenian assembly.

Second, modern societies feature an extensive **division of labor,** with people performing thousands of different and specialized jobs. To make a living, they must spend much time working; they lack the slaves who labored for many Athenian citizens. We cannot help relying, to a great extent, upon professional government employees and politicians to specialize in learning about and taking care of the complex business of government. Representative democracy allows us, however, to try to influence their decisions and to "fire" at least some of them when we don't like what they have done.

There are minor elements of directness in some present-day democratic systems—mainly **referendums,** in which citizens vote on policy proposals or constitutional amendments. Numerous state governments in the United States use this device. Even the British government, which has long insisted upon the full and undiluted authority of the elected executive (prime minister and cabinet) backed by a parliamentary majority, resorted to national referendums twice in the 1970s. Both involved highly controversial issues—continued membership in the European Common Market and a slight decentralization of authority toward regional governments—and the government considered them "too hot to handle."

The Swiss are the most frequent users of referendums, having held 297 such votes from 1866 to 1978.[17] The constitution of Switzerland makes calling a referendum relatively easy: any law passed by parliament can be challenged by a petition signed by 50,000 citizens within ninety days; its fate is then determined by popular vote. Constitutional amendments can be proposed by either house of parliament or by a petition signed by 100,000 citizens. All proposed amendments are put to a national referendum; passage requires both a national majority and approval within a majority of the twenty-three cantons (federal regions) into which the country is divided. Even in Switzerland, as in every other constitutional democracy, however, almost all the business of government is conducted by directly or indirectly elected representatives and the civil servants under their legal authority.

Qualified Majority Rule

Three centuries ago John Locke suggested a practical reason for **majority rule:**

> For when any number of men have, by the consent of every individual, made a community, they have thereby made that community one body, with a power to act as one body, which is only by the will and determination of the majority; for that which acts any community being only the consent of the individuals of it, and it being necessary to that which is one body to move one way, it is necessary the body should move that way whither the greater force carries it, which is the consent of the majority; or else it is impossible it should act or continue one body, one community, which the consent of every individual that united into it agreed that it should; and so one is bound by that consent to be concluded by the majority.[18]

That is, if a cooperative political body based on individuals' agreement to belong is to operate at all, it must move in the direction willed by the majority. The majority would have no interest in remaining voluntary members of an organized body continually dominated by a minority, and that body could not long continue. Majority rule has been generally accepted as a basic democratic procedure, both in private and in public governments, and mainly on the practical grounds that Locke suggested. No one has argued successfully that majorities are morally superior, always correct in their judgment, or more farsighted than minorities.

Both procedural rules and practice in every democratic system provide for important exceptions to majority rule. At the election stage, control of government is often won by candidates or parties receiving less than a majority of the popular vote. For example, in 1968 Richard Nixon won only 44 percent of the popular vote for the U.S. presidency but 56 percent of the electoral vote, making him the winner. In the 1987 British parliamentary election, the Conservative Party won 42 percent of the popular vote but a 58 percent majority of seats in the House of Commons, continuing its complete control of the Government.

How were these nonmajority victories possible in supposedly democratic systems? They were produced by electoral systems that existing political parties have a strong interest in retaining and that most U.S. and British voters accept as completely legitimate. Involved in each case is a form of the **single-member-district-plurality system.** To be elected U.S. president, a candidate must receive a majority of the electoral votes. Each state of the union operates as a voting district in which all of its electoral votes are cast as a single unit for the candidate who wins the most popular votes in that state. In 1968 there was a strong third candidate, George Wallace, and he drew enough votes from Republican Nixon and Democrat Hubert Humphrey so that a number of states were decided by small pluralities. The British system will be explained in the next chapter as the main historic model of one important type of democratic government.

In policy voting, both outside and inside legislative bodies, majority rule is likewise frequently qualified. The Swiss referendum vote on constitutional amendments enables a country-wide minority, if it is spread among a majority of the cantons, to defeat a proposal. It is not unusual for constitutional amendments to require extra-large majorities: in the United States, a proposal must receive a two-thirds favorable vote in each house of Congress and be approved by legislatures or special conventions in three-fourths of the states to become part of the Constitution. It was a procedure designed to assure that fundamental rules of government would be based on broad agreement in a large and diverse society.

Majority rule may also be qualified in order to protect distinct cultural groups, as we mentioned earlier. A specific example is Belgium, which is closely divided between a Flemish-speaking majority and a French-speaking minority. In 1970 the Belgian constitution was amended to provide that laws affecting the cultural and educational interests of language groups could be passed only if majorities of both the Flemish- and French-speaking parliamentary representatives voted for them.[19] Belgium has continued to be plagued by disputes, sometimes angry and even violent, between members of these two language groups. The majority principle may need to be qualified even further to preserve the country as a unified and democratic state.

In addition, constitutional protection for individual and minority-group

Enthusiastic support, such as these George Wallace backers display, enabled this third-party candidate to prevent both major party presidential candidates from receiving anything close to a majority of the popular vote in 1968. In the electoral college, however, Richard Nixon won a majority and the presidency.

political rights is an exception to majority rule that is absolutely essential to the existence of constitutional democracy. Use of temporary majority power to abolish those rights would mean the end of legitimate opposition and of truly competitive elections: the death of democracy.

Multiple Political Parties

"Liberty is to faction what air is to fire. . . ."[20] Given basic democratic freedoms to communicate, organize, and associate, people will inevitably establish cooperative groups—coalitions and organizations—to advance their interests by competing for control and influence over government. Among such groups are **political parties,** which present candidates and programs to voters in efforts to win elections, thereby gaining control over the machinery of government. Parties in government also organize, either to take charge of official business or to oppose the party or parties currently in power.

Political parties are essential to the functioning of constitutional democracy. According to an influential theory of democracy, "the democratic method is that institutional arrangement for arriving at political decisions in which individuals acquire the power to decide by means of a competitive struggle for the people's vote."[21] Without organizations to propose public policies and present candidates for public office, voters could have no idea of what they were deciding for or what to expect as a result of election outcomes. Nor could complicated governmental institutions function without organizations to take responsibility for running them while remaining accountable to the governed.

The first U.S. president, George Washington, warned against "the spirit of party" in the new republic, but with hindsight it is obvious that parties were inevitable. Washington's secretary of state, Thomas Jefferson, organized the first party outside government, the Republicans (later called Democrats); it helped him become the third president of the United States in 1801. In Britain, loose-knit parliamentary factions, Tories and Whigs, opposed each other in the eighteenth century, but there were no real political parties until the electorate began to be broadened in 1832. Tories and Whigs then developed into the modern Conservative and Liberal parties, with organizations outside parliament created to enlist members and conduct campaigns for party candidates.

Multiple parties have functioned in every modern democratic system. Since parties and party systems are critically important for defining the major types of constitutional democracy, they will be considered more fully in the next chapter.

Organized Interest Groups

Interest groups are the other major type of faction that political liberty makes possible and inevitable in democratically governed societies. The number of interest groups has increased significantly as governments have grown in size and scope. Given that important twentieth-century trend, more people now than in the earlier times see their interests threatened or potentially favored, or both, by government. So interest groups organize and multiply—business, labor, professional, religious, veteran, environmental, educational, self-styled "public interest." The United States has more such groups than any other country, in part because of its size and diversity. In addition, its federal system and separation-of-powers structure at every level of government provide numerous opportunities for interest groups to gain access to public officials. Organized groups are also extremely important actors in every other constitutional democracy.

Groups rely primarily on persuasion and inducements as they compete for influence, but their efforts sometimes also involve a degree of coercion. Persuasion may be aimed at the broad public, such as advertisements by the American Petroleum Institute in favor of ending price controls on oil. Most of the persuasive efforts are directed, though, at governmental decision makers. For example, before the Labor Government in Britain introduced its national health program in the late 1940s, several of its ministers and many top civil servants consulted at great length with the British Medical Association. This physicians' group desired to make the program as unobjectionable to its members as possible, and the Government wanted to implement the new service smoothly and effectively; to do so required the cooperation of British doctors.

That kind of organized, official consultation between governments, especially bureaucratic officials, and affected interests is an extremely common pattern in almost every democratic system. Organized groups always focus their efforts on the points of real decision-making power. As bureaucratic influence has grown, so have groups' efforts to persuade powerful civil servants and, through them, their political superiors. There is still considerable suspicion of this kind of activity in the United States, although it goes on continuously. Congress and state legislatures have much more independent power than do legislative bodies in other democratic countries, and they are naturally suspicious of bureaucratic policy making, even though their legislation makes it unavoidable.

It is not always easy to tell whether relations between interest groups and public officials amount to persuasion or inducement. Governments may sometimes offer modifications in a proposed program affecting members of a group to induce them to cooperate rather than making trouble. This was the case when the National Health Service was established in Britain. Inducements may also be used by interest groups and can assume more tangible forms: in West Germany, civil servants may take temporary leaves of absence, and some have done so in order to work for interest groups at considerably higher salaries. Some British trade unions pay election expenses and provide continuing subsidies for Labor members of parliament. In the United States, business, professional, labor, and other types of interest groups organize many political action committees (PACs), which raise funds for congressional candidates.

In most cases these material inducements should not be looked upon as virtual bribes; they seldom change an official's or candidate's policy views and usually go to those who fundamentally sympathize with the group's objectives in the first place. Groups feel the necessity of using inducements to assure ready access to decision makers. They also fear that if they stopped doing so, competitors who continued would gain an edge in the never-ending struggle for influence.

Sometimes persuasive activities may verge on or turn into coercion. Public officials are never enthusiastic about mass public demonstrations and rallies protesting current policies and government leaders. These activities are supposedly aimed at persuading the public of the justice and necessity of a particular cause—whether ending an unpopular war, protesting cuts in social spending, or demanding the deportation of foreigners. But any large crowd has a potential for violence, disorder, and trouble for the government. From the participating groups' perspective, this tactic can gain media attention for their cause, possibly conveying an impression of massive support among the public at large.

The record of semicoercive group tactics is quite mixed. Let's look at two British examples. In the winter of 1974 the mine workers' union shut down the coal mines with an illegal strike. Fuel shortages led to a temporary three-day week for industry and widespread shortages of electrical power. Conservative Prime Minister Edward Heath called an election on the issue of who should be in charge of economic policy, the government or a union in a state-owned industry. Heath's party lost, and the new Labor Government gave the miners a large increase in pay.

In the early 1980s a more desperate and grisly tactic aimed at changing British policy toward the ongoing conflict in Northern Ireland failed to move either Prime Minister Thatcher or most of public opinion. Hunger strikes in which several Irish Republican Army prisoners starved themselves to death did not noticeably advance this illegal group's policy aims.

Whether we like it or not, organized group activity will continue to be a central feature of democratic systems of all types. The nature of those types is the main topic of the next chapter, which also considers some troublesome problems of contemporary democracies and their at least equally significant strengths.

Summary

Democracy is a highly favored but much-abused term in contemporary politics. Constitutional democracy, though, is a specifically modern form of government. Its institutions differ greatly from the direct citizen-body rule of ancient democracies and medieval republics.

Modern constitutionalism grew out of European feudalism and attempts by the nobility to place enforceable restraints on royal power. These efforts were most successful in England, where, over several centuries, the medieval parliament evolved into a rival to the throne. From the Civil War and the Glorious Revolution in the seventeenth century, parliament emerged as the supreme governmental authority.

Table 5-3 Essential features of constitutional democracy

Elements	Importance	Checks/Balances
Effective constitution	Prevents governmental abuses of power	Independent courts, basic political rights, "loyal opposition"
Representative, accountable government	Guarantees citizens' right to change government	"Firing" government through defeat in election
Qualified majority rule	Implements prevailing will	Limited by individual and minority rights
Multiple political parties	Organize choices for voters' decision	Rights to organize, criticize, peacefully oppose
Organized interest groups	Maintain group influence and protection	Opposing groups limit each other

In the late eighteenth century the creation of the United States inaugurated broadly based popular government in a large and complex modern society. The right to vote was greatly extended both in the United States and in European constitutionalist systems in the nineteenth and twentieth centuries, converting them into inclusive constitutional democracies. These are states in which peaceful opposition to the current government is a basic right and in which all adults have an equal right to vote in free and competitive elections.

Constitutional democracy has never developed or has not survived in the great majority of countries. Certain conditions seem to favor democracy, and others make it very difficult or impossible to create or sustain. Gradual political change rather than revolutionary violence; decentralized control of economic, informational, and organizational resources; a relatively high level of economic development; a low level of ethnic group antagonism and conflict; broad and genuine democratic commitments by political elites—all favorably affect chances for the emergence and survival of democratic governments.

Constitutional democracies are by no means identical, but they do share certain features, summarized in table 5-3. An effective constitution is fundamental—one that provides enforceable restraints on the abuse of governmental power. The constitution must protect rights that are essential to a democratic political process: freedoms of expression, communication, association, and assembly and security against arbitrary arrest and punishment.

All modern democracies are representative: the people do not rule directly—with the minor exception of referendum voting—but hire and fire top officers of government through free elections. Majority rule is the basic voting procedure in elections and legislative bodies. It is often qualified, however, in order to protect regional, ethnic, or other minority interests, as well as individual rights, against a possible "tyranny of the majority."

Democratic political freedom inevitably leads to multiple and competing political parties representing different policy positions and interests. The same conditions give rise to organized interest groups who use a variety of techniques in attempting to influence official decision making in their favor.

Review List of Key Terms

democracy
"people's republic"
direct democracy
Magna Charta
Glorious Revolution
supremacy of parliament
law of nature
unalienable rights

extended republic
Voting Rights Act of 1965
fundamental trust
socioeconomic pluralism
socioeconomic development
zero-sum conflict

ethnic group conflicts
beliefs of political activists
effective constitution
basic political rights
basic political conventions
representation

division of labor
referendum
majority rule
single-member-district-plurality system
political parties
interest groups

Notes

1. Janos Kadar, address to Hungarian National Assembly, May 11, 1957; quoted in Anthony Flew, *The Politics of Procrustes: Contradictions of Enforced Equality* (Buffalo: Prometheus Books, 1981), p. 118.
2. Richard B. Lee, "Politics, Sexual and Non-Sexual, in an Egalitarian Society," *Social Science Information* 17(6) (1978): 884. The speaker was one of the !Kung people of Botswana.
3. Great Charter (Magna Charta), *Harper's Encyclopedia of American History*, vol. 4 (New York: Harper & Brothers, 1902), p. 150.
4. Alex N. Dragnich and Jorgen Rasmussen, *Major European Governments*, 6th ed. (Homewood, Ill.: Dorsey Press, 1982), p. 50.
5. From John Locke, *The Second Treatise of Government*, ed. Thomas P. Peardon, sec. 6 (New York: Macmillan Publishing Company, 1952), p. 5. Used by permission of the publisher.
6. See Louis Hartz, *The Liberal Tradition in America* (New York: Harcourt, Brace & World, 1955).
7. A leader in this effort is political scientist Robert A. Dahl. A superb critical review of much of the relevant research is found in his *Polyarchy: Participation and Opposition* (New Haven: Yale University Press, 1971); our discussion is heavily indebted to Dahl. See also his *Dilemmas of Pluralist Democracy: Autonomy versus Control* (New Haven: Yale University Press, 1982).
8. Dahl, *Polyarchy*, pp. 40–47; see also Robert A. Dahl, "Governments and Oppositions," in *Handbook of Political Science*, vol. 3, *Macropolitical Theory*, ed. Fred I. Greenstein and Nelson W. Polsby (Reading, Mass.: Addison-Wesley, 1975), p. 136.
9. See Dahl, *Polyarchy*, pp. 57–61; for a well-articulated collection of clashing views on this topic, see "Capitalism, Socialism, and Democracy: A Symposium," *Commentary*, April 1978, 29–71.
10. Dahl, *Polyarchy*, p. 64.
11. Robert Wesson, *Modern Governments: Three Worlds of Politics* (Englewood Cliffs, N.J.: Prentice-Hall, 1981), p. 223.

12. Dahl, *Polyarchy,* pp. 124–188.
13. Ibid., p. 140.
14. For a clear description of all the main elements of the British constitution, including important written components, see Dragnich and Rasmussen, *Major European Governments,* pp. 53–59.
15. Carl J. Friedrich, *Limited Government: A Comparison* (Englewood Cliffs, N.J.: Prentice-Hall, 1974), p. 121.
16. Giovanni Sartori, *Democratic Theory* (New York: Praeger, 1965), p. 66.
17. Austin Ranney, *Governing: An Introduction to Political Science,* 3rd ed. (New York: Holt, Rinehart & Winston, 1982), p. 152.
18. From John Locke, *The Second Treatise of Government,* ed. Thomas P. Peardon (New York: Macmillan Publishing Company, 1952). Used by permission of the publisher.
19. Arend Lijphart, *Democracy in Plural Societies: A Comparative Exploration* (New Haven: Yale University Press, 1977), p. 38.
20. James Madison, *The Federalist,* no. 10, in *The Federalist Papers,* ed. Clinton Rossiter (New York: New American Library, 1961), p. 78.
21. Joseph A. Schumpeter, *Capitalism, Socialism and Democracy,* 3rd ed. (New York: Harper & Row, 1950), p. 269.

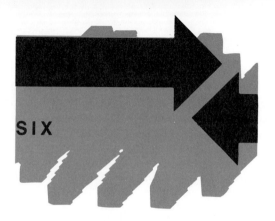

SIX

Constitutional Democracy: Types, Problems, Strengths

Many forms of Government have been tried, and will be tried in this world of sin and woe. No one pretends that democracy is perfect or all-wise. Indeed, it has been said that democracy is the worst form of Government except all those other forms that have been tried from time to time.
Winston Churchill, House of Commons, November 11, 1947

There is more than one way to construct and operate a democratic constitution. Historically distinctive balances of power among social and political groups, the use of certain countries as political models, and unique leaders and events combine to shape each democratic system. Most democratic regimes are faced today with similar problems in trying to govern effectively, but constitutional democracy has political and human consequences that lead many people to place a high value on its creation and preservation.

Types of Constitutional Democracy

Although there is no uniform method of classifying democratic regimes, widely used categories relate to two characteristics: the structure of the central government and the territorial organization of governmental authority. Figure 6-1 indicates that within each of these categories there are two major alternative patterns of organization. That makes possible four types of democratic constitution, and the examples show that each type actually exists. We will explain the meaning of the alternatives—presidential or parliamentary, unitary or federal.

Structures of Central Government

Are there constitutionally and electorally separated legislative and executive institutions that also check and balance one another? If so, the system is called a *presidential* government. But if voters elect only the national legislative body and it selects and can remove the executive, the government is *parliamentary*.

■ Presidential Government
The United States invented **presidential government,** and although the U.S. system has flourished for two centuries, the majority of democratic

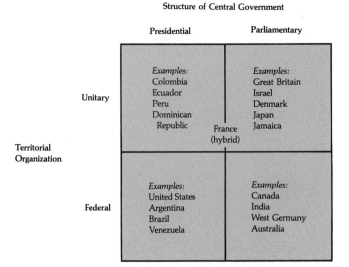

Figure 6-1 Types of constitutional democracy

systems are parliamentary. Most Latin American countries have tried presidential government more than once, but only a few, such as Costa Rica, Venezuela, and Colombia, have had much success in sustaining constitutional democracy.

"Separation of powers" and "checks and balances" are the defining features of presidential governments. The national legislature (the U.S. Congress, for example) and the president are elected separately, and neither depends upon the other to stay in office (with the exception of presidential impeachment and removal). Each is also given certain specific powers by the Constitution: the U.S. Congress declares war, but the president is commander-in-chief of the armed forces.

The United States Separation of powers might better be described as "separated institutions *sharing* powers,"[1] a relationship that makes **checks and balances** a reality. In the United States, only Congress can enact laws, but the president can veto acts of Congress. It takes a two-thirds majority both in the House of Representatives and in the Senate to overcome the president's official disapproval. The president proposes an annual budget for the entire government, but Congress determines how much money will be spent and for what purposes and who will pay what taxes. The president appoints Supreme Court justices, but the Senate has the power to approve or reject them. However, these high court judges serve for life and long ago established their authority to strike down as unconstitutional any official executive or legislative acts.

Although presidential systems formally concentrate executive power in a single office with a fixed term, presidential action is usually limited both by the independent legislative body and by the political party system. Separate elections make it possible for the presidency and the national legislature to be controlled by rival parties, and that situation frequently occurs both in the United States and in other presidential democracies.[2]

In the United States presidents probably have less effective control over their political party in Congress than is true in other presidential systems, even though presidents are the undisputed party leaders. There is a fair amount of **party cohesion** in Congress: majorities of Democrats and Republicans stick together in voting on most important policy questions.

This cohesion is far from complete, though, and a president has almost no means of enforcing **party discipline**—keeping members in line by threatening their political careers. Party structures are effectively decentralized; no national party leaders, including the president, have any part in deciding who can run for the House or Senate as their party's official candidates. These determinations are made at the level of each congressional district or state, sometimes by local party leaders but more often by voters in primary elections. U.S. party structures are the most decentralized among major contemporary democracies. Members of Congress often tend to go along with a president of their party, but mainly because they agree with presidential proposals or see their political interests as coinciding. The party "leader" can't compel them to do so.

A U.S. president, then, cannot count on getting administration policies enacted into law. Even if a president's party has a majority in Congress, enough members may vote with the opposition to reject presidential proposals frequently—the fate of national health insurance and federal aid to education when proposed by Presidents Truman and Kennedy, for instance. Conversely, a president whose party is in the minority in one or both houses of Congress can sometimes draw enough majority party support to achieve significant legislative successes—as happened with President Reagan's income tax cuts. The U.S. presidential system especially requires constant bargaining, compromising, and temporary coalition building between the president and members of Congress of both parties.

The U.S. Congress, because of its separate constitutional status and powers and the decentralized party system, is the most important and powerful legislative body in the contemporary world. A trend toward the rise of executive influence and the decline of legislative power has existed in all twentieth-century democracies, but it has gone less far in the United States than in any other country.

France In France a somewhat different kind of presidential government has developed since the Constitution of the Fifth Republic was adopted in 1958. That constitution replaced the parliamentary government of the Fourth Republic (1946–1958), which had proved too weak to cope with the threat of rebellion by the army over French policy in the Algerian war. The constitution was designed by associates of General Charles de Gaulle, a French national hero who had left France during the Second World War to rally support against the German occupiers. The constitution has continued to function since de Gaulle resigned the presidency in 1969, and it appears to be securely established.

In form, the **French constitution** is a hybrid of presidential and parliamentary systems, but in practice it has been strongly presidential. The president is directly elected by the people for a seven-year term, and the National Assembly is elected for a maximum five-year term. The Assembly cannot dismiss a president, but the president can dissolve the Assembly and call for new parliamentary elections—though not within a year of having done so.

The president appoints a premier and cabinet who can be voted out of office by an absolute majority of National Assembly members, but every premier until 1986 was very much the president's man and definitely the number two executive. The executive has substantial authority over the budget, very broad rule-making powers, and a sweeping emergency power that allows suspension of the constitution whenever the president perceives a severe threat to the independence or basic institutions of France.

French presidents have not hesitated to dissolve the assembly and seek greater support for themselves in new elections. Immediately after taking office in 1981, socialist President François Mitterrand dissolved a conservative-dominated assembly; in the subsequent election his party won an absolute majority in that body. In the 1986 National Assembly election, however, the president's party lost its majority. He appointed as premier a leader of the conservative coalition that had won a narrow majority in parliament, and the dual executive system was put to a real political test for the first time.

In the first year of divided party control of the government, the conservative premier took the lead in most policy areas. Backed by a National Assembly majority, he made this hybrid system operate more in a parliamentary than in a presidential fashion. The president did not give up his efforts to exercise authority, however.

Until 1986 the power to dissolve parliament and seek greater support worked to presidential advantage. The lack of a guaranteed term for the legislative body—a parliamentary feature of the French system—has put the French president in a much stronger position than any American president can hope to be. However much U.S. presidents might like to replace an existing Congress with a new one, they must try to live and work with it, whether backed by majority support or meeting frequent defeat.

■ Parliamentary Government

The basic principle of **parliamentary government** is fusion rather than separation of official powers: the executive (prime minister, premier, or chancellor, and cabinet) is voted into office by the popularly elected house of parliament and can be removed by that house also. The executive has no constitutionally guaranteed term of office, as does the president of France, Venezuela, or the United States. He or she remains continually accountable to the people's elected representatives in parliament.

Fusion of powers usually means also that the executive leader and cabinet ministers are selected from among members of parliament, continue to lead their parties in that body, and answer questions and participate in debates in parliament. There are exceptions: in the Netherlands, for example, cabinet officers cannot be members of parliament, although they may speak during its deliberations. A member of parliament selected to serve as a minister must resign his or her seat in the legislative body; in practice few are chosen.

Procedures for **parliamentary dismissal** of the executive (or the Government, as it is called in Britain) differ somewhat among countries and over time. In some countries simple defeat for any official government measure is enough to bring resignation, but in other cases formal parliamentary passage of a motion of censure or no-confidence is required. A distinctive provision of the West German constitution permits parliament (the popularly elected Bundestag) to dismiss a federal chancellor (head of government) only by electing a new chancellor with an absolute majority vote. This **constructive vote of no-confidence** was a reaction to the turbulent Weimar Republic, when chancellors were frequently forced out before a new majority coalition had developed to support a successor. The current procedure was not used to replace a chancellor until 1982.

Although more than three-fourths of existing democratic systems are parliamentary, there are important differences in how they actually work. Two broad categories can be distinguished—majoritarian, in which the government is normally backed by a majority of its own party in parliament, and representational, in which the government almost always represents a coalition of several parliamentary parties.[3]

Majoritarian parliamentary systems The political party system and the method of electing members of parliament together determine whether a parliamentary system will function as majoritarian or representational. In majoritarian systems, elections normally produce a single-party majority that can be counted on to stick together in support of the government that it elects. In parliamentary systems generally, parties tend to be more cohesive and disciplined than in presidential systems. A party's failure to support a government that it controls or in which it participates risks bringing that government down and replacing it with the opposition. This is especially true of parties in a majoritarian system. In a representational system, no party has a majority, and the leaders of a party may decide to desert their governing coalition in the hope of replacing it with a new one more advantageous to themselves.

The classic home of the **majoritarian parliamentary system** is Britain, where, since the latter part of the nineteenth century, one party—Conservative, Liberal, or Labor—has nearly always commanded a House of Commons majority. The leader of the majority party serves as prime minister and names other party leaders to head all government ministries. The prime minister selects certain ministers to serve in the cabinet and chairs its meetings, consults with ministers regularly, and leads and coordinates executive decision making. Coalition Governments have been extremely rare. For maximum national unity, however, all three parties were brought into the Second World War Government of Conservative Prime Minister Winston Churchill.

With a few notable exceptions, British parties have maintained strong cohesion and discipline in the House of Commons. Although candidates for parliamentary seats are usually nominated by local party organizations, national party officials have the authority to veto their choices. Any member of parliament (MP) who votes against the instructions of party leaders risks being denied the party's label at the next general election. Since most British voters decide on the basis of party or of candidates for prime minister, losing the party nomination could mean the end of a nonconforming MP's political career. As a result, MPs rarely break ranks in House of Commons votes, and national party officials seldom need to veto constituency party nominees.

As we suggested in chapter 5, the **single-member-district-plurality election system** is critical to producing a majority party in the House of Commons. Almost never does a single party gain a majority of the national vote in parliamentary elections, yet nearly always either Conservatives or Labor end up with a majority of Commons members. Why? The entire country is divided into 650 districts, or constituencies, each selecting one MP. However many candidates there may be in a constituency, the one who receives the most votes (a plurality) wins the seat. When there are three or more candidates, seats are frequently won with less than a majority vote.

The effects can be illustrated by comparing country-wide vote percentages and percentage of House of Commons seats won in the 1983 and 1987 parliamentary elections, as listed in table 6-1. These results dramatically show that the electoral system discourages third parties: in 1983 the Alliance of Liberals and the new Social Democratic Party received the highest vote for such a third force in sixty years, nearly as great as Labor's, yet won one-eighth as many seats as Labor. Alliance candidates defeated Labor candidates in many constituencies but still finished second to Conservative plurality winners.

The large Alliance vote also illustrates another tendency of plurality election systems: since the payoff is for winning seats and not merely for maximizing popular votes, any party that is considered extreme by very many voters will usually suffer. In 1983, that was the case with Labor, which had

Table 6-1 Results of the 1983 and 1987 British parliamentary elections

Party	1983		1987	
	Percentage of Votes	Percentage of Seats	Percentage of Votes	Percentage of Seats
Conservative	42	61	42	58
Labor	28	32	31	35
Liberal/Social Dem. Alliance	25	4	23	3
Others	5	3	4	4

become increasingly committed to ideologically pure socialism. Its vote declined by a greater percentage since the previous election than that of any other major party since the Second World War. Many voters who blamed the Conservative Government for recession and high unemployment were so unwilling to risk a Labor Government that they "wasted" their votes on the Alliance.

Plurality election systems tend to favor parties whose policies are perceived as moderate and centrist by most voters, since the **floating voters** who are not strongly committed to any party often determine the outcome of elections. Surveys indicate that most of these voters are hostile to extreme proposals and tend to favor only marginal changes in the status quo.

Party leaders, however, may find themselves pressured in the opposite direction by activist members and participants in party campaigns. **Party activists** tend to be much more concerned about ideological consistency and purity than ordinary voters; they want the party to stand for its supposed principles and not merely win elections. And parties need activists to do the grubby work of organizing, canvassing voters, and getting out the vote. But when activists gain dominant influence over party policies and candidates, parties tend to alienate centrist voters and lose.

With strong support from ideological activists, Michael Foot became Labor party leader in 1981. A long-time champion of thoroughgoing socialism and an opponent of British nuclear weapons, he was seen by many Britons as an impossible choice for prime minister. In the 1983 election he led Labor to its most one-sided defeat since the 1920s. In 1987, Labor was led by a skillful campaigner, Neil Kinnock, but continued to favor unilateral British nuclear disarmament, an unacceptably extreme position for many voters.

Outcomes of these British elections were comparable to similar experiences of the two major U.S. parties. In 1964, ideologically conservative activists dominated the presidential nominating process for the Republicans, and their candidate, Senator Barry Goldwater, lost overwhelmingly to Democratic President Johnson. Lopsided defeat was also the fate of ultraliberal Senator George McGovern, when his highly motivated ideological and anti–Vietnam War activists gained control of the Democrats' nominating process in 1972.

In general, the influence of political activists in several democratic systems in recent decades has tended to increase ideological and policy differences between rival parties. Activists, of course, are also interpreting and responding to events, such as the great increases in oil prices after 1973, hyperinflation, deep recessions and unemployment, and foreign policy conflicts and tensions. Sometimes the activists' candidate wins. Activist perseverance had much to do with the election of ideologically conservative government leaders in Britain in 1979, 1983, and 1987 (Prime Minister Thatcher) and in the U.S. in 1980 and 1984 (President Reagan) and an ideologically socialist president in France in 1981 (President Mitterrand). Tensions between party activists' demands and the need for attracting nonparty voters may continue to be an important feature of most sizeable parties in both presidential and majoritarian parliamentary democracies.

The influence of the British model is quite apparent in countries such as Australia, Canada, India, Jamaica, and New Zealand. They use essentially the same kind of electoral system and almost always have a Government backed by a single-party majority in parliament.

Not all majoritarian systems use the single-member-plurality system, which often produces large differences between percentages of the popular vote and of seats in parliament. the Federal Republic of Germany probably fits best into the majoritarian category, even though it has some traits of the representational type. These are an electoral system that produces approximately proportional results for each party and a government that has functioned as a coalition for all but a few years since 1949. One provision of the electoral law does push the political system strongly in the majoritarian direction: no party can obtain *any* seats in the national parliament (Bundestag) unless it receives at least five percent of the national vote.

In fact, there are only two major parties, the right-of-center Christian Democrats and the left-of-center Social Democrats. One of them always dominates the government, depending upon which of the large parties is currently joined in a coalition with the small but pivotal Free Democratic party (conservative economically but secular in orientation). This party has usually won enough votes to deny an outright majority to either major party and has collaborated at different times with each of them to control the government. The West German system has been quite stable and essentially majority oriented. The Free Democrats serve as a continual check on what their leaders might see as extremist influence among either Social Democrats or Christian Democrats.

Representational parliamentary systems In **representational parliamentary democracies,** the electoral system allows for representation in the parliament of almost any organized political group. That is the normal outcome of **proportional representation,** in which there are multimember districts, and seats are allocated more or less according to the percentage of the vote received by each party within a district. Table 6-2 demonstrates that proportional representation can produce an election outcome dramatically different from the result produced by a single-member-district-plurality system.

Revising an election system can have real and not merely hypothetical consequences. Before the 1986 parliamentary election in France, for example, the socialist majority in the National Assembly pushed through a change from single-member districts to multimember-district proportional representation. If the old system had remained in effect, the victorious coalition of conservative parties would have captured 350 to 400 seats in the election. However, with proportional representation they won only 291, a bare majority of the 577 seats. Although their leader became premier, he and his administration were in a much weaker position with the socialist president and parliamentary opposition than they would have been with a substantial majority in the Assembly.

Not all proportional representation systems are alike. In Israel and the

Table 6-2 Hypothetical outcomes of two election systems, assuming ten districts and three parties running in each district

	Parties		
	A	B	C
Districts			
1	4,000	3,600	2,200
2	3,800	3,700	2,200
3	1,500	4,600	1,700
4	3,600	3,300	3,500
5	4,200	3,900	2,700
6	2,000	4,000	3,700
7	3,700	3,600	1,200
8	3,500	3,400	2,800
9	3,300	3,200	3,100
10	3,900	3,500	3,700
Results			
Total votes	33,500	36,800	27,000
Percentage of votes	34.4%	37.8%	27.7%
Comparative outcomes			
Seats won under single-member district plurality system (of 10 total seats)	8	2	0
Seats won under proportional representation, with 10 election districts lumped together in one 10-seat district	3–4	4	2–3

Netherlands, for example, the entire country is one voting district, a party's proportion of parliamentary seats matches its nationwide percentage of the vote. This system obviously encourages multiple parties, since a tiny vote will win a party at least one or two spokesmen on the national political scene. In the Israeli Knesset (parliament) after the 1984 election, 15 parties were represented, ranging from 44 seats (among 120) down to a single seat. After the 1982 election in the Netherlands, 12 parties sat in the States General, the largest with 47 of 150 seats, the smallest with one. In most proportional representation systems, voting districts are much smaller than the country as a whole. Each district usually elects about six to twenty members of parliament.

It is extremely rare for a single party to gain a parliamentary majority in any country with proportional representation; as a result, a **coalition government** of two or more parties is common. Its head, the premier or prime minister, is usually leader of the largest party. Occasionally, precoalition bargaining among parties enables a smaller party's leader to gain that position. Cabinet and other ministerial positions are shared among coalition parties, and executive decision making tends to be more collective in character than it is with cabinets in majoritarian systems. As protectors of their parties' distinct interests, coalition partners have a strong incentive to watch each other closely.

Traditionally, most American and British political scientists have criticized proportional representation. Because it encourages a multiparty system in parliament, it increases the difficulty of providing a stable and reliable basis of support for the executive. A notorious example was the German Weimar Republic (1919–1933), in which pure proportional representation made possible increased parliamentary support for extremist parties in the early 1930s. Coalition bargaining became more and more difficult, leading finally to the horrendous mistake of entrusting executive leadership to Adolf Hitler as head of the largest party. Single-member-district systems, it is argued, may seem unfair to smaller parties such as the British Liberals who, unsurprisingly, favor proportional representation. However, single-member-plurality systems almost always produce a solid majority in parliament, ensuring the stability and presumably the effectiveness of the Government.

This argument may not stand up very well against the test of experience. Careful study has shown that the length of time a premier and cabinet remain in office *is* significantly shorter in representational than in majoritarian systems. But on three other measures of political effectiveness—voting turnout, political rioting, and political deaths—representational systems performed somewhat better overall from 1958 to 1976 than did either majoritarian or presidential democracies.[4] These differences are especially striking where representational parties have strong links with particular social groups such as Catholics, Protestants, or union members, and where "extremist" parties are small. These are parties that are generally perceived as a threat to democracy should they gain power, such as Communists or Fascists.

It seems possible that representational systems channel political demands and passions into legitimate electoral activities more effectively than do presidential or majoritarian systems. This channeling makes it less likely that demands will be expressed in rioting or other forms of violent protest. We should not assume that there is any single "best" way to organize a democratic system; in practice each type has both advantages and limitations.

Representational parliamentary systems also have built-in political guarantees against majority tyranny, since no clear-cut majority ever emerges from elections. At least two parties must compromise with each other even before they start governing and for as long as their coalition holds together.

A few parliamentary democracies have gone beyond even these kinds of mutual restraints on governmental power in trying to provide special protection for cultural groups. For instance, in both Belgium and Switzerland explicit constitutional and political guarantees make it possible for different language groups to remain together and cooperate within the same political system. The Belgian constitution provides that proposals affecting the cultural autonomy of the two language communities cannot pass without the approval of separate majorities among the members of parliament from each language group. Also, seats in the cabinet must be divided equally between Flemish- and French-speaking ministers.[5]

Since 1943, in Switzerland four major parties have staffed the seven-member federal council, the collective executive institution, in proportion to their electoral strength. The largely ceremonial presidency rotates among the members of this group, each serving for only a year. Council members also represent the major regional and language groups—a German-speaking majority, a sizeable French-speaking minority, and small Italian- and Romansch-speaking populations.

Special protections like these for minority cultural groups suggest that the translation of "popular will" into public policy is, for many people, not the main reason they value democratic government. Rather, they appreciate that constitutional democracy makes it possible to gain the benefits of social, economic, and political cooperation while protecting individuals and minorities against obnoxious and oppressive governmental actions. Strong constitutional barriers against official efforts to intrude on what people consider their most precious cultural rights and liberties appear to be essential components of democracy in societies divided by language.

Territorial Organization

What are the constitutional relationships between the central government and governments of the various territorial subunits of a country? Political scientists traditionally contrast "unitary" and "federal" systems of government.

■ Unitary Systems

In a **unitary system** the central government has full legal authority over all other governments—provincial, county, district, local—within the country. It may delegate some authority to lower levels of government, such as controlling local taxation and police functions, but it can regulate those governments as it sees fit, even removing their authority at any time. For example, every state in the United States has a unitary government, with complete authority to regulate, create, change, or even do away with any kind of local government within the state.

In practice, unitary governments are not all equally centralized. In Britain, for example, parliament has delegated extensive authority to elected local governments. In contrast, the French structure since Napoleon Bonaparte has been highly centralized: local governments have been treated as extensions of the central Ministry of the Interior. Most unitary governments are not democracies; about seven-eighths of contemporary sovereign states function in a unitary way.

■ Federal Structures

In our judgment, a state must be a constitutional democracy in order to *practice* federalism very effectively, whatever the language of its constitution. Some communist-ruled countries, such as the Soviet Union, Yugoslavia, and Czechoslovakia, have formally federal structures. They do not really comply, however, with this minimal definition of **federalism:** "a political organization in which the activities of government are divided between regional governments and a central government in such a way that each kind of government has some activities on which it makes final decisions."[6] In "federal" communist systems all levels of government are actually controlled by the centralized ruling party elite.

At any rate, in the present context we are considering federal structures as one of the two major ways of distributing governmental authority territorially in constitutional democracies. We believe that people need to be able to vote, organize, and express themselves freely in order to defend regional governments very effectively against efforts at centralized control.

Not many democratic states are federal, but some of the most populous are, including the United States, India, Brazil, and the Federal Republic of Germany. Just as they invented presidential government, the framers of the U.S. Constitution invented federalism. Before 1787 the only nonunitary territorial organization of government was the league or **confederacy,** a loose-knit cooperative alliance among essentially independent political units. Such a loose political bond joined the Swiss cantons from the thirteenth to the nineteenth century. Leagues involved relationships among governments, mostly for common defense, and individuals were subject only to the authority of the government of their own region.

Origins of federalism   The U.S. Constitution created a distinctive kind of government. Individual citizens were subject both to a central government and to smaller regional units of government (the states of the union), with both levels of government exercising some powers independently of each other.

Why federalism? At the Constitutional Convention in 1787, it was not proposed simply as an abstract idea; it emerged from hard bargaining within a particular balance of political forces. Each of the thirteen states was nearly autonomous under the government of the **Articles of Confederation,** established in 1781. They were equally represented in Congress, which had virtually no taxing, regulatory, or military powers, and the Articles could not be changed without the consent of every state. With almost all effective political power held by state governments, there was no possibility that they would willingly surrender it to a fully sovereign central government and agree to create a unitary system.

However, some state political leaders did feel the need for a stronger central government, mainly from fear of external attack. The British government might renew war with the Americans if they seemed weak and divided. Many leaders were also disturbed by "Shays' Rebellion," a debtors' revolt in Massachusetts in 1786, and desired a central government strong enough to put down internal disorder. The outcome of intense bargaining was a Constitution that gave broad authority to the new federal government but that guaranteed the continued independent exercise of important powers by state governments. This arrangement was an unavoidable price for a new and stronger central government but also a recipe for frequent conflict about the proper division of powers between the two levels of government.

Political scientist William Riker proposes a **political "threat" hypothesis:** every federal system has resulted from similar bargaining between would-be centralizers and political leaders of autonomous units. Those leaders fear a common external or internal threat but not enough to give up all effective authority to a unitary government. For example, in 1867 the largely separate provinces of British Canada established a new federal government for more effective defense against a possible effort by the United States to annex its neighbors to the north.[7]

In short, whether a federal system is established depends on how political leaders respond to apparent threats to the existing balance of power, both among the units involved in political bargaining and between them and other states. Riker further contends that political "threats" result in federalism only where no group has sufficient power to impose centralized government without excessively high risks or political costs. It seems likely, though, that the origin of West German federalism in 1949 does not fit very well the "threat" scenario. Rather, it was imposed by the victorious Western Allies—Britain, France, and the United States—with the aim of permanently weakening the government of Germany.[8]

Characteristics of federal systems Whatever their particular origins, all democratic federal systems share three legal-structural features designed to protect the basic central–regional division of authority. These features are a written constitution, a **bicameral** (two-house) national legislature in which the smaller regions are disproportionately represented, and participation of regional governments or voters in the process of amending the federal constitution.[9]

A written constitution is necessary to spell out the territorial division of powers, some exclusive to each level of government and others overlapping (**concurrent powers**). Written rules never prevent all conflicts over this primary feature of federalism, and high courts of appeals usually have authority to decide jurisdictional disputes, as in the United States, Canada, West Germany, Australia, and India.

One house of the federal legislature is designed mainly to represent the regions rather than the population at large. The United States Senate, in which each state, regardless of size of population, has two senators, is the classic example. The federal legislative body that probably most consistently represents and protects regional interests is the ***Bundesrat*** (federal council) in West Germany. Each state (*Land*) has at least three members and none more than five. In addition, each state delegation must vote as a bloc as instructed by its state government. Since the *Bundesrat* must approve all legislation affecting state interests, more than half of all bills, it is a powerful and important body in the Federal Republic of Germany.

Federal constitution-amending procedures always provide distinctive authority for regions; in the United States amendments can be approved only with favorable votes in legislatures or special conventions in three-fourths of the states. In Canada the Constitution Act of 1982 is even more restrictive: amendments require approval in at least two-thirds of the ten provincial legislatures, and the people in the approving provinces must constitute at least 50 percent of the total Canadian population. Amendments concerning some matters, such as changes of provincial boundaries or the use of English or French within a province, cannot pass without approval of the legislature of each province to which the amendments apply.

In every federal system that has been in effect for very long, a trend has developed for policy-making and financial powers to become more centralized in the federal government. On the average, however, this **centralizing of functions** has proceeded more slowly in federal than in unitary systems.[10] More important, no federal system in a democratic state has been transformed, either constitutionally or in practice, into a unitary system. This fact points up the enduring importance of federalism as one way of qualifying majority rule and enabling people with diverse regional and cultural interests both to cooperate and to regulate their conflicts within a single political system.

Federalism can be most realistically seen as a political bargain and not as a magic formula for assuring harmonious cooperation. Until recent decades, federalism in the United States often enabled state governments to discriminate against people on the basis of race; for example, blacks in the South and Chinese immigrants in California. That kind of "state's right" had to be overcome in order to protect the democratic rights of individual citizens. But federalism is not about to disappear. Regionally oriented politicians and interest groups will not voluntarily surrender their power, and a federal structure can function as a useful mechanism for limiting conflict within plural societies.

Problems of Democracy: Factions and the Economy

We limit our brief discussion of problems to those that seem to be built into universal-suffrage–mass-media constitutional democracy, which has fully emerged only in the past few decades. No one knows how stable and durable it will be over the long run or even whether its problems will become fatal defects. Will it, for example, be able to survive the challenge of rival states whose leaders are not restrained by legal opposition and freely expressed public opinion? Autocratic power may permit such regimes to concentrate singlemindedly on military and manipulative techniques of competing for world power.[11] Will democracies produce too many leaders skilled at winning elections but lacking the knowledge and political skills needed to govern effectively?

These are bothersome questions. Many others could be raised, but we will focus on some recent discussions of the oldest problem of democracy—**factions.** Chapter 5 referred to James Madison's famous analysis of this problem and used the term *faction* to label organizations, such as parties and interest groups, that attempt to control or influence government on behalf of their members.

Madison proposed a more specific and unflattering definition:

> By a faction I understand a number of citizens, whether amounting to a majority or minority of the whole, who are united and actuated by some common impulse of passion or of interest, adverse to the rights of other citizens, or to the permanent and aggregate interests of the community.[12]

Of course, there is never general agreement about which groups should be considered Madisonian "factions," seeking to infringe on other people's rights or damage the public interest. Obviously, though, the interests and objectives of organized groups are often in conflict.

Discussion and disagreement continue endlessly about the impact of factions and factional conflict on the economy and society. As Madison shrewdly observed, "the most common and durable source of factions has been the various and unequal distribution of property."[13] Election campaigns, debates in legislative bodies, and the writings of political commentators and partisans frequently focus on disagreements about current economic policies and sometimes about the basic organization of the economy.

Critics of the Market Economy

Left-of-center democratic commentators contend that business groups and corporations are the main barrier to democratic equality and progress. Although everyone may have equal political rights, enormous inequalities in wealth lead to grossly unequal amounts of influence on government among organized and unorganized groups. Campaign contributions and party subsidies, dependence of voters on private corporations for jobs, the dominance of the media by consumer-capitalist images and values, the ability of wealthy groups to hire the best professional lobbyists—all give the economic "haves" much more political clout than the "have-nots." That influence is used to protect and reinforce economic inequality through taxation that favors wealthy interests and welfare policies that barely allow the poor to survive.

Political scientist Robert Dahl argues that if democracy means self-rule, it cannot be truly realized until democratic processes are extended to the workplace and the economy in general. Employers, market forces, and corporate managers control more of people's lives than do elected public officials but are not subject to democratic checks and controls. As long as business interests generally call the political tune in capitalist societies, there is little hope of progressing toward **economic democracy**.[14]

Advocates of the Market Economy

Many other political analysts, however, favor the market economy, with greater or lesser degrees of governmental regulation and social spending.

This combination of private enterprise and government activity is often called a *mixed economy*. Its partisans claim that it produces a better standard of living for most people than does any other type of economic organization. It also assures pluralistic control of resources and jobs, a precondition for effective political opposition. From this perspective, economic democracy is utopian—impossible to achieve. Efforts to bring it about would almost certainly concentrate more power and resources in the central government, especially in an ever-mushrooming bureaucracy.

However, champions of **democratic capitalism** also worry about the impact of factional demands and pressures on the economy and the political process. Economist Mancur Olson contends that over time, organized interest groups have an increasingly negative impact on economic growth, productivity, and efficiency. Given democratic liberties, all kinds of groups will eventually organize and develop more and more effective techniques of trying to influence public policy.

The trouble is that leaders of organized groups have a direct and immediate interest in gaining specific benefits for their members but no such motivation for promoting efficiency and productiveness in the economy as a whole. Therefore economic groups tend to push for policies like these:

- protecting monopolies
- limiting competition through licensing
- restricting imports from competitors who produce more cheaply
- paying farm subsidies that encourage wasted production
- exempting some kinds of income from taxation
- setting minimum prices through government regulation
- exploiting union bargaining strength to gain inflationary wage increases.

Such policies instantly and obviously benefit members of interest groups who promote them. The costs are much less apparent because they are spread across the whole society and operate in the longer run. They are real, however: "The great majority of special-interest organizations redistribute income rather than create it, and in ways that reduce social efficiency and output." Disputes about the distribution of national income are extremely divisive and tend to increase the level of hostility in public life.[15]

Competing for votes, democratic politicians and parties may tend to exaggerate the benefits of programs they favor and play down the costs. Economist Samuel Brittan suggests a long-term result: many voters expect too much from government at too little cost. Constant deficits result, followed by inflation, then by rising unemployment created by desperate inflation-fighting policies.[16] Anxiety about the economic future, resentment and envy of the better off, and reckless mortgaging of the future by running ever-larger deficits are all potentially dangerous effects of group pressures and democratic political competition. They could help create a downward economic spiral, intensifying conflict among groups and threatening to destroy the mutual toleration that constitutional democracy absolutely requires.

We suspect that warnings about the economic and social effects of factional conflict are worth thinking about very seriously but are usually exaggerated. Charges about "unfairness" and "favoring the rich" can inspire feelings that the democratic system is illegitimate and biased. No doubt that is an important reason why even conservative parties in power continue sizeable commitments to welfare and other social programs. As one would expect, however, data from a number of democracies indicate that left-of-center party control of governments has had more of an equalizing impact on taxes and income distribution.[17]

If voting majorities become worried about increased government spending for domestic programs, they are free to elect more conservative leaders, as they did with Margaret Thatcher in Britain (1979, 1983, 1987) and with Ronald Reagan in the United States (1980, 1984). Whatever the effects of these leaders' policies, their election and reelection showed that majorities were not immovably locked into support for more and larger redistribution programs. Many voters try to respond sensibly to changing circumstances and may often show more prudent judgment than academic theorists—whether left or right—are inclined to recognize. We doubt very much that factional conflict alone can destroy either a modern industrial economy or a well-established constitutional democracy.

Strengths of Democracy

The major positive effects of constitutional democracy are extremely important to most members of democratically governed societies. So we are constantly told by people who have lived under autocratic regimes or have witnessed the death of democracy in their own countries. We will summarize these strengths under four headings: **personal freedom and autonomy, governmental responsiveness, absence of mass coercion,** and **peaceful change.**

Personal Freedom and Autonomy

The ability to do and say what you want most of the time without fear of official punishment or censorship is the essence of the personal liberty protected by genuine constitutionalism. However questionable John Locke's concept of a "natural right" to personal liberty may seem, we believe that human beings have a natural urge to be free of coercive restraints.

This desire is strongly felt even by poor people whom the nonpoor sometimes believe care only about food, not freedom. In 1977 the Govern-

Criticism of the expanding economic role of government has struck a responsive chord in both Britain and the United States in recent years. Two of the main political beneficiaries of this trend, Prime Minister Thatcher and President Reagan, are shown here at a 1985 meeting in Washington.

ment of Prime Minister Indira Gandhi of India called an election. It followed a state of emergency that she had declared earlier, suspending political rights and jailing many opposition leaders. She expected that the mass of poor voters who had traditionally supported her Congress Party would do so again, approving the emergency declaration after the fact. But her party lost, in part because of the attitude expressed by one old peasant: "'Just because a man is poor and maybe cannot read does not mean that he cares nothing for his human rights. The Congress Government has tried to shut my mouth this last year and one-half, and therefore the Congress loses my vote.'"[18]

Governmental Responsiveness

If people are free to express their policy views, organize to advance them, and vote for public officials, their interests are much more likely to be taken into account by government policy makers than if they are denied political rights. Officials' claim to represent the "true" interests of the people is no substitute for people's ability to make them known freely: "If there is an inviolable rule, in life as in politics, it is that no interest is ever protected if the interested party cannot express his interest. Those who are absent are always wrong."[19]

Of course, democratic governments cannot and do not respond equally to all interests. Some groups have an advantage over others in most circumstances, and policy must usually represent a compromise among the demands of conflicting interests. Because of the relative openness of democratic politics, however, no substantial interests are forever prevented from making some impact on public policy.

Democratic leaders do not always act in response to public opinion or to the demands of organized groups. Sometimes their own judgment of what the situation demands leads them to go against current opinion. President Franklin Roosevelt, for example, gave military aid to Britain in 1941, which placed the officially neutral United States squarely on the British side in the war with nazi Germany. At the time, public opinion polls showed that three-fourths of the American public opposed U.S. entry into the war. In 1986 President Reagan fought successfully for congressional approval of aid to the anti-Marxist "contras" in Nicaragua, despite sizeable majorities' opposing that policy in public opinion polls. Each president felt compelled to act on his own beliefs and judgment about the national interest.

Absence of Mass Coercion

The more fully and freely people in a country can participate in policies and peacefully oppose the government, "the more difficult it is for the government . . . to adopt and enforce policies that require the application of extreme sanctions against more than a small percentage of the population; the less likely, too, that the government will attempt to do so."[20] The horrendous mass political murders of this century indelibly underline the tremendous importance of this protective function of democracy.

Where semidemocratic systems have not prevented large-scale persecution and discrimination, such as the treatment of blacks in the South under slavery and state-enforced segregation, the victims were actually excluded from exercising basic political rights. As southern blacks finally obtained those rights in the 1960s, coercive violence against them rapidly declined.

Peaceful Change

Constitutional democracy creates procedures that make political and social change possible without violent upheaval and terrifying disorder. These processes do not always work smoothly and seldom "efficiently" from an abstract point of view, but they usually enable societies to cope with conflict while avoiding the dangers of political violence.

In the terminology of political science, "Democracy—as an ensemble of behaviors and practices, institutions and rules, ideas and ideals—is replete with tensions, trade-offs, dilemmas, incompatibilities, and conflicts."[21] Yet we believe that it is worth taking to heart Winston Churchill's famous remark about democracy, quoted at the head of this chapter. For all the imperfections, injustices, and frustrations of constitutional democracy, it has proved much less damaging to most of the people it governs than has any other type of government.

In historical perspective, that generalization is surely correct. As we have pointed out frequently, the evolution of states has mainly produced more effective techniques of domination. The same has been true of much political change in the twentieth century, as will become apparent when we examine contemporary autocracies. Constitutional democracy is the only kind of large-scale governmental structure yet developed that can actually minimize government by coercion, manipulation, and permanent elimination. No majority in a democratic country has ever voted to replace it with another form of government; killing democracy has always been the work of self-chosen elites. We will examine the various ways of conducting nonaccountable elite rule in the following three chapters.

Summary

Basic differences in the structures of central governments can be used to classify democratic governments as presidential or parliamentary. Presidential systems feature separate elections and separate but overlapping constitutional powers for the executive and legislative branches. In the United States, for example, the president and Congress check and balance each other, and the independent judiciary can check both of the other branches. It is not uncommon for the presidency and the legislative body to be controlled by opposing parties, imposing an additional limitation on executive leadership. When parties are not subject to effective discipline, as in the United States, a president cannot count on solid support from legislators of his own party. The chief executive must work constantly at building temporary supportive coalitions on specific issues.

The French government is presidential but has some parliamentary features. The president appoints a premier and cabinet and maintains general control over the executive branch. Popularly elected for a seven-year term, the president cannot be removed by parliament but can dissolve the legislative body and call for new elections. The Fifth Republic's norm has been unified party control of presidency and parliament.

Parliamentary systems feature a fusion of executive and legislative offices and powers. The executive leader and cabinet are voted into office by the popularly elected house of parliament and can be voted out by the same body. As a rule, leading executive officials are chosen among members of parliament; they continue as members of the legislative body and participate in its debates.

In majoritarian parliamentary systems, a single party normally has a majority in the popularly elected house and monopolizes executive leadership posts. Britain provides the classic example: its single-member-district-plurality election system makes it possible and normal for one party to win a majority of seats in the House of Commons with less than a nationwide voting majority. This kind of electoral system tends to favor long-established parties with a substantial following and, in most elections, disfavors parties that many voters perceive as extreme. Party activists, both left and right, have become increasingly influential in pushing party positions toward ideological extremes in Britain and the United States.

In representational parliamentary systems, national elections are based on proportional representation. This method encourages multiple parties to seek places in parliament, and almost never can any single party gain a majority of seats. Executive leadership always involves a coalition of two or more parties. Bargaining among party leaders determines the makeup of the cabinet and the distribution of all ministerial posts. Coalition governments tend to have shorter lives than single-party governments, but most representational democratic regimes are not noticeably less effective or stable than majoritarian systems. In countries such as Belgium and Switzerland, multiparty governments provide special guarantees to distinct language and cultural groups, enhancing support for the constitutional system.

Another common method of classifying democratic governments refers to the territorial organization of official powers. In unitary systems the central government has complete legal authority over all regional units of government. Within federal systems the main territorial units—states, provinces—have some degree of independent authority that cannot be altered simply by decisions of the central government.

Most democratic states are unitary, but some of the largest are federal. Federalism was invented by the framers of the U.S. Constitution as a political compromise inducing strong state governments to accept a significant increase in the legal powers of the central government. Federal systems have often been created when societies faced possible external dangers or internal disorder but already existing regional governments were not willing to surrender all their authority.

All federal systems have written constitutions, bicameral legislative bodies with smaller regions disproportionately represented in one house, and a distinctive role in the constitutional amending process for regional governments or voters. These measures aim to spell out—not always successfully—the central–regional division of authority and to guarantee that regions and their governments can guard against domination by the central government.

Present-day democracies, like all other governments in all times, have many problems, and there is considerable disagreement on how to diagnose and treat them. A recurrent concern is the impact of factions—self-seeking organized groups—on economic and social structures, prosperity, and welfare. Critics from the democratic left contend that economic inequalities usually override political and legal equality, with business groups exploiting their wealth and economic control as potent political resources. Democracy requires that economic decision making, both in the workplace and in society at large, become accountable to the entire citizen-body.

Critics of factionalism also speak out from the center and right of the democratic ideological spectrum. They worry that organized group pressures will lead to so many policies designed to protect existing economic interests that the general competitiveness and efficiency of the economy will steadily decline. Parties and candidates promise benefits from governmental policies but minimize the costs. Huge and persistent deficits, inflation, panicky austerity policies, rising and persistent unemployment, a decline in living standards—all may stem from factional conflict and pressures and democratic electioneering. As a result, conflict among groups and alienation from the political system may increase and pose a long-term threat to the mutual toleration that undergirds the practice of democratic politics.

However, the strengths of constitutional democracy are considerable and tend to provide a degree of support for the system that normally enables it to survive dissatisfaction with current governmental performance. Personal freedom and autonomy, the ability to assure a degree of responsiveness by government, political and constitutional protections against mass coercion, and the routine possibility of producing political and social change through peaceful rather than violent methods are the bedrock advantages of democracy. When democratic governments are compared not with an ideal of perfect justice but with the actual performance of modern autocratic regimes, practical judgment strongly tends to favor constitutional democracy.

Review List of Key Terms

presidential government
separation of powers
checks and balances
party cohesion
party discipline
French constitution
parliamentary government
fusion of powers

parliamentary dismissal
constructive vote of no-confidence
majoritarian parliamentary systems
single-member-district-plurality system
floating voters

party activists
representational parliamentary democracies
proportional representation
coalition government
unitary system
federalism
confederacy

Articles of Confederation
political "threat" hypothesis
bicameral
concurrent powers
Bundesrat
centralizing of functions
factions

economic democracy
democratic capitalism
personal freedom and autonomy
governmental responsiveness
absence of mass coercion
peaceful change

Notes

1. A phrase suggested by political scientist Richard Neustadt, in *Presidential Power: The Politics of Leadership* (New York: Wiley, 1960), p. 33.
2. G. Bingham Powell, *Contemporary Democracies: Participation, Stability, and Violence* (Cambridge, Mass.: Harvard University Press, 1982), p. 153.
3. These two labels are suggested in Powell, *Contemporary Democracies*, p. 60. Powell's is one of the most thoroughgoing empirical, comparative analyses of the functioning and effects of the major types of democratic government.
4. Powell, *Contemporary Democracies*, pp. 61–62, 109–110, 125–132.
5. Arend Lijphart, *Democracy in Plural Societies: A Comparative Exploration* (New Haven: Yale University Press, 1977), p. 97.
6. William H. Riker, "Federalism," in *Handbook of Political Science*, vol. 5, *Governmental Institutions and Processes*, ed. Fred I. Greenstein and Nelson W. Polsby (Reading, Mass.: Addison-Wesley, 1975), p. 101.
7. Ibid., pp. 119, 120.
8. Ibid., pp. 98–101.
9. Arend Lijphart, "Consociation and Federation: Conceptual and Empirical Links," *Canadian Journal of Political Science* 12 (September 1979): 502.
10. Ibid., 503–504.
11. See Samuel P. Huntington, *American Politics: The Promise of Disharmony* (Cambridge, Mass.: Harvard University Press, 1981), pp. 237–259.
12. James Madison, *The Federalist*, no. 10, in *The Federalist Papers*, ed. Clinton Rossiter (New York: New American Library, 1961), p. 78.
13. Ibid., p. 79.
14. Robert A. Dahl, *Dilemmas of Pluralist Democracy: Autonomy versus Control* (New Haven: Yale University Press, 1982).
15. Mancur Olson, *The Rise and Decline of Nations* (New Haven: Yale University Press), 1982, esp. pp. 41–47.
16. Samuel Brittan, "The Economic Contradictions of Democracy," *British Journal of Political Science* 5 (1975): 129–159.
17. Powell, *Contemporary Democracies*, pp. 188–195.
18. *New York Times*, March 3, 1977.
19. Giovanni Sartori, *Democratic Theory* (New York: Praeger, 1965), p. 432.
20. Robert A. Dahl, *Polyarchy: Participation and Opposition* (New Haven: Yale University Press, 1971), p. 27.
21. Eric A. Nordlinger, *On the Autonomy of the Democratic State* (Cambridge, Mass.: Harvard University Press, 1981), p. 219.

SEVEN

Authoritarianism

Those who carry arms can always determine the fate of the constitution.
Aristotle, Politics

When nothing else is turned up, clubs are trumps.
Thomas Hobbes, Behemoth

Autocratic government consists of a true "power elite," rulers who are not accountable to the governed or effectively limited by the law and who try to prevent real challenges to their control of the government. Historically, most states have been governed autocratically, and about two out of three countries still are today.

This chapter considers the more common type of autocracy—authoritarianism—which, as we explained in chapter 4, features a more limited scope of centralized political control than do totalitarian regimes (go back and study figure 4-3 again). There is much variety among authoritarian governments: most don't allow any kind of political competition that could threaten the rulers' power, but some do sponsor certain types of political pluralism. Within the sole legal parties of Tanzania and the Ivory Coast, for example, candidates compete for parliamentary positions, and incumbents often lose. The corporate-military government that ruled Brazil from 1964 to 1985 allowed limited party competition in congressional elections, and the ruling party of Taiwan has long sponsored fair and competitive local elections; in 1986 it allowed an opposition party to compete in a general election for the first time.

However, authoritarian governments seriously restrict oppositional activity, and they don't permit electoral competition in which their opponents might win power.

Classification

To be as specific as possible, we are using the *authoritarian* category to include all contemporary governments that don't function as constitutional democracies and aren't ruled by communist elites. Countries having authoritarian regimes are shaded in figure 7-1. It is possible that a few communist-ruled states, such as Hungary, Yugoslavia, and China, have come to allow their citizens enough cultural, personal, and economic au-

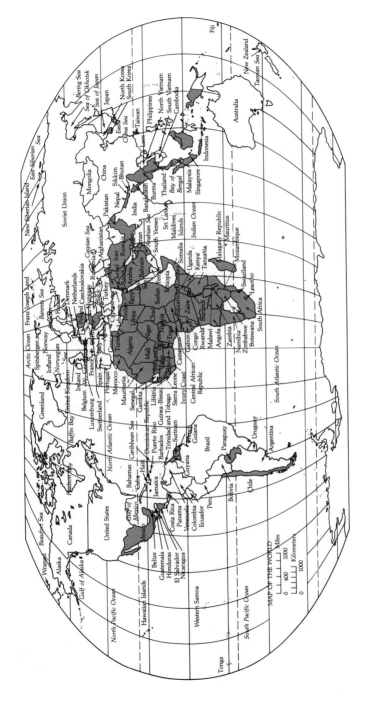

Figure 7-1 Authoritarian regimes (based mainly on authors' interpretation of 1987 Freedom House classifications)

tonomy to be classified as semiauthoritarian rather than totalitarian regimes. They do retain politically intolerant party-monopoly systems of control, however, and allow less oppositional criticism and organizing than do a great many authoritarian regimes. They also continue to claim authority based on the totalist ideology of Marxism-Leninism, which is explained in chapter 8. We are impressed by their practical differences from typical communist patterns, though, and inclined not to classify these autocratic regimes as totalitarian.

In this chapter, however, we focus on noncommunist authoritarianism. All present-day regimes of this type are located in the Third World—Africa, Asia, the Middle East, Latin America, and the Caribbean.

The Third World

Third World can be a confusing term, but it is used so often that it seems unavoidable. It began to appear in the 1950s to refer to countries that were not aligned either with the United States and Western Europe (the "First World") or with the Soviet bloc (the "Second World"). But it is no longer restricted to that meaning. Certain Soviet client-states, such as Cuba, Ethiopia, and Angola, and certain states aligned with the United States, such as South Korea, Taiwan, and El Salvador, are nearly always included in the vague "Third World" category.

Third World often refers to the "developing" countries—those that have much less industrialized economies than the United States and Europe. Yet there is a tremendous range of economic development among Third World countries, extending from the phenomenal industrial progress of Taiwan to the stagnation and decay of the once-flourishing agricultural economy of Ghana.

Geography alone is no sure clue to Third World membership. Although Japan is Asian, its economy—the third most productive in the world—places it clearly outside the Third World category. Nor is South Africa, under its white-dominated regime, ever so categorized. The more recently fashionable identification of the "developing" Third World with the geographical "south" of the globe as contrasted with the developed "north" is also misleading. Afghanistan, Iran, Korea, and most of China are as far north as the United States but are usually called *Third World*. States with highly developed economies such as South Africa, Australia, and New Zealand are located far to the south of most Third World countries.

All these labels—*Third World, developing,* and *south*—were coined originally for propaganda purposes, and it is not surprising that they remain imprecise and misleading. In addition, it would be a serious mistake to identify all the states within these vague categories as authoritarian. As we pointed out earlier, some Third World states—such as India, Sri Lanka, and Venezuela—are constitutional democracies. We would classify others—Cuba and Ethiopia, for example—as totalitarian.

■ Approach to Classification

But even in categorizing regimes as authoritarian by a process of elimination, we are still left with well over half the independent states of the world within this broad category. There is great variety among them in governmental structures, policies, and stability. There are nearly as many systems of classifying them as there are political scientists writing about "political development," and we suggest our own simple classification scheme very tentatively. It is nothing more than a preliminary effort to make some sense of empirical complexity by pointing up what seem to be the dominant characteristics of different regimes.

Traditional authoritarianism is a nearly vanished political species, but the other three types—personal-rule, corporate-rule, and party-rule—are alive and flourishing. Almost every nontraditional authoritarian government has an individual head of government, some degree of corporate (collective elite) decision making, and an official political party. These governments differ a great deal, though, in the extent to which one of these three features tends to predominate.

Tanzania, for example, has an elaborate official party organization yet probably fits best within the "personal rule" category, because of the overwhelming influence of its first president, Julius Nyerere. His 1985 retirement from office is too recent to make possible any judgment yet about reclassifying the Tanzanian regime. The Syrian government maintains an official party and has a forceful president, but it is probably best understood as a corporate-military regime. Some states are difficult to classify using these categories: is South Africa a corporate-racial or a dominant-party authoritarian regime? There is considerable room for disagreement about both individual governments and our classification system; at best we hope that it casts a little light on a much-obscured subject.

Why Authoritarianism?

Before analyzing the major types of authoritarian government, we need to consider an important and puzzling question: in an age when everyone publicly favors democracy, why are most governments in fact authoritarian? We cannot provide a definitive answer—so far no one has. But some helpful clues to thinking seriously about this question are provided, we suggest, by the great seventeenth-century English political theorist Thomas Hobbes.

Hobbes and the State-of-Nature Problem

As we noted in chapter 1, Hobbes argued forcefully that human beings are competitive power seekers by nature. It follows, then, that in any society that lacks a government strong enough to limit and regulate competition for power, no one's life or possessions will be secure. Actual or threatened violence will dominate everyone's existence in this **state of nature,** and life will be "solitary, poor, nasty, brutish, and short."[1] To escape this terrifying condition, people should be willing to accept the right to rule of anyone who can mobilize enough coercive power to enforce law and order, assuring social peace and personal security. Protection—against both external attack and internal disorder—is the central purpose of government, although rulers who hope to remain in power very long will also try to promote their subjects' economic well-being.

In this century many Third World peoples have seen the decay, disappearance, or revolutionary overthrow of stable, order-enforcing governments, whether traditional monarchies, landowner oligarchies, or European-imposed colonial regimes. The resulting absence of strong governments encourages new and intensified power competition, a game in which, as Hobbes observed, it is often true that "clubs are trumps." Authoritarian rulers rely heavily on controlling the biggest and most intimidating clubs—military force. With various degrees of success, they also use inducements and persuasion to build support and legitimacy for their regimes.

Creating effective governments that can maintain social peace and promote prosperity has never been easy or painless, and it has usually been a long drawn-out process. The relatively prosperous, strong, and stable democratic states of Western Europe and of such European offshoots as the United States, Canada, and Australia are products of many centuries of wars, forced border changes, political oppression, rebellions, massacres, revolutions, famines, religious persecution, and mass exterminations. Even in the twentieth century, Europe has been the center of the two most deadly wars in history.

Is it really surprising, then, that transitions from traditional or colonialist political orders should have produced a great deal of conflict, violence, and military rule in Third World countries? From an historical perspective, the existence of some orderly, stable, and relatively effective governments should seem much more remarkable.

Historical perspective is not the long suit, however, of the mass media or of most working politicians. Moreover, conflict and violence can create problems for governments other than those immediately involved, as well as opportunities for regimes whose leaders want to extend their power and influence. The world is much more politically interdependent today than when feudal princes were slugging it out with each other in the twelfth century.

The "Political Lag" Explanation

For explaining present-day disorder and authoritarianism in the Third World, most political scientists favor some version of the **political lag** hypothesis: "The primary problem of politics is the lag in the development of political institutions behind social and economic change."[2] In addition to the general danger that political competition will become violent when power is up for grabs and the stakes are high, most countries of Asia, Africa, and Latin America face more specific problems of late development.

When Britain and France began what we can now look back upon as their long progress toward unity, commercial and industrial development, and world empire, no one knew that they were headed toward any particular future condition. What they and other highly industrialized countries have achieved—usually referred to as **modernization**—is strongly desired, at least in part, by significant groups within every developing country.

Political elites' quest for modernization doesn't necessarily mean that they want their countries to become just like the United States or West Germany. But even when they would like to preserve much of their traditional social structure and culture, they consider it essential to build up a modern industrial economy. Industrial capacity provides the necessary basis for sufficient military strength to defend their states against domination by the major industrial powers.

Japan remains the prime example of such reactive or **defensive modernization**. The Japanese were able to keep Western traders and missionaries out of their country until threatened with superior U.S. naval force in the the mid-nineteenth century. Japanese political elites responded by reorganizing an already centralized government and embarking on an all-out industrialization drive accompanied by educational and other social changes. Within a few decades Japan was the military leader of Asia; its leaders' attempt to create an empire by military conquest was halted only by overwhelming U.S. might in the Second World War. The economic success of Japanese modernization has become quite apparent, though, in the years since its military forces were defeated.

In recent decades, rising economic expectations among Third World peoples have also become a powerful influence on their politics: "The demand that Third World countries should traverse the road to modernity rapidly is the most important source of the political unrest that makes many Third World countries so explosive."[3] Many people live in poverty

This sharp contrast between modern luxury and a shantytown in Acapulco, Mexico, is typical of rapid urbanization in much of the Third World.

in these countries, but they always have. What becomes "explosive" is the contrast between mass poverty and awareness of what looks, comparatively, like mass prosperity in the industrially advanced countries.

This awareness is felt first and most keenly by students, journalists, and other would-be intellectuals who are exposed to Western-style education, perhaps in mission schools or in European or U.S. universities. Awareness and resentment spread to larger and larger portions of the population through exposure to Western films and television programs, political propaganda promising rapid development, and expanding systems of primary education.

As a result, political participation increases rapidly. Students demonstrate and sometimes riot. Peasants clamor for land and occasionally kill landlords. Merchants pressure the government to prevent competition from modern retailers and foreigners. Religious leaders mobilize zealous followers offended by Western-style entertainments, education, and practices such as women's emancipation. Hordes of job seekers press the government to provide them with secure positions in the bureaucracy. Military leaders insist that their forces become better prepared, professionally competent, and respected as the ultimate guardians of the state.

It is not easy to develop governments that are strong and well organized enough to cope with so many demands and pressures through compromise, favoritism to critical groups, and credible threats of coercion against persistent "troublemakers." Governments that are relatively new and whose principles of authority are nontraditional may receive little respect or general support if they cannot "deliver the goods" and seem to be weak and inept. Effective political party organizations, politically experienced interest group leaders, and adaptable and unified governmental institutions are rarely found in countries undergoing the difficult transition from traditional to modern societies.

Frustrated expectations, reasonable or not, can lead to riots, terrorism, military takeovers, revolutionary movements—in general, to intense political conflict and instability. As we noted in chapter 6, even well-established democratic governments in advanced industrial societies have been experiencing great difficulty in coping with the many conflicting demands made upon them. It should not be surprising that governments with far fewer economic resources and often very little legitimacy are even more vulnerable to violent opposition and sudden changes of ruling elites or regimes.

(For examples of both typical and exceptional relationships between income levels and governmental systems in a variety of countries, see table 7-1.)

Types of Authoritarian Government

We will consider four kinds of authoritarian regimes: traditional, personal-rule, corporate-rule, and party-rule. These categories are not clear-cut and mutually exclusive; particular regimes may be plausibly fitted into more than one classification. However, there is a basic logic to the categories and to the order in which we discuss them. They begin with regimes that have the least-modernized institutions, and each successive type has attained, broadly speaking, a progressively greater degree of political modernization.

Modernization is a difficult and slippery term when applied to politics and government. It has a reasonably clear socioeconomic meaning, entailing a money-based economy, a sizeable industrial sector, an urban population much larger than the rural, an extensive system of formal education, a relatively high level of social mobility based on individual training and ability, and specialization of functions according to job categories and by organizations designed for specific purposes.

Political modernization refers first of all to the principles of legitimacy that rulers use to justify their authority. Nontraditional regimes do not appeal to rights of inheritance or to divine right—with the possible exception of the Iranian "Islamic Republic." A modernized regime features complex institutions—numerous government ministries and departments staffed by a more or less merit-based civilian bureaucracy, a professional military establishment, an executive establishment well supplied with ad-

Table 7-1 Economic development and governmental systems

Typical Patterns			
Relatively Low Income, Authoritarian Government		*Relatively High Income, Democratic Government*	
Country	GNP* per capita	Country	GNP* per capita
Zaire	$ 170	Spain	$ 4,780
Tanzania	240	Italy	6,400
Ghana	310	Belgium	9,150
Kenya	340	Britain	9,200
Indonesia	560	Japan	10,120
Egypt	700	France	10,500
Ivory Coast	710	West Germany	11,430
Cameroon	820	Australia	11,490
Syria	1,760	Canada	12,310
Chile	1,870	Sweden	12,470
South Korea	2,010	United States	14,110
Mexico	2,240	Switzerland	16,290
Exceptional Patterns			
Low-Income Democracies		*High-Income Authoritarian Regimes†*	
India	$ 260	Oman	$ 6,250
Sri Lanka	330	Libya	8,480
Senegal	440	Saudi Arabia	12,230
Philippines	760	Kuwait	17,880
Jamaica	1,300		

*Gross National Product, 1983: *World Development Report 1985* (published for the World Bank by Oxford University Press, 1985).
†All major exporters of oil.

visers and support staffs, a legislative body that may have an important symbolic role even if it lacks real law-making power, and a professional judiciary with legal expertise and some degree of independence.

Modern governmental institutions have reasonably specific responsibilities and, as a rule, the capabilities to discharge them. Their functions may frequently overlap, but organized methods are used in attempting to coordinate and direct their activities as the top authorities desire. Among the most important of modernized institutions are well-organized political parties that provide direction, a degree of unity, and support for official policies both inside and outside the government.

Finally, a modernized and thoroughly institutionalized regime outlasts its founders. Rules prescribing how new government leaders should obtain their offices prove effective in channeling the competition for power. Predictable and peaceful **leadership transitions** add an important degree of stability to the system.

(For summary descriptions and examples of the four types of authoritarian regimes, arranged according to their degree of political modernization, see figure 7-2.)

Traditional Authoritarianism

Traditional authoritarianism means hereditary monarchy, the most ancient type of centralized state regime. In a discussion of contemporary authoritarianism, there is little point in dwelling long upon monarchies, a dying political species. Governments in which the monarch exercises real decision-making power include such states as Swaziland and Morocco in Africa and Jordan, Saudi Arabia, and the Persian Gulf sheikdoms in the Middle East. All the Arab monarchies are more or less seriously threatened; since the Second World War, monarchical governments have been overthrown in Egypt, Iraq, and Libya and in the important non-Arab Middle Eastern state of Iran.

Traditionally, monarchies have depended on support from royal officials, aristocratic landholders, and a politically ignorant and uninvolved mass peasantry. They have usually proved unable to absorb or accommodate new groups who have received a modern type of secular education. Such people tend to be strongly influenced either by democratic or by Marxist-Leninist ideologies; in either case they vehemently reject claims to legitimacy based on divine right and inheritance. They seek to bring into existence a new kind of regime in which "modern" people like themselves will have broadened opportunities to wield power and move their countries toward catching up with the industrially advanced societies.

Twentieth-century experience suggests that traditional monarchs probably can't save their regimes either by refusing to initiate modernizing reforms or by trying to act as modernizers themselves. The first approach was tried by the imperial Chinese government, which was fairly easily overthrown by nationalist would-be modernizers in 1911. The modernizing path was followed, to a significant extent, by Reza Shah Pahlevi of Iran, whose regime collapsed in 1979.

A briefly sketched case study of Ethiopian politics should point up the perils of traditional monarchy in the late twentieth century. Ethiopia is an ancient state in northeastern Africa, though its territory tripled in size through conquests as recently as the late nineteenth century. Its forceful subjection of neighboring peoples eventually produced separatist movements and warfare.[4]

The last Ethiopian emperor was Haile Selassie, who ruled from 1930 until removed by a military revolt in 1974. The emperor claimed all powers of government, and his rule was sanctified by the official Coptic Christian Church. In practice, the monarch ruled by shrewdly manipulating pow-

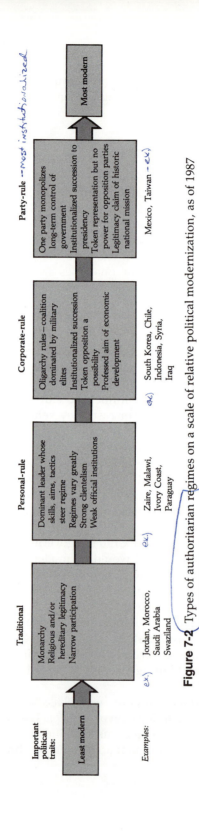

Figure 7-2 Types of authoritarian regimes on a scale of relative political modernization, as of 1987

erful forces such as the landowning nobility, the church (also a major landholder), provincial governors, court and administrative officials, and military officers.[5]

After the Second World War, the emperor began to employ Westerneducated experts in his bureaucracy, but eventually the universityeducated segment of the population outgrew the capacity of the government to absorb them. Intellectual, professional, and trade union leaders became extremely hostile to the traditional regime. They did not believe in its religious legitimacy or in its ability to move the country toward economic modernization. The fundamental incapacity of the government was demonstrated in its reaction to a terrible drought that hit much of the country in 1972–1973. It did almost nothing except try, unsuccessfully, to cover up the news that as many as 100,000 peasants had starved to death. It also proved powerless against inflation that strongly affected city populations in 1973–1974. Urban riots and military rebellions broke out, and the emperor's attempt to appease the protestors by changing prime ministers only demonstrated his vulnerability.

The year 1974 in Ethiopia proved to be "a rare moment in history when existing political and social authorities are discredited and irresolute and the state is vulnerable to expropriation by the boldest and strongest adventurer. . . . the boldest and the strongest were soldiers in arms."[6] After much violence and bloodshed within the military, a group of formerly lowranking officers took charge, headed by Lt. Col. Mengistu Haile Mariam. Thousands of the students who had backed the overthrow of the monarchy were sent to the countryside to help implement the new regime's radical land reforms. These measures destroyed the power of the traditional landowning nobility and of the church hierarchy.

Leaders of the revolutionary regime first identified themselves as "Ethiopian socialists," but by 1976 the survivors of a fierce power struggle at the top were calling themselves "Marxist-Leninists." Yet they bloodily suppressed efforts by civilian Marxists to organize political parties. The ruling soldiers' ideological self-identification was probably helpful, though, in securing massive military aid from the Soviet Union. Sovietbloc advisers and thousands of well-trained Cuban troops enabled the new regime to avoid defeat by armed ethnic secession movements and the army of neighboring Somalia.[7]

The Ethiopian monarchy's dependence on traditional social forces proved incompatible with its limited encouragement of Westernized education and its buildup of substantial U.S.-armed professional military forces. The narrowness and shallowness of support for the monarchy doomed it to rapid destruction once its weakness and incapacity had been exposed.

Monarchs elsewhere have no doubt tried to learn from experiences such as the overthrow of the Ethiopian and Iranian monarchies. The traditionalist Saudi Arabian royal family, for example, has attempted to import nothing but technical knowledge and expertise from the West and to maintain a society guided by a puritanical Islam. Saudi rulers have feared both the subversive effects of untraditional ideas of legitimacy and the enmity of the radical "more-Islamic-than-thou" Iranian regime. Iran's leaders have constantly denounced the Saudi authorities as hypocritical puppets of the United States. It seems entirely possible that no traditional authoritarian monarchies will remain by the end of the twentieth century. Their disappearance will close a nearly six-thousand-year political epoch that began in ancient Sumeria and Egypt.

Personal-Rule Authoritarianism

"Military rule" is not one of our three categories of nontraditional authoritarianism, even though most authoritarian rulers have come to power through military takeovers (coups d'état). "Military regime" is such a broad category and military officers as rulers differ so much in objectives, skills, approaches, ideologies, policies, and allies that it tells us little about a government to know that its top leaders are military professionals. In addition, regimes that begin with a military takeover tend to become increasingly dependent on civilian experts, advisers, and officials if they last very long.[8]

Military officers who seize ruling power inevitably claim to act as guardians of the nation, saving it from the selfish, corrupt, or subversive politicians who have too long violated their public trust.[9] In fact military rulers are not "above politics"; they are simply skillful or inept politicians in uniform. Military leaders often predominate but do not monopolize power in both personal-rule and corporate-rule authoritarian regimes. Their governing role is considerably smaller in party-rule systems.

■ Power without Limits

Personal-rule authoritarianism refers to a system in which there are no long-established, secure political institutions that predictably channel or constrain the actions of the top ruler. Since this type of rule is typical of relatively new states or governments, they have no framework of rules and procedures that have gained acceptance through generations of practice. The personalities, political skills, and beliefs of individual leaders always make some difference in every political system, no matter how stable or institutionalized; policy making involves much more than following established routines. The personal-rule authoritarian leader, though, is so little hemmed in—or helped—by political traditions that he or she can be relatively more influential than any British prime minister, U.S. president, or

Soviet general secretary. This kind of ruler comes closer to the traditional strong monarch than does any other type of present-day political leader.

Personal-rule authoritarianism was common in most Latin American countries in the nineteenth century, after they had won independence from Spanish control. Power was typically gained by a military coup, and the leading general would rule as he saw fit—often to enrich his family and friends as rapidly as possible—until overthrown by another military plot. This phenomenon extended into the twentieth century: the Somoza family ruled Nicaragua from 1936 until 1979, exploiting their control of government to enrich themselves through corruption and favored treatment of their own agricultural and commercial enterprises. As we will point out in the next section, though, most Latin American military governments became more corporate and less personal in recent decades.

The sub-Saharan states of Africa, largely because of the recency of their political independence and their limited political experience, provide most examples of personal-rule authoritarianism in the contemporary world. Although withdrawing colonial governments, especially the British and French, usually left behind Western-style democratic constitutions in African states, few governments have actually functioned as democracies. In some cases the party in power at independence soon declared a one-party state, as it did in Kenya and Tanzania. In others the government's weakness and poor performance invited military overthrow, which by 1980 had occurred more than forty times in twenty-one of these countries. Occasionally both occurred, as in Ghana, where a military coup in 1966 overthrew the one-party government of Kwame Nkrumah.

As we explained in chapter 3, the recently independent African states emerged from colonialism with boundaries originally drawn to reflect the relative power and interests of European states, not traditional African politics or ethnic territories and relationships. With little or no common noncolonial political experience and with many divisions in their societies—among ethnic groups, between Western-educated elites and nonliterate majorities, between cities and countryside—these states have not proved easy to govern or to organize. The weakness of most governments has made politics an inviting arena for ambitious individuals seeking power, fame, and fortune—similar to the attractions of the rich and powerful medieval European church.[10]

Most of the more successful African rulers have incorporated strong elements of traditional kingship into their regimes—especially the claim to rule like a stern but wise father deeply concerned for the people's welfare. In societies still based to a great extent "upon kinship and primordial ties, embedded in tradition,"[11] rulers' cultivating a paternal image can greatly enhance their authority.

Jomo Kenyatta, for example, the first president (1963–1978) of independent Kenya, drew upon his age and long experience as a nationalist political leader to present himself as the "patriarch" of all Kenyans. He achieved some success in bridging deep ethnic divisions. Ahmadou Ahidjo, president of Cameroon from 1960 to 1982, ruled firmly, presenting himself as a stern father commanding obedience from his children–people. He viewed the state as "the family writ large." However, his political shrewdness, effective management of the economy, and willingness to use force were also extremely important for holding power. His use of secret police and detention of several thousand political prisoners suggest that paternalistic ideology may also need to be supplemented by effective coercion.[12]

■ Characteristics

These personal-rule regimes are authoritarian in that the rulers are not effectively restrained by laws; they seek to monopolize governmental power; and other groups and individuals have no real opportunities to compete effectively for control of the government. Kenya, for instance, has emphasized the importance of the law more than most African states. Yet President Kenyatta's "emergency" powers were so broad that in 1975 he was able to get the constitution amended in order to pardon members of parliament convicted of violating election laws.[13]

The authoritarian rather than totalitarian nature of most personal-rule African regimes is shown by their general **nonpolitical tolerance** of citizens' rights. These include freedom of religion and of occupational choice and—in a majority of the states—freedom to own private property and to buy and sell as one pleases. It is mainly the rights to form new political parties and express open political opposition that are severely curbed or eliminated.[14]

Obviously, personal-rule regimes depend very much on support from the armed forces; when they lose it, a military coup is likely to bring in a new government. They also rely heavily on selective inducements as a method of building and keeping adequate support. This amounts to **clientelism,** a system of reciprocal exchanges between leaders and selected followers. Leaders provide government jobs, contracts, or kickbacks and other illegal payments in return for followers' loyal political support, even when material rewards are temporarily unavailable.[15]

As you may recall from reading chapters 1 and 2, sharing the fruits of dominant political power—land, slaves, taxes and tributes, delegated power—is an ancient technique exploited by the earliest chiefs and kings. They also needed cooperative clients to support and defend their governments and implement their laws and policies. In some form, clientelism has persisted in every state. Urban political machines in the United States that assured jobs to the politically faithful in return for their votes and campaign assistance provide a much more recent and familiar example.

Most African personal-rule governments depend very heavily on dispensing **patronage** to supporters, in the forms of official jobs and special economic opportunities. Even low-paying government positions—police officer, license clerk, customs officer—can be fairly lucrative, because people generally expect to pay bribes in order to evade regulations or speed their business through bureaucratic roadblocks. The more laws and regulations multiply, the greater the opportunities for civil servants to supplement their salaries.

In many African countries the government owns and operates important enterprises, such as the copper industry in Zaire and Zambia. In East Africa many Indian-owned small businesses and in West Africa Lebanese-owned shops have been confiscated in the name of "Africanization." Policies like these provide economic resources that rulers can distribute among their faithful followers. The corrupt exploitation of public office is extremely widespread in Africa, as it has been in many other countries in various times and circumstances, including the United States.

■ Kleptocracy

A relatively low level of corruption may do little harm and even help hold a regime together as it develops increasing competence over the years. Bribes may sometimes clear the way for both foreign and domestic business firms to develop operations that help promote national economic development. Taken to extremes, though, corruption can turn a regime into a tyrannical **kleptocracy**—rule by thieves[16]—that can do great economic and human damage.

In Ghana, for example, Kwame Nkrumah's government (1957–1966) controlled all cocoa exports, siphoning off most of the profits from farmers in order to reward political clients. Virtual bankruptcy led to a military takeover in 1966, but a successor president, Ignatius Acheampong, learned too well from the earlier regime. In six years of office in the 1970s, he reportedly built a personal fortune of $100 million. His financial success was accompanied by hyperinflation and severe shortages for most citizens of Ghana, and a 1979 military coup led to the execution of Acheampong and two other former heads of state.[17]

Not all kleptocracies are quickly or easily overthrown. The regime of Mobutu Sese Seko, who engineered a military takeover in Zaire in 1965, is a spectacular example of clientelism run wild.[18] In seeking loyal helpers, Mobutu cared little about ability. An economically incompetent political elite has developed; its members are totally dependent on the ruler and entirely dedicated to self-enrichment. Through bribes, payoffs, and holdings in state-owned enterprises, plus salaries and perquisites of office, this elite misappropriates an estimated 60 percent of the annual budget. Although Mobutu has tried to exalt himself above his own government and occasionally criticizes his subordinates in the name of "the people," he has also become incredibly rich. He has bloodily suppressed protests and opposition. Mobutu's regime starkly illustrates that the "generalized loyalty of a wider public to a personal ruler is probably less important than the more immediate and direct loyalty of lieutenants and clients."[19]

■ Beneficial Effects

Not all African personal-rule regimes have resembled those that have burdened Ghana and Zaire. Partly because this kind of government depends so heavily on a particular individual, recent African regimes have varied widely in quality, stability, and effectiveness. Governments in the Ivory Coast, Cameroon, and Kenya have been stable and not terribly repressive, and they have promoted a significant amount of economic development. Their leaders have been shrewd, skillful, and determined politicians concerned with more than self-enrichment.

A particular example of stable, moderate, and politically intelligent personal rule was provided by Léopold Sedar Senghor, President of Senegal after that West African country became independent from France in 1960 until his retirement in 1980. Before Senghor entered politics, he had made a reputation as a leading African intellectual and French-language poet. He permitted a great deal of intellectual and press freedom in Senegal, even though it was in reality a one-party state from 1963 to 1978. Carefully and shrewdly outmaneuvering potential rivals and maintaining a kind of royal "court" in which he served as the supreme dispute settler, Senghor avoided serious challenges.

There was a kind of institutionalized corruption in his regime, but it was kept well below kleptocratic levels and probably helped strengthen the government's position. Islamic religious leaders and chiefs of political "clans" in the countryside acted as patrons of many peasant clients. In return for a share of the harvest, these patrons channeled government agricultural services to "cooperative" peasants. Since the Senegalese are strongly Muslim, this system prevented traditionalist opposition to the government.

Perhaps Senghor's most notable political contribution to his country was gradually moving its government toward constitutional democracy. By 1978 three licensed opposition parties were functioning, and in 1980 Senghor voluntarily stepped down in favor of his constitutionally designated successor, Prime Minister Abdou Diouf. In truly competitive elections Senghor's and Diouf's Socialist Party has won overwhelming support, even though opposition parties have multiplied. On the whole, it appears that Senghor's personal-rule authoritarianism benefited Senegal by providing peace, order, intellectual openness, and a politics of accommodation leading to a peaceful transition of power and fledgling democratic institutions.[20]

At least one other African personal-rule regime may also have moved significantly toward a fully institutionalized constitutional system. When Kenyan President Kenyatta died in 1978, Vice President Daniel arap Moi succeeded him and soon won a special presidential election. President arap Moi legally gained and held office even though he is not of Kenyatta's numerically dominant ethnic group. Opposition to him was successfully contained within the ruling party, and he was careful to maintain proportional regional-ethnic representation within his government.[21] It seems probable that with time and political experience, African personal-rule governments will move toward highly institutionalized political systems. They are likely to take a variety of forms—democratic, corporate- or party-authoritarian, or even totalitarian.

Corporate-Rule Authoritarianism

Corporate-rule authoritarianism refers to a particular kind of **oligarchy**—rule by the few. The regime is an oligarchic coalition dominated by the top ranks of the military. They act as a corporate professional group whose first priority is to protect the interests of the military elite. Less powerful partners in the ruling coalition, acting as cabinet ministers and advisers, may include high-ranking bureaucrats, technocrats (economic and technological experts) from inside or outside the bureaucracy, representatives of important economic groups (usually not including independent labor unions), leaders of the official party (if there is one), and occasionally representatives of the dominant church, if any.

Regimes of this general type have existed in Europe in the recent past—in Spain from 1939 to 1975, in Portugal from 1931 to 1974, in Greece from 1967 to 1974. In Asia, governments in Pakistan, South Korea, Indonesia, and Thailand probably fit into this category. The main geographic strongholds of corporate-military authoritarianism recently have been the Middle East and Latin America, and our discussion will focus on examples from those regions.

■ Military Leadership

In practice, the major Middle Eastern regimes—in Egypt, Iraq, and Syria—have strongly resembled personal-rule authoritarianism because of the strong influence of their presidents. Each of these regimes began in a military takeover directed against traditional political and social elites and led by officers who promised radical change, development, and **Arab socialism.** This ideology "might be described as an aspiration to instant modernization. The elements . . . seem to be Islam, militarism, nationalism, harmony among the classes in the interest of national unity, a single party that all are invited to join, and state direction of the economy."[22]

Attempts have been made to establish ruling coalitions including both the military **Revolutionary Command Council,** originally leaders of the coup, and officials of a mass party. In each case, however, the party remains definitely subordinate to the military leadership. Efforts to build well-organized and effective parties have either been pushed inconsistently, or, in Syria for example, halted and undone. Rulers have tended to see strong parties as potential rivals to the military and have used their leadership of the parties mainly to control them. In Syria, army officers have been strongly urged to join the official Ba'ath socialist party, but mainly to indoctrinate them with the wisdom and necessity of obedience to President Assad, simultaneously head of government, armed forces, and party.[23]

According to a Lebanese social scientist, these "Arab socialist" regimes have failed to impose a national pattern of modernization on their societies. At the village level, people continue to be strongly attached to traditional religious and "folk" values and to political groupings based mainly on kinship. Party organization does not really penetrate to the countryside where most people live. Military leaders remain intolerant of deviation and discord, especially political dissent. They try constantly to indoctrinate the population through the mass media and to control them by using coercive force and extensive intelligence networks.[24]

In the absence of strong, modernized political parties, whether competitive or monopolistic, these "army-party" regimes strongly favor the interests of the military. As a result, they feature large and well-armed military forces, costing up to 70 percent of the national budget. For individual officers, a military career holds out the promise of upward social mobility; its financial rewards and potential political influence look very attractive within the context of largely peasant societies.[25] The decades-old Arab–Israeli conflict, which occasionally breaks into open warfare, also provides a reasonably effective rationale for large military establishments.

Clientelism and nepotism are probably as important in the organization of these "army-party" corporate regimes as in African personal-rule systems. During Anwar Sadat's presidency in Egypt (1970–1981), the "people recruited into the most intimate structure of power—the presidential office—came from the patrimonial network of family, village, and kinship relationships." The bureaucracy and the military also provided many jobs for officeholders' relatives and for people whose primary loyalties were owed to their military, bureaucratic, or party patrons.[26]

Similar tendencies in Syria are complicated by religious divisions between the three-fifths of the population who are orthodox Sunni Moslems and the one-tenth who are members of the Alawi Islamic sect. Ancient disputes and hostility persist between these groups. President Assad is Alawi, and as many as eighteen of the top twenty-five armed-forces positions have been held by military colleagues from that minority group. The key positions in internal security and intelligence organizations also tend to be reserved for Alawis closely tied to the president. His 20,000-man palace guard has been commanded by one of his brothers.

None of the "Arab socialist" regimes tolerates very much political opposition, although control of criticism is usually not very tight in Egypt. They have all been very tough on religious dissent, because most of it has been antisecular Islamic fundamentalism, from both the long-illegal Moslem Brotherhood and more recent Iranian-inspired movements. A conspiracy by one such Egyptian group engineered President Sadat's assassination. As for Syria: "Faced with a rebellion by Muslim fundamentalists early [in 1982], [President] Assad besieged the city of Hama and slaughtered more than 20,000 of his foes."[27] Tight control of loyal troops, opponents who seemed threatening, and total ruthlessness combined to produce a politics of physical elimination.

In a number of Latin American countries the military has a longer history as a corporate profession than is generally true in the Middle East. *Caudillismo*—rule by a military strong man—became quite common in Latin America soon after those countries won their independence early in the nineteenth century. By the early twentieth century, governments in Argentina, Bolivia, Chile, Peru, and Brazil had imported professional military advisers and instructors from Germany or France to begin developing a modern, well-disciplined officer corps. Military academies and advanced training schools were established. Since the Second World War, the United States has become the major foreign trainer and supplier of Latin American armed forces.

■ Alternation with Democracy

Most Latin American countries have alternated between unstable democracy and military-dominated regimes. Military officers have often become disgusted with the pulling and hauling, empty rhetoric, and frequent immobility of democratic politics and presented themselves as guardians of the whole nation, standing above politics: "Order, obedience, authority, and stability—cherished values of the Hispanic socioeconomic elites—not only dovetailed neatly with the spirit of military training, but also provided easy rationalizations for military rule."[28]

With few exceptions, military-controlled regimes have supported the predominant economic interests in their societies, often big landowners and recently the more modern sectors of the business community. However, the military power wielders no longer seek merely to keep order through coercion; they also want to promote rapid economic development. In 1952, a top Brazilian officer summed up the typical Latin American military view of recent decades: "National security lies in the battle for production, in the tranquility of the population, and in the provision of stability and a reasonable standard of living."[29]

The revolutionary regime in Cuba, which Fidel Castro identified in 1961 as "Marxist-Leninist," added a strong sense of urgency to this military ideology. It seemed very probable that Castro, with massive assistance from his Soviet sponsor, would encourage, train, and arm guerrilla movements attempting to produce communist revolutions in most Latin American countries. This threat led military leaders to see political conflict, especially if participants included leftist or populist parties, trade unions, or peasant movements, as even more menacing than in earlier times.

Against this background, between 1964 and 1976 military coups overthrew shaky and conflict-ridden democratic governments in Brazil, Chile, Uruguay, and Argentina. The new regimes represented much more the corporate interests and viewpoint of the professional officer corps than the ambitions of particular "strong men." These governments struck some Latin American and foreign social scientists as a new type of military regime, which they labeled **bureaucratic authoritarian.** This term refers to a coalition among the professional military, selected economic experts (technocrats), the permanent state bureaucracy, and, to a disputed extent, the business community. Its purpose was to implement a capitalist development program that required denying political or economic power to labor movements.[30]

Brazil, starting in 1964, was the first Latin American country to be ruled by one of these more highly organized, corporate-military regimes. A formally civilian government was retained, with an elected president and congress, but an informal "college of generals" made up of the high-ranking military officers actually controlled the government. A regime-sponsored party was established, as well as a "tolerated" opposition party, which the military rulers carefully prevented from winning real power.

Election procedures were rigged to assure that the generals' presidential candidate would win easily. The presidents were all military officers and in practice had to accept the decisions of the corporate **"college of generals."** That group did not allow any president to be reelected, and only once did they favor the presidential candidate preferred by the outgoing president. In each case their collective judgment prevailed.

Congress had no effective power to check the president, and restrictions on parties and voting kept the official party in the majority. The president claimed sweeping powers against "subversive" individuals and groups and over the legislative process. Brutal methods—torture, long imprisonment without trial, "disappearances" arranged by security forces or officially tolerated vigilantes—were sometimes used to prevent political opposition. The rights of labor unions to organize, strike, and engage in political activities were severely restricted or eliminated.

However, the regime could not suppress all criticism and opposition, and, after enjoying considerable success in promoting economic growth, it ran into severe financial difficulties in the late 1970s. In that same period, the military rulers began to permit a greater degree of political freedom, including almost unlimited press criticism of the government. Several new political parties were allowed to form. In 1982, five parties participated in truly competitive elections for the federal Congress and for state and local offices. The government's party received only 40 percent of the total vote but apparently held onto control of a congressional majority and of the electoral college that would select the next president.

From the generals' standpoint, political developments had escaped their control by 1984. Public agitation for direct election of the president, involving hundreds of thousands of urban demonstrators, helped persuade some government party legislators to break with their leaders. The votes that these dissidents cast in the electoral college in 1985 helped elect a popular opposition candidate as the first civilian president in twenty-one years. The military establishment accepted the result, and constitutional democracy was restored in Brazil.

When they seized control of the government in 1964, Brazilian military leaders claimed to be saving democracy from populist chaos and the threat of communism. Mainly they established tightly organized corporate military-technocratic-bureaucratic control. After about a decade they gradually loosened political controls and ultimately permitted the reemergence of democratic politics. It seems likely that they did so, however, mainly because economic problems had become so serious as to threaten permanent damage to the reputation and prestige of the Brazilian military profession.

Under similar but more severe circumstances, military officers in Argentina, who had ruled since 1976, returned control of the government to a democratically elected president late in 1983. Not only did this corporate-military regime also face a foreign debt crisis, but in 1982 its leaders had tried to rally patriotic opinion to its support by occupying the British-controlled Falkland Islands. Argentina had long claimed sovereignty over what its government called the Malvinas Islands, but the few inhabitants were strongly pro-British. The Argentine move backfired when British Prime Minister Margaret Thatcher decided to defend British sovereignty by military means, and Argentine forces were defeated within a few days after fighting began. The demonstrated incompetence of the military weakened Argentines' fear of the regime, and massive demonstrations and protests helped persuade the generals to allow free elections and turn over the frustrations of governing to civilians.

■ Inherent Weakness

The recent political experience of the two largest South American countries suggests a fundamental problem of corporate-rule authoritarianism: the great difficulty it has in generating legitimacy or loyalty among the people whom it rules. That seems especially true when those regimes impose themselves upon previously democratic countries. Even many people who agree with the economic objectives of the military government are alienated by its coerciveness and its refusal to allow even non-"subversives" to speak and publish their political ideas in public. Franco's authoritarian regime in Spain (1939–1975) was in many ways a forerunner of Latin American corporate-military rule. Though it lasted a long time, its legitimacy was so feeble that it could not survive the death of the founder.

A good deal of experience suggests that corporate-rule authoritarianism can lead to the reemergence of democracy. That happens not necessarily because the government plans such a transition but in part because it never gains very effective control of potential bases of political opposition such as churches and universities. When military rulers become terribly frustrated that big problems can't be solved by giving orders, they may become willing to give up and let their critics and other civilian politicians try again. Only in rare circumstances has modernized authoritarianism become effectively institutionalized, highly durable, and relatively legitimate for the bulk of its population—by means of a well-organized ruling party.

Party-Rule Authoritarianism

The two most clear-cut and longest-lived examples of **party-rule authoritarianism** are Mexico and Taiwan (Nationalist China). Tanzania and Tunisia might qualify, but they have yet to show that they can long outlast their founders without fundamental changes. We will focus our attention on the Mexican system.

■ Development in Mexico

There has not been a successful military coup in Mexico since 1920. Starting in 1934, a new president has been elected every six years and peacefully served out the single term allowed him by the constitution. The Mexican regime is probably the most fully institutionalized modern authoritarian system. Its foundation is the Party of Revolutionary Institutions (PRI), established in 1929 and given its present name in 1946.

The PRI is best described as a **hegemonic party.** This label means that it "neither allows for a formal nor a de facto competition for power. Other parties are permitted to exist, but as second class licensed parties; for they are not permitted to compete with the hegemonic party in antagonistic terms and on an equal basis." The existence of multiple parties and regular elections seems to contradict the *authoritarian* label for the regime, but in Mexican politics, "where contradictions exist, democratic elements can safely be ascribed to façade and authoritarian ones to reality."[31]

The PRI always wins presidential elections with 80-plus percent of the vote, and it always maintains an overwhelming majority in Congress.

Even after changes in election law designed to help minor parties, the PRI still won three-fourths of seats in the chamber of deputies.[32] PRI support is probably broad and genuine, but it has been persuasively claimed that when its opponents do too well, ballot boxes are stuffed or replaced. In some cases elections won by opposition candidates have been nullified as "fraudulent."[33]

The PRI is broadly based and organized into three sectors: labor, agrarian, and popular. Officially approved trade unions and agricultural organizations make up most of the first two membership sectors, and the large corps of civilian civil servants dominates the third. The president of Mexico functions almost as a temporary dictator over both the government and the party, which is dominated also by a powerful executive committee. Nominations for governmental positions and official party policies are determined by the top leadership. Rank-and-file party organization functions to transmit complaints to the leadership and to mobilize mass opinion on behalf of the regime.[34]

Because of the presidency's broad powers, which are not limited by congress or the courts or by the threat of being voted out of office, that office dominates government at every level. A president is limited to a single six-year term, however, which prevents the development of personal tyranny. Political stability is also promoted by a procedure that guarantees peaceful succession to the top office: each outgoing president has an uncontested right to select the next PRI presidential candidate, usually a loyal cabinet minister. After the minister's inevitable election victory the new president has no obligations to the man who selected him. He brings his own close circle of political friends and clients into the top positions of government and often takes a somewhat different policy line from the last president's. This system encourages ambitious politicians to work hard and loyally at their political and government jobs. Such efforts may persuade their superiors to select them for the cabinet, perhaps eventually for the presidency. The system also decreases incentives to attempt a forceful takeover of the government.

The Mexican regime grew out of the "Revolution of 1910," which led to nearly two decades of intense conflict, fighting, assassinations, popular banditry, and social turmoil, although it started simply as a demand for regular free elections. Promises of land redistribution, trade union rights, and social services quickly became part of an explosive and confused political struggle that ultimately cost several million lives.[35]

After the postrevolutionary regime had begun to become institutionalized, President Cardenas (in office from 1934 to 1940) decreed the redistribution of much land to peasant communes, nationalized the railroads, and expelled foreign (mainly U.S.) oil companies. He also established a government-monopoly petroleum corporation. Over the years, the government has become more deeply involved in the economy, through complex regulations, tax policies, tariffs, subsidies, and control of credit and of some prices. Wholly or partially state-owned firms produce about ten percent of industrial output. Official control of the oil business increased governmental leverage over the economy with the discovery of huge new reserves and great increases in world oil prices in the 1970s. According to political scientist Martin Needler, "the general picture . . . is of a socialist-minded government trying to run a generally capitalist economy."[36]

■ Mexican Popular Support

From the mass of the population, inducements such as land reform, economic growth, and social services have helped sustain popular support for the PRI regime. More obvious inducements are available to talented and cooperative politicians, who can readily see that their ambitions are most likely to be fulfilled in the PRI, and to civil servants who staff the sizeable bureaucracy.

Coercion also plays a role in propping up support for the PRI regime. The government often uses or threatens negative sanctions such as selective law enforcement to bring business interests into line. It routinely treats peasant protests as insurrections and puts them down by military force. In 1968, an originally trivial dispute between government officials and students escalated into a deadly confrontation. Soldiers with tanks and automatic weapons attacked a massive demonstration by students and their sympathizers. Hundreds were killed, and the president in office at the time became immensely unpopular. This massacre clearly demonstrated, though, that leaders of the regime were inclined to use any level of violence they believed necessary to preserve their power.[37]

The "ruling class" PRI elite tries to mobilize persuasive power to sustain support for its regime. It dominates or manipulates the mass media in order to indoctrinate and propagandize the general population constantly with the official viewpoint. These efforts gain some persuasiveness from the party's claim to represent both the spirit and achievements of "the Revolution" and to embody the true expression of Mexican nationalism—especially against the Yankee colossus to the north. The official colors of the PRI are even identical with the red, white, and green of the national flag.[38] Both the stabilized ruling party organization and the claim to be *the* legitimate expression of revolutionary nationalism give the Mexican regime enormous advantages in the struggle for political survival.

Problems of Legitimacy

Certain kinds of governmental institutions tend to predominate in all types of authoritarian regimes—strong and domineering executive leadership, a sizeable bureaucracy staffed by patronage from the top, a more or less active and violent security police, and pseudodemocratic political trimmings. These are not sufficient, however, to guarantee a stable and orderly system. Even if the rulers are relatively moderate and can take credit for a degree of economic progress, they will have great difficulty in building up legitimacy for their regimes. This is especially the case among the more modernized sectors of the population, in the absence of a persuasive ideology.

In recent years, for example, South Korea experienced phenomenal economic growth and a rising standard of living. Yet the corporate-military regime was often challenged by student-led crowds protesting its authoritarian rule and demanding democratic government. Widespread economic satisfaction no doubt helped to contain the spread of political discontent but couldn't prevent it. Massive student demonstrations in 1987 finally led the authoritarian president to move toward restoring democratic rights, institutions and processes. Mexico is a rare exception to the general principle that modern authoritarian regimes are not very good at generating ideological rationalizations for their type of rule.[39]

Political sociologist Juan Linz suggests why: "In the modern world, all **legitimacy formulas** refer in some way to the authority coming from . . . the people. Who 'the people' should be and how they should transfer their authority to the rulers are the great questions of politics."[40] Authoritarian rulers cannot establish their legitimacy with people who believe that only competitive democratic elections can express the will of "the people." Nor can they appeal to the kinds of political intellectuals who seek supreme power as self-appointed representatives of the "true" will and interests of the people in order to produce the revolutionary transformation of society. As a result, Linz observes, all authoritarian regimes ultimately face a **legitimacy pull** toward the democratic or the revolutionary totalitarian model.[41]

We suspect that there is much wisdom in this analysis, and the revival of democratic government in most of Latin America in the 1980s bears out its shrewdness. Of course, "ultimately" can be a long time coming when a politically skillful authoritarian ruler lives on and retains control for decades.

Both problems of legitimacy of some authoritarian regimes and their relatively limited scope of control over society can result, whatever their rulers' intentions, in their actually setting the stage for the emergence or reemergence of political democracy. That outcome seems especially likely when a long-time leader dies or military leaders become discredited and frustrated by the messiness of politics. In some circumstances, however, politically inept, increasingly violent, and narrowly based authoritarian regimes can unintentionally promote the emergence of a more highly organized and thoroughgoing type of autocracy—totalitarianism.

Summary

Authoritarianism is the more common type of autocracy—a government in which the ruler isn't limited by law or held accountable to the people. Authoritarian regimes try to organize and control fewer areas of life than do totalitarian systems, but they don't permit effective political opposition. All noncommunist authoritarian governments are currently found in Third World countries, although not all Third World countries have authoritarian regimes.

There are several plausible reasons for the prevalence of authoritarianism in the Third World. Many of these countries are relatively new, and new governments cannot depend on tradition and habit for legitimacy and popular support. The weakness of postcolonial regimes opened the door to ambitious competitors for power, with the advantage often going to military leaders. In most developing countries the building of stable and effective political institutions lags behind social and economic change. Shaky and inexperienced governments can be overburdened with demands; their failure or inability to respond to them can lead to more frustration, conflict, and violence. In turn, such developments may encourage military takeovers.

Authoritarian regimes can be grouped into four loosely defined categories: traditional, personal-rule, corporate-rule, and party-rule. Of the traditional form, hereditary monarchy, few examples remain in which the monarch has real executive power. Modern secular education and demands for broader participation in government undermine belief in divine and hereditary right and contradict ruling systems based on traditional social pillars such as an established church and landed estates.

Personal-rule authoritarianism is similar to monarchy in the critical role played by the individual ruler. It differs, though, in the absence of traditional rules and institutions of government, including the inheritance of authority. Forceful and ambitious leaders often present themselves as the stern but wise fathers of all the people in an effort to bridge deep divisions. They tend to place themselves above the law but usually do not interfere persistently with nonpolitical rights and activities. In addition to relying on military backing, personal rulers depend on clientelistic systems in which they trade patronage for political support. Taken to extremes, these practices produce kleptocratic corruption that drains off an enormous proportion of national wealth to a tiny political elite. Some African personal-rule systems have not been especially repressive or corrupt, and some authoritarian leaders have moved governments in the direction of constitutional democracy.

Corporate-rule authoritarianism refers to oligarchic rule dominated by military elites who bring in technocrats and top bureaucrats as their coalition partners. Top military leaders' power greatly outweighs the influence of official party organizations. Clientelism is as prominent as in personal-rule systems, and the interests of the corporate military take first priority in official decision making. In Latin America, recent military rule has usually been much more corporate than personal. High-ranking military officers, impatient with the messiness of democratic politics, overthrew elected governments and created corporate-rule oligarchies. Economic reverses and, in Argentina, military humiliation led military rulers to return power to elected civilian politicians by the mid-1980s (except in Chile).

It is rare that authoritarian systems become fully and durably institutionalized, but there are at least two such "party-rule" systems—in Taiwan and Mexico. The Mexican government features apparently democratic institutions: multiparty elections, a limited presidential term, an elected congress. However, the hegemonic Party of Revolutionary Institutions controls and operates the system in authoritarian fashion. The PRI-controlled government has created a sizeable public sector and uses economic influence and pressures to sustain its dominant position. The government does not hesitate to use deadly force to put down threats to its legitimacy or control. The ruling party prevents the rise of personal dictatorship by limiting every president to a single six-year term. It has developed a stable system of succession by permitting each outgoing president to select his successor.

Sooner or later, most authoritarian governments confront serious problems of legitimacy. People affected by modern political ideas and propaganda are strongly inclined to believe that authority should come from "the people." That belief leads them to favor either constitutional democracy or revolutionary movements whose leaders claim to seek sweeping changes in the interests of "the people." Stable and long-lived authoritarian systems are rare, but unstable and short-lived ones are likely to keep on appearing and disappearing for a long time to come.

Review List of Key Terms

Third World
"state of nature"
political lag
modernization
defensive modernization
political modernization
leadership transitions
traditional authoritarianism
personal-rule authoritarianism
nonpolitical tolerance
clientelism
patronage
kleptocracy
corporate-rule authoritarianism
oligarchy
Arab socialism
Revolutionary Command Council
caudillismo
bureaucratic authoritarian regimes
"college of generals"
party-rule authoritarianism
hegemonic party
legitimacy formulas
legitimacy pull

Notes

1. Thomas Hobbes, *Leviathan*, ed. Michael Oakeshott (Oxford: Basil Blackwell, 1960), p. 82.
2. Samuel P. Huntington, *Political Order in Changing Societies* (New Haven: Yale University Press, 1968), p. 5.
3. Anthony James Joes, *Fascism in the Contemporary World: Ideology, Evolution, Resurgence* (Boulder, Colo.: Westview Press, 1978), p. 102.
4. Crawford Young, *Ideology and Development in Africa* (New Haven: Yale University Press, 1982), pp. 69–72.
5. Robert H. Jackson and Carl G. Rosberg, *Personal Rule in Black Africa* (Berkeley: University of California Press, 1982), pp. 122–123.
6. Ibid., p. 125.
7. Young, *Ideology*, pp. 74–83.
8. Juan J. Linz, "Totalitarian and Authoritarian Regimes," in *Handbook of Political Science*, vol. 3, *Macropolitical Theory*, ed. Fred I. Greenstein and Nelson W. Polsby (Reading, Mass.: Addison-Wesley, 1975), p. 275.
9. Amos Perlmutter, *The Military and Politics in Modern Times* (New Haven: Yale University Press, 1977), pp. 113–114; see also Brian Loveman and Thomas M. Davies, Jr. (eds.), *The Politics of Antipolitics: The Military in Latin America* (Lincoln: University of Nebraska Press, 1978), pp. 3–13.
10. This analogy is suggested in Jackson and Rosberg, *Personal Rule*, pp. 14–15. Their excellent study alerted us to the importance of "personal rule" as a basic type of authoritarianism.
11. Giovanni Sartori, *Parties and Party Systems: A Framework for Analysis*, vol. 1 (Cambridge: Cambridge University Press, 1976), p. 247.
12. Jackson and Rosberg, *Personal Rule*, pp. 99, 152–156.
13. Ibid., p. 25.
14. Ibid., p. 24.
15. Our discussion of African clientelism is based primarily on Jackson and Rosberg, *Personal Rule*, pp. 38–47.
16. Amos Perlmutter, *Modern Authoritarianism: A Comparative Institutional Analysis* (New Haven: Yale University Press, 1981), p. 41.
17. Young, *Ideology*, pp. 5–6.
18. See Jackson and Rosberg, *Personal Rule*, pp. 167–181.
19. Ibid., p. 41.
20. Ibid., pp. 89–97.
21. Ibid., pp. 108–111.
22. Joes, *Fascism*, p. 182.
23. Perlmutter, *Modern Authoritarianism*, pp. 148–151; Alasdair Drysdale, "The Syrian Armed Forces in National Politics: The Role of the Geographic and Ethnic Periphery," in *Soldiers, Peasants, and Bureaucrats: Civil–Military Relations in Communist and Modernizing Societies*, ed. Roman Kolkowicz and Andrezej Korbonski (London: George Allen and Unwin, 1982), pp. 69–70.
24. Fuad I. Khuri, "The Study of Civil-Military Relations in Modernizing Societies in the Middle East: A Critical Assessment," in *Soldiers, Peasants, and Bureaucrats: Civil–Military Relations in Communist and Modernizing Societies*, ed. Roman Kolkowicz and Andrezej Korbonski (London: George Allen and Unwin, 1982), pp. 18–21.
25. Ibid., pp. 21–24.
26. Perlmutter, *Modern Authoritarianism*, p. 150.
27. *Newsweek*, November 21, 1983, p. 52.
28. Loveman and Davies, *Politics of Antipolitics*, pp. 4–5.
29. Quoted in Loveman and Davies: *Politics of Antipolitics*, p. 8.
30. For a variety of interpretations of "bureaucratic authoritarianism," see David Collier (ed.), *The New Authoritarianism in Latin America* (Princeton: Princeton University Press, 1979).
31. Sartori, *Parties and Party Systems*, p. 230; Martin C. Needler, *Mexican Politics: The Containment of Conflict* (New York: Praeger, 1982), p. 6.
32. Needler, *Mexican Politics*, pp. 86–87.
33. Sartori, *Parties and Party Systems*, p. 234.

34. Needler, *Mexican Politics*, pp. 67–69.
35. For a summary account, see Needler, *Mexican Politics*, pp. 17–25.
36. Ibid., pp. 25–27, 98.
37. Ibid., pp. 74–76, 32–33.
38. Ibid., pp. 73–74.
39. See Sartori, *Parties and Party Systems*, pp. 222–225.
40. Juan L. Linz, "The Future of an Authoritarian Situation or the Institutionalization of an Authoritarian Regime: The Case of Brazil," in *The Political Influence of the Military: A Comparative Reader*, ed. Amos Perlmutter and Valerie Plave Bennett (New Haven: Yale University Press, 1980), pp. 290–291.
41. Ibid., p. 296.

Totalitarianism: Ideological Domination

"Fear prophets, Adso, and those prepared to die for the truth, for as a rule they make many others die with them, often before them, at times instead of them."
Umberto Eco, The Name of the Rose

He who has power has it by historical logic.
Respectfully bow to that logic.
Let your lips, proposing a hypothesis,
Not know about the hand faking the experiment.
Let your hand, faking the experiment,
Not know the lips proposing a hypothesis.
Czeslaw Milosz, "Child of Europe"

Totalitarianism is a twentieth-century form of autocracy. It uses techniques, ideas, and institutions from earlier times, but it combines them with modern technology to produce a new kind of regime. In it, "all aspects of political, social, economic, and cultural life are subject to control, no limits to governmental interference are admitted, no political opposition or independent organization is permissible, and all citizens are expected to accept official, infallible doctrine."[1] A similar definition emphasizes the techniques of rule: "A totalitarian society is one where a small ruling elite controls the means of coercion and persuasion and in the name of some ideal uses police and propaganda to stamp out dissent and reduce social and cultural space to a minimum."[2]

Totalitarian regimes are created by ideological movements whose leaders seek supreme and unlimited governmental power. They scornfully reject traditional authority based on divine right and inherited status but are equally contemptuous of constitutional democracy. Instead, they promise a revolutionary transformation of society so that it will reflect the purified will and true historic interests of the people. Individuals gain value only by committing themselves to the great collective movement for total change; personal sacrifice is justified by the ultimate triumph of the cause, whether rule by a master race or by the working class. From the ideologically correct perspective on history, there can be no conflict of interests between rulers and ruled. Guided mass participation is essential, so that totalitarianism "signifies the specific form of mass dictatorship in a democratic age."[3]

As we pointed out in chapter 4, Italian dictator Benito Mussolini first brought to prominence the term *totalitarianism* in reference to his regime in the 1920s and 1930s. He proclaimed, for example, that "for the Fascist, everything is in the State, and nothing human or spiritual exists, much less has value, outside the State. In this sense Fascism is totalitarian. . . ."[4] A few political analysts, noting basic similarities among the Italian fascist, German national socialist, and Soviet communist regimes in the 1930s, began to classify all three as totalitarian. As a category of scholarly political analysis, totalitarianism became prominent only in the 1950s, initially as "a summary of the judgments contained in the bulk of the literature devoted to fascism, national socialism, and bolshevism."[5]

The most influential scholarly concept of **totalitarian autocracy** was first proposed by political scientists Carl Friedrich and Zbigniew Brzezinski in their 1956 book *Totalitarian Dictatorship and Autocracy*. As summarized by Friedrich:

> The features which distinguish these regimes from other and older autocracies . . . are six in number . . . (1) a totalist ideology; (2) a single party committed to this ideology and usually led by one man, the dictator; (3) a fully developed secret police; and three kinds of . . . **monopolistic control:** namely, that of (a) mass communications; (b) operational weapons; (c) all organization, including economic ones, thus involving a centrally-planned economy.[6]

It is the combination of all these features that makes a regime totalitarian. The secret police is an ancient institution, and even most democratic governments today control all weapons that might be used to overthrow the regime. But totalitarian rulers develop the secret, or political, police to previously unknown levels of size, complexity of organization, and penetration of society. Their weapons monopoly is enforced in an equally thoroughgoing way.

The "Totalitarianism" Controversy

In the 1960s a scholarly and political debate erupted on the concept of totalitarianism. Critics charged that the term had been defined in so many ways and applied to such different regimes that it could not be scientifically useful. It had become mainly a term of abuse and an ideological weapon in the Cold War because its main purpose was to assert an essential identity between the horrific Nazi regime and the Soviet and other communist systems. Yet since Stalin's death in 1953, the all-pervasive state-sponsored terror had declined in the Soviet Union; ideological controls on culture had been relaxed somewhat; Stalin had been criticized; and more liberalization seemed entirely probable. It was most reasonable, then, for political scientists to give up a concept with such "ideological and emotional overtones."[7]

Yet defenders of the descriptive usefulness of *totalitarianism* pointed out that the term originated long before the onset of the Cold War soon after the Second World War. They also argued that discussing politics intelligibly requires that we use a number of terms—such as *democracy, peace, dictatorship*—having emotional and ideological overtones.

By the 1970s it became clear that autocracy was not withering away in the Soviet Union, as ideological, police, and party controls remained comprehensive and tight. Differences of interests and views were not permitted to break out into public debate, much less evolve into political pluralism, but remained restricted to secret deliberations within circles of the ruling elite. Public criticism or attempts to open up the Soviet or Eastern European communist states to a diversity of views or to establish nonofficial organizations were met with persistent and generally successful repression.[8]

As they do in most scholarly debates about politics, ideological beliefs played a large role on both sides, and few minds seemed to be changed by logic or evidence. The titles of this chapter and the next show that we accept the usefulness of the "totalitarian regime" category. We believe that there is massive evidence of fundamental distinctions between such systems and all other autocracies, which we classify as authoritarian.

We think that improved empirical understanding of politics requires the use of more than one category for contemporary autocratic systems. Some commentators do refer to the Soviet and similar regimes as "authoritarian," but to do so obscures important distinctions.

If we were to classify the Soviet regime as "party-rule authoritarian," it would be lumped with the governments of Mexico and Taiwan. In those countries, though, the dominant party does not utterly monopolize politics: opposition parties exist and function, though they are not allowed to win power at the national level. Unofficial and critical ideas can be published, within fairly broad limits, without leading to punishment for their authors. Government officials don't try to coordinate, control, and direct most of cultural and social life according to an official ideology for which they claim infallibility and a monopoly. There are large and important private sectors in the economies. These strike us as important differences. In fact, the Soviet-type system functions in ways that are quite distinct from those in Mexico or Taiwan or from any other regime that we have classified as authoritarian in chapter 7.

We agree with two political scientists who conclude their carefully balanced and unpolemical introduction to Soviet politics by declaring that "the totalitarian concept seems to us still to offer the best framework for the beginning student to understand the Soviet system."[9]

This chapter will deal mainly with the longest-lived and most common type of totalitarianism: communist regimes, especially in the Soviet Union. The other systems most frequently labeled *totalitarian* are Mussolini's **Ital-**

ian fascism, and, in Germany, Hitler's national socialism. We focus on contemporary politics, and those two regimes were destroyed by the Second World War. In addition, nearly all students of Italian fascism agree that Mussolini's control over Italy was far from total, despite his boastful claims. He was significantly limited by the prestige of the monarch, the state bureaucracy, the Catholic Church, and the business community, as well as by his laziness, impulsiveness, and impatience with planning and detail.[10]

As we pointed out in chapter 3, the Ayatollah Khomeini's revolutionary regime in Iran claims guidance by a totalist ideology based on fervent religious convictions. There can be no doubt that this government allows people a great deal less personal and group autonomy than did the shah's authoritarian rule; it is actively intolerant of any ideas or behavior that its leaders consider incompatible with their interpretation of Islam. It is also a militant religious-political faith, inspiring organized efforts to spread it to other Islamic countries. This movement and regime are discussed as revolutionary in chapters 12 and 13, but it is not yet clear whether they should be classified as a new and distinctive type of totalitarianism.

Totalitarian is probably best understood as a relative or comparative term; a slackening of ruling-party cultural and social control can mean that a regime becomes in practice merely authoritarian (look back at figure 4-3). On the other end of the spectrum, something close to the inescapable controls on individuals depicted in George Orwell's *1984* existed for many years under Stalin, in Hitler's wartime empire, and in Pol Pot's Cambodia.

By no means are all contemporary communist regimes equally "total" in their degree of control over society. As we indicated in chapter 4, the governments of Hungary and Yugoslavia allow some degree of economic and cultural freedom, as well as freedom to travel abroad and emigrate. Chapter 13 will briefly consider how the Chinese regime has moved far from Mao Zedong's totalitarian ideal since his death in 1976, especially in allowing an increasing amount of private economic activity.

On the dimension of centralized control these regimes may differ enough from Soviet, Rumanian, Czech, and Cuban practices to justify including Hungary and Yugoslavia and possibly China within the "party-rule authoritarian" category. Yet the basic institutions and ideology of the "totalitarian syndrome" remain nearly intact. The ruling elites are limited mainly by their own judgment about the most effective ways to retain power.

For several reasons our discussion will focus mainly on the Soviet Union. It was the first totalitarian state and has continued to claim legitimacy and guidance from the longest-lived, most influential, and most ambitious of totalist ideologies. It rules the most extensive land mass and one of the largest populations among the states of the world, as well as a substantial European empire, and its political-military aid and influence penetrate nearly every region on earth. It is also one of the two most powerful states and has had and continues to have an enormous influence on shaping the contemporary scene. We will point to some parallels with other communist systems, as well as to the Hitler regime in Germany.

Two Phases of Totalitarian Development

The Soviet and other European communist systems have existed long enough that it is useful to differentiate between two stages in their development, which we will call the *revolutionizing* and the *institutionalized* phases of totalitarianism. Hitler's Third Reich did not last long enough to move beyond the initial stage; it was destroyed in the course of his attempt to bring the Nazi revolution to the entirety of Europe through military conquest.

Revolutionizing Totalitarianism

The **revolutionizing phase** begins with the seizure of autocratic power by leaders of a totalitarian movement, which is normally organized on the model of a disciplined military hierarchy. The new rulers are determined to implement their comprehensive ideology, which includes total rejection of the existing sociopolitical order. They attempt to crush every actual or potential opponent and either destroy or purge and bring under secure control all existing institutions of government.

After their successful armed takeover in November, 1917, for example, the Russian **Bolsheviks** virtually outlawed private property, although economic disasters forced some moderation in that policy after they had won the Civil War in 1921. In Germany, Hitler moved in stages after 1933 to destroy the citizenship status and economic position of German Jews, as a prelude to their eventual extermination. Totalitarian movements promise a wholly new order of things, and they prove to be deadly serious about destroying the old (although they never succeed completely).

Of enormous importance for revolutionizing totalitarianism, as a rule, is **the leader** of the movement that becomes the sole legal party. Lenin, Stalin, Hitler, Mao, and Castro played absolutely critical roles in shaping the revolutionary regimes that they headed. They became strongly dominant over the party apparatus and largely succeeded in making its other leading figures dependent on their favor. Hitler and Stalin, for example, carried out bloody purges of their parties. Mao stirred up the turbulent, chaotic, and destructive **Great Proletarian Cultural Revolution** in the late 1960s, inspiring youthful Red Guards to attack party officials who had attempted to decrease Mao's control over official policy.

In each case the leader came to be portrayed as the all-wise and all-knowing fount of ideological truth and virtue and as the essential protector of the revolution against all enemies, foreign and domestic. Some of the official rhetoric about Stalin and Mao, for example, suggested virtual deification, and the mummified remains of Lenin have been preserved in the holiest shrine of the Soviet revolution since his death in 1924.[11]

Even at the pinnacle of the leader's power, however, the totalitarian regime is creating new institutions of governance and control. Hitler and Stalin needed loyal officials and organizations such as the secret police and propaganda agencies to implement their policies. Stalin especially required a vastly enlarged and elaborately organized Communist Party to supervise governmental control and direction of the entire economy. If the regime outlives the leader, as was the case with Stalin but not Hitler, this kind of organization can become the nucleus of an institutionalized totalitarian system.

Institutionalized Totalitarianism

The second phase of development is **institutionalized totalitarianism.** The power of the party leader is greatly reduced, with personal dictatorship essentially giving way to rule by a party-elite oligarchy. Leaders in such key institutions as the military, foreign and economic ministries, and the party bureaucracy have a common interest in preventing the rise of another supreme leader who can discharge, imprison, or execute them at will. They collaborate to make all important decisions of government, keep the security forces under their firm control, and bring more stability and predictability to the elaborate network of interlocking bureaucracies that aim at continued thorough control of society.

Under this coalitional leadership the interests and routines of institutions become increasingly important in determining how the system functions, and the desires and ideological aspirations of individual leaders much less so. In China, Mao's "cultural revolution" interrupted this process, which he fiercely opposed, but it resumed even before his death. The individual and collective interests of party and bureaucratic elites in preserving their own institutionally based power become an irresistible force once the revolutionizing supreme leader is gone.

It even seems possible that in the Soviet Union unwritten rules for **regularized succession** to the top leadership position—general secretary of the Communist Party—have become institutionalized in the 1980s. After 1953, succession to Stalin was decided by intraelite intrigue and struggle, with Khrushchev quickly pushing aside Malenkov, facing down a serious challenge in 1957, but finally falling victim to a successful plot by Politburo colleagues in 1964. Under the general secretaryship of Leonid Brezhnev, the leader of that political coup, institutionalization of the regime proceeded rapidly.

When Brezhnev died in 1982, his successor, Yuri Andropov, was quickly agreed to by the Politburo, and Andropov's death in 1984 produced an equally rapid decision on Konstantin Chernenko as party leader. Soon after the 73-year-old Chernenko took over, his health declined rapidly. A man twenty years his junior, Mikhail Gorbachev (b. 1931), apparently began to supervise Politburo business and was formally named general secretary a few hours after Chernenko died in 1985. Intraelite bargaining now seems to deal smoothly with the question of succession. Institutions originally created to revolutionize society have become bulwarks of the political status quo.

Why Totalitarianism?

Our discussion of the causes of totalitarianism is necessarily brief. The subject is enormous, highly controversial, and extremely complex, and there is no generally persuasive theoretical explanation for this critically important political development. The following remarks will focus on circumstances that significantly influenced the capacity of totalitarian movements to attain, use, and retain supreme power.

One important factor was the persuasive power of revolutionary worldview ideologies. Political doctrines totally hostile to the existing order and promoting the development of rationally organized societies of equality, harmony, peace, and universal happiness began to appear in eighteenth-century Europe. They received considerable publicity—pro and con—during the era of the French Revolution in the 1790s. The main ideological legacy of that great political upheaval, however, was the belief in some minds that deeply rooted social institutions must be uprooted by armed violence and that centralized political power can remake not only government but economic and cultural institutions as well.[12]

Ideologies of total transformation became more clearly articulated in the nineteenth century with the emergence of a variety of socialist theories. Over the long run, the most influential of these was Marxism, which emphasized the significance of the great changes brought by industrialism and was adopted as official doctrine by German trade unions and Social Democrats in the late nineteenth century. Marx emphasized the critical importance of the revolutionary movement's gaining supreme political power, which appealed greatly to revolutionary activists.

A second contributing factor was nationalism, discussed in chapter 3. Nationalism helped undercut the legitimacy of traditional regimes in Central and Eastern Europe in the nineteenth century, intensified rivalry among the great powers early in the twentieth century, and set the stage for the First World War. In the aftermath of that conflict, nationalism served as the most appealing component of Mussolini's fascism and Hitler's national socialism.

Third, and possibly most critical, were the unexpected consequences of twentieth-century wars. The First World War had a disastrous impact upon the tsarist government in Russia, yet the provisional government that replaced it in early 1917 insisted on honoring Russian commitments to continue in the war. These unusual circumstances made it possible for a small revolutionary group, the Bolsheviks, to seize power and defend it successfully. Fear of bolshevism then contributed enormously to support for fascism and national socialism, as did Hitler's appeals to nationalist anger at losing the war. The Second World War brought Soviet troops into Eastern and Central Europe and northern Korea, where they simply remained and made it possible for Stalin to impose new communist regimes on the local populations.

In China, nearly four decades of internal war and disorder followed the collapse of the traditional empire in 1911. Lack of a strong central government and exploitation of nationalist and social discontents by the communist party and Red Army in wars with Japan and with the Nationalists made possible the communist takeover of the entire mainland in 1949.

Finally, weak, relatively incompetent, and fatally indecisive regimes often contributed unintentionally to seizure of power by totalitarian movements. This was certainly true of the inexperienced Russian provisional government in 1917, the Italian constitutional monarchy in 1922, and the harassed and unpopular Weimar Republic in 1933. In Cuba in 1958, the inept and embarrassingly corrupt Batista dictatorship rapidly lost middle-class support, making it possible for Fidel Castro's guerrilla movement to gain control of the government. Before coming to power, though, Castro had portrayed himself as a democratic revolutionary; otherwise it seems unlikely that Batista's support would have collapsed so suddenly and completely.[13]

In view of the sweeping and traumatic changes that totalitarian revolutionaries bring to their societies, at great human cost, a more fundamental question than how they gain power is how they manage to keep and increase it. Discussing that question requires that we examine the power strategies and tactics of totalitarian regimes.

We will focus mainly on how their rulers employ various forms and combinations of coercion, persuasion, and inducements and attempt to generate and appeal to authority in order to perpetuate their regimes and implement policies. Our discussion will be organized around the four strategies of power competition described and analyzed in chapter 2. The remainder of this chapter will consider structures and techniques of domination, and chapter 9 will analyze the power strategies of cooperation, toleration, and elimination in their totalitarian versions.

Domination

Totalitarian regimes present the most extreme historical instances of societies dominated by centralized and concentrated political power. Leaders of revolutionary totalitarian movements have possessed an overwhelming determination to gain supreme power in order to destroy opposition and reconstruct society according to their ideological designs. They conceive of power mainly as the ability to dominate; in practice, gaining and holding onto absolute power become the most basic and durable political goals of these movements and their regimes. We will consider how totalitarians achieve dominant power, the coercive methods they use to consolidate and keep it, and the role of ideology in reinforcing their ruling monopoly.

Winning Supreme Power

Of Lenin's and Hitler's seizures of power in Russia and Germany, respectively, historian Paul Johnson has aptly remarked: "Both show how irresistible is clarity of aim combined with a huge, ruthless will to power."[14] Of course, both also confronted weak governments that could not cope with overwhelming problems—war and shortages of food in Russia, mass unemployment and street violence in Germany. By no means, though, do all such crises give rise to totalitarian regimes; Lenin and Hitler were power seekers of genius.

Both leaders were determined not to share power with any group or party but their own. In their quest for monopolistic control of government they entered into coalitions with other parties, only to desert and destroy them once the coalition's enemies had been overcome. This tactic has been a standard feature of the rise to power of virtually every successful totalitarian movement.

Hitler used **coalitional tactics** to gain high office in the first place. Several conservative and nationalist politicians, as well as key military leaders, decided to enter into alliance with the leader of the largest party (about one-third of the seats) in the German parliament in early 1933—the Nazis. These politicians believed that they could easily control the Austrian demagogue, whose tactical skills they grossly misjudged. Although there were only three Nazis in the twelve-man cabinet that took office on January 30, Hitler was chancellor, with authority to issue sweeping emergency decrees, and his two party colleagues controlled most of the police organizations in the country.

Within five months Hitler had destroyed constitutional democracy in Germany through a combination of official decrees, intimidation and expulsion of numerous members of parliament, and an **Enabling Act,** which passed 441 to 94 with the support of Right and Center parties. This act suspended the constitution and gave Hitler supreme power to legislate and conduct foreign policy. The governing coalition was destroyed by Hitler's outlawing all non-Nazi parties in June and declaring the National Socialists the sole legal party in July. Hitler's suppression of the Communists, his decisive dismissal of the widely hated politicians of the Weimar parties on behalf of "national unity," and his rapid takeover and expansion of police agencies made his movement the undisputed master of Germany.

Sixteen years earlier, a much smaller movement had attained supreme power in Russia with no pretense of legality. Lenin's Bolsheviks did, however, make limited use of the device of temporary coalition in order to consolidate their hold on power. In February 1917 the tsarist regime had collapsed as a result of massive protests and street demonstrations against lack of food in the cities. A provisional government drawn from the previously powerless parliament took over. Lenin was not able to reach Russia from his exile in Switzerland until April, and most of his party's leaders on the spot were inclined to support the provisional government. Upon his arrival he vehemently rejected that policy and insisted that the Bolsheviks exploit the virtual anarchy in Russia by organizing an armed seizure of power.

In the *soviets*—workers' and citizens' councils that had sprung up in urban areas since the "February Revolution"—the Bolsheviks collaborated with other radical parties to attack and undercut the indecisive and ineffective government. It was easily overthrown by a Bolshevik armed force that seized key points in the capital city of Petrograd (now Leningrad) in late October of 1917 (November 7 in the current calendar).

The new Bolshevik regime allowed one competitive national election that had previously been scheduled to select an assembly to draw up a new Russian constitution. In this November voting, the Bolsheviks obtained only 175 seats out of 707; the peasant-based Social Revolutionary Party had a majority of 410. The **Constituent Assembly** met for one day in January 1918; on one vote the Bolsheviks lost, 237 to 138, and Lenin dissolved the Assembly by force.

For some months after they seized power, the Bolsheviks tried to broaden their support by including several left-wing Social Revolutionaries in the government. Although it was a coalition government in form, the Bolshevik leaders were in complete control. The democratic socialist **Menshevik** party was tolerated until the Bolsheviks had won the Civil War. Early in 1921, two thousand Mensheviks, including all party leaders, were arrested, and the Bolsheviks definitively established their one-party monopoly.

A more recent use of coalitional takeover tactics succeeded in South Vietnam. In 1960, a politically diverse **National Liberation Front** (NLF) was established, with the aim of overthrowing the authoritarian U.S.-supported regime. Although Communists participated in the NLF and communist-ruled North Vietnam supported it, most of its leaders were democrats and nationalists. North Vietnamese officials repeatedly assured them that once the Americans were driven out, South Vietnam would be independent and free to practice internal democracy. In 1969 the NLF set up a secret provisional revolutionary government in the jungle, only a few of whose cabinet members were Communists.

After U.S. forces withdrew from Vietnam in 1973, the North Vietnamese army assumed more and more of the military role against the South Vietnamese government. Most provisional government leaders were hoping to create a genuine coalition government in South Vietnam. However, when military resistance to the North Vietnamese suddenly collapsed in the spring of 1975, leaders of the victorious communist forces quickly took over complete control and began at once to dissolve the NLF. Disillusionment came rapidly to its noncommunist former officials when a united Vietnam under one-party communist rule soon emerged. As in other totalitarian takeovers, manipulative persuasion had worked to gain coalition partners and broaden popular support until circumstances allowed the best-organized and most determinedly power-oriented movement to gain total control.[15]

Coercion

As minority movements determined to gain complete control of their societies and remold them according to an ideological design, totalitarian movements inevitably meet with opposition and resistance to their rule and policies. They have proved able and willing to organize and apply effective violence in order to get their way. Upon becoming German chancellor, Hitler quickly expanded the state security policy (**Gestapo**) and removed all legal barriers to its operations. He built up a special Nazi party military organization, the SS, as both a security force and a band of elite troops who undertook to "pacify" defeated populations by mass shooting, torture, and deportations. They were also charged with executing the genocidal "**Final Solution**" of the "Jewish problem." Political opposition or dissent within Germany was almost nonexistent, and the Nazis had no trouble in procuring enough loyal, obedient officers and troops to carry out Hitler's pathological schemes.

Among the first institutions created by the new Bolshevik regime in 1917 was the All-Russian Extraordinary Commission for Combating Counter-Revolution and Sabotage, known, after its Russian initials, as the *Cheka.* This was the first form of the massive security police organization that has continually served as a pillar of the Soviet regime: its present incarnation is the **KGB** (Committee for State Security). Growing rapidly in the midst of civil war and assassinations, the *Cheka* exercised sweeping powers bestowed upon it by Bolshevik leaders. They shot thousands of prisoners without trial and punished groups of people categorized as bourgeois and therefore hostile, rather than worrying about individual guilt.

With 15,000 employees, the tsar's secret police had been the largest in the world, but in 1920 the *Cheka* had grown to about 250,000. By 1922 it had set up 132 forced labor camps, with 60,000 inmates, mainly workers or peasants. It is estimated that in four years the *Cheka* executed 140,000 people, compared with 14,000 during the last half-century of tsarist rule.[16]

Stalin's use of security forces to unleash incredible violence against elements of the population in the Soviet Union was mentioned in chapter 2 and will be explored further. In the present context, we would suggest that the memory of Stalin's mass killings has long served to intimidate many would-be critics of the regime—especially since Khrushchev's brief de-Stalinization campaign was halted by the men who ousted him from office in 1964.

Today the KGB employs tens of thousands of agents (estimates range from 50,000 to 150,000), plus a very large corps of border guards.[17] In practice, it is commanded solely by the ruling Politburo of the Communist Party. The job of the KGB is to deal with "'state crimes,' such as espionage, anti-Soviet agitation and propaganda, violation of law governing separation of church and state, formation of 'anti-state' organizations."[18] All these offenses are interpreted very broadly to include any criticism of the regime or its policies. The KGB also acts as the main Soviet foreign intelligence and espionage agency.

Critics and dissenters can expect in almost every case to be arrested by the KGB, tried and convicted on some such charge as "slandering" the state, and sent to very grim prisons or labor camps. By a U.S. Central Intelligence Agency (**CIA**) estimate, there are at least 10,000 political prisoners in the USSR.[19] We believe that this summary observation from the early 1970s continues to apply to the Soviet Union: "There is no reason to underestimate the power of the KGB and the relationship between its existence and the modesty of political expectations of the Soviet masses. . . . The odds are overwhelming that a person will not escape retribution for any sustained political dissent."[20]

An especially dramatic example of the effectiveness of well-organized security forces in protecting a threatened communist regime was the imposition of martial law in Poland late in 1981. Since the summer of 1980 the unofficial Solidarity trade union had grown to massive proportions and clearly reflected general rejection of the regime. Most analysts believed that only a huge Soviet invasion could suppress Solidarity, but the Polish security police, modeled on and trained by the KGB, proved totally loyal to the ruling party and broke up the Solidarity organization. The security forces so obviously monopolized effective armed force that they were able to subdue opposition almost entirely by intimidation rather than bloodshed.

We are not contending that more or less institutionalized totalitarian systems rest *only* upon the coercive institution of the security police. We simply point out that the security police—and its associated network of informers—is always one of the first institutional creations of newly established communist regimes (the KGB model is most popular). No such regime has ever disbanded or even failed to make persistent use of this kind of organization.

Economic coercion is a mechanism of control available to communist regimes because of their ideologically motivated efforts to own, control, and direct almost the entire economy. Practically speaking, there is only one employer in most communist-ruled countries—the party-state. This is as true for lawyers, doctors, sculptors, poets, and composers as for auto mechanics, retail sales clerks, factory workers, and truck drivers. To be critical or nonconformist is to risk losing one's chance to work and earn a livelihood anywhere. Furthermore, any unemployed person risks arrest as a "parasite."

The coercive effects of this arrangement are well summarized by the Russian physicist and Nobel Prize-winning human rights activist Andrei Sakharov:

> A complete state monopoly inevitably entails servitude and compulsory conformism. Each person is completely dependent upon the state. . . . [The Russian] has not forgotten how his grandfather was dispossessed as a kulak [under Stalin]. And he knows that even today his personal fate depends wholly upon the state: upon his immediate or remote superiors; upon the chairman of the housing committee; upon the chairman of the trade union committee, who may or may not decide to get his child into kindergarten; and possibly on the KGB informer working next to him.[21]

Ideological Monopoly

What are the sources of this drive for supreme power by a totalitarian movement and its ongoing effort at complete domination of society? The nature and uses of comprehensive worldview ideology take center stage at this point. We will focus on the longest-lived, most elaborate, and most influential of these political doctrines, **Marxism-Leninism,** the official ideology of communist regimes.

Marxism Karl Marx (1818–1883) and Friedrich Engels (1820–1895) were German revolutionary socialists, most of whose political activity consisted of writing books, articles, and pamphlets explaining, applying, and promoting Marx's theory of history. In all its variations and complexities, this theory contains obscurities and ambiguities that are still being reinterpreted and debated. Marx's popularized writings, especially *The Communist Manifesto,* which he and Engels issued in 1848, exerted by far the greatest influence on political activists, and they do present a reasonably clear set of ideas.

Marx emphasized the material, economic basis of life as the ultimate cause of every characteristic of society, including ideas and beliefs. The particular forms taken by the **forces of production**—land, labor, capital, technology—determine the **relations of production**—the property system—of any given society. Peasant agriculture in the Middle Ages, for example, gave rise to feudalism, the effective control of productive property and the peasant serfs by landlords with the military capacity to defend their domains.

Marx declares that sweeping, long-term transformations of societies begin with changes in the forces of production. In the modern era, such a change has occurred and is advancing rapidly; namely, the development of mechanized industrial production. The old feudal relations of production—the private-property system—continue to dominate society, but in the long run they will prove to be incompatible with industrialism. This new mode of production represents the greatest progressive development in human history; it makes possible fantastic increases in human productiveness and ultimately the abolition of poverty and even of material scarcity.

Before the full potential of industrialism can be realized, however, the private-property system must be destroyed and replaced with social ownership and control of the means of production. History has been a record of unending **class conflict,** with a minority always controlling and profiting from the productive system. The vast majority, whether slaves, serfs, or wage workers, have suffered exploitation by the economically **dominant class.** Members of that class always control and use the coercive state to keep the impoverished majority powerless and helpless.

Within newly industrializing societies, the dominant class consists of **bourgeois capitalists,** the businessmen who own and control factories. Their private-property system is doomed; it will inevitably be destroyed and replaced by a new social property system. In fact, the capitalist system produces its own "gravediggers": the propertyless factory workers, or **proletariat.** Their hard labor turns raw materials into marketable commodities, but their efforts are repaid with only a small proportion of the value that they create—at best only enough to keep them alive and reproducing more potential proletarians.

The competitive market system of capitalism requires every capitalist to squeeze maximum production for the lowest possible wages out of the workers; anyone who doesn't will be undersold and put out of business by lower-wage competitors. Capitalism makes poor and miserable wage-slaves of the exploited proletariat. Even their meager employment is insecure; capitalist industrial production inevitably outruns its capacity to sell more products, in large part because of the low wages earned by most consumers. The result is periodic collapse of the economy—depressions and financial panics—with massive unemployment, bankruptcy of the weaker capitalist firms, and an increasing concentration of productive wealth in the hands of an ever-shrinking bourgeois class.

In the meantime, industrial development brings together great masses of workers within individual factories and in the rapidly growing cities. Common experience and constant communication create in them a proletarian **class consciousness,** an awareness that their interests are radically opposed to the bourgeois bosses' interest in exploiting their labor for private profit. Workers begin to organize, aided by a few bourgeois intellectuals who have attained a theoretical understanding of the direction of historical development and seek to shorten the birth pangs of the new social order.

Eventually, a tiny bourgeois class will confront a massive majority of proletarians who will refuse any longer to tolerate a system that impoverishes and enslaves them. The workers will forcibly overthrow the bourgeois government and with it the capitalist private-property system. The inner contradictions of bourgeois society make its self-destruction as inevitable as the periodic return of Halley's comet; proper scientific understanding leads to a correct prediction in each case.

After the proletarian revolution, government will take the temporary form of a **dictatorship of the proletariat** in order to suppress any counter-revolutionary efforts by the dispossessed bourgeoisie. This regime will be truly democratic, however, because it will represent the workers, who make up the vast majority of the population.

At this point Marx's forecast becomes extremely general and sketchy. All productive property will be socialized and operated in the interests of the total society. The potential benefits of industrialism will no longer be blocked by self-seeking competition and wasteful depressions. Some kind of central planning will lead both to steady increases in production and to the distribution of its benefits to everyone. Eventually, scarcity will be ended forever, and equality and abundance will result from implementing the rule "From each according to his ability, to each according to his needs."

With the end of competition for wealth and possessions, the class system becomes extinct. Since the essential purpose of the state has always been to protect the interests and position of the dominant class, the state as a repressive apparatus will no longer be necessary: "State interference in social relations becomes . . . superfluous, and then dies out by itself; the government of persons is replaced by the administration of things and by the conduct of the processes of production."[22] Material security, complete equality, the end of coercion, and a harmonious and cooperative society amount to the emergence of true communism, the final outcome of the unstoppable progessive march of humanity. This goal will be reached, though, only by passing through the valley of deadly class conflict: the "haves" will never give up without a fight.

Marx and Engels died still waiting for the "inevitable" proletarian revolutions in the most advanced and therefore most conflict-ridden bourgeois societies, but they have never occurred in such countries. The failure of Marx's most fundamental "scientific" prediction did not, however, cause Marxist ideology to die out. By the late nineteenth century Marxism had become the official doctrine of the German Social Democratic Party, the largest socialist party in Europe, as well as the socialist theory with the broadest appeal to anticapitalist European intellectuals.

Lenin and Leninism It was one of those intellectuals, son of a bourgeois Russian school inspector, whose version of Marxism inspired the first self-styled socialist revolutionary movement to gain and hold supreme political power. V. I. Ulyanov (1870–1924) took the party name of Lenin. An heir to a generations-long student revolutionary culture in tsarist Russia, he was converted to Marxism as a young man and became an activist in the illegal Russian Social Democratic Workers' Party. After spending some time in prison and in Siberian exile for illegal political activities, Lenin spent most of the years from 1900 to 1917 in Western Europe, where he could produce clandestine propaganda for Russian consumption.

At a secret conference of Russian Social Democrats in 1903, the party split over questions of organization and tactics; Lenin led the Bolshevik ("majority") faction, which was opposed by the Mensheviks ("minority"). He was utterly determined that his ideas would prevail and always dogmatically asserted that only his interpretation of Marxism could be correct. He accused all Marxists who disagreed with him of rejecting the "scientific truth" of Marxism and attacked them with unrelenting hostility and sarcasm.

Yet there can be no serious question that Lenin revised Marxist doctrine in very important ways (see figure 8-1). He was most concerned to explain why Marx's predicted proletarian revolutions had not occurred and what their absence implied for the strategy of revolutionary socialism. The nonrevolutionary character of Western working classes showed that the workers' own knowledge and experience could awaken in them mere **trade-union consciousness** rather than proletarian class consciousness. Workers would readily organize to bring pressure upon their employers for better

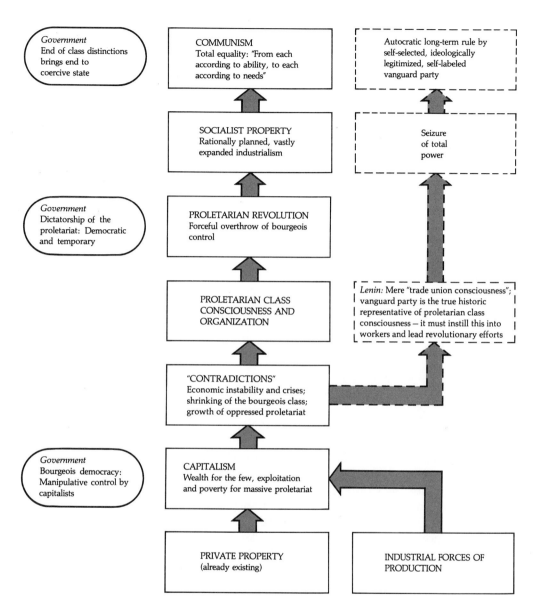

Figure 8-1 Marx's theory of revolutionary change, with Lenin's amendments

working conditions and wages, but material improvements would leave unionized workers uninterested in destroying the capitalist system.

Yet how could wages be raised, given the cutthroat competition with which Marx had charged capitalism? Lenin claimed that the more advanced capitalist states had conquered large overseas empires, which they exploited to earn "superprofits." Capitalists used a portion of this loot to buy off their workers on the home front, making them "labor aristocrats" in comparison with the incredibly impoverished laborers and peasants of the colonial world. The lack of empirical evidence of massive investments of capital in European colonies didn't change Lenin's mind or diminish the appeal of his idea that imperial rule stems from capitalist exploitation.

His main interest lay in designing and supervising an effective revolutionary party; only through proper organization and tactics and ideological uniformity could it possibly gain power. Its leading element, the **vanguard,** must be made up of fulltime, well-trained, thoroughly dedicated professional revolutionaries acting in disciplined obedience to the highest party authorities:

> The proletarian consciousness necessary for the socialist revolution could only be brought to the working class from without, by the self-selected vanguard of revolutionary Marxists . . . composed of declassed bourgeois intellectuals who were capable of correctly anticipating events because of their superior theoretical insight. They addressed themselves to the real and ultimate, if still unconscious, will of the masses. They could anticipate history.[23]

Lenin believed with evident sincerity that the party could and would educate the workers to understand their true historic interests and so gain their willing support. Before 1917, most of his writings anticipated a considerable period of parliamentary "bourgeois" democracy in Russia as a necessary prelude to socialism. However, when chaotic circumstances presented his well-disciplined group with an opportunity to seize power in 1917, he brushed aside all theoretical doubts and objections and established the world's first self-proclaimed socialist regime.

In *State and Revolution,* written just before the Bolshevik coup, Lenin expressed contempt for **capitalist democracy** as "a democracy for the minority, only for the propertied classes, only for the rich." He asserted that the postrevolutionary "dictatorship of the proletariat, i.e., the organization of the vanguard of the oppressed as the ruling class for the purpose of suppressing the oppressors . . . *for the first time,* becomes democracy for the poor, democracy for the people. . . ." The means of production will become social property, and the workers' state, having crushed the violent resistance of the former exploiters, will work toward a vast expansion of production and of all-round equality. Over an indeterminate period of time, "people will gradually *become accustomed* to observing the elementary rules of social intercourse that have been known for centuries . . . without force, without compulsion, without subordination, *without the special apparatus* for compulsion which is called the state."[24]

In the meantime a powerful workers' state must be created, controlled exclusively by the party—Bolshevik, soon renamed Communist—that possesses true theoretical understanding of Marxism, the only scientific interpretation of history and socialism. The Leninist "vanguard" concept has remained the essential rationale for the Soviet Communist Party's political and governmental monopoly since 1917. If actual workers or peasants object to party policies, they must be educated to accept them as consistent with their true interests or, if necessary, forced to accept them. Thus the *Cheka* and, today, the KGB.

Stalin When Lenin suffered a serious stroke in 1922, his active leadership was nearly ended, and he died in January 1924. His long-time follower Joseph Stalin was appointed general secretary of the party in 1922. He effectively used this bureaucratic post to build his personal power, mainly by appointing his loyalists to key positions in the rapidly growing bureaucracy of the Communist Party.

The struggle among party elites to succeed Lenin as top leader lasted about four years. Although relying heavily on his organizational strength, Stalin also used ideological persuasion to discredit his competitors within higher party circles. Against Leon Trotsky, his primary rival, Stalin argued for his main theoretical concept, **"socialism in one country."**

Grossly exaggerating their differences, Stalin claimed that Trotsky had so little faith in the capacity of Russian Communists to construct a socialist system that he wanted them to mark time until the revolution had spread to the more industrialized countries of Europe. Stalin denounced this supposed defeatism and asserted that the heroic workers and peasants of Russia could and would build socialism on their own, as the essential first step to its spread to other countries. Stalin's "message of sturdy confidence in 'the internal forces of our Revolution'" strongly appealed "to the pride of political virility in the rising Soviet ruling class, its will to believe in the potency and world mission of the Russian Revolution." In contrast, he effectively painted his rivals as weak ("castrated"), passive, and lacking confidence in Russian communism.[25]

Stalin's successful power strategy combined ideological persuasion, making and breaking coalitions with other party leaders, and exploitation of his organizational strength. In 1926 he was able to have Trotsky expelled from the Politburo, in 1927 from the Communist Party, and in 1929 from the Soviet Union. As an exile, Trotsky vigorously criticized Stalin's rule until he was assassinated in Mexico in 1940, undoubtedly on Stalin's orders.

As he approached supreme power, Stalin declared that Soviet socialism must secure itself against the menace of **capitalist encirclement** by rapidly developing heavy industry as the basis for greatly increased military strength. This goal would be achieved through centralized planning and control of the entire economy, including agriculture. In 1929 Stalin decreed an end to private ownership of land, and all peasants were compelled to join government-directed collective farms. Allowing peasants to secure their own land had gained vital support for the Bolsheviks in the Civil War, but many party leaders remained uneasy about creating a class of rural capitalists. Stalin moved with brutal relentlessness—millions of peasants died—to establish socialism in the countryside.

Stalin's career starkly illustrates an important kind of relationship between ideological commitment and political power. One typical view of him was expressed by Dmitri Shostakovich, a famous Russian composer who had been ferociously criticized and put in fear of his life for displeasing the supreme leader: "Stalin never had any ideology or convictions or ideas or principles. Stalin always held whatever opinion made it easier for him to tyrannize others, to keep them in fear and guilt. . . . He never cared what he said, as long as he held on to his power."[26]

In contrast, a careful scholar asserts that Stalin was not a mere power-mad paranoid but rather "a dedicated revolutionary who unambiguously expressed a perfectly clear conception of the historically unprecedented society his labors were to bring into existence. This new society was to be communism, the ideal order of human life envisioned by both Marx and Lenin. . . ."[27] For example, once his power had been consolidated, Stalin suddenly reversed the **New Economic Policy** that Lenin had grudgingly implemented to overcome economic disaster in the early 1920s. This policy had allowed not only private farming but also a limited range of small-scale private business. It had brought economic improvement, but in 1929 Stalin moved decisively toward the ideologically Leninist policy of state ownership and control of the total economy.

Although these two interpretations seem incompatible, we believe that there is some validity in both. Everything we have learned about Stalin's personality suggests that his personal drive for power was about as extreme as can be imagined. His intolerance of opposition or criticism, whether real or imagined, was virtually unlimited, and he certainly changed and manipulated policy ideas to gain support. However, his basic economic policy would almost certainly not have taken the shape it did outside the framework of Marxism-Leninism.

In practice, Stalin's ideological commitments and his overwhelming need to dominate constantly reinforced each other. Concentrating decision-making power in the party leader could be seen as necessary for the iron discipline required to build and protect "socialism in one country." His domination of foreign communist parties supposedly served the same purpose, and his extension of party control over the economy and society reinforced his supremacy. Within Stalin's mental universe, any threat to his power was readily identified as a threat to the world's first socialist state and therefore to mankind's march toward the ultimate goal of perfect communism. No matter how murderous his policies, Stalin found plenty of followers, both in his country and abroad, who accepted his self-serving ideological claims. They proved willing to kill or even to sacrifice their own lives in defense of the historic cause that he claimed to embody.

Khrushchev Although Stalin came as close to one-man tyranny as is possible within a large and complex state, he continued to claim authority on the basis of his leadership of the Communist Party. In fact he totally dominated the party and decimated both its top leadership and its bureaucracy in his Great Purge of 1935–1938. After Stalin's death, members of the Politburo, the committee at the summit of the party's command structure, closed ranks to prevent another abitrary dictatorship that might threaten their careers and even their lives. They arrested and secretly executed Lavrenti Beria, Stalin's last chief of security police, and apparently agreed that no future losers in their political struggles would suffer imprisonment or death. As Nikita Khrushchev intrigued his way to top leadership, his rivals were relegated to obscure bureaucratic posts. His own lack of Stalin-like power was decisively demonstrated when a Politburo majority led by Brezhnev removed him from office in 1964.

On the ideological front, Khrushchev attempted to gain support through his sensational—though not public—denunciations of Stalin, focusing mainly on his destructive impact upon the Communist Party. Khrushchev also sponsored an elaborate "**New Program of the Communist Party**," issued in 1961. It promised that the Soviet economy would surpass U.S. per capita production by 1970, leave the United States far behind in total industrial output by 1981, and exceed U.S. productivity by 100 percent. In that same period all consumer goods would become plentiful for Soviet citizens, as would comfortable, rent-free housing. At the same time, income differences would shrink; in short, "The party solemnly proclaims: the present generation of Soviet people shall live under communism."[28]

The party elite welcomed Khrushchev's efforts to restore the supremacy of party organization in the Soviet Union, but his denunciations of Stalin threatened to undermine their own legitimacy: they had risen to power as faithful servants of the late dictator. In addition, Khrushchev's explicit promises to the Soviet people were potentially troublesome.

Brezhnev and beyond Under Brezhnev and his successors, a truly oligarchic or collective leadership structure has developed, centered in the dozen or so full members of the Politburo. Their official announcements, campaigns, and programs suggest that the present-day operational ideology of Soviet Marxism-Leninism can be summarized in five fundamental principles:[29]

1. The absolute primacy and sanctity of the Communist Party. Article 6 of the 1977 Soviet Constitution declares:

> The leading and guiding force of Soviet society and the nucleus of its political system, of all state and public organizations, is the Communist Party of the Soviet Union. The CPSU exists for the people and serves the people.
>
> The Communist Party, armed with Marxism-Leninism, determines the general perspectives of the development of society and the line of domestic and foreign policy of the USSR, directs the great constructive work of the Soviet people, and imparts a planned, systematic, and theoretically substantiated character to their struggle for the victory of communism.

This principle is readily exportable, as seen in a 1974 statement by Cuban Communist Party official Armando Hart. He claimed that party authority "is based on the party's own history; on the fact that it always marches at the vanguard; on its knowledge and interpretation, in the face of any situation, of the ideology and the interests of the proletariat; and on its accurate decisions in relation to diverse problems."[30]

2. Socialist ownership of the means of production, meaning state ownership and direction of almost all legal economic activity. Small private plots of land conceded to collective farmers for individual cultivation are the main exception to the rule.

3. Anti-individualism or **collectivism.** Soviet citizens are officially discouraged from asserting individual desires and ambitions, which should always be subordinated to the needs, goals, and norms of the *kollektiv*, the peer group. Starting in nursery school, extending through one's entire educational career, and continuing in the place of employment, each person's *kollektiv* has a right to judge his or her conduct according to standards laid down by the party.

4. Atheism. Both Marx and Lenin viewed religion as illusory consolation for oppressed classes, promoted by and justifying their overlords. Religious belief would die out after the proletarian revolution had ended class tyranny and spread scientific enlightenment to the masses. The Soviet Constitution guarantees citizens "freedom of conscience, that is, the right to profess or not to profess any religion and to conduct religious worship or atheistic propaganda." In practice, the regime strongly favors and constantly pushes atheistic propaganda. The degree and harshness of religious persecution have varied over time, but severe limits on religious activities are the standard rule. In some cases, for example, children of Baptists have been removed from their parents by officials who were enforcing the official ban on teaching religion.[31]

5. Antagonism toward other sociopolitical systems. Soviet leaders since Khrushchev have stressed the necessity of **peaceful coexistence** between socialist and capitalist states, mainly because of the nuclear threat of mutual destruction. At the same time they have persistently emphasized that preventing World War III in no way implies the possibility of **ideological coexistence** between their system and the "capitalist" world. "Internal contradictions" will continually weaken "bourgeois imperialism," and it will ultimately give way to Soviet-style socialism. Marxist-Leninist leaders persistently express confidence in the inevitable triumph of communism and present themselves as the historic carriers of human progress. In the meantime, they must prevent "decadent" Western ideas, publications, and other cultural products from seducing and corrupting the Soviet people. They also wage political warfare through propaganda and espionage and provide military and organizational assistance to Marxist "liberation movements" in the Third World. These tactics serve a strategy for hastening the inevitable demise of historically senile world capitalism.

This operational ideology of official Soviet Marxism-Leninism differs radically from Marx's vision of proletarian self-rule, followed by the withering of the state in a realm of spontaneous cooperation and harmony. The Soviet Constitution declares: "The aims of the dictatorship of the proletariat having been fulfilled, the Soviet state has become a state of the whole people. The leading role of the Communist Party, the vanguard of all the people, has grown."

This **"state of the whole people"** is in fact controlled by a self-selected, self-perpetuating political elite, as we explain in chapter 9. The original political means for realizing "socialism" en route to the building of communism—the self-proclaimed "vanguard" party's total power—long ago displaced the revolutionary ends proclaimed by Marx and passionately reaffirmed by Lenin on the eve of his seizure of power. The operational ideology functions first and foremost to rationalize and legitimize the political monopoly of the Communist Party and its control of economic, social, and cultural life.

Indoctrination

Methods of indoctrination Ideologically oriented controls work mainly through organized indoctrinational persuasion linked closely with officially sponsored political participation and an official communications monopoly. Political controls extend not only to news media but also to the content of popular culture and the arts.

Official ideological indoctrination begins in kindergarten. Every Soviet classroom has portraits of Lenin, and a typical children's song proclaims:

Citizens of the Soviet Union begin to be exposed to systematic, pervasive, lifelong political indoctrination at an early age. Here, a portrait of Lenin looks down on children in a nursery school.

In many countries children live,
And everywhere all children love Lenin.
We children live better than anybody on earth,
Our country is happy and lucky.[32]

Political emphases became more sophisticated, but even more persistent, all the way from elementary through graduate school. Ideological training includes "mixing of patriotic and communist symbols so that the difference between the Soviet Union as a country and communism as an ideology is blurred into near invisibility, and finally by mystical appeals to the sanctity of the motherland in bold contrast with the frightening, alien, hostile world outside."[33]

In addition to specific political lessons, textbooks in almost every field, however technical, include Marxist-Leninist examples and references to Lenin and other ideological symbols. University students are required to take courses in Marxist-Leninist doctrine; even candidates for the highest graduate degrees must pass an advanced examination in that subject, whatever their fields of study.

Paralleling and extending beyond the school experience are the mass children's and youth organizations of the Communist Party. Almost all five-to-nine-year-olds are enrolled in the Young Octobrists, and the Young Pioneers include ages ten to fifteen. These organizations sponsor sports and hobby programs, outdoor recreation and children's libraries, art and music groups—nearly every kind of activity in which most parents might want their children to be involved. The political purpose of the children's participation is exemplified in the new members' pledge of the Pioneers: "'I, a Young Pioneer of the Soviet Union, solemnly promise in the presence of my comrades to warmly love my Soviet motherland, to live, to study, and to struggle as Lenin willed and as the Communist Party teaches.'"[34]

The most important party auxiliary organization is the **Komsomol** (Young Communist League), open to individuals who are fifteen to twenty-seven years of age. Membership is not universal, as it nearly is with the two younger groups, though the Komsomol is about forty million strong. It provides a somewhat less demanding, apprentice-type experience modeled on the Communist Party, and it supplies almost all of the constant inflow of new members to the Party. Komsomol members are expected to be politically active, to volunteer for extra work where needed, and above all to act as vigilant and loyal Communists. Membership can boost a young person's chances for admission to desirable educational programs and for the best job openings.

Participative political training is by no means limited to young people; it is an official way of life for all Soviet adults. In 1977, for example, Communist Party schools and courses enrolled 21 million adults, including 8 million nonparty members. In addition, 35 million received official economic training. These programs were managed by 2.2 million trained party propagandists. Among the working population there were 3.1 million "agitators," responsible for talking up official policies among their fellow workers, 1.8 million political informants who gave ideological talks, and 300,000 full-time party lecturers. During that typical year, then, some 8 million people were "permanently charged with supervising and instructing Soviet society."[35]

Party members are expected to enroll frequently in political courses, and those who want to improve their career prospects do so more often than the average. Everyone, party member or not, is expected to attend officially sponsored meetings after hours at the workplace or with local councils (soviets) to hear lectures and engage in discussions of current party policies. Some 140 million Soviet citizens are supposed to have discussed the proposed 1977 constitution, and so far as was reported, they all endorsed it. Unanimity is the expected outcome of this kind of meeting. This essentially **compulsory participation** is a distinctive mark of totalitarianism. As the late Russian dissenter and political prisoner Andrei Amalrik observed, "The regime is not content that anyone simply be 'not against' it: everyone must be 'for' it and must demonstrate this from time to time."[36]

Consistent with the enshrinement of an official, purportedly scientific, and infallible ideology, all the media of communications—newspapers, magazines, books, pamphlets, movies, radio, television—are controlled by the party and the state. Officials not only censor all media but in effect dictate their contents. Prohibitions against unauthorized publication are almost always enforced, even against passing typewritten documents from hand to hand.

News is reported according to the line and direction of party leaders; its preparation, control, and dissemination are among the most important functions of several party and government departments. Most stories highlight current official policies, feature supposedly serious problems of the decadent West, or celebrate Soviet economic achievements.

Soviet journalists are restricted from referring to an enormous list of subjects, such as detailed military information and agricultural and industrial shortfalls. Taboo subjects have also included earthquakes and other natural disasters in the USSR; fires, murders, airplane, train, and industrial accidents; figures on the earnings of party and government officials; reports of food shortages in the country; and names of politically disgraced leaders of the past, including five former premiers of the Soviet government.[37] Whether the 1986 reporting of the deadly breakdown of the Chernobyl nuclear power plant and a fatal Soviet cruise ship disaster could foreshadow a long-term policy of greater openness in the media remains to be seen.

Not only the mass media but all the arts—painting and sculpture, literature, film, drama, even music—are also subject to official ideological control. No one can legally attempt to make a living as any kind of artist if not a member of an official writers' or artists' or composers' union, which completely controls whose work may be published, shown, or performed. Generally, all artists have been expected since the 1930s to practice the basic principles of **Socialist realism:** "1. Their work must be realistic in content and form; 2. It must have mass appeal; 3. The message must be an optimistic one; 4. And it must follow the party line."[38]

In practice, *Socialist realism* means not only that all works must be free of criticisms of the regime but they must positively support it. Literary works cannot even be *non*political. Following many precedents in Soviet history, for example, a Cuban poet who had been imprisoned for nine years after seeking permission to emigrate to the United States was jailed again in the late 1970s. He was accused of allowing "an anthology of his elegiac, apolitical poetry" to be published abroad.[39]

Enforcement of these standards in the Soviet Union has varied in strictness. During the Khrushchev years (1955–1964) a slight thaw in the cultural climate was permitted to occur, and a few works honestly depicting the Stalinist past were published or performed. The cultural climate was quickly refrozen when Khrushchev was removed from power. Under Gorbachev, tentative signs of a new thaw in Soviet culture may be appearing, but the brevity and tentativeness of the earlier period of greater artistic freedom must temper any judgments about its depth, effects, or durability.

Effects of indoctrination An important question about institutionalized totalitarian systems, especially that of the Soviet Union, is how effective these massive and persistent efforts at ideological indoctrination actually are. The only honest answer is that no one knows; in the absence of unofficial and risk-free opinion studies, actual data to answer that question are not available. What we have instead are conflicting impressions and assertions.

An American student of the Soviet Union, for example, suggests that indoctrination has considerable success: "Incessant ideological indoctrination, despite its inconsistencies with reality, has a very strong effect on its captive audience, which is largely deprived of alternative sources of information." An experienced foreign correspondent believes that it is common for Soviet citizens to learn, as they grow up, not to think seriously about discrepancies between official political teachings and their own experience: "This, I came to feel, was one of the earliest lessons of Soviet childhood, and it helps keep many, perhaps most, adults in a spirit of political comfort with their country and their system."[40]

In contrast, two former Soviet citizens critical of the regime downplay the persuasiveness of official indoctrination. According to satirist Vladimir Voinovich, "over the years of its existence Soviet propaganda has completely exhausted the reserves of belief among its consumers. Through persistent lying and unscrupulousness it has achieved a staggering effect: Soviet man is attracted by everything it rejects and repelled by everything it extols." Ex-political prisoner Vladimir Bukovsky bitterly declares: "From top to bottom, no one believes in Marxist dogma any more, even though they continue to measure their actions by it, refer to it, and use it as a stick to beat one another with: it is both a proof of loyalty and a meal ticket."[41]

There are a few fragmentary Soviet opinion surveys relevant to this question, probably undertaken and published in order to improve the efforts of party propagandists. These studies suggest that the effects of indoctrination fall well short of what party leaders undoubtedly desire. Large numbers of respondents said that they attended political meetings and training sessions because they felt compelled to do so but were indifferent to the content. A survey of political propagandists revealed that more than half of them doubted that students remembered anything they were told. Surveys of the values and desires of young people have revealed an almost total aversion to political work and strong interest in a satisfying private life rather than in service to the broader community. In sum: "If we analyze the interests of Soviet citizens in detail, we note that they prefer anything that is distant from ideological education."[42]

These sparse data seem to provide considerable support for the above-quoted views of Soviet dissidents. The scholar whose analysis of opinion studies we have reported suggests, however, that the massive, never-ending Soviet effort at political socialization must have some intended effects: "On certain points—patriotism, fear or distrust of the external world, the assurance of security in everyday life (even at a low level)—society has internalized the official culture."[43] Her assertion may be correct, but it is still nothing but a plausible guess.

Certain rapidly developing and explosive political events should give us pause in trying to estimate the persuasiveness of official indoctrination. The Czech people in 1968 and the Poles in 1980 had been subjected to decades of indoctrinational persuasion on the Soviet model, but movements that challenged communist ideological and political monopoly quickly gained overwhelming popular support. Both were suppressed only by armed force, not persuasive propaganda. Of course, these movements appealed enormously to nationalist antagonism toward Soviet domination, and, as noted, Soviet ideology skillfully incorporates Russian patriotism and nationalism.

What we can safely conclude about Soviet ideological indoctrination is that it combines coercion and persuasion: "Both education and propaganda in the Soviet Union have a coercive character, insofar as they are government monopolies which simultaneously restrict access to unorthodox ideas and make exposure to the officially approved ones inescapable."[44]

We doubt that Soviet leaders are cynical hypocrites; it is usually not difficult for people to believe in doctrines that justify their power and privileges. Even if they were cynics, enforcement of ideological uniformity would be enormously useful to them—"as a kind of early-warning system. Those who are unwilling to communicate within the ideological framework are exposed and denied any role in politics. This is a positive factor in helping to maintain control, no matter how empty the ideology might become."[45] Persistently, then, ideologically oriented indoctrinational persuasion works in tandem with coercion to sustain and protect Communist Party leaders' domination of Soviet politics and society.

Summary

Totalitarian regimes are unique to the twentieth century. They are created by movements whose leaders seek total power in order to remold entire societies according to their ideological designs. In addition to an official ideology, totalitarian systems feature an elite-controlled ruling party; a sizeable and active security police force; and monopolistic regime control of mass communications, weapons, and nearly all kinds of organizations.

In the 1930s *totalitarianism* began to be used as a label encompassing the regimes in Nazi Germany, fascist Italy, and the Soviet Union. The concept has become controversial since the 1960s, with critics calling it a Cold War propaganda term outmoded by post-Stalin changes in the Soviet Union. It has since become clear, however, that the Soviet and most other communist regimes are much more tightly organized for control of society and hostile to dissent than are most noncommunist autocracies. "Totalitarianism" still seems a necessary descriptive category.

It is helpful to distinguish two phases in the development of a totalitarian regime: revolutionizing and institutionalized. The first phase begins as the movement secures absolute power. Its leaders move to destroy the old political and social systems, eliminate all opposition, and implement their ideological program. In almost every case a supreme leader personifies the regime in its initial phase, inspiring and dominating officials and members of the monopoly ruling party.

When the leader is gone, the party apparatus takes over. A self-perpetuating oligarchy of top party officials commands the regime by means of the party bureaucracy, the party-controlled government, and the security police and armed forces. This second phase, institutionalized totalitarianism, has proceeded furthest in the Soviet Union.

There is no scholarly consensus on why totalitarian regimes have arisen in this century. Four political factors can be highlighted as helping to make them possible. First, ideologies of total social transformation emerged in the wake of the great French Revolution. In the nineteenth century these ideologies inspired the formation of countless parties and movements, with Marxist socialism becoming the most influential of such worldviews.

Second, the rise of nationalism helped undercut the legitimacy of traditional European regimes, set the stage for the First World War, and contributed mightily to the appeal of fascism and Nazism.

Third, twentieth-century wars have frequently changed the distribution of power, both within and among states. Some war-induced changes have made it possible for totalitarian movements to gain dominance or to expand their rule to additional countries.

Fourth, in some critical cases, governmental incompetence and indecisiveness have contributed greatly to the success of totalitarian takeovers.

Our analysis of totalitarianism is organized according to four basic categories of competition for power. Domination takes first priority, for totalitarianism represents the most thoroughgoing control of entire societies ever attempted or achieved by autocratic rulers.

In order to gain power initially, totalitarian movements almost always need and use assistance from other groups and parties. Totalitarians never share power once they have consolidated it, however; takeovers by Hitler's Nazis in Germany, the Bolsheviks in Russia, and the North Vietnamese Communists in South Vietnam exemplify the manipulation of coalition partners or allies. All were wholly excluded from power when the totalitarian movement no longer needed their help.

Ideological elites' attempts to dominate society are met with some degree of resistance. The rulers rapidly build and deploy large security forces to suppress all actual or anticipated opposition. Security organizations continue to function beyond the revolutionizing stage as institutions essential for preserving totalitarian regimes.

Economic coercion is also an effective instrument of control, especially in communist systems. Where the state is the sole employer, political nonconformists can readily be punished by depriving them of all opportunities to make a living.

Totalitarian rulers always justify their domination in terms of an ideology, the most influential of which is Marxism-Leninism. In the nineteenth century Karl Marx produced an elaborate theory of history not merely to explain the past but to predict the future. He forecast the inevitable self-destruction of capitalism, the socioeconomic system combining industrial production with market competition. Pressed by competitors, bourgeois manufacturers exploit their workers unmercifully to squeeze out higher profits. Poverty, insecurity, economic slumps, shrinkage of the bourgeois class, and ever-growing proletarian class consciousness must lead to anti-capitalist revolution made by and for the workers.

After a temporary "dictatorship of the proletariat" has put down desperate bourgeois resistance, postrevolutionary society will move toward abundance and equality for all. Property will become exclusively social, and eventually everyone will work according to ability and be rewarded according to need. In the absence of a dominant class, the coercive state will wither away as communism flourishes.

V. I. Lenin led the Russian political group that produced the first revolution in the name of Marxism. He believed that, left to themselves, workers could develop only trade-union consciousness, a desire to organize but merely in order to press for higher pay and not to overthrow capitalism. A militant, tight-knit, hierarchically organized party made up exclusively of professional revolutionaries must act as the vanguard of the proletariat to organize for and lead a socialist revolution.

A few years after he led his vanguard party to seize control of the Russian state, Lenin died and was succeeded as leader of the communist regime by Joseph Stalin. Stalin brought the peasantry under his firm political control through forced and murderous agricultural collectivization. He also built up heavy industry to support a rapid increase in military power and killed off his former rivals and millions of others in a bloody purge of the Communist Party.

Three years after Stalin's death, party general secretary Nikita Khrushchev denounced the late dictator's destructive effects on the party in a speech delivered in secret but soon widely known. His Politburo colleagues removed Khrushchev from office in 1964, and de-Stalinization ended.

Under Khrushchev's successors, oligarchic leadership and the party bureaucracy became more thoroughly institutionalized and entrenched. The ruling elite has continued to justify the system by promoting an official ideology. It emphasizes five principles: the absolute primacy of the "vanguard" Communist Party, socialist ownership of the economy, collectivism in all spheres of life, atheism, and ideological antagonism toward all noncommunist sociopolitical systems.

In communist-ruled societies ideological indoctrination is a major official undertaking, and it affects everyone from cradle to grave. Education, the workplace, all media of communications, and even the arts function as ideological transmission belts and reinforcers of the official version of reality.

In the absence of nonofficial opinion studies or free elections, it is impossible to evaluate adequately the effectiveness of communist political indoctrination. As regime monopolies, which severely limit access to alternative ideas and guarantee endless exposure to the official worldview, both education and propaganda function as coercive components of the total system of control.

Review List of Key Terms

totalitarian autocracy
monopolistic control
Italian fascism
national socialism

Enabling Act
Constituent Assembly
Mensheviks

class conflict
dominant class
bourgeois capitalists
proletariat

New Economic Policy
New Program of the Communist Party
collectivism

revolutionizing phase
Bolsheviks
the leader
Great Proletarian Cultural Revolution
institutionalized totalitarianism
regularized succession
ideologies of total transformation
coalitional tactics

National Liberation Front
Gestapo
"Final Solution"
the *Cheka*
KGB
economic coercion
Marxism-Leninism
forces of production
relations of production

class consciousness
dictatorship of the proletariat
trade-union consciousness
vanguard
capitalist democracy
"socialism in one country"
capitalist encirclement

peaceful coexistence
ideological coexistence
"state of the whole people"
Komsomol
compulsory participation
Socialist realism

Notes

1. Michael Curtis, "Retreat from Totalitarianism," in *Totalitarianism in Perspective: Three Views*, Carl J. Friedrich, Michael Curtis, and Benjamin Barber (New York: Praeger, 1969), pp. 58–59.
2. Barrington Moore, Jr., *Injustice: The Social Bases of Obedience and Revolt* (White Plains, N.Y.: M. E. Sharpe, 1978), p. 483.
3. Karl Dietrich Bracher, "Totalitarianism," in *Dictionary of the History of Ideas*, vol. 4, ed. Philip P. Wiener (New York: Scribner's, 1973), p. 409.
4. Benito Mussolini, "The Doctrine of Fascism," *Enciclopedia Italiana*, 1932; reprinted in *Modern Political Ideologies*, ed. Alan P. Grimes and Robert H. Horowitz (New York: Oxford University Press, 1959), p. 412.
5. A. James Gregor, "Totalitarianism Revisited," in *Totalitarianism Reconsidered*, ed. Ernest A. Menzel (Port Washington, N. Y.: Kennikat Press, 1981), p. 143.
6. Carl J. Friedrich, "The Evolving Theory and Practice of Totalitarian Regimes," in *Totalitarianism in Perspective: Three Views*, ed. Carl J. Friedrich (New York: Praeger, 1969), p. 126.
7. Benjamin R. Barber, "Conceptual Foundations of Totalitarianism" in *Totalitarianism in Perspective: Three Views*, ed. Carl J. Friedrich et al. (New York: Praeger, 1969), p. 47 fn. See also Curtis, "Retreat," pp. 53–121; and Herbert J. Spiro, "Totalitarianism," in *Encyclopedia of the Social Sciences*, vol. 16, ed. David L. Sills (New York: Macmillan and Free Press, 1968), pp. 106–113.
8. See, e.g., Bracher, "Totalitarianism"; Friedrich, "Evolving Theory"; Andrew C. Janos, "Group Politics in Communist Society: A Second Look at the Pluralistic Model," in *Authoritarian Politics in Modern Society*, ed. Samuel P. Huntington and Clement Moore (New York: Basic Books, 1970), pp. 437–450; Alexander J. Groth, "USSR: Pluralist Monolith?" *British Journal of Political Science* 9 (1979): 445–464; Maurice Cranston, "Should We Cease to Speak of Totalitarianism?" *Survey* 23 (3) (Summer 1977–1978): 62; Paul Hollander, "Bureaucracy, Totalitarianism, and the Comparative Study of Communism," in *The Many Faces of Socialism: Comparative Sociology and Politics* (New Brunswick, N. J.: Transaction Books, 1983), pp. 67–77.
9. Donald D. Barry and Carol Barner-Barry, *Contemporary Soviet Politics: An Introduction*, 2nd ed. (Englewood Cliffs, N. J.: Prentice-Hall, 1982), p. 353. They specifically endorse Carl Friedrich's above-quoted description of the essential features of a totalitarian system. For a knowledgeable defense of the necessity and usefulness of the "totalitarianism" concept, see Walter Laqueur, "Is There Now, or

Has There Ever Been, Such a Thing as Totalitarianism?" *Commentary,* October 1985, pp. 29–35.
10. See, e.g., Alberto Aquarone, "The Totalitarian State and Personal Dictatorship," in *Totalitarianism Reconsidered,* ed. Ernest A. Menzel (Port Washington, N. Y.: Kennikat Press, 1981), pp. 83–92.
11. For well-informed discussion of the central role of the leader, see Leonard Schapiro, *Totalitarianism* (New York: Praeger, 1972), pp. 20–29; Robert C. Tucker, "Does Big Brother Really Exist?" in *1984 Revisited: Totalitarianism in Our Century,* ed. Irving Howe (New York: Harper & Row Perennial Library, 1983), pp. 89–102.
12. See James H. Billington, *Fire in the Minds of Men: Origins of the Revolutionary Faith* (New York: Basic Books, 1980).
13. For an account, based on interviews with the Cuban dictator and a number of his close collaborators, of Castro's successful exercise in manipulative persuasion, see Tad Szulc, "Fidel Castro's Years as a Secret Communist," *New York Times Magazine,* October 19, 1986, 47 ff.
14. Paul Johnson, *Modern Times: The World from the Twenties to the Eighties* (New York: Harper & Row, 1983), p. 282.
15. See the account by former NLF and Provisional Government official Truong Nhu Tang, "The Myth of a Liberation," *New York Review of Books,* October 21, 1982, pp. 31–36.
16. Leonard Schapiro, "The Triumph of Lenin and Stalin," *Encounter,* March 1984, pp. 63–64; see also Johnson, *Modern Times,* pp. 66–71.
17. See Vadim Medish, *The Soviet Union,* 2nd ed. (Englewood Cliffs, N. J.: Prentice-Hall, 1984), p. 124.
18. Frederick C. Barghoorn and Thomas Remington, "Politics in the U.S.S.R.," in *Comparative Politics Today: A World View,* 3rd ed., ed. Gabriel A. Almond and G. Bingham Powell, Jr. (Boston: Little, Brown, 1984), p. 346.
19. Ibid., p. 347.
20. Paul Hollander, *Soviet and American Society: A Comparison* (New York: Oxford University Press, 1973), p. 392.
21. Andrei D. Sakharov, *My Country and the World* (New York: Vintage Books, 1975), pp. 14–15, 29–30.
22. Friedrich Engels, "Socialism: Utopian and Scientific," in *Essential Works of Marxism,* ed. Arthur P. Mendel (New York: Bantam Books, 1961), p. 78.
23. A James Gregor, *The Fascist Persuasion in Radical Politics* (Princeton: Princeton University Press, 1974), p. 106.
24. V. I. Lenin, "State and Revolution," in *Essential Works of Marxism,* ed. Arthur P. Mendel (New York: Bantam Books, 1961), pp. 169, 171, 172. (Italics in original.)
25. Robert C. Tucker, *Stalin as Revolutionary, 1879–1929: A Study in History and Personality* (New York: Norton, 1973), pp. 303–304, 383–389.
26. *Testimony: The Memoirs of Dmitri Shostakovich,* as related to and edited by Solomon Volkov (New York: Harper & Row, 1979), p. 187.
27. C. W. Cassinelli, *Total Revolution* (Santa Barbara, Calif.: Clio Books, 1976), p. 82.
28. "The New Program of the Communist Party of the Soviet Union," in *Essential Works of Marxism,* ed. Arthur P. Mendel (New York: Bantam Books, 1961), p. 486.
29. Spelled out in Barry and Barner-Barry, *Contemporary Soviet Politics,* pp. 34–37.
30. Quoted in Jorge I. Dominguez, *Cuba: Order and Revolution* (Cambridge, Mass.: Harvard University Press, 1978), p. 337.
31. Hélène Carrère d'Encausse, *Confiscated Power: How Soviet Russia Really Works* (New York: Harper & Row, 1982), p. 216.
32. David K. Shipler, *Russia: Broken Idols, Solemn Dreams* (New York: Times Books, 1983), p. 101.
33. Ibid., pp. 106–107.
34. Quoted in Barry and Barner-Barry, *Contemporary Soviet Politics,* p. 63.
35. d'Encausse, *Confiscated Power,* pp. 219–222.
36. Andrei Amalrik, *Notes of a Revolutionary* (New York: Knopf, 1982), p. 5.

37. Barry and Barner-Barry, *Contemporary Soviet Politics*, pp. 65–66.
38. Medish, *Soviet Union*, p. 242.
39. Carlos Ripoll, "Censors and Dissenters in Cuban Culture," in *Cuban Communism*, 5th ed., Irving Louis Horowitz, ed. (New Brunswick, N. J.: Transaction Books, 1984), p. 404.
40. Medish, *Soviet Union*, p. 73; Shipler, *Russia*, p. 97.
41. Vladimir Voinovich, "The Trouble with Truth," *New Republic*, November 28, 1983, pp. 28–29; Vladimir Bukovsky, "The Soul of Man Under Socialism," *Commentary*, January 1979, p. 40.
42. d'Encausse, *Confiscated Power*, pp. 238–244.
43. Ibid., pp. 245–246.
44. Hollander, *Soviet and American Society*, p. 159.
45. Barry and Barner-Barry, *Contemporary Soviet Politics*, p. 39.

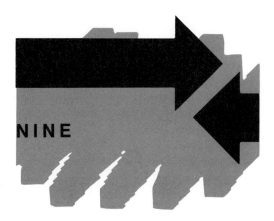

NINE

Totalitarianism: Organization and Problems

Under the dictatorship of the proletariat, proletarians are supposed to exercise power; since we claim this is a dictatorship of the proletariat, those who wield power here must be proletarians; but if those who wield power are proletarians, then this must indisputably be the dictatorship of the proletariat.
**George Konrad and Ivan Szelenyi,
The Intellectuals on the Road to Class Power**[1]

However relentlessly totalitarian rulers attempt to dominate government and society, they can't rely completely on the whip of coercion. They must also use the carrot of selective inducements to attract and hold collaborators whose cooperation is essential for implementing policies dictated from the top of the political pyramid. In this chapter we examine the structure of the ruling Communist Party in the Soviet Union and the inducements that make it work.

We also consider the strategy of toleration, but briefly, in keeping with its minimal role in totalitarian systems. Consistency requires that we give more attention to political and physical elimination as totalitarian strategy. We conclude by discussing problems of legitimacy that seem most typical of institutionalized totalitarian regimes.

Cooperation: Party and State

In the Soviet Union and other communist systems, the central focus of organized cooperation is the ruling party. Coercion is certainly not absent from relationships within the party, for there are enormous differences in power among its members and officials. Severe sanctions are now much more likely to involve demotion or expulsion from the party than execution or imprisonment in a forced labor camp, as were common under Stalin.

Party Membership

The Communist Party of the Soviet Union (CPSU) is a very large organization—about 9.7 percent of the adult population, more than 18 million members in the mid-1980s. Yet it is also rather exclusive; by no means are all applicants accepted. Most new members are recruited ("co-opted") by party or Komsomol officials. Their applications must be sponsored by three party members of at least five years' standing who know them personally and can attest to their personal abilities and political zeal and loyalty. In practice, the recommendations of fulltime party officials at the level of the primary (lowest level) unit, plus approval of officials at the next higher level, determine an applicant's success.

After admission, an individual serves a year as a candidate member, during which he or she is expected to be an enthusiastic political activist. At the end of this probationary period the entire application process must be repeated. The failure rate for candidate members is reported as 3 percent. The average new member is about 22 to 25 years old and has had seven to ten years of Komsomol training.[2]

Party membership involves duties. All members are expected to take on unpaid social assignments and must have at least one regular spare-time task. Examples include helping with the organizational work of the member's primary unit, giving talks on current events to co-workers, and heading a neighborhood committee. But there are inducements as well: "In return for these obligations, rank-and-file party members enjoy privileges such as better career chances, better housing and material goods, and access to party channels of information."[3]

Party Structures

Two organizational features essentially determine the functioning of the CPSU: a professional bureaucracy of perhaps 250,000 officials who supervise the operations of party organizations at every level, and full command of this bureaucracy by the few top party officials who are members of the **Politburo** and the **Secretariat.** In theory, the party is democratically controlled by its members through elections of representatives and officials. Elections begin at the base of the organization, the 420,000 or so **primary party organizations** located mainly in workplaces, and extend through several progressively larger geographic regions to the CPSU Party Congress held every five years (see figure 9-1).

In practice, though, the Leninist principle of **democratic centralism** means that power in the party flows from the top down, not from the bottom up. Party rules define democratic centralism as involving four elements: "All leading party bodies are elected; party bodies report periodically to their organizations and to higher bodies; there is strict party discipline and subordination of the minority to the majority; the decisions of higher bodies are obligatory for lower bodies."[4]

In fact, reports and decisions by party organs are always received with unanimous approval by groups at their level or below it in the chain of command. Since all nominations and elections are controlled from above, there is always a 100 percent majority supporting the leadership at every level. Organization is highly centralist but not in the least democratic.

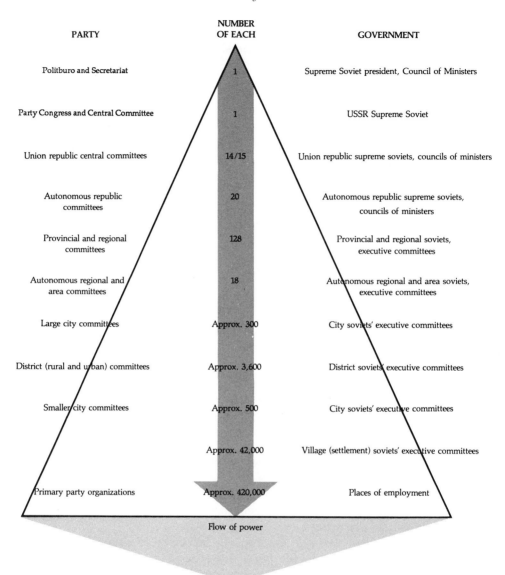

Figure 9-1 Soviet Communist Party and government parallel structures (From Vadim Medish, *The Soviet Union,* copyright 1984, p. 136. Adapted by permission of Prentice-Hall, Inc., Englewood Cliffs, New Jersey.)

"The other two elements—discipline and the binding nature of decisions upon lower bodies—are, by contrast, firmly applied. . . ."[5]

At the top of the formal structure the **Party Congress** "elects" a **Central Committee** of about 500 members mainly representing the higher levels of party and government officialdom from all the regions of the Soviet Union. This body usually meets twice yearly to "represent" the Congress between its infrequent sessions. The Central Committee supposedly elects an "administrative body," the Politburo, to carry on daily party business. In reality the reverse is normally true: the Politburo determines all appointments to the Central Committee and dictates whom that body will select for the Politburo.

With rare exceptions, which have involved leadership struggles behind closed doors, the Central Committee elects and approves only as recommended by the Politburo. The same is true without exception of the Party Congress; it casts nothing but unanimous votes and echoes with unbroken praise of party leaders and their policies. The **general secretary** of the party chairs the Politburo and also heads the Central Committee Secretariat, a committee of ten or so, including several Politburo members. Members of the Secretariat command the various departments that make up the vast bureaucracy of the party, assuring strict control of all subordinate officials from the top and center.

The structure of the Politburo has changed little since 1917, when Lenin began to use it as the central decision-making body. In the post-Stalin era it has become the supreme focus of ruling power: "In the crucially important sense of decision-making and policy determination, the Politburo is the government of the USSR, deciding priorities, allocating resources and defining broad policies and perhaps occasionally dealing with specific items of business that require quick, authoritative resolution."[6]

The size of the Politburo varies slightly from time to time, but it usually has about a dozen full members and half as many "candidate"—nonvoting—members. It is made up of the highest party and government officials, and since the early 1970s the KGB and the military establishment have usually been represented by the inclusion of their chiefs in the Politburo. No group or department has any formal right to representation at this level, since the Politburo is in the most literal sense autocratic. It has complete control over the selection and removal of its own members and is accountable only to itself. Its members cooperate with each other to rule the Soviet Union. They always present a united front in public, though behind-the-scenes bureaucratic and personal struggles for power and advantage are a normal feature of Politburo life.

By controlling the entire process of bureaucratic appointments and removals within the structures of party and government, the Politburo secures the cooperative helpers it needs. The state apparatus is huge and all-encompassing, since it directs almost all economic activity as well as the basic functions common to all modern governments. However, "the state is merely the administrative arm of the Party, which absorbs within itself all political life."[7]

Party and state structures stand almost precisely parallel to each other, from local soviets to the one-party "parliament," the USSR **Supreme Soviet,** which votes and praises as unanimously as the Party Congress. It is *party* bureaucrats—directed by and accountable to the Politburo-Secretariat elites—who are responsible for assuring that party policies are implemented in every office and enterprise within each territorial unit. Governmental officials and economic managers are party members, but party leaders do not consider membership sufficient to guarantee faithfulness to their policies. Although party secretaries are not supposed to interfere in "routine" management, their bureaucratic superiors hold them accountable for governmental operations within their jurisdictions. The result is some degree of "interference" and tension between party and state bureaucrats.

The Nomenklatura

The key to the control of this enormous **dual bureaucracy** is the **nomenklatura** ("nomenclature") political patronage system. All party committees, directed by their professional secretaries, have lists of specific political and administrative posts and of persons who are considered suitable for appointment to those positions. Party officials determine the appointees. The more politically sensitive the position, the more likely it is to be on the nomenklatura roster and to be open only to party members; for example, senior officers of state bodies, directors of economic enterprises, journalists, army and secret police officers. But probably nearly all positions with authority—middle managers, heads of academic institutes and departments, directors of schools and hospitals—are included on nomenklatura lists.

These lists are highly secret, and few people know how many positions they include. Two British political scientists refer to a 1969 estimate of 3 million executive positions. Michael Voslensky, a historian who left the Soviet Union, also suggests the 3 million figure—but includes both the nomenklaturists and their families. Members of this "ruling class," he estimates, total about 750,000. About one-third, or 250,000, make significant policy decisions and constitute the **political nucleus** of the nomenklatura. The other half-million hold executive posts in industrial and agricultural enterprises, research institutes, and educational institutions. Including families, the Soviet "ruling class" consists of 1.5 percent of the total population.[8]

Whatever the exact number of nomenklaturists, together they make up an enormous patronage system. It assures that nearly all desirable and important jobs will be held by individuals whom party leaders consider politically reliable. Since there is no guaranteed **bureaucratic tenure** in either party or government, fear of removal strongly reinforces political control from the top.

Inducements for cooperative reliability include a higher standard of living, chances for foreign travel, improved educational opportunities, access to publicly unavailable news and information—and the pleasures of exercising power over other people. In Voslensky's judgment, this last inducement is the cornerstone of the entire system: "The nomenklatura is a bastard kind of feudalism; every nomenklaturist is granted a fief, just as every vassal was granted a fief by the crown. . . . The nomenklatura fief is power."[9]

The distribution of tangible rewards in the Soviet and similar systems is highly unequal and corresponds closely to the effective distribution of political power. These inequalities are not so apparent in published salary figures; they consist mainly of privileged access to consumer goods, health care, and housing that are not available to the general population. Various types and gradations of "special" shops, restaurants, and clinics are open only to families of political and administrative elites. This privilege frees them from the daily standing in line for scarce food and other consumer goods that is the lot of ordinary citizens. Using their influence and connections, nomenklaturists have enormous advantages in getting their children into the best schools and most envied university programs, perpetuating privilege into the next generation.[10]

One fairly typical example of the unseen luxuries enjoyed by the most privileged elites was reported by a Soviet emigré who had visited a special farm as the husband of a general's daughter. He saw women in white smocks carefully examining, measuring, and sorting individual tomatoes: "The farm director explained proudly that the perfect ones went to the highest generals' families, the others to other officers, censors, the chief prosecutor, and so on." Within the officers' corps of the army, "stratification was so refined that a colonel general had a five-room apartment and a lieutenant-general . . . had a four-room apartment. . . ."[11]

Not the least valued privilege is access to accurate news drawn mainly from foreign media reports. Information officials prepare bulletins containing news that is unavailable or distorted in the Soviet media and distribute them to eligible party and government officials. These documents come in several editions differing in completeness; the higher an official's rank, the broader and franker the coverage of the news bulletins. This knowledge serves as both an instrument and a reward of power.[12]

Members of the nomenklatura elite, whatever their personal and institutional rivalries, are bound together by a common **nomenklatura class interest:** to sustain the autocratic, hierarchical political system that provides them with material advantages and at least a sliver of power. The threat of losing these privileges and power operates as a strong deterrent to displacing their superiors: inducements shade into coercion.

Inducements offered in exchange for the cooperative support of nonelite citizens are considerably skimpier but not insignificant. Probably the most important is **basic economic security** through guaranteed employment (however inefficient), provision of education and health services of some sort for everyone, subsidized vacations, and retirement benefits.

By one rough quantitative estimate, the average standard of living in the USSR is only one-third to one-half of that in the United States, and much worse if the quality of goods is considered. But few Soviet citizens know much about conditions in other countries, and they are most likely to compare their standard of living with their own past. For the last three decades or so, average real income has gone up a small amount nearly every year, and there have been some improvements in consumer goods and services.[13] Soviet citizens presumably view as relative progress conditions that would be intolerable in the West or provoke rebellion even in such communist countries as Poland. Consumers' choices are determined largely not by their demands or desires but by the wielders of autocratic political power.

Toleration

Ruling elites in the Soviet and similar communist regimes explicitly reject the political strategy of toleration. Lenin's charge that the power of bourgeois money actually dominates the politics of parliamentary republics, despite trivial competition between parties, remains the orthodox ideological line. Official ideologists claim that the absence of distinct economic classes in the Soviet Union and kindred **"people's democracies"** guarantees that the vanguard party will represent the interests of *all* the people.

If there is no competitive democracy, still there are numerous elections in all communist countries. In the Soviet Union alone some 2.3 million people are elected by universal suffrage to formal legislative institutions, from the local to the national level. More than 20 million are involved as candidates, their agents, members of electoral commissions, and turn-out-the-vote "agitators"—one for every eight voters.

Elections are massively publicized, and voting is proclaimed to be every citizen's urgent moral duty. On election day each "agitator" is responsible for getting a particular group of voters to the polls, if necessary seeking them out personally. It might be difficult for voters to work up a great deal of enthusiasm otherwise, since there is always only one Communist Party-approved candidate for each position, and these elected bodies have no decision-making powers.[14]

Why do Soviet leaders invest so much time and effort in noncompetitive elections for powerless offices? The reported turnout is usually about 99.9 percent of eligible voters, and only a handful of voters cast negative ballots by crossing out the candidate's name. We agree that a basic political function of Soviet-style elections is to demonstrate to everyone the ideologically claimed complete cohesion of the society, serving as "a means of social pressure, probably as powerful as coercion. How can one escape from the unanimity, from the feeling of belonging to a system supported by everyone?" In addition, Soviet rulers "find in elections a source of legitimacy. What counts . . . is not the representation of those elected but the **demonstration of unanimity** around the leaders and the Party program, for which elections are the pretext."[15]

The leaders' desire for unanimous support does not mean that they allow absolutely no criticisms of the government or the party. Complaints about local problems and officials are usually permissible and may even be published. This is a means of releasing some popular antagonisms and of permitting superior officials to check on their subordinates.

Early in his tenure as general secretary, Mikhail Gorbachev proclaimed a new openness (*glasnost*) in public airing of Soviet problems. Information about such formerly taboo subjects as drugs began to appear in the media, as did a greater volume of exposés of and complaints about bureaucratic failures, foul-ups, and disasters. There was no sign, however, that toleration would be extended to criticisms of top policy makers, their policies, the system of government, or the party.

In the economy, the Soviet regime grudgingly tolerates, out of necessity, certain practices that seem inconsistent with the official ideology. **Private plots** tilled by collective farm families are legal, and, though comprising only 4 percent of farm land, they produce 25 percent of Soviet crops. Agricultural bureaucrats resist the expansion of these plots, however, because their existence makes it even more difficult to get peasants to work on collective farm projects.

In addition, there is a sizeable **second economy** that involves trading and bartering of goods and services, as well as securing and selling items otherwise unavailable to nonelite consumers. Much of this activity is illegal, and there are occasional arrests, sometimes even executions to deter large-scale operators. Usually, though, party and government elites tolerate illegal activities that may add up to a quarter of the total economy. One component of the second economy—moonlighting by regularly employed workers—was legalized in 1987, but the income it produced was also taxed for the first time. The second economy meets a part of the consumer demand ignored by official emphasis on heavy industry and the military. There is also evidence, even from Soviet arrests and trials, of nomenklatura profiteering from the black market.[16]

Elimination

Totalitarian regimes have implemented the physical removal of opponents, whether actual or simply as defined by ideological categories, on an astonishing scale. Hitler's armed crusade for creating a new racial order in

Europe cost perhaps 50 million lives through warfare and his racist "purification" program of systematically murdering 6 million Jewish men, women, and children.

For the Soviet and other communist systems we do not have nearly as accurate data as for the Nazis, whose defeat brought their records into Western hands. In the 1970s a Russian geophysicist, Iosif Dyadkin, attempted to estimate the number of **"unnatural" deaths in the USSR** during the Stalin era, using nothing but published census data. For writing and sending this document abroad he was arrested and imprisoned for "defaming" the Soviet state.[17]

Dyadkin estimated that from 1929 to 1936, when massive collectivization was accomplished in the countryside, 10 to 16 million people perished as "class enemies" or as victims of deliberately engineered famine. About 1.5 million died in Stalin's blood purge of the Communist Party in the late 1930s, 30 million in the Second World War, half a million or more in labor camps after the war. A substantial percentage of the war deaths—perhaps half or more—resulted not from German hostilities but from Stalin's policies, which included mass deportations of "suspect" ethnic groups and imprisonment of people reported by informers.

Anton Antonov-Ovseyenko, son of a Bolshevik military leader and diplomat who was killed in Stalin's great purge, contends that Stalin's victims were even more numerous. Apparently drawing upon information from high-ranking Soviet officials who knew his father, he also cites a study of Stalin's murderous record supposedly commissioned by the Politburo under Khrushchev but never completed or made public. Antonov-Ovseyenko concludes that the collectivization drive took 22 million lives; the 1930s party purge brought the arrest of 19 million, most of whom perished; repression during and after the Second World War resulted in 9 million deaths. He agrees with Dyadkin that at least 15 million wartime Soviet fatalities should be attributed to Stalin's policies.[18]

We shall probably never be able to check these or other estimates against official records. It has gradually become apparent, though, that Stalin and his collaborators were responsible for the deaths of tens of millions of defenseless civilians.

Estimates of regime-inflicted deaths range widely for Maoist China, although tens of millions seem likely if famine caused by ideologically inspired efforts to revolutionize the countryside overnight is factored into the grisly equation. A massive apparatus of penal and labor camps, as well as an admission by Mao's successors of the famine deaths caused by his policies, began to come to light in the 1970s. Again, no archives are available; one cautious estimate of the Mao regime's defenseless victims is 33.5 million.[19]

In Cambodia: "From the middle of 1975 to the end of 1978, between one million and three million Cambodians, out of a population of about seven million, died at the hands of Pol Pot's Khmer Rouge." The **Khmer Rouge** was a communist movement "run by Paris-educated ideologues" who sought total transformation of Cambodian society; their first step was to execute former government employees, army personnel, and "intellectuals"—almost any literate person—by the hundreds of thousands. Others died from disease, exhaustion, and malnutrition during forced evacuations of cities and labor performed at gunpoint.[20]

Totalitarian mass killing has resulted in each case from revolutionizing elites' ideological fanaticism and determination to seize, protect, and maximize their power. Leaders advancing radical policies meet with opposition (or, as Hitler and Pol Pot did, anticipate it) and counter it with overwhelming coerciveness and brutality. The immense human costs are "willfully and premeditatively incurred by groups of self-appointed visionaries who have scorned the methods of experimentation and adjustment and who have openly believed that they act on a historical level beyond the conscious comprehension of the ordinary person."[21]

Elimination as totalitarian strategy does not necessarily involve mass killing. In Castro's Cuba there have been many political executions since 1959, but nothing on the Nazi, Soviet, Chinese, or Cambodian scale.[22] Instead, about 10 percent of the 10 million Cubans have emigrated, mainly to the United States. The willingness of the U.S. government to accept anticommunist Cubans allowed Castro to get rid of large numbers of actual

The most murderous noncommunist totalitarian regime was Hitler's Nazi Germany. In this horrifying photograph taken by U.S. soldiers who liberated the Buchenwald prison camp in 1945, we see a small sampling of the millions of innocent victims of Nazism.

or potential opponents without "engaging in mass extermination . . . or worse, genocidal decimation of a large chunk of the Cuban population. Thus Cuba's Stalinization has been comparatively benign: **Stalinism with a human face.**"[23]

Since the mid-1960s Castro has been heavily subsidized and advised by the Soviet Union, and his less bloody but unrelenting efforts to eliminate opposition may reflect the post-Stalin strategy of Soviet elites. They have replaced Stalin's massive, unpredictable, and universally menacing police terror with a more limited and relatively predictable use of official terror against actual critics and opponents. As a dissenter and victim of this **rationalized repression** observes, "It's enough to arrest one out of every ten and of those who have seen the light—the most uppity ones—to frighten all the others. It's not like the old days."[24]

By one CIA estimate, there are about 10,000 political prisoners in the USSR, plus an unknown number of "troublesome" people forcibly held and "treated"—very painfully—in mental hospitals. Not much confidence can be placed in this figure, which "is far lower than some cited by informed Soviet dissidents."[25] Post-Stalin experience suggests that the number arrested and imprisoned may be less significant than the virtual certainty that open protest against the regime, its leaders, or its policies will be severely punished.

Finally, the Soviets have eliminated the influence of some dissidents by exiling them, either against their will or as a coerced alternative to a labor camp. This is an effective tactic because Westerners usually pay little attention to exiled Soviet writers and intellectuals.

Problems of Legitimacy

Difficult problems for the rulers of institutionalized totalitarian systems grow out of those regimes' relationship to one of the basic forms of political power—authority. To conclude our discussion of totalitarianism, we will focus on this issue with particular regard to the Soviet Union.

Science and Soviet Ideology

Permit us a preliminary comment on the intellectual authority of Soviet Marxism-Leninism. Official communist terminology calls this ideology **scientific socialism,** or, as the 1977 constitution has it, *scientific communism.* The label alludes to Engels's claim that Marx was the Darwin of the social and historical sciences, discoverer of the true laws of motion of human societies. Given the enormous achievements and prestige of modern natural science, it is not surprising that this claim contributed to the intellectual appeal of Marxism over many decades. Other nineteenth-century theorists, whose ideas differed from Marx's, also claimed for them scientific truth. Some of these writers helped construct a racist ideology that eventually formed the basis of Hitler's Nazism, a doctrine he firmly believed to be based on the most important scientific truth about humanity.

Leaving aside the still-debated issue of the scientific usefulness of Marx's approach to historical interpretation, we believe that Soviet Marxism-Leninism is no more scientific than was Hitler's national socialism. Both are **closed doctrinal systems** backed by claims of finality and infallibility, subject to interpretation and application only by autocratic rulers. Whatever the disagreement among modern philosophers of science, none contends that a scientific theory or hypothesis is final and complete truth not open to question.

A scientific outlook requires that all ideas be subject to analysis, criticism, and refutation on the basis of sound logic and relevant empirical evidence. Authority—whether political, religious, or academic—cannot dictate scientific truth; it is never final and infallible but only the best we can currently formulate and cannot yet disprove. However fiercely individual scientists may sometimes defend their own theories and irrationally reject contrary evidence, the process of scientific inquiry legitimizes rational-empirical criticism of all claims to truth. It is completely incompatible with totalitarian rigidity and hostility toward scientific criticism of official claims and doctrines. There is at least impressionistic evidence that the scientific claims for Soviet ideology are no longer taken very seriously even by many communist intellectuals or by natural scientists in the Soviet Union.

The most elementary truths about the nature of science, however, do not prevent Marxist-Leninist ideologues from claiming exclusive *scientific* validity for their doctrines. For example, in a 1981 secret speech to Sandinista army and militia officers in Nicaragua, Defense Minister Humberto Ortega declared: "Marxism-Leninism is the scientific doctrine that guides our revolution, the instrument of analysis of our Vanguard for understanding [the revolution's] historic process and for carrying out the revolution. . . ."[26] For some people, apparently, the very word *science* is still magical, however unscientifically and manipulatively it may be used.

An Ideological Power Elite

On the larger question of how to understand the problems of political authority in the Soviet political system and how they affect its operations and prospects, scholarly views and opinions differ. The interpretation that best fits our understanding of and emphasis on political power might be called the **ideological power elite** interpretation.[27] Historical experience strongly suggests that elites who hold and benefit from concentrated political power do not voluntarily limit it, much less intentionally give it up.

We also believe that the ideological power elite interpretation has best stood the test of experience since Stalin's death in 1953. At that time many Western analysts predicted significant liberalization of the Soviet system and its evolution toward political pluralism and constitutionalism. Mass terror was ended, but neither substantial cultural tolerance nor acceptance of peaceful criticism and opposition has been allowed to develop. As we suggested in chapter 8, large-scale state terror was halted because the new rulers were determined to prevent the emergence of another Stalin. From their perspective, his major crime had been to attack the party, including its highest ranks. But enforceable constitutional restraints on state coercion would undercut their supreme power.[28] Their solution was, of course, the turn to "rational," more limited, but inescapable state terror. It proved adequate for virtually eliminating the "democratic movement" of human rights activists and peaceful dissenters in the 1970s.

As we have explained, the Soviet and other communist systems are ruled by a pyramid-shaped political organization, the party. Policy-deciding power is monopolized by the self-perpetuating elites—the Soviet Politburo, for one—who control all appointments, promotions, and removals within the bureaucratic apparatus that in turn controls the pyramid. Party and governmental leaders cannot and do not claim legitimacy on the basis of public choice in contested elections.

Sometimes that lack of choice is deliberately obscured by Soviet spokesmen, as when General Secretary Gorbachev declared, in a 1985 interview, that there must be no "confrontation" between the Soviet Union and the United States: "This is a reflection of the interests of our two peoples and of the politicians who represent them. It is after all the people of the two countries who put the politicians into the positions they hold today."[29] Gorbachev was in fact selected only by his Politburo colleagues, who owed their positions to no one except other Politburo members.

More comprehensively speaking, the total Soviet power elite is virtually synonymous with the political nucleus of the nomenklatura, which includes all executive decision makers in party and government. Whatever their rivalries—and they are numerous, as every bureaucrat tries to protect and advance the interests of his or her own office or department—they have a fundamental shared interest in preserving the system of autocratic party control of government and society.

Those at the very top are likely to feel this concern most keenly, for they have devoted their lives to the system, and it has richly rewarded them with power and a luxurious standard of living. It is not surprising that they should show great concern for propagating an official ideology that identifies their organization as the supreme agent of inevitable human progress and therefore one that is entitled to rule as its leaders see fit.

Table 9-1 Party preferences of Eastern Europeans traveling in Western Europe

Home country:	1974–1977			1978–1981		
	Czech.	Hungary	Poland	Czech.	Hungary	Poland
Communist Party	4%	8%	4%	3%	7%	4%
Democratic Socialist Party	43%	42%	46%	43%	42%	35%
Christian Democratic Party	25%	25%	28%	29%	26%	34%
Peasant Party	5%	17%	11%	3%	11%	15%
Conservative Party	7%	5%	4%	8%	10%	7%

Adapted from Henry O. Hart, "The Tables Turned: If East Europeans Could Vote," *Public Opinion,* October/November 1983, pp. 53–57; reprinted with permission of the American Enterprise Institute.

Legitimacy and Nonelites

How successful have ruling communist parties been in generating genuine authority for themselves—broad belief in their right to rule and the citizens' obligation to obey? That is the main purpose of the massive organized efforts at nursery-to-grave indoctrination. Since unofficial, uncontrolled social science research is not allowed in such countries, relevant opinion data are hard to find.

One suggestive source consists of Radio Free Europe polls of visitors to Western Europe from Czechoslovakia, Hungary, and Poland, three countries with Soviet-style communist regimes. They allow considerably more foreign travel than do the Soviets, although ordinary citizens are usually restricted to one exit visa every three years. Tourists in the opinion surveys conducted from 1974 to 1981 were asked what kind of party they would vote for in a free election.

Table 9-1 shows that respondents who favored a communist party ranged from 3 to 8 percent of the sample. Overwhelming majorities would vote for a democratic socialist or a Christian democratic party, such as those that predominate in most Western European countries. These fragmentary data suggest enormous **problems of legitimacy** for long-established communist regimes. So also did the quick disintegration of party control in Hungary in 1956, Czechoslovakia in 1968, and Poland in 1980–1981.

Similar opinion data are not available for the Soviet Union, and scholars disagree about the degree of legitimacy accorded the regime by its subjects. The classic Marxist-Leninist claims to authority—that the party is leading in a movement toward equal abundance for all, direct self-rule, and the withering of the state—are no longer stressed in official indoctrination. As recently as Khrushchev's 1961 New Program of the Communist Party those themes were reemphasized, but in 1985, "Gorbachev announced that the embarrassing document [the 1961 Program], technically still in effect, had been rewritten to excise parts that in his view 'have not stood the test of time.'"[30]

If nearly everyone today, communist and noncommunist, recognizes that the "withering of the state" is nothing but nineteenth-century mythology, why don't Soviet leaders attempt to provide consumer abundance for their people as an authority-building inducement? After all, the Hungarian regime has taken that approach and has had some success with its "goulash communism."

A partial answer is that the centralized, party-dominated Soviet economic system is too inflexible, providing no rewards for risk and innovation but only for quantitative plan fulfillment. In order to meet consumer demands, individual plant and store managers would need to be given much more authority, and market relations between buyers and sellers would have to be tolerated on a much broader scale. Very modest changes in these directions have been proposed occasionally by Soviet economists and even tried briefly on a small scale. But they have been fiercely resisted by party bureaucrats threatened with losing their directive power over economic operations and the accompanying rewards and privileges.[31]

If the consumer-abundance route to building legitimacy is rejected as threatening the power of ruling elites, is indoctrination sufficient? Their actions suggest that Soviet elites don't think so. If they could count on nearly everyone for willing obedience, they wouldn't need the vast security police apparatus, and peaceful criticism could be shrugged off rather than treated as a deadly threat. The consistent practice of most communist regimes most of the time inclines us toward Paul Hollander's view that

> the massive presence and apparent permanence of coercive institutions "legitimate" Marxist societies by making them seem immovable and basically unchangeable, by eliminating the prospect of alternatives. Consequently, people will accept the system and bring their discontent or frustrations under control; most certainly they will not entertain ambitions to change their society. The result is a kind of "legitimacy"—the passive acceptance of the immovable object. Hence Marxist societies, and especially those which have been in existence for several decades, unexpectedly acquire certain attributes of a traditional society: they are accepted because the citizens, living in an environment from which conceptions of alternatives have been carefully removed, cannot conceive of other ways of being governed and regard the system as "natural."[32]

Even Seweryn Bialer, a political scientist who believes that in the Soviet Union "broad strata of the population exhibit a basic identification with the Soviet system as it is," describes this identification as "unconscious, amorphous, and unfocused." It leads not to an active willingness to sacrifice oneself for the system but to a **political apathy** that doesn't threaten it. Bialer emphasizes mainly the legitimacy the regime enjoys among the strategic political and military elites, since it is open disagreements within the elite that are most likely to weaken a political system fatally (see chapter 12). Elite consensus seems very strong in the Soviet Union, and it includes not only the "leading role" of the Party but "deep-seated nationalism and a great-power orientation which provides the major effective durable bond among the elites and between the elite and the masses."[33]

Problems of Legitimacy and Soviet Foreign Policy

In our judgment, Soviet rulers have attempted in part to cope with their regime's problems of legitimacy by building up military power and expanding their political influence abroad wherever possible without great risks. Since Stalin's time the regime's top economic priority has been heavy industry, creating the essential basis for an ever-expanding military establishment. Its growth is another basic reason for the constant shortage of many consumer goods for nonelites.

Stalin rallied support by pointing to the supposed threat of "capitalist encirclement," and decades later his successors justify an enormous military buildup by raising the specter of "imperialist aggression." Long after the end of the Second World War, the Soviet Union's costly and heroic victory in the "Great Patriotic War" with Nazi Germany is one of the most common themes in all political education and indoctrination. Clearly implied is the ongoing necessity of patriotic enthusiasm for the heroic Soviet armed forces.

At the core of the Soviet regime is a **"defense-heavy industry complex"** that many members of the top elite serve or have served at some point in their careers. Giving its interests first priority constitutes for them "a value, belief, and policy orientation that cuts across the organizational and functional lines of the elite establishment."[34]

The Soviets' large and diversified military capability enables top elites to pursue policies that reinforce their ideology. The survival, increasing strength, and multiplying of Soviet-style communist regimes prove to them that they are the historically inevitable **wave of the future.** Soviet leaders have essentially continued Lenin's policy of helping the inevitable to happen by seizing opportunities for power, however unripe for a proletarian revolution a country may be. At the same time, military might provides an ultimate weapon for elites against potential trouble on the home front: "Soviet citizens know that the Soviet authorities do not want to use coercion against them but that they have the military means to crush any mass movement."[35] Such movements were put down by Soviet military forces in Hungary in 1956 and in Czechoslovakia in 1968. The threat of Soviet military intervention enabled Polish security forces to crush the independent mass trade union, Solidarity, in 1981 without provoking a general uprising.

Soviet responses to challenges to their political orthodoxy in Eastern Europe and in 1979 in Afghanistan provide strong support for the ideological power elite interpretation. Rumanian leaders have differed frequently with the Soviets on foreign policy, ranging from a refusal to provide troops for the Warsaw Pact invasion of Czechoslovakia in 1968 to participation in the Soviet-boycotted Olympics in 1984. In post-1956 Hungary, party head Janos Kadar has allowed the reestablishment of small-scale private business, and much of the economy operates according to market principles rather than centralized planning. In neither case has the Soviet regime intervened to halt these **ideological deviations.** In 1968 in Czechoslovakia the reform-minded Communist Party leaders pledged to remain faithful to the Warsaw Pact, but the Soviets invaded and replaced them with "reliable" men.

Why this difference? Essentially because the Communist Party power monopoly seemed threatened in Czechoslovakia: a new party program had even denounced the "dictatorship of the proletariat" as a "false thesis." Freedom of speech and other political freedoms were under serious consideration within the party. That was not the case in Rumania, which has at least as totalitarian a system of control as the Soviets'. Neither is it true of Hungary, where the 1956 Soviet invasion forced Hungarians to accept one-party rule as an unchangeable fact of life.

After the invasion of Czechoslovakia, the Soviet general secretary proclaimed his **Brezhnev doctrine.** It declares that every "socialist" country has a "fraternal duty" to prevent the triumph of "counterrevolution" in any member of the socialist commonwealth.[36] This means any departure from ideological communism, which the Soviets interpret as requiring uncontested rule by the vanguard party. That kind of rule is the defining feature of a truly socialist revolution, which is historically "irreversible." In Afghanistan also, it was apparently popular resistance to a new and very shaky "vanguard" regime that prompted Soviet military intervention.

For the same reason, the Soviets could not tolerate Polish Solidarity. Its mass appeal, broad-scale organization, and determined leadership not only suspended for fifteen months the party's domination of Polish politics but threatened to eclipse the party's influence permanently. As a former U.S. correspondent in Poland observed, the Soviets were unquestionably willing to use their military power, if necessary, to eliminate any Polish "movement dangerous to Soviet interests as the Soviet Union sees its interests. And that means any . . . movement that would demonstrate . . .

that the core of the Soviet power structure—a self-perpetuating party leadership in control of all aspects of life—could be successfully challenged."[37]

In addition to the resolute defense of "fraternal" party-monopoly systems in neighboring countries, the Soviets seek to provide **ideological dynamism** for a domestically immobile regime by supporting communist movements and regimes in the Third World. In countries such as Cuba, Angola, Ethiopia, Vietnam, South Yemen, and Nicaragua, they have used military and economic aid and advisers and trainers for military and security forces to help create and protect regimes ideologically and organizationally similar to their own (see chapter 11).

Some people in such countries have been attracted by the Soviet political model. It seems to assure well-organized elite control along with ready-made ideological justifications for destroying the old order and establishing their own autocracy. The more the model is imitated, however imperfectly, and especially with Soviet aid and sponsorship, the more convincing the ideological argument of historic inevitability may seem. At the same time, this line of policy extends the influence of Soviet ruling elites to additional countries and presumably reinforces their own ideological self-confidence. It may also make it seem increasingly hopeless to resist their already established domination.

None of this discussion implies that totalitarian communist systems are unchangeable or necessarily permanent. Neither does it suggest that problems of legitimacy alone will lead to sweeping changes in these regimes. On the one hand, the communist systems in Hungary, Czechoslovakia, and Poland went far toward unraveling and undergoing political transformation as a result of elite disagreements or of mass protest and counter-organization. In those countries there proved to be limits to the capabilities of domestic coercion. On the other hand, their communist regimes survived because they were supported by the military power of their huge Soviet neighbor.

Communist governments beyond Soviet control, such as those in China and Yugoslavia, have introduced significant doses of "capitalism" into their economies. In neither case, though, is there real freedom from the central control of the Communist Party, whose political monopoly remains intact.

The central question about change in contemporary totalitarian systems concerns the Soviet Union. We are inclined to doubt that significant change in the ideological power-elite-dominated system is likely so long as organization and policies function to reward and protect the power of the nomenklatura from top to bottom of the bureaucratic pyramid. Only overwhelming economic problems or the failure of high-risk foreign policy initiatives might shake elite confidence enough to produce a public split, with unpredictable consequences for the system. That possibility seems very remote.[38]

The internal system of competing for positions at the top level of decision making strongly discriminates against innovators and favors supreme commitment to preserving autocratic nomenklatura power. Institutionalization of the Soviet totalitarian system seems to have increased its capacity for self-perpetuation. Politically speaking, the most likely prospect is for more of the same.

Summary

The central ruling, directing, and controlling organization in a totalitarian communist system is the official party. It has a large membership, but applicants are screened carefully to assure their loyalty and willingness to engage in party work. Many people join mainly to improve their career prospects.

The party is run by a fulltime professional bureaucracy headed by an autocratic, self-perpetuating oligarchy of top leaders. Party structure is formally democratic, but in reality all elections of party officers and delegates are dictated by higher-level officials. Party members are expected to support the party's policies unwaveringly and to obey absolutely all orders from their superiors.

In the Soviet Communist Party the Politburo, a committee of about a dozen members headed by the general secretary, is the supreme directing and policy-making body for the government and society, which the party apparatus dominates. The Politburo in fact determines the membership of the Central Committee, which formally elects members to the Politburo. The Politburo also decides who its own members will be, including the general secretary.

In large measure, top officials control the enormous party-government dual bureaucracy through the nomenklatura system. It is a massive but secret system of patronage that presumably covers all executive positions within the society. Political loyalty and reliability as interpreted by party elites are absolute requirements for appointment to these posts—and for keeping them, since there is no guaranteed bureaucratic tenure.

Nomenklaturists have much more power, a much higher standard of living, and many more privileges than ordinary party members, and incomparably more than nonparty citizens. So long as they follow orders and please their superiors, nomenklaturists have some prospect of rising even higher in the steeply graded pyramid of power and privilege. These rewards operate as powerful inducements for their recipients to support strongly the system of autocratic party rule. Inducements for ordinary citizens consist mainly of economic security, provided at a standard that is quite low for an industrialized society but represents some improvement over the past.

Although the ruling party tolerates no public political criticism or opposition, it sponsors numerous elections for party and government offices and puts pressure on everyone to vote. The voting ritual reinforces the message of complete party domination and provides autocratic rulers with some semblance of legitimacy.

As a rule, totalitarian rulers determinedly pursue the power strategy of elimination, as exemplified by Hitler's ideologically motivated mass murder of 6 million Jews. In the Soviet Union Stalin eliminated tens of millions of "enemies of socialism" through false charges and political trials, disappearances and executions, and fatal confinement in labor camps. Similar policies produced millions of deaths in Maoist China and in Khmer Rouge-controlled Cambodia. Castro's strategy of elimination has mainly involved exporting a million Cubans to the United States.

In the post-Stalin era the Soviet regime has switched from Stalinist mass murder to rationalized repression, imprisoning or confining to mental hospitals only actual critics and dissenters. The number of political prisoners is secret but substantial.

Totalitarian regimes tend to have real difficulty in getting people to think of the autocratic elites as morally entitled to rule. They always claim legitimacy on the basis of ideology, but over time that claim loses much of its original persuasiveness. Instead of dying out, the state grows tremendously and becomes much more coercive, and equality and abundance for all fail to develop. Marxism-Leninism increasingly functions as mere rationalization for the dictatorial power and privileged status of the self-appointed vanguard. The claim of scientific truth for the official ideology becomes entirely hollow and ritualistic, since science requires that all claims to truth be open to criticism and rational argument.

In our view, the defining and most enduring feature of Soviet-style communist systems is domination by a determined and tenacious ideological power elite—the nomenklatura. They monopolize political power and possess strong individual and class interests in protecting, expanding, and legitimizing it. They try to do so in part through semicoercive and inescapable ideological indoctrination. Questionnaire data from Eastern Europeans touring in the West and fragmentary reports of Soviet opinion studies suggest a low level of enthusiasm for the ruling elites and their ideological definition of good citizenship. A semitraditional kind of legitimacy, which accepts the political system because it seems impossible to move or change it, encourages apathetic obedience from the bulk of the population.

The nomenklatura elites presumably regard the Soviet regime as highly authoritative because their whole lives are devoted to serving the system, enjoying its benefits, and striving for even greater rewards. They have supported a continuous emphasis on heavy industry and military growth, as well as political, secret-police, military, and economic aid to "fraternal" regimes in the Third World. These policies enable the elites to protect their

European empire and to project their system as the inevitable wave of the future in the rest of the world. Soviet rulers react most strongly against any threat to the political monopoly of a ruling communist party in Eastern Europe, fearing the spreading consequences if any such system proves not to be irreversible.

Some communist regimes have experimented with certain ideologically deviant policies, although none has relaxed the most basic Marxist-Leninist requirement of autocratic rule by the official party. The Soviet Union is the linchpin of present-day institutionalized totalitarianism; its power-monopolizing and highly privileged nomenklatura class is likely to keep it that way into the indefinite future.

Review List of Key Terms

Politburo
Secretariat
primary party organizations
democratic centralism
Party Congress
Central Committee
General Secretary
Supreme Soviet
dual bureaucracy
nomenklatura

political nucleus
bureaucratic tenure
nomenklatura class interest
basic economic security
"people's democracies"
demonstration of unanimity
private plots

second economy
"unnatural" deaths in the USSR
Khmer Rouge
"Stalinism with a human face"
rationalized repression
scientific socialism
closed doctrinal systems

ideological power elite
problems of legitimacy
political apathy
"defense-heavy industry complex"
wave of the future
ideological deviations
Brezhnev doctrine
ideological dynamism

Notes

1. Trans. Andrew Arato and Richard E. Allen (New York: Harcourt Brace Jovanovich, 1979). The authors are Hungarian intellectuals.
2. Ronald J. Hill and Peter Frank, *The Soviet Communist Party* (London: George Allen & Unwin, 1983), pp. 21–25.
3. Frederick C. Barghoorn and Thomas Remington, "Politics in the U.S.S.R.," in *Comparative Politics Today: A World View,* 3rd. ed., ed. Gabriel A. Almond and G. Bingham Powell (Boston: Little, Brown, 1984), p. 309.
4. Hill and Frank, *The Soviet Communist Party,* pp. 71–72.
5. Ibid., p. 72.
6. Ibid., p. 65.
7. Annie Kriegel, "The Nature of the Communist System: Notes on State, Party, and Society," in *The State,* ed. Stephen R. Graubard (New York: Norton, 1979), p. 146.
8. Hill and Frank, *The Soviet Communist Party,* pp. 41–42, 86; Michael Voslensky, *Nomenklatura: The Soviet Ruling Class,* trans. Eric Mosbacher (Garden City, N. Y.: Doubleday, 1984), p. 95.
9. Voslensky, *Nomenklatura,* pp. 71–72.
10. See Walter D. Connor, *Socialism, Politics, and Equality: Hierarchy and Change in Eastern Europe and the USSR* (New York: Columbia University Press, 1979).
11. David K. Shipler, *Russia: Broken Idols, Solemn Dreams* (New York: Times Books, 1983), pp. 222–223.
12. Paul Lendvai, *The Bureaucracy of Truth: How*

Communist Governments Manage the News (Boulder, Colo.: Westview, 1981), pp. 129–130.
13. Vadim Medish, *The Soviet Union*, 2nd ed. (Englewood Cliffs, N. J.: Prentice-Hall, 1984), p. 159. There is some evidence that ordinary people's standard of living may have declined in recent years, especially with respect to medical care and food supplies; see Andrew Nagorski, *Reluctant Farewell: An American Reporter's Candid Look inside the Soviet Union* (New York: Holt, Rinehart & Winston, 1985), pp. 78–106.
14. See Hélène Carrère d'Encausse, *Confiscated Power: How Soviet Russia Really Works* (New York: Harper & Row, 1982), pp. 255–257; Donald D. Barry and Carol Barner-Barry, *Contemporary Soviet Politics: An Introduction*, 2nd ed. (Englewood Cliffs, N. J.: Prentice-Hall, 1982), pp. 91–93.
15. d'Encausse, *Confiscated Power*, p. 261.
16. See Marshall I. Goldman, *USSR in Crisis: The Failure of an Economic System* (New York: Norton, 1983), pp. 55, 83–85.
17. Iosif G. Dyadkin, *Unnatural Deaths in the USSR, 1928–1954* (New Brunswick, N. J.: Transaction Books, 1983).
18. Anton Antonov-Ovseyenko, *The Time of Stalin: Portrait of a Tyranny* (New York: Harper & Row, 1981), esp. p. 307. The greatest work inspired by the Stalin horrors was written by a survivor of the prison camp network (the "gulag") who conscientiously collected the stories of hundreds of innocent victims and incorporated them into a literary, psychological, and moral masterpiece. The author is Nobel Prize winner Alexander Solzhenitsyn; the work is *The Gulag Archipelago*, 3 vols., trans. Harry Willetts (New York: Harper & Row, 1976). This work is banned in the Soviet Union.
19. C. W. Cassinelli, *Total Revolution* (Santa Barbara, Calif.: Clio Books, 1976), pp. 186–187.
20. David Hawk, "The Killing of Cambodia," *New Republic*, November 15, 1982, pp. 17–21.
21. Cassinelli, *Total Revolution*, p. 243.
22. Many political prisoners have died of torture and general maltreatment in Castro's prisons. For the harrowing story of a Cuban poet's twenty-two years of incarceration, see Armando Valladares, *Against All Hope*, trans. Andrew Hurley (New York: Knopf, 1986).
23. Irving Louis Horowitz, "Introduction," in *Cuban Communism*, 5th ed., ed. Irving Louis Horowitz (New Brunswick: N. J.: Transaction Books, 1984), p. 8.
24. Vladimir Bukovsky, "The Soul of Man under Socialism," *Commentary*, January 1979, p. 38.
25. Barghoorn and Remington, "Politics in the U.S.S.R.," p. 347.
26. Quoted in Shirley Christian, *Nicaragua: Revolution in the Family* (New York: Random House Vintage Books, 1986), p. 222.
27. Examples include d'Encausse, *Confiscated Power*; Alain Besancon *The Soviet Syndrome* (New York: Harcourt Brace Jovanovich, 1978); R. V. Burks, "The Arcane Art of Kremlinology," *Encounter*, March 1983, pp. 20–30; Leszek Kolakowski, "Totalitarianism and the Virtue of the Lie," in *1984 Revisited*, ed. Irving Howe, (New York: Harper & Row Perennial Library, 1983), pp. 122–135.
28. For the reasons we have already elaborated, as well as those discussed in the remainder of this chapter, we are unconvinced by political scientist Jerry Hough's contention that something roughly comparable to enforceable constitutional restraints may be developing in Soviet politics. See Hough's fundamental revision of Merle Fainsod's classic text *How Russia is Ruled*, which Hough has retitled *How the Soviet Union is Governed* (Cambridge, Mass.: Harvard University Press, 1979), esp. pp. 554–555. A persuasive reply to Hough's claim that intraelite conflicts place some basic restraint on the exercise of power is presented in George Breslauer's studies of political disagreement among Soviet elites, especially "Khrushchev Reconsidered," *Problems of Communism*, September/October 1976, pp. 18–33.
29. Interview with Mikhail Gorbachev, *Time*, September 9, 1985, p. 26.
30. *Time*, October 28, 1985, p. 62.
31. See Goldman, *USSR in Crisis*, p. 123.

32. Paul Hollander, *The Many Faces of Socialism: Comparative Sociology and Politics* (New Brunswick, N. J.: Transaction Books, 1983), pp. 211–212.
33. Seweryn Bialer, "The Question of Legitimacy," in *States and Societies,* ed. David Held et al. (New York: New York University Press, 1983), pp. 421, 424.
34. Ibid., p. 427. Note also: "There is no doubt that the U.S. has a military-industrial complex, but its power relative to the total GNP pales compared to its Soviet counterpart" (Goldman, *USSR in Crisis,* p. 120).
35. d'Encausse, *Confiscated Power,* p. 331. She seems to mean that the "authorities" don't want to feel a *need* to use military force internally, not that they would hestiate to do so if threatened.
36. See Peter Zwick, *National Communism* (Boulder, Colo.: Westview, 1983), pp. 108–116.
37. A. M. Rosenthal, "The Trees of Warsaw: A Return to Poland," *New York Times Magazine,* August 7, 1983, p. 31.
38. For well-informed and somewhat dissimilar speculations on the possible unintended political consequences of Gorbachev's "reform" campaign, see Vladimir Bukovsky, "Will Gorbachev Reform the Soviet Union?" *Commentary,* September 1986, pp. 19–24; Seweryn Bailer, "How Far Can Gorbachev Go?" *Dissent,* Spring 1987, pp. 188–194.

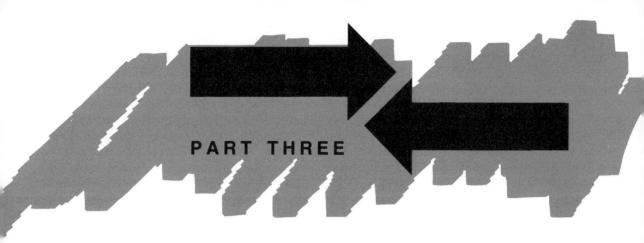

PART THREE

POWER AND INTERNATIONAL POLITICS

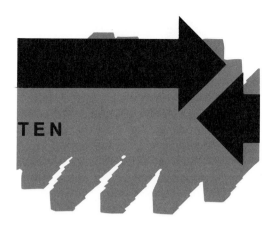

International Politics: Sovereign States and Security

For I dipt into the future, far as human eye could see,
Saw the Vision of the world, and all the wonder that would be;
. . . .
Till the war-drum throbb'd no longer, and the battle flags were furl'd
In the Parliament of man, the Federation of the world.
There the common sense of most shall hold a fretful realm in awe,
And the kindly earth shall slumber, lapt in universal law.
Alfred Lord Tennyson, "Locksley Hall"

In all times kings and persons of sovereign authority, because of their independency, are in continual jealousies and in the state and posture of gladiators, having their weapons pointing and their eyes fixed on one another—that is, their forts, garrisons, and guns upon the frontiers of their kingdoms, and continual spies upon their neighbors—which is a posture of war.
Thomas Hobbes, Leviathan

The preceding chapters have focused mainly upon power, political relationships, and governmental structures within the boundaries of individual states. In Part Three we will consider some important features of political relations among states. These international relationships differ somewhat from politics within a state, most importantly in the absence of centralized government.

As we stated in chapter 1, *the* government is the only institution in a complex society that claims the right to have the final word on how physical force may be legitimately used to enforce society-wide rules. Since *the* government of each state claims this exclusive authority over its citizens, it follows that none recognizes any higher authority, or international government. As we indicated in chapter 2, authority in the full sense does not play a large role in relations among states. To understand what this lack of governmental authority implies for the political interactions of 160-plus states, we need to consider the development and main structural characteristics of present-day international politics.

The Sovereign State in International Politics

Nation-states ("states" for short) emerged as the principal units of government and main actors on the international stage from the sixteenth through the eighteenth centuries in Europe. In our discussion of nationalism (chapter 3), we saw that centralized governments developed more or less gradually in England and France in the medieval period and later in other regions of Europe. In general, successful centralizing monarchies laid the groundwork for statehood by using their armies to pacify the countryside and by erecting defensive barriers against external threats. In these circumstances, "central governments and their creations at lower levels of administration were the only rule-making and rule-applying bodies in defined territories. On the inside, political units such as duchies or walled cities were incapable of challenging central authorities."[1]

Improvements in military technology and capabilities played an important part in transforming the European territorial landscape, in time broadening the range of enforceable law and order. Within the new centralized state, European peoples began to experience a greater degree of physical security in their daily lives.

State authority became consolidated not only domestically but in its relations with such supposed external authorities as the pope and the Holy Roman Emperor. An important milestone in the achievement of the new state's autonomy was the **Treaty of Westphalia,** which in 1648 concluded the devastating Thirty Years War in Central Europe. The war had involved bitter religious conflicts between Catholics and Protestants. It had been fought mainly on German soil by the forces of the Holy Roman Emperor, German princes, and rulers of other continental states.

In the peace treaty, rulers of the surviving German states declared that they would no longer acknowledge the Holy Roman Emperor's authority over them. The parties to this agreement also pledged that the religion of each territorial state would be determined by its ruler. As heads of emerging states, the rulers who signed the treaty had strong personal and collective interests in establishing mutual respect for state autonomy as promised in this document.

The doctrine of **sovereignty** had already been formulated in the sixteenth century by Jean Bodin (1530–1596), a political theorist and legal adviser to the French monarchy. His conception emphasized sovereignty as a government's supreme authority over its own inhabitants and the essential foundation of every state. Later writers broadened this internal legal concept so that it came to include external sovereignty—the legal independence of each state from the authority of any other state or political entity.

Present-day use of the term *sovereign states* refers both to supreme internal authority and to external relationships, with the emphasis on the latter in an international context. To be sovereign is to be subject to no superior authority. Two important implications follow. First, each state should be free from intervention in its internal affairs by other states and should practice nonintervention in return. Respecting the territorial integrity of all states, then, is a basic rule of sovereignty. Second, all states are formally equal, meaning, most importantly, that each has an equal right to defend itself by **self-help.**

In practice, the **equality of states** has been much more easily claimed than secured. The most obvious fact of international life is substantive inequality among states—extreme differences in territorial size, population, resources, wealth, and arms. Generally speaking, "The only equality [that international society] has known has been a rough, precarious equality of the strong."[2]

Yet great and powerful states have not been the only self-interested advocates of sovereignty. When we look at the contemporary **state system**—by which we mean nothing more than the coexistence of independent states—we find the sovereignty concept staunchly defended by rulers of nearly all states, old and new, strong and weak.

Expansion of the Modern State System

The earliest modern states were located in Western Europe and Russia, and their philosophical and legal ideas about statehood derived from European thought. Some sense of cultural commonness assisted the conduct of diplomatic relations among these states and encouraged their mutual acceptance of each other's independence. Since the eighteenth century many states have been formed with non-European cultural and political traditions, but without basic revision of the originally European rules of sovereignty.[3]

The first states outside Europe that European governments regarded as independent members of the state system were their former colonies in North and South America. For example, the United States, Mexico, Brazil, and Haiti extended the geographical scope of that system in the late eighteenth and early nineteenth centuries. Other British colonies settled primarily by Europeans, such as Australia and New Zealand, gradually gained internal self-rule. They readily achieved international acceptance and were able to join the newly formed League of Nations as sovereign states in 1920.

The African state of Liberia, which had developed as a settlement of freed slaves from the United States, declared its independence in 1847. It was quickly recognized by several European governments, although the United States withheld recognition until the Civil War period. The prominence of Christianity in Liberia, as well as in Haiti, helped considerably to encourage European recognition of these non-European states.

More fundamental questions about statehood on European terms arose in the latter half of the nineteenth century, when frequent political and economic contacts developed between Europeans and non-European regimes such as the **Ottoman Empire** (Turkey), China, Japan, Persia (Iran), Siam (Thailand), and Ethiopia. These involvements brought a growing network of treaties and eventually mutual recognition, but not until the non-Europeans had adapted to European diplomatic forms. Brief looks at European relations with the Ottoman Empire and the entry of China and Japan into the state system illustrate these adaptations.

For centuries the Ottoman Empire had been a dominant political force in sizeable regions of Europe and the Near East. Until the nineteenth century it occupied and administered nearly a third of the European continent. Ottoman theories of state and government derived from the Islamic faith and contrasted sharply with the European concept of the state.

Ottoman doctrine held that God is the source of all authority and that law and government exist to enable believers to fulfill their obligations to God. The true Muslim polity is a community of all believers, not confined to any particular territorial state. God's ultimate intention is a universal true-believing community under a single ruler and divine law. Until it can be established, the world will continue to be divided into two spheres, Islamic and infidel. This doctrine doesn't really seem compatible with principles of the equality and territorial integrity of sovereign states.

Yet Ottoman rulers dealt increasingly with European states on European terms, mainly because of the Ottoman Empire's growing military and political weakness. Its envoys began to travel frequently to European capitals to express concern about colonial rivalries affecting Ottoman territories and potentially the very survival of the empire. Its government was gradually drawn into treaties of alliance with various European states, at first produced by negotiations but, as the Ottomans grew weaker, dictated to them by their more powerful partners. By necessity, the Ottoman rulers overlooked their principle of the infidels' inferior political status. In return, the Ottoman regime received recognition as a formally equal sovereign state, signified by its participation in the process of ratifying treaties.

In 1856, when the Treaty of Paris concluded the Crimean War, the Ottoman government was represented at the proceedings and signed the agreement. In that brief war, Britain and France had joined the Turks in turning back a threat of Russian domination over most Ottoman territory in Europe. The empire's more powerful European allies formally pledged to respect and guarantee Ottoman independence and territorial integrity. Though necessarily recognizing its allies' dominance within the treaty relationship, the Ottoman Empire at least gained their explicit commitment to protecting its independence. Actual power differences compromised that independence, but Ottoman rulers believed that relative inferiority was more acceptable in an alliance with Britain and France than within a Russian sphere of influence.[4]

In Asia, China and Japan joined the international state system after long enjoying predominance in their regions. Together with Persia and Siam they sent delegates to the 1899 and 1907 Hague conferences, which discussed limiting armaments and agreeing on practices to be considered as valid **international law.**

The Chinese were accustomed to thinking of their land as the **Middle Kingdom,** center and summit of the entire political universe. In the nineteenth century this ancient sense of superiority had been severely shaken by the Western "barbarian" states' imposing unwelcome treaties upon the Chinese by force of arms. These accords actually required China to acknowledge what Western states had long viewed as obligations of sovereignty. Their effect in China, though, was mainly to promote and protect Western commerce. Treaty provisions required, for example, that China guarantee the lives, liberty, and property of foreign nationals and observe Western standards of diplomatic practice.

In the latter decades of the nineteenth century Japan also reluctantly abandoned self-imposed isolation from the West. Because of its successful "defensive modernization," discussed in chapter 7, Japan was much less vulnerable to Western coercive pressures than was China. In fact, when the Japanese surprisingly won a war with Russia in 1904–1905, Japan was quickly established as a "great power" in the European sense. Whether they were equal or not, the Asian states' presence in the developing international state system began to undercut those sources of unity that had derived exclusively from European history and culture.

When the **League of Nations** was formed after the First World War, 42 states became members. Eventually 63 joined, but some withdrew also. Although the League was originally designed as a worldwide organization, not all states were permitted to join, and some of the eligible states chose not to become members.

The standards actually applied to candidates for admission were political, not necessarily emphasizing careful tests of sovereign independence: "The League . . . emerged from its birthplace as a voluntary association of sovereign and almost-sovereign or prospectively sovereign entities which had not been found on the 'wrong' side in World War I."[5] Germany and the Soviet Union were deliberately excluded at the start, and the United States excluded itself.

As we pointed out in chapters 3 and 7, a spectacular proliferation of new sovereign states has occurred since the Second World War. As the European colonial powers withdrew from their overseas empires, the new nationalist leaders insisted that only sovereign and equal statehood could fulfill their peoples' national aspirations. Nearly all the new states soon became members of the **United Nations** (UN), where they were advantaged by the **"one state, one vote"** decision-making formula in the General Assembly. Ultimately forming a majority bloc, the new Third World states increasingly focused UN debate on decolonization and their economic demands. Originally 51 states, the UN grew in membership to 157 by 1982.

Continuing State-Centeredness of International Relations

Modern states have never been the only participants in international relations. More than three centuries ago the Treaty of Westphalia successfully asserted sovereign states' independence of the papacy, but popes continue to play an active part in international affairs. They try to exert some influence over various actors on the world scene, whether the Polish government or the Palestine Liberation Organization.

On occasion some prominent students of international politics have predicted the demise of the sovereign state.[6] A few contemporary American commentators have contended that the emergence of entities such as multinational corporations, transnational revolutionary movements, and international organizations points to a fundamental transformation of the role of states in a more **"interdependent" world.**[7] A comprehensive and accurate account of international politics can't afford to omit these kinds of groups and organizations.

We believe, however, that a state-centered view of international politics still provides the most realistic perspective; the state system is by no means on the verge of disappearing or losing its importance. As political scientist Kenneth Waltz reminds us, "The death rate among states is remarkably low. Few states die; many firms do."[8]

Two contemporary situations illustrate the continuing primacy of statehood. First, the Palestinian movement is a transnational force that does have an impact on international politics even though it lacks statehood. The central stated objective of all Palestinian factions, however, has been to secure an internationally recognized Palestinian state. In part, they seek statehood because of rivalry with the state of Israel. Also, Palestinian groups have not always been able to rely on Arab states for political support or even for survival. Leaders of those states do not see their interests as identical with the aims of Palestinian organizations. Open and deadly conflict has sometimes erupted between them, as it did in Jordan in 1970 and in northern Lebanon in 1985.

Second, events in Lebanon after 1975 have shown dramatically the practical, protective importance of statehood. Bitter and interminable conflict has brought anarchy to Lebanese society: "Of a state that defends, adjudicates, taxes, heals, educates, governs, there [is] no trace at all."[9] Another observer, trying to explain the power struggle among Lebanese religious communities, remarks on the terrible consequences of the demise of state authority: "The power has come to the Shia during a time of ruin. All in Lebanon battle one another, a vicious cycle of helplessness. In a world of states, the lives of men and sects without a state of their own are chronicles of futility."[10]

In the Marxist-Leninist "socialist" world, the state form is certainly not dying out. In addition to championing the all-encompassing role of the state within their societies, Marxist-Leninist rulers remain committed advocates of state sovereignty. They consider the socialist state to be the only reliable vehicle for participation in world affairs.[11]

For governments in states of all shapes, sizes, and types, claims to sovereign status remain a compelling and mutual self-interest. Transnational corporations, movements, and organizations play their roles in international politics *within* a state-dominated framework.

International Anarchy and the Primacy of Security

The traditional state-centered system of international relations established the concept of sovereignty as a basic decentralizing principle. In political relations among states a key word is *self*: self-limitation, self-judgment, and self-help, which includes the possible use of force. Some kinds of international cooperation and institutions have developed, but **anarchy is the persisting political condition among sovereign states**. Anarchy sometimes implies the complete absence of order, such as has accompanied the endless political violence in Lebanon after 1975. Among states there is always the possibility of violence and war, but complete disorder doesn't prevail, nor is there constant warfare. **International anarchy** is most appropriately defined as the absence of government.[12]

This anarchy produces a persistent insecurity that government leaders responsible for national security can never afford to ignore. They may strongly desire to concentrate their efforts and resources on domestic problems in areas such as the economy, education, or ethnic group relations. Yet they will have no chance to make headway on the home front unless they keep the country secure against coercive threats from foreign powers. Defense against external attack has always been the most fundamental problem and the indispensable function of the territorial state in all of its historic forms.

What is it about **problems of national security** that make government leaders ever sensitive to them?[13] Most important, the costs of wrong decisions in this area can be truly terrible. Even if dire consequences are infrequent, memories of past disasters persist as stern reminders to present-day leaders. They naturally try to draw analogies between earlier crises and the present, seeking to avoid previous mistakes but sometimes making new ones.

Crucially influential twentieth-century experiences of this type include British and French efforts to appease Hitler, as described in chapter 2, and Stalin's attempt to collaborate with the Nazi dictator, referred to in chapter 4. A more recent misjudgment was made by the Israeli government in 1973; its leaders did not realize until too late that their country was about to be attacked by Egyptian forces.

In each of these cases, states whose leaders had erred on the side of optimism about their rivals' intentions eventually defeated their attackers, but only after paying very high prices in lives and resources. Of course, viewing later situations as substantially similar to earlier crises could prove to be a mistake. In new circumstances lack of preparation might have little effect, and there could be a danger of overreacting to a perceived threat. But government leaders must always worry that their failure to be prepared for a security showdown could have disastrous consequences that might have been avoided.

Those who make decisions concerning national security know that errors can have awful results, yet they must decide in the midst of much uncertainty and ignorance. The intentions of other governments are critically important information for decision makers but are often impossible to determine. Even more sophisticated technology and techniques for detecting the development and deployment of weapons cannot provide definitive evidence of political intentions and eliminate **decision-making uncertainty.** For example, since the early years of the Cold War, Western analysts of Soviet intentions have been divided. Some contend that the persistent buildup of Soviet weapons systems should be interpreted as evidence of aggressive and expansionist intentions. Others argue that increases in Soviet military capabilities reflect a defensive paranoia rather than an assertive, offensive stance toward other states.[14]

Twentieth-century developments in military technology have also heightened anxieties about national security. As offensive weapons improved, aggressor states appeared to gain a critical edge, increasing apprehension among leaders of potential target states. This trend has culminated in the development of horrendously destructive nuclear weapons propelled by rocket systems that can deliver them within minutes. Natural boundaries that once afforded time to mobilize a nation to fight an attacker no longer provide protection. The North American continent, previously isolated from European wars, can now be targeted and quickly reached by the ultimate weapon.

National security is always a relative and never an absolute condition. States are unavoidably interdependent in determining their security requirements. If one state seeks additional protection, its neighbors or potential rivals face a **security dilemma.**[15] Even if the new military measures are intended as nothing more than prudent defensive precautions, their very existence could pose a potential threat to other states, whose leaders might then consider it necessary to respond with their own military improvements.

This cycle of defensive and competitive arms increases might conceivably be avoided by the negotiation of mutual limitations. However, trust is difficult to achieve in matters of basic security, even among allies, much less between adversaries. In the absence of political trust and confidence, it is not very likely that negotiations or even treaties will reliably enhance national security. The security dilemma is inescapable. Because of this primary, competitive concern for security, governments' relative power plays an absolutely critical role in international politics.

Power Resources and Effective Power

Justifiably wary about security for their states, governments seek power. Sometimes political actors strive for power as an end in itself. But even government leaders who are not personally obsessed with power seeking can't help recognizing that their states must pursue and use power as the essential means of maintaining their territorial integrity and political independence.

Problems arise in trying to understand or forecast the effects of states' relative power resources in international affairs. There is no consistent, predictable relationship between those resources and the amount of influence that a state actually wields.[16] Many textbooks have carefully enumerated the supposedly objective **elements of national power,** such as population, geographical location and size, natural resources, industrial capacity, technological capabilities, weapons systems, and armed forces. Yet attempts to assess the effectiveness of these potential power resources are seldom successful outside the context of specific policy situations. In practice, large gaps often appear between a state's measurable power resources and the degree of success its government has in getting its way with other states.

In the period between the world wars, any attempt to evaluate national power resources comparatively and objectively would have ranked the United States in first place among the world's states. However, largely because of its isolationist foreign policy, the U.S. government's impact on world politics was minor in comparison with its power potential.

Decades later, when the United States was both much more powerful and much more committed to using its power in international politics, the United States was defeated in its major policy objective in Vietnam. Because of a variety of complex political circumstances, it failed to prevent the military conquest of South Vietnam by communist North Vietnam. Not only, then, do objectively stronger states not always get their way but states "with very weak capabilities are often able to resist the demands of the strong and sometimes achieve their own demands at the expense of the interests of major powers."[17]

Why, then, does a state *need* power resources? A persuasive answer comes from Kenneth Waltz, who suggests four ways in which power capabilities help a state:

1. Power gives a state the means to protect its autonomy when confronted with other states wielding force; more powerful states have better chances of surviving.
2. Greater power provides a government with a wider range of policy choices, even though the outcomes of action remain uncertain.
3. More powerful states enjoy wider **margins of safety**, and weaker states operate on narrower margins.
4. Leaders of states with greater power find that they have a large stake in the existing international system and are inclined to try to "manage" it as much as possible.[18] They invariably find, however, that full-fledged *control* over the system is beyond the means of the most powerful state.

Great Powers in International Politics

A common use of the term *power* in discussions of international politics is to designate some states as **great powers**. For three centuries this term has clearly implied that certain states far exceed all others in whatever counts for international power. In the nineteenth century Prussian historian Leopold Ranke wrote a treatise, *The Great Powers*, defining those states in terms of military capability. A state is a great power, he concluded, when it can maintain its independence even against a sizeable alliance of other states.[19] Ranke's Prussia had entered the ranks of European great powers by militarily winning and holding new territories, gaining recognition of its acquisitions by previously established great powers.[20] As a rule, "Self-revelation of a great power is completed by war."[21]

Nearly all definitions of a great power since Ranke's have identified military might as an essential criterion. A more comprehensively political definition is proposed by Jack Levy:

> A Great Power is defined here as a state that plays a major role in international politics, especially with respect to security-related issues. The Great Powers can be differentiated from other states by their military power, [but also by] their interests, their behavior in general and interactions with other Powers, other Powers' perception of them, and [by] some formal criteria . . . including identification as a Great Power by an international . . . organization.[22]

Traditionally, the major political significance of great powers has been their leading role in efforts to manage and maintain the structural order of the international system. They have acted in that way not for noble or disinterested reasons but to protect their vital interests. In fact, great powers have participated in a disproportionate share of modern wars and largely shaped the postwar peace settlements.

These states also project military power beyond their own borders, sometimes in defense of allies, sometimes to make or protect a conquest. In defining their interests, governments of great powers always interpret security as going beyond territorial protection to include in some cases maintenence of a continental or even a global balance of power. As a rule, with rare but terrible exceptions, great powers have tried to avoid war-provoking crises among themselves. They tend especially—again with exceptions—to avert collisions in regions that any great power considers its own special **sphere of influence.**

Governments of great powers tend to claim that they have a special responsibility for protecting international order. In some cases governments of weaker states expect and are even eager for a great power to intervene constructively in their affairs. The U.S. Marshall Plan, which involved large-scale economic and security assistance to Western European countries starting in the late 1940s, was eagerly encouraged by European governments. At various times United States intervention in the Middle Eastern political morass, whether to provide military aid or to try to revive the "peace process," has been solicited both by Israel and by Arab states such as Egypt and Saudi Arabia. In cases like this, governments of lesser powers still expect a great power to fulfill certain special responsibilities.

Figure 10-1 provides an abbreviated perspective on how the universe of great powers has changed over the past four centuries. It shows that some states holding that rank for centuries—most notably France and Britain—do so no longer and that the Second World War changed the great-power lineup much more drastically than did the First. In fact, the most stunning change was the sudden reduction of great powers from the usual half-dozen or so to only two. Today there is no complete agreement on what states might be classified as "middle powers," but hardly anyone doubts that there are only two great powers, the United States and the Soviet Union.[23] The common term *superpower* signifies that their power status is categorically superior to that of all other states.

In recent years high Soviet officials have increasingly made public claims to great-power status. In a 1971 speech to the Twenty-Fourth Party Congress, then–Foreign Minister Andrei Gromyko declared: "Today there is no question of any significance which can be decided without the Soviet Union."[24] Since that pronouncement, Soviet leaders have not always seemed entirely confident that all other states recognize their equality with the United States as a superpower. According to political scientist Seweryn Bialer, "Soviet leaders and analysts do not use the term 'political parity.' But from what they say and write there clearly emerges a picture of their global *political* expectations which should naturally follow their global *military* attainments."[25]

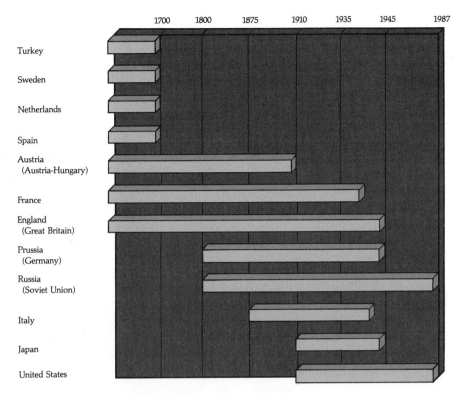

Figure 10-1 Great powers, 1700–1987 (Adapted from Kenneth Waltz, *Theory of International Politics*, New York: Random House, 1979, p. 162.)

Mikhail Gorbachev, general secretary of the Soviet Communist Party, put the "great" or "super" power issue into a slightly different context when he spoke to the press at the 1985 Geneva summit meeting:

> Of course, the Soviet Union and the United States, the two most powerful states with their global interests, with their own allies and friends, they all have their own priorities in matters of foreign policy, but the Soviet leadership sees this not as a source of confrontation but rather as a source of particular responsibility that our countries hold. The Soviet Union and the United States of America and their leaders are responsible for the future of the world; that's how we see it.[26]

Despite general agreement that the United States and the Soviet Union are the greatest of great powers today, scholars differ sharply on the usefulness and effectiveness of superpower military capabilities. We will consider that important question in the next chapter. It doesn't seem at all debatable, though, that there is a very unequal distribution of power in international politics and that it structures and conditions both cooperation and competition among sovereign states.

International Anarchy and International Law

As a rule, great powers have a distinct advantage in competing with other states. International disputes tend to be settled more often on the basis of the predominant power of one or more of the states involved than according to theoretical standards of justice. International norms do exist in the body of international law that has evolved since the fifteenth century. It lays down certain rights and duties of all states in their mutual relations. It is, however, a primitive kind of law, strongly marked by the decentralized character of international relations.

Main Traits of International Law

First, its primary "subjects" have always been states acting through their recognized governments. These subjects have rights, are bound by legal obligations, and can enter into legal relationships with other parties. The category of subjects has been broadened somewhat in the twentieth century. In the Nuremberg and Tokyo trials after the Second World War, for example, individuals were charged with and convicted of what were termed war crimes, crimes against humanity, and crimes against the peace.

However, even while international law is developing to encompass new subjects, it is extremely difficult to extend effective rights beyond states to individuals. A broad Declaration of Human Rights was passed by the United Nations General Assembly in 1948 but has not assured that states will actually respect those rights. The Cambodian mass murders in the 1970s stand as the starkest possible testimony that human rights are infinitely easier to proclaim than to protect internationally.

Second, the most important sources of international law are customs and treaties or conventions in force among states. Others include "general principles," judicial decisions made by national or international tribunals, and the writings of legal scholars.

Customs and treaties are most influential because they develop through the consent of governments, as reflected in persistent common practices or formal agreements. Examples of international legal practices established by these means include a host government's granting immunity from prosecution to foreign diplomats and recognition of the neutrality of noncombatant states in wartime. Clearly, most of what states tend to recognize as binding international law derives from their own practices and explicit agreement—by no means from world legislative or judicial bodies.

Third, international legal institutions do exist, most prominently the **International Court of Justice,** or World Court. It was created by a separate agreement entered into when the United Nations was established. The court, which sits at The Hague, consists of fifteen judges who are elected by the United Nations and serve nine-year terms.

Only states may appear as parties before the World Court. It has no compulsory jurisdiction, so it can consider only cases presented to it by consenting states. Some forty-five states have signed agreements conceding compulsory jurisdiction in cases involving themselves. Most have attached so many reservations that the concession is meaningless.[27] The court is also authorized to issue advisory opinions on international legal questions as requested by organs of the United Nations. Since its creation in 1946, this tribunal has heard few cases.

A 1980 case exemplifies the weakness of the World Court. The United States government requested that it rule on the legality of Iranians—backed by their government—seizing U.S. diplomatic personnel and holding them as hostages in the Teheran embassy. The court ordered the Iranian government to release the hostages and pay reparations to the U.S. government. The government of Iran had denied the court's jurisdiction in the first place and simply ignored its ruling.

The hostage case demonstrates that on some subjects international law is quite well known and almost universally recognized. The legal immunity of diplomatic personnel has become so firmly established in the mutual practices of states that Iran had virtually no international support for its hostage taking. However, the World Court had no authority or any other kind of power to enforce its ruling against the offending Iranians. In short, "even the most charitable apologist for the Court would have to conclude that it has been an extremely ineffective, largely ignored international institution."[28]

Fourth, the principle of self-help authorizes an aggrieved state to retaliate against what its government regards as illegal acts—with either nonviolent or forceful sanctions. This principle reemphasizes the highly decentralized character of international law.

There are traditional standards for judging reprisals, the most important of which is **proportionality:** retaliation must have "some degree of equivalence with the alleged breach."[29] Of course, what one state considers retaliation proportional to the supposed provocation may be denounced by another as unjustified aggression. In 1986 President Reagan ordered air raids on Libyan targets as retaliation for Libyan-sponsored terrorist attacks on U.S. citizens; responses to his action clearly exemplify this point. Ideology and political calculations seemed much more important than legal considerations in determining whether governments approved the attacks as legitimate self-help or attacked them as imperialist aggression—or something in between.

At least some of the founders of the League of Nations and the United Nations hoped to create effective mechanisms for collective action against violations of international law, as we will explain. But many decades after those efforts were launched, self-help has not been displaced as the primary means of enforcing international law.

Criticisms of International Law

The body of international law today continues to be dominated by Western customs and principles developed over the past four centuries. Revolutionary ideologists and regimes often denounce the Western origins of international law and claim that it mainly protects the interests of privileged classes in capitalist states. That is the Soviet view, and their legal theorists insist that a distinctively "socialist" kind of international law applies to relations within their bloc of states.

Soviet understanding of that law is exemplified in the **Brezhnev doctrine,** discussed in chapter 9. It declares that the Soviets have a right, in fact a "fraternal duty," to intervene militarily in other "socialist" countries when socialism is threatened with destruction. It is the Soviet government, of course, that defines *socialism* and decides when this kind of threat exists and what to do about it. In relations with nonsocialist countries the Soviets have adapted somewhat to the diplomatic norms of traditional international law. Some of their legal experts have called this adaptation a prudent course of action to help resist "encirclement" by capitalist states.

Various Third World governments have objected that the rules of international law favor former colonial states and the powerful Western-based multinational corporations. Yet these governments hold strongly to at least some elements of that body of legal principles. The Chinese, for example, have long complained about the **"unequal treaties"** forced on them by Western powers in the century or so before the 1949 communist revolution. Chinese rulers have insisted upon full observance of the "equality of states" principle, although it has often been nullifed in practice by inequalities of power among states: "China's interest is not so much in expanding its rights as in attempting to restrict, and formalize the obligations, of other major powers that have interests in Asia."[30]

Other Third World governments have expressed a central reservation about the concept of sovereignty: it is too abstract. Legal sovereignty does not confer on a state economic means for gaining the relative self-sufficiency that states of the developed world seem to enjoy. The sovereignty principle does provide a certain kind of international sanctity for territorial borders inherited from former colonial overlords. It may help some very weak states to maintain themselves politically, despite inability to protect their boundaries with armed force.[31] As a rule, Third World leaders desire to strengthen their states and enhance their independence.

Challenges do exist to specific traditional principles of international law—for example, the longstanding rule that the territorial jurisdiction of a state extends outward from its shores for only three nautical miles. It was first rejected by states heavily dependent on fishing, such as Iceland and Peru. Gradually many other states saw advantages in unilaterally claiming more extensive territorial waters, and differing official views on this matter have not yet been reconciled.

A multilateral treaty on the law of the sea was negotiated in the 1970s, incorporating a twelve-mile limit for territorial waters. However, it ran into U.S.-led opposition to provisions for international control over resources of the deep seabed. The treaty has not been ratified by a number of technologically advanced states whose industries are most capable of recovering those resources.[32]

The most basic function of any legal system is protection against aggressive attacks, violence, and disorder. It is in this vital sphere that international legal processes are very weak, verging on impotence. International aggression, stockpiles of enormously destructive weapons, terrorist acts against innocent civilians—all remain as dangerous threats to peace and safety. Nothing remotely resembling effective domestic enforcement of law and order exists on the world scene, despite varied efforts starting in the early nineteenth century to create international peacekeeping mechanisms.

Security through International Organization?

With the end of the Napoleonic wars in 1815, government leaders of the European great powers were willing to consider modifications in the decentralized international system. They had been very slow to recognize the threat of French political domination and barely averted it through long and costly warfare. As a result, the idea of cooperating for mutual security seemed practical and appealing. Their cooperative arrangement, however, required no basic changes in the state-centeredness of international politics.[33]

Origins of Modern International Organization

This initial effort to create some kind of international structure for mutual security was called the **Concert of Europe.** It was essentially an exclusive club for the great powers that had triumphed over Napoleon. They pledged to uphold the territorial and political settlements on which they reached agreement at the 1815 Congress of Vienna. The great powers also asserted the right to approve any future changes in those arrangements, even if making good on that claim would require them to intervene within a state to prevent revolution.

The prospect of cooperative intervention was not equally appealing to all of the great-power governments, and gradually their differences about managing European political affairs became apparent. The cooperative efforts of the Concert didn't survive the 1850s, but in the short run it functioned as a joint venture among great powers resting on a nearly unprecedented sense of shared political interests.

The Concert-initiated practice of convening diplomatic gatherings to deal with international issues was continued with conferences at The Hague in 1899 and 1907. They focused on efforts to create a written code of international law and to discuss possible disarmament. As we have mentioned, representation at these conferences was broadened so that Europeans first met on an equal footing with diplomats from non-Western states.

The League of Nations

In the twentieth century, two world wars have inspired efforts to create new institutions for dealing with international security questions in a permanent diplomatic forum. After the First World War, a special commission chaired by U.S. President Woodrow Wilson drew up the Covenant of the League of Nations. Its machinery was designed to implement Wilson's concept of **collective security,** which he publicized with the slogan "peace is indivisible."

Wilson contended that if all governments would agree in advance to isolate and punish any state that committed international aggression, those pledges would threaten any would-be aggressor with overwhelming force. If that possibility failed to deter an aggressor state, the Council of the League would organize joint sanctions for effective punishment of the international lawbreaker. Under those circumstances aggression could not succeed.

In practice, the League's collective security system was a failure. Efforts to mobilize sanctions against Japanese and Italian aggression in the 1930s proved totally ineffective. The United States had refused from the start to join the League and wouldn't participate in its sanctions. The British and French governments weren't sure in 1936 that they really wanted to punish Italy for its invasion of Ethiopia and risk pushing Mussolini closer to Hitler's Germany. Soon thereafter a clear pattern of expansionist German aggression developed, and in 1939 the USSR, a League member, signed a nonaggression treaty with Germany and proceeded to occupy Finland. The members of the League had proved unable, unwilling, or both, to implement the principle of collective security.

The United Nations

In 1945 the architects of the United Nations didn't abandon the concept of collective security but did try to modify it according to more realistic assumptions about the self-interest of sovereign states. The UN Charter clearly assigned responsibility for implementing collective security to its **Security Council,** giving special voting rights to the great-power members of the council—the United States, the Soviet Union, Great Britain, France, and China. As the only permanent members of that body, each great-power government could defeat by its negative vote any proposal for collective action.

Fully aware that this **veto power** would prevent the Security Council from acting against any of the permanent member states, the framers of the charter recognized that collective security could never work against a great power. In 1945 most leaders of the victorious allies of the Second World War assumed that the most likely threat to peace was a resurgence of Germany or Japan. Against those defeated but potentially dangerous powers the five permanent members would surely vote unanimously for sanctions. Postwar political developments soon nullified those assumptions.

By and large, the United Nations has been no more effective in implementing collective security than was the League. Its only action along the lines of the original conception was the **Korean "police action"** from 1950 to 1953. When communist North Korean forces massively invaded South Korea in June 1950, the Soviet Union was boycotting Security Council meetings. As a result, the council was able to vote for a collective military response to what it declared an act of aggression. When the Soviet delegate quickly returned to block further actions, the council could not sustain its original policy.

The United States then persuaded a General Assembly majority to pass the **"Uniting for Peace"** resolution, calling for the assembly to assume responsibility for collective security if a veto blocked Security Council action. However, General Assembly resolutions are nonbinding recommendations, and whether to support them depends entirely upon the decision of each member state.

From the perspective of the original Security Council resolution, the Korean War ultimately realized the goal of thwarting aggression. The fighting ended with an uneasy armistice, but it assured continued South Korean control of all territory below the boundary dividing the two Koreas before the war began in 1950.

However, the "Uniting for Peace" resolution had raised two problems from which collective security has never really recovered. The first, a UN

Charter "constitutional" problem, was whether it was proper to go around both the Security Council and the deliberately designed great-power veto. Second was the great practical difficulty facing even a majority of states in taking military action against a well-armed and determined minority—North Korea supported by Soviet military aid and communist Chinese troops. Even though the prewar status quo was restored, the UN majority coalition had not been able to mobilize the kind of overwhelming coercive force originally assumed in the concept of collective security.

Both of these problems reappeared in 1960 when the General Assembly passed a resolution authorizing a voluntarily constituted United Nations force to restore peace in the former Belgian Congo (now Zaire). The colonial authorities had withdrawn with startling suddenness, and a civil war was raging in the Congo. The military situation was chaotic and confused, and it was extremely difficult to know how to go about restoring order.

Even more damaging for the United Nations effort, however, the Soviet and French governments labeled the General Assembly action an "unconstitutional" violation of the charter. Those governments backed up their objection by withholding financial support from the UN, bringing on a serious financial crisis for the organization. It was overcome only by means of a political understanding that the Security Council could not be circumvented in the future—even if that meant the end of UN collective security actions.

UN and Other "Peacekeeping" Efforts

After the Congo crisis, the UN has retreated to a more modest type of international security activity: peacekeeping. It was conceived by Dag Hammarskjold, UN secretary general from 1953 until his death in a Congo plane crash in 1961. Experience had convinced him that his organization's role in international security must be quite limited, perhaps at most to prevent local conflicts from flaring into confrontations between the great powers. The secretary general would engage in "preventive diplomacy," and the UN would use force only to limit or contain crises.

Since the 1960s the Security Council has generally limited itself to organizing small-scale peacekeeping forces to serve as a buffer between opposing sides. In practice, not to use force has become the first rule of peacekeeping. A small multinational force may be deployed to observe a cease-fire but not to confront an aggressor. The observers are restricted to using force only in self-defense.

A second rule, practically speaking, is that no peacekeeping operation will be undertaken or continued without the explicit consent of the host government. The critical precedent for this rule was the secretary general's quick agreement to the Egyptian government's 1967 request for the withdrawal from Egypt of a **UN peacekeeping** force.

Part of the UN force originally placed in Lebanon in 1978—depicted here in 1986—to observe implementation of military disengagement agreements in southern Lebanon and on the Lebanese–Israeli border.

Third, UN peacekeeping forces almost always consist of troops from smaller countries remote from the dispute in question. It is very unusual for the permanent member states of the Security Council to furnish peacekeepers, as the British did with a troop contingent on Cyprus. U.S. and

Table 10-1 United Nations peacekeeping operations

Dates	Names and Assignments of UN Peacekeeping Groups
1948–	UN Truce Supervision Organization (UNTSO)—to report on armistice between Egypt and Israel, Syria and Israel
1949–	UN Military Observer Group in India and Pakistan (UNMOGIP)—to report on cease-fire observance in Kashmir by Indian and Pakistani forces
1956–57	UN Emergency Force (UNEF I)—to supervise armistice on border between Egypt and Israel
1958	UN Observer Group in Lebanon (UNOGIL)—to investigate Lebanese government charges of Syrian border violations
1960–64	UN Operations in the Congo (ONUC)—to help keep order, prevent secession and external intervention in former Belgian Congo (now Zaire)
1962–63	UN Temporary Executive Authority (UNTEA)—to observe cease-fire and keep order during transition from Dutch to Indonesian sovereignty in West New Guinea (now West Irian)
1963–64	UN Yemen Observation Mission (UNYOM)—to report on withdrawal of Saudi troops from Yemen civil war
1964–	UN Force in Cyprus (UNFICYP)—to prevent fighting between Greek and Turkish communities
1965–66	UN India-Pakistan Observation Mission (UNIPOM)—to supervise cease-fire and troop withdrawal on Indian–West Pakistan border
1973–79	UN Emergency Force (UNEF II)—to verify cease-fire and disengagement agreements in Suez and Sinai regions
1974–	UN Disengagement Observer Force (UNDOF)—to observe compliance with Syrian–Israeli disengagement agreements on Golan Heights
1978–	UN Interim Force in Lebanon (UNIFIL)—to observe disengagement agreements in Southern Lebanon and on Lebanese–Israeli border

Soviet forces are never included.[34] Table 10-1 lists peacekeeping operations carried out under the auspices of the UN.

In the early 1980s, two peacekeeping forces were created outside the UN framework, both in the Middle East. A force made up of Italian, French, and U.S. troops was deployed in Beirut when the Israeli invasion of Lebanon compelled Palestinian forces to withdraw from that country in 1982. The threat of a Soviet veto had prevented the Security Council from sending a UN peacekeeping force into the political and military chaos of Beirut. The multinational force soon departed, only to return quickly to Beirut after political massacres in two Palestinian refugee camps. The non-UN force withdrew again in 1984 after suffering severe losses in terrorist attacks and becoming briefly involved in the fighting.

Another **multinational peacekeeping** force, which included troops both from the United States and from a number of smaller states, was placed in the Sinai Desert in 1982. In this case also the Security Council had been unable to act because of threat of a Soviet veto. The Sinai force functioned smoothly and without violent incidents, probably because it was not a mere cease-fire agreement that produced it. Its mission rested on a full-fledged Egyptian–Israeli peace treaty, which had brought the return of the Sinai to Egypt. It is sobering to conclude that international peacekeeping works best to safeguard a mutually agreed peace arrangement, not as a means of creating peace in the first place.

This chapter begins with two contrasting quotations. The first records a nineteenth-century poet's vision of a peaceful future world ruled by a parliamentary federal government and universal law. The second, written two centuries earlier by a hard-headed political philosopher and observer of political conflict, seems considerably less dated as a description of international politics.

As we pointed out in chapter 1, there is no historical record of any government's giving up what Hobbes calls its sovereign "independency" unless compelled to do so by the actuality or dire threat of coercive force. Despite all the poets' dreams, international conferences and institutions, and cooperative treaty arrangements in the contemporary world, state sovereignty remains the most basic structural feature of the international system. Realistic efforts to manage and limit deep conflicts of interests and ideologies among states and blocs cannot assume that it is about to disappear.

Summary

Modern sovereign nation-states first emerged in sixteenth- to eighteenth-century Europe. Gradually they succeeded in putting an end to centuries of decentralized feudal rule and so could provide their subjects with increased security and order. Strengthened by the religious wars of the sixteenth and seventeenth centuries, rulers of the new states could fend off efforts to dominate them by international authorities such as the pope and the Holy Roman Emperor. The "sovereign state" had come to maturity.

The doctrine of sovereignty, first formulated in the sixteenth century, holds that there must be a final absolute authority within a state and that every state is legally independent from all the others. Rules of nonintervention and formal equality of all states follow from these premises, although actual inequalities among states make for many deviations from the rules.

The modern state system has expanded enormously from its European origins. Beginning with former European colonies in the Americas, countries with very different cultural backgrounds, such as the Islamic Ottoman Empire, China, and Japan came to be included in it in the nineteenth century. The League of Nations, decolonization, and the United Nations provide important landmarks en route to the current system with more than 160 internationally recognized sovereign states.

In recent decades many commentators have suggested that the sovereign state has become outmoded and that new kinds of international organizations and political entities will come increasingly to dominate the world scene. However, international relations continue to be state-centered. A stateless revolutionary group such as the Palestine Liberation Organization operates transnationally but mainly seeks its own state. Breakdown of state authority in Lebanon has graphically illustrated the desperately important protective function of sovereign states for their inhabitants. Governments of all ideological stripes have a strong mutual self-interest in continuing to proclaim allegiance to the sovereign equality of states.

That principle is extremely decentralist, and self-help, including the use of force as determined by the government of each state, prevails in the international system. It is a condition of anarchy, chiefly in the sense of an absence of government beyond the authority of sovereign states. Anarchy means that leaders of all governments must be perpetually concerned about basic national security. Memories of earlier crises always color their response to current situations, though drawing such analogies can sometimes lead to new mistakes.

The consequences of not coping effectively with perceived threats to security, plus the difficulty or impossibility of knowing competing governments' intentions, generally push government leaders toward attempting to build up their own protective capabilities. Sometimes that effort leads rival governments to feel compelled to match it with their own buildup. Problems of security constantly emphasize the importance of each state's power resources.

Those resources—such as large population and territory, a highly productive economy, advanced technology, and sizeable armed forces—do not translate into effective power in all circumstances. U.S. isolationism before the Second World War and unfavorable political circumstances during the Vietnam War had strong negative effects on the actual international power of the United States. Nevertheless, substantial power resources can give a state a better chance to preserve its autonomy, a broader range of policy choices, and a wider margin of safety in its relations with potential adversaries.

Some states are clearly much more powerful than others and are generally called *great powers*. Traditionally their leaders have considered the national interest to require them to play a leading role in efforts to manage and maintain the structure of the international system. Such states always have very substantial military power and tend to project it beyond their borders to defend what government leaders define as their legitimate interests. As a rule they try to avoid dangerous collisions with other great powers, especially by refraining from interference in their particular spheres of influence.

Governments of great powers often claim for themselves a special responsibility for the international order. Occasionally governments of weaker states agree to and even welcome intervention by a great power, as they have done with the Marshall Plan in post–World War II Europe and some U.S. mediation efforts in the Middle East.

Most analysts of international politics agree that during the past several decades the great-power universe has shrunk to include only two superpowers, the United States and the Soviet Union. There is no agreement on the rankings of all the other states, but no one doubts that a hierarchy of power persists among them.

Normally, the relative power of states has a great deal to do with the outcome of disputes among them, despite the existence of international law. International law is a body of principles that apply almost exclusively to states and is derived mainly from long-established customs and formal international agreements. The International Court of Justice has the duty of interpreting it, but that court has little effective jurisdiction, no power of enforcement, and few cases. The principle of self-help permits a state to retaliate against injuries, but according to a standard of proportionality. In practice, international rules and standards are interpreted by each affected state, predictably in its own interests.

Criticisms of traditional, Western-based international law come mainly from Third World figures, revolutionaries, and ruling Communists. However, they tend to support its basic principles of the sovereignty and equality of states, at least where their own interests are involved. Weaker states especially cling to those international norms. In no effective sense does international law provide the kind of basic, enforceable protection against aggression and violence that characterizes a domestic system of law and order.

Cooperative efforts to increase international security have involved the establishment of various multistate organizations, starting with the Concert of Europe in 1815. It helped enforce the great powers' version of peace for some decades and started the continuing practice of holding international conferences to consider common problems.

In the twentieth century the League of Nations and later the United Nations were created to enforce the principle of collective security—confronting an officially labeled "aggressor" state with the overwhelming force of most other states. Neither world organization has been able to realize that goal, despite sporadic efforts and limited success in the Korean War "police action."

In the 1960s the United Nations retreated to a more modest goal of peacekeeping in a few zones of dangerous conflict. Even that very limited kind of activity has run afoul of superpower disagreement in the Security Council, and more recent multinational peacekeeping efforts have taken place outside the UN framework. Despite myriad dreams, schemes, and good intentions, state sovereignty and ever-present threats to basic security remain defining features of international political life.

Review List of Key Terms

nation-states
Treaty of Westphalia
sovereignty
self-help
equality of states
state system
Ottoman Empire
international law
Middle Kingdom
League of Nations

United Nations
"one state, one vote"
"interdependent" world
international anarchy
problems of national security
decision-making uncertainty
security dilemma

elements of national power
margins of safety
great powers
sphere of influence
International Court of Justice
proportionality
Brezhnev doctrine
"unequal treaties"

Concert of Europe
collective security
Security Council
veto power
Korean "police action"
"Uniting for Peace"
UN peacekeeping
multinational peacekeeping

Notes

1. K. J. Holsti, *International Relations: A Framework for Analysis,* 4th ed. (Englewood Cliffs, N.J.: Prentice-Hall, 1985), p. 83.
2. Robert W. Tucker, *The Inequality of Nations* (New York: Basic Books, 1977), p. 4.
3. The following discussion draws upon Hedley Bull and Adam Watson, eds., *The Expansion of International Society* (Oxford: The Clarendon Press, 1984); for the editors' conclusions, see esp. pp. 425–435.
4. Thomas Naff, "The Ottoman Empire and the European State System," in *The Expansion of International Society,* ed. Hedley Bull and Adam Watson (Oxford: The Clarendon Press, 1984), pp. 142–169.
5. Inis Claude, *Swords into Plowshares,* 4th ed. (New York: Random House, 1984), p. 86.
6. Two influential arguments of this type were those of E. H. Carr, *Nationalism and After* (London: Macmillan, 1947), and John Herz, "The Rise and Demise of the Territorial State," *World Politics* 9 (July 1957): 473–493. Two decades later, Herz admitted that his earlier expectation had proved a misjudgment; see "The Territorial State Revisited," *Polity* 1 (Fall 1968): 11–34.
7. See Robert O. Keohane and Joseph S. Nye, *Power and Interdependence* (Boston: Little, Brown, 1977).
8. Kenneth Waltz, *The Theory of International Politics* (Reading, Mass.: Addison-Wesley, 1979), p. 95.
9. John Keegan, "Shedding Light on Lebanon," *The Atlantic,* April 1984, p. 43.
10. Fouad Ajami, "Lebanon and Its Inheritors," *Foreign Affairs,* Spring 1985, p. 799.
11. Michael Howard, *The Causes of Wars* (Cambridge, Mass.: Harvard University Press, 1983), pp. 33–34; Terry Nardin, *Law, Morality, and the Relations of States* (Princeton, N.J.: Princeton University Press, 1983), p. 43.
12. For a classic statement of this point, see Inis Claude, *Power and International Relations* (New York: Random House, 1962), pp. 205–271.
13. This discussion draws upon the writings of

Robert Jervis, e.g., "Cooperation under the Security Dilemma," *World Politics* 30 (January 1978): 167–214; and "Security Regimes," in *International Regimes,* ed. Stephen D. Krasner (Ithaca, N.Y.: Cornell University Press, 1983), pp. 173–194. See also Charles Lipson, "International Cooperation in Economic and Security Affairs," *World Politics* 37 (October 1984): 12–23.
14. This disagreement first developed among U.S. policy makers in 1949, as the Truman administration engaged in defense planning in the aftermath of the Soviets' Berlin blockade and the test detonation of their first atomic bomb. George F. Kennan, director of the State Department Policy Planning Staff, criticized an inclination to base planning on the Soviets' capabilities rather than their "real intentions," which he did concede were "unsusceptible to exact determination." See his *Memoirs: 1925–1950* (Boston: Little, Brown, 1967), pp. 474–475. Secretary of State Dean Acheson found Kennan's approach to evaluating the Soviet threat "obscure" and "esoteric" and not helpful for making policy recommendations to the president and Congress. See his *Present at the Creation* (New York: Norton, 1969), pp. 346–347.
15. This term was first used by John Herz, in "International Politics and the Security Dilemma," *World Politics* 2 (January 1950): 157–180.
16. Holsti, *International Relations,* pp. 149–150.
17. Ibid.
18. Waltz, *The Theory of International Politics,* pp. 194–195.
19. Cited in Hedley Bull, *The Anarchical Society* (New York: Columbia University Press, 1977), p. 201.
20. Gordon Craig and Alexander George, *Force and Statecraft* (New York: Oxford University Press, 1983), pp. 17–27.
21. Martin Wight, *Power Politics* (New York: Holmes and Meier, 1978), p. 46.
22. Jack Levy, *War in the Modern Great Power System, 1495–1975* (Lexington: University of Kentucky Press, 1983), pp. 16–17. Levy's chapter 2, "The Modern Great Power System," is the most thorough contemporary discussion of great-power status and roles.
23. For a sensible scheme differentiating among states' power levels, see Carsten Holbraad, *Middle Powers in International Politics* (New York: St. Martin's Press, 1984); for one scholar's explanation of why he classifies Britain, France, West Germany, and China as great powers, see Levy, *War,* pp. 24–49.
24. Quoted in Vernon V. Aspaturian, "Soviet Global Power and the Correlation of Forces," *Problems of Communism,* May/June 1980, p. 1.
25. Seweryn Bialer, *Stalin's Successors* (Cambridge: Cambridge University Press, 1980), p. 237, n. 5. (Italics in original.)
26. Transcript of press conference, *New York Times,* November 22, 1985.
27. Frederic S. Pearson and J. Martin Rochester, *International Relations* (Reading, Mass.: Addison-Wesley, 1984), pp. 302–303.
28. Ibid., p. 303.
29. Oscar Schachter, "Self-Help in International Law: U.S. Action in the Iranian Hostage Crisis," *Journal of International Affairs* 37 (Winter 1984): 231–246.
30. Walter Jones, *The Logic of International Relations,* 5th ed. (Boston: Little, Brown, 1985), p. 518.
31. See Robert H. Jackson and Carl S. Rosberg, "Why Africa's Weak States Persist," *World Politics* 35 (October 1982): 1–24.
32. Theodore A. Coulombis and James H. Wolfe, *Introduction to International Politics,* 3rd ed. (Englewood Cliffs, N.J.: Prentice-Hall, 1986), pp. 262–266.
33. Claude, *Swords into Plowshares,* pp. 21–80.
34. For a discussion of peacekeeping, both under the United Nations and outside it, see Richard W. Nelson, "Multinational Peacekeeping in the Middle East and the United Nations Model," *International Affairs* 61 (Winter 1984–1985): 67–89.

ELEVEN

International Politics: Statecraft and the Balance of Power

It may be that when the advance of destructive weapons enables everyone to kill anybody else no one will want to kill anyone at all.
Winston Churchill, 1953

After a certain point has passed, it may be said, the worse things get the better. . . . Then it may be that we shall, by a process of sublime irony, have reached a stage in this story where safety will be the sturdy child of terror, and survival the twin brother of annihilation.
Winston Churchill, 1955

Traditionally, efforts by governments of sovereign states to use power in their relations with other states are called **statecraft.** In this chapter we will examine some of the main instruments and techniques of statecraft, attempting to understand their political uses and limitations. We will also try to explain how some of these practices can help produce a degree of security and order despite the anarchy, conflicts of interests, and endless competition for power that characterize international politics.

Difficulties of International Power Wielding

The exercise of influence in international politics is not a predictable, mechanical enterprise. As an economic resource, currency is called *liquid* because it can be reliably and repeatedly exchanged for given amounts of commodities. Power resources don't work the same way: economic and military strength, for example, sometimes enable a government to get its way with another state, but by no means always. Crucial differences in circumstances and in target can determine whether the power potential of a state translates into effective power or a power failure. Two examples of U.S. foreign policy making illustrate some of the difficulties and complexities of trying to bring a government's power resources to bear upon opposing sovereign states.

As the Second World War wound down, U.S. policy makers became increasingly concerned about the prospect of a continued Soviet military presence in Eastern Europe. U.S. diplomats in Moscow urged their government to consider offering postwar economic and reconstruction assistance to the Soviets as inducements for cooperating in a European political settlement acceptable to the West. Presidents Roosevelt and Truman both laid some groundwork for postwar aid but assumed that they would withhold it until the Soviets agreed to satisfactory political arrangements. No final decision was ever made about U.S. assistance because the Soviets never showed any interest in bargaining about it.

"One thing I'll say for him. He does have a <u>coherent</u> foreign policy!"

With hindsight, it is still not possible to know for certain how the prospect of reconstruction aid might have affected U.S.–Soviet relations. It is most unlikely, though, that the Soviets would have given up domination of Eastern Europe in exchange for postwar economic assistance. In the prewar period Stalin had attempted to develop an autarkic—nationally self-sufficient—economy, and he pushed toward **autarky** again after the war. At the same time he launched an intense campaign to purge Soviet culture of all foreign influences. It appears extremely doubtful that he could have been induced to yield any political concessions—much less his new European empire—in return for economic help.[1]

The second example involves President Johnson's program of expanded U.S. bombing raids on North Vietnam in 1964. It had been under discussion for some time within the administration and was implemented in the guise of retaliation for alleged North Vietnamese torpedo boat attacks on U.S. ships in the Gulf of Tonkin.

The bombing was intended to have several effects favorable to U.S. objectives. First, it was designed to impose severe costs on North Vietnamese military involvement in the south. Second, policy makers hoped that this use of military force would deflate U.S. and South Vietnamese pressures for deploying U.S. ground forces in South Vietnam. Third, they intended the bombing to demonstrate political resolve and U.S. support for the South Vietnamese government.[2]

What were the effects of the U.S. bombing program? It is clear that it stiffened rather than weakened the resolve of the North Vietnamese government to persist in its involvement in the south: the main military objective was not achieved. As for the South Vietnamese government, it experienced a new political crisis a few months after the bombing began, as military rulers replaced civilians. Conditions were too unstable for the U.S. use of force against the north to have any marked effect on morale in the south. The bombing did postpone commitment of a large U.S. combat force to the conflict, but only for a few months.

Both of these cases illustrate some of the difficulties and complexities of trying to influence policies of other states. A common explanation of foreign policy failures is policy makers' lack of will or skill, but often that kind of charge is somewhat beside the point. There are many circumstances—possibly including these two cases—in which even determined and skillful leaders cannot convert power resources into effective power. Their difficulties can become insurmountable when rulers of target states define their vital interests as utterly incompatible with submitting to the would-be power wielders.

Instruments and Techniques of Statecraft

Despite frustrations and failures, however, governments continually find it necessary to try to influence policies and actions of other sovereign states. Most contemporary governments have developed specialized bureaucracies for conducting statecraft, which can be usefully classified under four main headings: propaganda, diplomacy, economic statecraft, and military statecraft.[3]

Various types of statecraft are frequently intermingled in specific circumstances. For example, an economic boycott may be declared not mainly to damage the target state's economy but to signal to other states that the power wielder is determined to act and reserves the possibility of using more forceful sanctions.

Propaganda

Propaganda, or verbal persuasion, can be an essential complement to other varieties of power. In the 1962 **Cuban missile crisis,** U.S. President Kennedy effectively used public and private messages to define and respond to the threat of Soviet medium-range missiles in Cuba. His very clear insistence, both spoken and written, that the missiles could not be tolerated contributed significantly to his success in getting them removed—especially with the backing of U.S. military superiority.

Diplomacy

To a great extent **diplomacy,** attempting to achieve objectives through negotiations, involves official exchanges of views, enabling governments to learn about and probe each other's intentions. As a negotiating process diplomacy is considerably more complex. If the objectives and approaches of the parties involved are fundamentally incompatible, talks alone are not likely to produce much influence for either side. Successful bargaining usually begins only when one or both parties are inclined toward agreement in the first place. In that case rational persuasion may prove sufficient, although it is more probable that inducements and coercion will play some part in the outcome.

Economic Statecraft

Economic statecraft involves material sanctions and inducements. Of the four techniques under discussion, it has probably been most heavily discounted by scholars and commentators as a means of exercising international power. Klaus Knorr, a leading analyst of international politics, clearly states the prevailing view: "The most conspicuous thing about . . . attempts at coercion by economic means is that they nearly always fail to coerce."[4]

More recently, political scientist David Baldwin has emphasized the possible effectiveness of economic sanctions. He warns that in the nuclear age it is especially important to find alternatives to military statecraft. Two examples illustrate his attempt to evaluate sanctions by more discriminating political standards than have usually been applied to them.

First, as we mentioned in chapter 10, the League of Nations voted economic penalties against Italy for its invasion of Ethiopia in 1936. Failure of this effort was not, Baldwin asserts, because of inherent flaws in economic sanctions. In fact, he contends that the Italian economy would have been highly vulnerable to international sanctions. However, the governments of Britain and France, the two great-power members of the League, feared that if the sanctions succeeded Italy would be driven into a closer political relationship with Nazi Germany. In their judgment, that development would have been more of a threat to their vital interests than was the Italian war in Africa. That is why they failed to give practical force to the League's decision, ruining its chances of success. Baldwin argues that it could well have succeeded if the British and French governments had cooperated.

Second, U.S. President Carter declared an embargo on American grain sales to the Soviet Union in response to the Soviet invasion of Afghanistan in 1979. Generally derided as ineffective, the embargo was lifted by President Reagan in 1981. However, "the grain embargo was probably highly effective in impressing the Soviets with the grave implications of the invasion, minimally effective in imposing significant costs for refusal to withdraw, and moderately effective in demonstrating [the U.S.] commitment to resist further Soviet moves to the allies and other countries."[5] These conclusions remain highly debatable, but Baldwin's analysis at least suggests that there may be circumstances in which economic sanctions can function as instruments of statecraft.

Military Statecraft

The utility and effectiveness of military power, used or threatened, have long been assumed in the study and practice of international relations. It has been regarded as the ultimate guarantor of physical security and a sometimes useful means of securing economic and territorial gains. In recent decades, however, some analysts have contended that **military statecraft** is declining in usability and effectiveness.

Decline of force? In 1966 Klaus Knorr published the first influential statement of the view that force is on the decline, although he has since revised his conclusions. He originally asserted that the utility of armed force would decline if the costs of using it increased while its benefits in attaining valued goals decreased. In his judgment, both conditions prevailed in the 1960s.

Costs were rising as the extreme danger of using nuclear weapons became more and more apparent. A conflict originally fought with conventional weapons might well escalate into nuclear confrontation. Public opposition to any use of military force was increasing out of fear that it could lead to a nuclear holocaust.

Knorr concluded that armed force was losing its traditional attractiveness as a means of seizing and controlling territory. In addition to costs related to nuclear weapons, nationalism had increased the inclination of weaker states to resist militarily stronger foreigners. In sum, "the costs of using [military] power have risen, its effectiveness has decreased. The world has become less coercible."[6]

Knorr has subsequently conceded that he overestimated the trends pointing to a decline in military force and that his conclusions have proved mistaken in crucial respects. Drawing on his and other observers' later analyses, we will consider two questions implied in the **decline of force hypothesis**: Is the use of armed force actually decreasing? Is it less effective than it used to be?

Maintaining and using military power Whether armed force is used less in contemporary international relations than in earlier eras is impossible to determine with any precision. It *is* certain, though, that the largest proportion of the world's 160-plus states are sustaining their military power at substantial levels. The United States has not stopped expanding its military capability. The Soviet Union has engaged in a huge military buildup over the past few decades. Third World military spending has proceeded at a faster pace than world military expenditures generally. In 1960 military budgets of developing states represented less than 5 percent of the world total but by 1982 had risen to 23 percent.[7]

As for the use of military force, violence and warfare obviously continue to feature prominently in international relations. In the 1980s, wars were under way in Southeast Asia, the Persian Gulf region, North Africa, and Central America, and many other armed struggles continued at lower levels of violence. There were border and territorial conflicts, as in the Spanish Sahara; civil wars, as in Lebanon and Eritrea; and many conflicts occasionally interrupted by uncertain truces, as in Cyprus and, most uneasy of all, between Israel and Arab states such as Syria. Governments have continued to accumulate armaments and in many cases put them to use.

There *has* been a sharp decline in wars among major powers since the end of the Second World War (see table 11-1). Most notably, in that period war has been absent from Europe, and Japan has had no involvement in armed conflict, despite the frequent use of force by Western European states and Japan before 1945. Britain's brief Falklands–Malvinas Islands war with Argentina in 1982 and occasional, limited French intervention in several African states represent something close to great-power projections of military force beyond territorial defense and deterrence.

With those minimal exceptions, Western European governments have lost interest in actually using force, mainly because they have no concern about renewed military aggressiveness among themselves. Their interests are overwhelmingly economic and domestic. For example, in 1973 there was a bit of unofficial discussion in the United States of possible military retaliation against Arab governments that were refusing to export oil to states supporting Israel. Even with economies much more dependent upon Arab oil than was the United States, Western European leaders were completely unwilling to consider any military action.

That kind of aversion to using military force is not, however, evenly distributed around the globe. It is not at all apparent in much of the Third World, and there is no discernible revulsion in world opinion when two Third World countries fight each other.

As for communist states, the Soviet regime has repeatedly demonstrated its determination to use or threaten military intervention to maintain its domination of Eastern Europe. In 1979 it sent large numbers of troops into a neighboring Asian state, Afghanistan, apparently to rescue a puppet communist regime and consolidate Soviet-sponsored communist rule for the long term.

Soviet-armed, -trained, and -sponsored Cuban troops have fought in the African countries of Angola and Ethiopia since the mid-1970s to preserve insecure Marxist-Leninist regimes aligned with the USSR. Soviet advisers and trainers have also participated in those military efforts. In addition,

Table 11-1 Wars fought since the Second World War, with starting dates

Syria–Lebanon	1945	India–Pakistan	1965		
Indonesia	1945	Indonesia	1965		
China	1945	Biafra	1966		
Malaya	1945	Israel–Arab states	1967		
Indochina	1946	Czechoslovakia	1968		
Greece	1946	Malaysia	1969		
Madagascar	1947	El Salvador	1969		
India–Pakistan	1947	Chad	1969		
Kashmir	1947	Northern Ireland	1969		
Philippines	1948	Ethiopia (Eritrea)	1970		
Israel–Arab states	1948	Cambodia	1971		
Hyderabad	1948	Bangladesh/Kashmir	1971		
Burma	1948	Burundi	1972		
Korea	1950	Israel–Arab states	1973		
Formosa	1950	Iraq (Kurdish)	1974		
Tibet	1950	Cyprus	1974		
Kenya	1952	Angola	1975		
Guatemala	1954	Timor	1975		
Algeria	1954	Lebanon	1975		
Sudan	1955	Spanish Morocco	1976		
Cyprus	1955	Somalia–Ethiopia	1977		
Sinai	1956	Ethiopia (Eritrea)	1977		
Hungary	1956	Syria–Lebanon	1977		
Suez	1956	Libya–Egypt	1977		
Lebanon	1958	Iran	1978		
Cuba	1958	Nicaragua	1978		
Vietnam	1959	Vietnam–Laos	1978		
Himalayas	1959	Chad	1978		
Rwanda	1959	Zaire	1978		
Laos	1959	Rhodesia (Zimbabwe)	1978		
Congo	1960	N. Yemen–S. Yemen	1979		
Colombia	1960	Uganda–Tanzania	1979		
Cuba (Bay of Pigs)	1961	China–Vietnam	1979		
Goa	1961	Vietnam–Kampuchea	1979		
Angola	1961	Nicaragua	1979		
Yemen	1962	South Africa–Angola	1979		
West New Guinea	1962	USSR–Afghanistan	1980		
Portuguese Guinea	1962	Iran–Iraq	1980		
Algeria–Morocco	1963	El Salvador	1980		
Cyprus	1963	Britain–Argentina			
Malaysia	1963	(Falkland Islands)	1982		
Somalia–Kenya	1963	Israel–Syria–PLO			
Zanzibar	1964	(in Lebanon)	1982		
Thailand	1964	Kampuchea–Thailand	1983		
Mozambique	1964	Sri Lanka	1983		
Dominican Republic	1965	US–Grenada	1983		

Adapted from Walter S. Jones, *The Logic of International Relations*, 5th ed., p. 271. Copyright © 1985 by Walter S. Jones. Reprinted by permission of Little, Brown and Company.

Cuban and other Soviet bloc military personnel have played substantial roles in organizing and training the vastly expanded armed forces of the Nicaraguan Sandinista regime since 1979.

Most Third World and all communist military enterprises are not open to political criticism and opposition by domestic public opinion. Foreign criticism seems seldom, if ever, to have any deterrent effect upon autocratic policy-making elites and usually has little staying power on the international scene.

Alliances and deterrence Even if most states continue to cultivate military strength, how useful and effective is it? Its most important use remains, as always, to undergird basic national security by deterring attacks from other states. It is arguable that because of their massive military capabilities the United States and the Soviet Union have achieved a greater degree of physical security and defensive self-sufficiency than great powers in any previous era.[8] The existence of nuclear-armed ballistic missiles may weaken the argument somewhat; we will consider the significance of those weapons systems shortly.

The militarily based security of the two superpowers has been extended in distinctive ways to the states that make up the core of their spheres of influence. For the United States, as Robert Art has observed, "American power has created and sustained the political preconditions necessary for the evolutionary intertwining of the American, Canadian, Japanese and Western European economies. . . . America's military preeminence politically pervades these relations. It is the cement of economic interdependence."[9]

Likewise, the Soviets have forged military and **economic interdependence** among Eastern European states—mainly through a highly coercive military presence backed by their demonstrated willingness to use force in that region. From the perspective of Soviet rulers, military force is both effective and essential for maintaining what they consider their most vital sphere of influence.

Since the Second World War, there has been a drastic decline in the usefulness of military force for changing the political and territorial status quo among the states of Europe. This dramatic contrast to the extreme instability of the post–World War I treaty settlements stems mainly from the existence of nuclear weapons. Their possession by the rival superpowers has worked to perpetuate political boundaries originally determined by the locations of Soviet and Western troops when Nazi Germany surrendered in 1945. Even the unnatural division of Germany has been essentially legitimized in treaties between West Germany and the Soviet Union and Eastern European states, and in the **Helsinki Accords** signed by the United States and thirty-five European governments in 1975.

The absence of international war in Europe for more than four decades

Table 11-2 Techniques of statecraft

Technique	Definition	Comment
Propaganda	Verbal persuasion	Most effective with coercive threat
Diplomacy	Official negotiations	Success usually requires initial inclination toward agreement
Economic statecraft	Material sanctions, such as trade embargo	Requires international cooperation, usually fails
Military statecraft	Use or threatened use of armed force	No evidence of decline in nuclear age

does not guarantee that war *cannot* occur in that critical region. But so long as the structure of superpower deterrence remains intact, the nuclear threat effectively prevents yet another world war. There seems to be no good reason to conclude that military capability has declined in significance as a basis of power in international politics. (See table 11-2 for a summary of the techniques of statecraft.)

Balancing Power among States

Given their inescapable concern for security, combined with international anarchy, governments have traditionally tried to practice balance-of-power politics. Above all, each attempts to make certain that its own defensive power is not overwhelmed by an imbalance strongly favoring adversary states. Treaties of alliance are often motivated by that overriding concern, as are military buildups.

Balance-of-Power Politics

Balance of power is a traditional term that is not used consistently and uniformly.[10] Some scholars believe that it has become so ambiguous as to be useless. They would restrict it to such historic circumstances as the prevailing relations among major European states in the eighteenth and nineteenth centuries. As we noted in chapter 2, that state system represented, with exceptions, an example of the strategy of toleration: European governments tended to assume the legitimacy and ongoing existence of all other European states, even their current rivals.

We believe, however, that balance-of-power politics continues to be fundamentally important, despite drastic changes in the world since 1914. The term can usefully refer both to a *situation* and to a kind of *policy*.[11] In the first sense it means a power relationship of **equilibrium** among states or alliances, a rough equality that governments of the affected states generally accept. It involves, of course, not only the distribution of power resources but also leaders' perceptions of each others' intentions in foreign policy. A balance-of-power policy, then, would aim at creating or preserving a perceived condition of power equilibrium, and above all, at preventing the rise of a potentially dominant adversary.

For understandable reasons, balance-of-power policies have had a long run in international politics. As we emphasized in chapter 10, international institutions and mechanisms do not effectively regulate the uses of power among sovereign states. In their absence, self-help requires each government to focus on its power situation relative to neighboring states, allies, and potential enemies. Decisions in this vital sphere are and must be determined by each government in its own interests.

Moreover, the primary traditional objective of balance-of-power policies has been to preserve the independence of states. Government leaders do not fear international anarchy so much as the threat that one state may try to end it by establishing imperial rule over others. For that reason, balance-of-power policies have proved to be a resilient mutual interest that states can pursue both independently and in alliances. So long as coercive power remains a reality or a constant possibility in international relations, governmental leaders will continue to assume that nothing but effective power can offset its threat to their independence.

Status Quo and Revisionist States

Balance-of-power policies are most severely tested by a state or states not willing to accept an established equilibrium. **Status quo states** are those whose governments accept and wish to continue the existing power ratios among the states with which they are likely to interact. **Revisionist states**, however, seek to improve their relative power position substantially, in some cases drastically. Competition among status quo and revisionist states tends to be highly unstable and can most readily lead to war.

For example, in the early 1790s the status quo states of Europe, such as Britain, Austria, and Prussia, began to feel distinctly menaced by the new revolutionary regime in France. They feared that its attacks on the legitimacy of monarchical government would inspire disorder and upheavals throughout Europe and acted to signal their concern. Faced with threats from abroad, the new French regime declared war and inaugurated a period of European armed conflict that ended only with the final defeat of Napoleon in 1815. French revisionism had eventually taken the form of imperial conquest, and the status quo allies had been compelled to fight long and costly wars in order to restore a condition similar to the pre-1790s balance of power in Europe.

In more recent times, Hitler's Germany and imperial Japan pushed hard to revise the international power distribution in their favor. The defensive, status quo powers, as we noted in chapter 2, were extremely reluctant to recognize the thrust of German and Japanese revisionism. When they finally did feel compelled to resist it with armed force, the result was the Second World War.

War

Clearly, balance-of-power policies don't necessarily prevent war, and as a rule that has not been their primary objective. Eighteenth-century European heads of state regarded warfare as an indispensable means of preserving or adjusting the balance, although their wars were relatively low cost and were fought mainly by professional armies. As wars have become much more expensive and deadly, practitioners of statecraft have more rarely advocated war as desirable policy. Practice, of course, has often failed to match their public expressions of undying affection for peace. On the whole, balance-of-power policies have been aimed more at preventing domination or hegemony than at avoiding war.

Particular wars and warfare in general have been much discussed and analyzed by historians and political scientists. However, "No widely accepted theory of the causes of war exists, and little agreement has emerged on the methodology through which these causes might be discovered."[12] Within the context of international power competition, we would endorse the view of an eminent military historian: "When [wars] do occur, it is for a very simple reason: one side believes that it can win."[13]

For instance, in 1980 Saddam Hussein, the autocratic ruler of Iraq, ordered his armed forces to attack Iran. Apparently he had calculated that his army could quickly compel the Iranian government—weakened by revolutionary turmoil—to return to Iraq disputed border territory that the shah had earlier forced Iraq to concede to Iran.[14] He may even have believed that he could destroy the Iranian revolutionary Islamic regime, a possible future threat to his own hold on power. As we will explain in chapter 13, Hussein grossly miscalculated. The Iranians resisted effectively, and after more than half a dozen years of terrible human and material losses on both sides the war was dragging on with no end in sight. That outcome illustrates a most important point about choosing specific strategies and tactics of power competition with other states: they can be disastrously mistaken.

Benefits of Balance of Power

If government leaders of each state try to calculate and act on their own judgments of how best to protect and enhance their state's relative power, but those judgments may be wrong, how can balance-of-power policies actually be successful? For one thing, they have often prevented wars when the potential instigator believed it impossible to win. The nuclear "balance of terror" between the United States and the Soviet Union certainly appears to be the main reason why there has been no third world war.

Balance-of-power policies aim above all at protecting the very existence of sovereign states that pursue them. The threat that the strategy of elimination will be implemented against states with grossly inferior power is no paranoid fantasy, given thousands of years of wars of conquest and annexation of losers' territory by the victors.

Sometimes elimination has involved the dismemberment of a defeated state: partial loss of territory, population, and jurisdiction. Prussian seizure of Alsace-Lorraine in the Franco-Prussian War of 1870, followed by French retaking of that disputed territory nearly half a century later, exemplifies successive dismemberments. Pakistan's loss of its eastern half after defeat in a brief war with India in 1971 also illustrates partial elimination of a state.

Total elimination of sovereign states is somewhat rarer in the modern era. However, Poland was partitioned among Austria, Prussia, and Russia in the late eighteenth century and did not reappear as a sovereign state until the end of the First World War. The Baltic states of Estonia, Latvia, and Lithuania were annexed by the Soviet Union under terms of the Hitler–Stalin pact of 1939 with no likely prospect of regaining independence. China invaded and proclaimed its sovereignty over Tibet in 1959. In 1975 South Vietnam ceased to exist as a sovereign state when it was conquered by the North Vietnamese and incorporated into their Democratic Republic of Vietnam.

Adequate defensive power—its own, its allies', or that of a larger "protector" state—remains the most basic security for any state against the possibility of partial or total elimination. As a rule, balance-of-power policies succeed in that minimal but fundamental purpose.

Policies of that kind also frequently frustrate attempts at international domination. Resisting such a threat with defensive power doesn't always succeed, but without it, coercive domination would almost certainly become the universal relationship among sovereign states. Effective defense, of course, sometimes means fighting. The wars against Napoleon, Hitler, and the Japanese imperialists demonstrate that threats and good intentions aren't always sufficient to halt aspiring conquerors.

In the contemporary world the threat of war on a previously unimaginable scale of death and destruction has brought into sharp relief worries about balance-of-power politics. If that line of policy has not prevented war in the past, shouldn't it be replaced with some new approach to prevent the ultimate disaster of nuclear war? This frequently posed question leads us to examine some basic features of the present-day balance of world power.

The Bipolar Balance and International Stability

We have already referred to the United States and the Soviet Union as superpowers, a cliché term of contemporary journalism. It fits when we consider how the nuclear and other military capabilities of either of these states dwarf those of all other states—except its main adversary's. Allies of necessity against Nazi Germany, these two powers have had essentially antagonistic relations for more than four decades, without actually fighting each other.

The clustering of two blocs of states around the superpowers is known as **bipolarity**, in contrast to a condition of **multipolarity**, in which several states have roughly equivalent power and individual states may sometimes change allies in an attempt to tip the balance in their favor. That classic European pattern has given way to a more rigid and enduring alignment.

In our judgment, the U.S.–Soviet bipolar balance of power has two basic defining features. First, since 1945 the United States has been essentially a status quo state with respect to the international distribution of power, and the Soviet Union has been persistently revisionist—outside its own sphere of domination. Second, in this bipolar power relationship, also in contrast to the classic European pattern, the main participants do not assume the legitimacy and ongoing existence of the rival regimes. Each has at best a grudging toleration of the other and frequently probes for points of possible vulnerability. Because of the Soviets' revisionist perspective, this probing has more typically characterized, we believe, their attitudes and policies than those of the United States.

In short, there is a substantial degree of **instability** in the bipolar balance of world power. We will point out, however, certain **elements of stability** in this relationship, which remains the most potent shaping force in contemporary international politics.

Sources of Instability

Ideological incompatibility Profound differences in ideologies and governmental systems are the most basic source of antagonistic competition between the Soviet Union and the United States. The Soviets continue to profess belief in the "scientific" claim of Marxism-Leninism that all bourgeois capitalist systems will eventually self-destruct and be replaced by vanguard-led revolutionary socialist systems similar to their pattern-setting example. The United States has no official, comprehensive worldview ideology, but its leaders have consistently denied the **historical inevitability** of communism, and some have declared that freedom and democracy will yet prove to be the actual wave of the future.

Differences in political systems and pressures More obviously and immediately relevant to U.S.–Soviet hostility are differences in political systems, which give rise to contrasting pressures on top policymakers. Chapters 5, 6, 8, and 9 have explained the major features of the two systems, and there is no need to repeat them here. We would make the somewhat controversial but, we believe, historically defensible claim that public opinion, electoral, and interest-group pressures usually push governments of large-scale, mass-opinion representative democracies away from risking armed hostilities abroad.

Democracies and foreign policy problems In the absence of enemy attack or an obvious military threat, the sacrifices and mortal dangers of war strongly repel most voters within a democracy. In addition, many interest groups support domestic programs that may be threatened or cut if military spending is increased, as do large proportions of the electorate.

Certainly the interests of the **military-industrial complex**—in defense contracts, jobs for constituents and union members, profits for affected corporations—favor substantial defense programs. Groups representing those interests defend them, however, not as preparations for war but as contributions to preserving peace through strength. Military spending is also subject to constant and outspoken criticism and possible reductions, depending upon outcomes of elections.

British and French policies of appeasing Hitler, discussed in chapter 2, were motivated in part by strong public revulsion against any prospect of war and by fears that rearmament would greatly reduce governmental efforts to cope with urgent domestic problems. The costly, stalemated Korean War became distinctly unpopular in the United States after initial support for President Truman's decision to counter North Korean invaders with U.S. combat forces. Domestic opposition to the U.S. military role in Vietnam was unprecedented in its breadth, depth, diversity of expression, and traumatic impact upon the American body politic. Foreign policy debaters of all stripes wrangle endlessly about the **lessons of Vietnam,** but all agree that that failure continues to place special inhibitions on the ready resort to U.S. military force abroad.

Foreign policy and the Soviet nomenklatura In the Soviet Union, however, the impact of general public opinion on the autocratic government is very small, and the influence of independently organized groups is nonexistent. Top decision makers' isolation from popular influences gives them a greater capacity for long-range planning and persistence in pursuing policy objectives than democratic governments generally have. Riding out occasional setbacks and displaying tactical flexibility, they have maintained over the long haul a persistently revisionist policy of expanding the domain of Soviet power.

Public opinion, both supportive and critical, is an important factor in foreign policy making by democratic governments, though it seldom restrains autocratic regimes. Here, some Americans exercise their democratic right to attack the president's foreign policy in 1983.

We believe that this policy is a fundamental interest of the nomenklatura, the ruling class described and analyzed in chapter 9.[15] Soviet rulers face serious problems in trying to generate authority for their regime. The large role played in that system by physically and mentally coercive institutions and techniques suggests continuing elite concern about political self-preservation.

Under those circumstances, the nomenklatura's best defense is a good offense: constantly, though opportunistically and cautiously, seeking to expand Soviet power abroad, in part to demonstrate its irresistibility and inevitability. As historian Richard Pipes explains:

> The Soviet government lacks a legitimate **mandate to rule** and can never risk putting its credentials (that is, force) in question. Failure effectively to apply power abroad would at once raise doubts in the minds of Soviet citizens about the regime's ability to cope with internal opposition, and any loss of public faith in the omnipotence of the regime (and hence in the futility of resistance to it) might prove the beginning of the end. Thus the Soviet regime finds itself in the extremely difficult situation of having to create the impression of a relentless advance forward as it in fact moves very cautiously and slowly.[16]

We would add that Soviet rulers have always *needed* an external enemy, whether the motives of foreign governments were actually hostile, as were Hitler's, or relatively benign or indifferent. Stalin warned continuously of the menace of "capitalist encirclement" in order to justify his key policies: total centralized control and mobilization of the economy, a strong emphasis on heavy industry and military production at the expense of consumer goods, and mass official terror against falsely accused "traitors." Stalin's successors have constantly emphasized the threat of "imperialism," led by the United States, to justify similar economic priorities, as well as the costs and risks of their revisionist, opportunistic foreign policy in remote areas of the world.

For decades the external threat, genuine or not, has functioned to rationalize the rigid hierarchical system of control that pervades the Soviet political system. After all, the rulers constantly tell the Soviet people, if we are relentlessly under siege, don't we need a military type of command and discipline? Isn't dissent equivalent to traitorous dissension in the ranks, threatening to weaken resolve and morale and give aid and comfort to the imperialist enemy?

According to Michael Voslensky, a former Soviet historian, the Soviet ruling class cannot afford to adopt a policy of genuine "live and let live" toleration toward the West. Its freedom and prosperity stand as a perpetual challenge to the nomenklatura regime, demonstrating that an alternative to rationalized repression and consumer scarcity is possible. Although information about the West is tightly rationed and distorted, Soviet citizens know that an alternative exists, and their rulers know that they know it. Therefore, "no amount of detente or 'good conduct' on [the West's] part will cause the Soviet leaders to depart from their general line and abandon their objective of destroying the Western system."[17]

Whether or not one agrees with Voslensky, his point is at least a plausible explanation of the official Soviet view that **"ideological coexistence"** is impossible. He makes clear, and we agree, that destruction of Western democracy is a very long-term goal of the nomenklatura. Furthermore, they consider war with the U.S.–West European NATO alliance to be much too dangerous a way of trying to achieve it. Their autocratic power and its privileges are far too precious to put at serious risk. As a result, "everything depends on the balance of power, for the nomenklatura itself admits that peaceful coexistence is a function of the relations of strength between the two systems."[18]

Chapters 12 and 13 will discuss the kinds of revolutionary movements and regimes in various regions of the world that the Soviets have aided and continue to support. In the present context it is important to note that Soviet-backed revolutionaries are uniformly hostile to the United States and do whatever they can to damage its interests. The Soviets certainly have not created all such movements and revolutionary situations, at least not on their own, but they have persistently tried to exploit them to damage the interests of the United States and its allies.

Controversies in U.S. foreign policy We do not mean to imply that the United States and other Western governments have never acted aggressively, disruptively, or nastily during this period of worldwide bipolar rivalry. The U.S. Central Intelligence Agency, for example, played a critical role in overthrowing elected leaders considered hostile to U.S. interests in Iran in 1953 and Guatemala in 1954. It also provided aid to opponents of President Allende of Chile in the early 1970s, and his government fell to a military coup in 1973. In the 1960s the CIA tried to arrange for the assassination of Fidel Castro in Cuba, at one point making a contract for this job with the Mafia and at another point planning to do in the Cuban dictator with a poisoned cigar. Obviously, this agency hasn't been uniformly successful, but presumably it has had some still-secret successes in helping to destablilize unfriendly governments.

On the whole, we believe, U.S. decision makers have felt it necessary to engage in such activities, and other forms of **political warfare,** to defend the status quo power interests of the United States against perceived Soviet or other communist threats. Since the late 1960s there has been a good deal of debate—some of it quite bitter—about the morality, legality, wisdom, and necessity of clandestine CIA operations. Members of Congress have become more active in oversight of the agency, and more legal restrictions than before now apply both to the president and to the CIA. Sharp differences about the intelligence agency and its secret operations are likely to continue as long as Americans disagree about the nature, avoidability, and possibilities of negotiating an end to the U.S.–Soviet rivalry for international power.

For a variety of reasons the U.S. power position relative to the Soviet Union has declined significantly since the end of the Second World War. The Soviets' revisionist policies have had some success in changing what they call the "correlation of forces" in the world, although the United States is far from becoming, in former president Richard Nixon's phrase, a "pitiful helpless giant."

If, then, the bipolar U.S.–Soviet balance-of-power relationship seems to be rooted in uncompromisable conflicts of political interests, mutual hostility, insecurity, and suspicion, is the world destined to end with a nuclear bang?

Nuclear Deterrence and Stability

This terrifying question leads us, finally, to consider the critical degree of stability in the highly competitive bipolar balance of power. Beyond any doubt, it is based on mutual fear of the self-destructive consequences of all-out nuclear war:

> When the decision to go to war involves the likelihood, if not the certainty, that the conflict will take the form of an exchange of nuclear weapons from which one's own territory cannot be immune, then even for the most [warlike] of leaders, even for those most insulated from the pressures of public opinion, the calculation that they have more to gain from going to war than by remaining at peace and pursuing their policies by other means will, to put it mildly, not be self-evident.[19]

The main effects of the U.S.–Soviet nuclear standoff on the politics of the "central balance" between the superpowers have been analyzed and clarified by Australian scholar Coral Bell.[20] She points out that the most threatening confrontations between the giant rivals occurred in the first seventeen years after the Second World War, culminating in the Cuban missile crisis of 1962. Policy-making establishments in both countries apparently learned two important lessons from those early crises: the dire necessity of avoiding serious direct clashes and how to avoid escalating conflicts to the flashpoint.

Within the all-important framework of **nuclear deterrence,** Bell gives major credit for avoiding a U.S.–Soviet war to **alliance stability** and prudent **crisis management.** Membership of a state in one of the main superpower alliances, the Soviet-led Warsaw Treaty Organization or the U.S.-centered North Atlantic Treaty Organization (NATO), signals that the Soviets or the United States regard it as vital to their security. This awareness imposes special restraints upon efforts to detach an alliance state from its giant ally.

Despite great U.S. sympathy for East German, Hungarian, Czech, and Polish attempts during the past few decades to achieve freedom from Soviet-imposed communism, the United States did little or nothing to counter coercive Soviet intervention that ended those efforts. Rightly or wrongly, U.S. administrations of both parties decided that Soviet rulers consider communist rule in Eastern Europe a vital interest that they might well go to war to protect.

Crisis management since the early 1960s has been greatly assisted by the development of ever more ingenious **surveillance technology,** especially in space, plus powerful computers to process the flood of data. These systems also provide subtle ways of sending signals to the adversary; for example, observable weapons or troop deployments can communicate an intention not to escalate a particular conflict to the point of all-out warfare.

Finally, policy makers on both sides seem to observe an unwritten rule of decoupling their own antagonistic relationship from Third World conflicts in which they have a part. At least this **decoupling of conflicts** has been the case since the terrifying 1962 confrontation over Cuba. Wars in

Vietnam, the Middle East, Afghanistan, the Persian Gulf, and Central America have often involved fighting between rivals backed by the superpowers.

In no case have these regional or internal conflicts led to a crisis truly threatening a U.S.–Soviet war, despite many dire predictions of its probability. Soviet–U.S. competition in the Third World will probably remain persistent and often intense but seems most unlikely to lead to the sort of "crisis slide" toward great-power conflict that preceded both world wars.

In short, what has developed over time is a minimal but critical degree of cooperation between mutually hostile superpowers. It is not based to any significant extent on the treaties, arms control and otherwise, that they have signed with each other. Rather, its foundation is their common interest in survival, "the twin brother of annihilation," as Churchill termed it early in the nuclear age.

Far from being outmoded, balance-of-power politics remains the core reality of the contemporary international system: "The 19th-century system of conventions of crisis management . . . operated to limit or avoid hostilities in central balance crises for an entire century before 1914. The present system might do as well, if the valuable and essential **sense of jeopardy** is not lost."[21] That sense seems certain to persist, given the nuclear arsenals of mutually distrustful superpowers with radically incompatible aims and governmental systems, both competing for power in a world of sovereign states.

Summary

The exercise of power in the relations of sovereign states is called *statecraft*. It is a difficult and often unsuccessful enterprise, even for great powers. The United States considered giving economic inducements to Stalin after the Second World War but didn't; it is doubtful that they would have changed his policy of dominating Eastern Europe. Nor did U.S. bombing of North Vietnam in 1964 succeed militarily or politically. When rulers define their vital interests as immune to influence by adversary states, they can seldom be moved by anything less than the application of overwhelming power.

The main types of statecraft can be grouped under four headings: international propaganda, diplomacy, economic statecraft, and military statecraft. Most controversy surrounds economic and military techniques of influence. Economic sanctions have a mediocre track record, at best, although President Carter's embargo on U.S. grain shipments to the Soviet Union following its invasion of Afghanistan may have had some minimal success.

In the 1960s some analysts of international politics claimed to spot a trend toward the declining use of military force. Growing awareness of the catastrophic consequences of nuclear warfare, popular fear that any fighting could lead to that end, and nationalist resistance to militarily stronger states supposedly made the benefits of using force much lower than the costs and risks.

However, since that time there has been no discernible decline in military capabilities worldwide and probably even an opposite trend. Regional and internal wars have occurred in many places, although once-belligerent European states and Japan have engaged in few or no hostilities in the postcolonial era. The United States, however, continues to be a military superpower and has fought in two sizeable if "limited" wars since the Second World War, plus a number of smaller military engagements. The Soviet Union and other communist states have been directly or indirectly involved in warfare in Africa, Asia, and Latin America. Third World ruling elites in many places have shown no inclination to avoid armed hostilities.

Armed might continues to serve as bedrock national security insurance for most states. U.S. and Soviet military capabilities reinforce, in different ways, their leadership of alliances that also have important economic dimensions. Their nuclear standoff has been critical in preventing renewed war in Europe and freezing boundaries determined by military positions at the end of the Second World War. Military force has declined neither in quantity nor in political significance.

Because they are ultimately dependent upon themselves for protection in an anarchic world, most states have long engaged in some form of balance-of-power politics. The term implies an equilibrium, a rough equality that interacting states accept in their mutual self-interest. It also connotes a policy of trying to create or preserve such an equilibrium, above all by preventing the rise of a conquering imperial state. Governments have not feared international anarchy so much as becoming victims of foreign domination.

Status quo states defend the existing international distribution of power, whereas revisionist states seek to improve their own relative power position. Their attempts to do so can lead to severe conflicts, sometimes war. However complex their motives, rulers tend finally to go to war when they think they can win; miscalculation is frequent and sometimes disastrous.

Yet balance-of-power policies can prevent war and often have. They also aim at preventing the dismemberment or total elimination of a sovereign state or its domination by a much more powerful revisionist state. Such policies sometimes require a willingness to fight a war, and they have not been uniformly successful in preventing its occurrence.

Since the Second World War the global balance of power has become essentially bipolar, with the United States and the Soviet Union confronting each other as military and political superpowers. Each heads a central alliance, with cooperation among Warsaw Pact members based more on coercion than it is among NATO members. On the whole, the United

States has pursued a status quo policy with respect to the distribution of power among states, while the persistent thrust of the Soviets has been revisionist—except within their own sphere of domination.

There are deep sources of instability within this bipolar competition. Ideologically, Soviet leaders continue to assert the scientific inevitability of their brand of socialism everywhere. U.S. leaders deny that claim and profess to favor the expansion of democracy and liberty.

More significantly, the two political systems impose radically different pressures on top decision makers. Freedom of expression and organization, direct accountability to the electorate, and domestic competition for government resources produce constant pressures on democratic governments to avoid war-threatening foreign involvements. Leaders sometimes respond to contrary pressures and circumstances, but most wars continue to generate political controversy within democracies.

In the Soviet Union the autocratic regime stifles the expression of public opinion and can largely ignore it. The nomenklatura ruling class has a strong interest in expanding its power—to validate its dubious right to rule as the wave of the future and to intimidate potential opponents by demonstrating its willingness and ability to use massive coercion to protect and advance its vital interests. Its unremitting hostility to U.S. "imperialism" also legitimizes the semimilitary command and obedience structures that implement its total control of Soviet society.

Yet there are also elements of stability in the U.S.–Soviet bipolar balance, based on the mutual threat of nuclear destruction. It has inspired increasingly prudent management of crises by both Soviet and U.S. leaders, deployment of vastly improved technological means of surveillance, and a decoupling of Third World conflicts from the central bipolar confrontation. Given the profound political differences between the United States and the Soviet Union, their competition for power appears certain to continue indefinitely. So also does the deterrent effect of their leaders' mutual desire to avoid nuclear suicide.

Review List of Key Terms

statecraft
autarky
propaganda
Cuban missile crisis
diplomacy
economic statecraft
military statecraft
decline of force
economic interdependence

Helsinki Accords
balance-of-power equilibrium
status quo states
revisionist states
bipolarity
multipolarity
instability
elements of stability
historical inevitability

military-industrial complex
lessons of Vietnam
mandate to rule
"ideological coexistence"
political "warfare"
nuclear deterrence
alliance stability
crisis management

surveillance technology
decoupling of conflicts
sense of jeopardy

Notes

1. Vojtech Mastny, *Russia's Road to the Cold War* (New York: Columbia University Press, 1979), pp. 215–216. He mentions an occasion when the Soviet foreign minister told U.S. officials that a loan to the USSR would benefit its economy less than it would the recovery of a capitalist economy.
2. Larry Berman, *Planning a Tragedy* (New York: Norton, 1982), pp. 31–52.
3. See David Baldwin, *Economic Statecraft* (Princeton, N.J.: Princeton University Press, 1985), pp. 13–14.
4. "Is International Coercion Waning or Rising?" *International Security* 1 (Spring 1977): 103.
5. Baldwin, *Economic Statecraft*, pp. 51–59.
6. Klaus Knorr, *The Power of Nations* (New York: Basic Books, 1975), p. 318; pp. 107–126 develop this thesis, as does Knorr's earlier study, *On the International Uses of Military Power in the Nuclear Age* (Princeton, N.J.: Princeton University Press, 1966).
7. Charles W. Kegley, Jr., and Eugene T. Wittkopf, *World Politics: Trend and Transformation* (New York: St. Martin's Press, 1985), p. 378.
8. Robert Art, "To What Ends Military Power?" *International Security* 4 (Spring 1980): 21–23; Kenneth Waltz, *Theory of International Politics* (Reading, Mass.: Addison-Wesley, 1979), pp. 168, 193.
9. Art, "To What Ends Military Power?" 29.
10. Historical development of the various meanings is reviewed in Martin Wight, *Diplomatic Investigations: Essays in the Theory of International Politics* (Cambridge, Mass.: Harvard University Press, 1966), pp. 149–175; their political significance is explored in Ernst Haas, "The Balance of Power: Prescription, Concept, and Propaganda," *World Politics* 5 (July 1953): 442–477.
11. Inis Claude, *Power and International Relations* (New York: Random House, 1962), pp. 13–20.
12. Jack Levy, *War in the Modern Great Power System, 1495–1975* (Lexington: University of Kentucky Press, 1983), p. 1.
13. Michael Howard, "Is Arms Control Really Necessary?" *Harper's*, May 1986, p. 13.
14. Jonathan Farley, "The Gulf War and the Littoral States," *World Today*, July 1984, pp. 269–276.
15. Two instructive uses of the "ideological power elite" interpretation of the Soviet political system to analyze its foreign policy are Michael Voslensky, *Nomenklatura: The Soviet Ruling Class* (Garden City, N.Y.: Doubleday, 1984), chap. 7, "The Claim to World Hegemony"; and Richard Pipes, *U.S.–Soviet Relations in the Era of Detente* (Boulder, Colo.: Westview, 1981).
16. Pipes, *U.S.–Soviet Relations*, pp. 87–88. (Emphasis added.)
17. Voslensky, *Nomenklatura*, p. 326.
18. Ibid., p. 334.
19. Michael Howard, *The Causes of Wars* (Cambridge, Mass.: Harvard University Press, 1984), p. 22.
20. Coral Bell, "Managing to Survive," *The National Interest*, Winter 1985/1986, 36–45. See also John Lewis Gaddis, "The Long Peace," *International Security* 10 (Spring 1986): 99–142.
21. Bell, "Managing to Survive," 45.

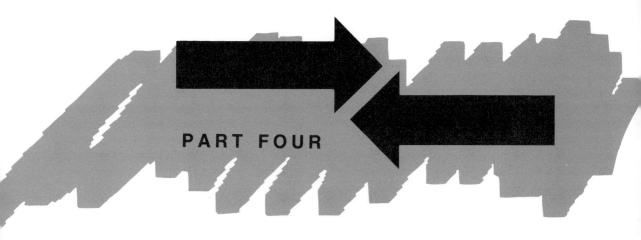

PART FOUR

POWER AND REVOLUTIONARY CHANGE

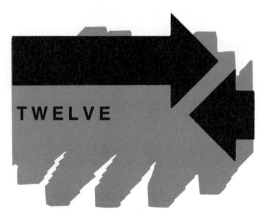

Revolution: Concepts and Causes

> *The primary aim of politics is the acquisition or the preservation of power. Consequently, the aim of revolutionary phenomena, the goal for which they strive, whether consciously or not, whether effectively or not, is power, power that will enable them to build a new social order.*
> *Jean Baechler,* **Revolution**

Like *democracy, revolution* is one of the magic words of contemporary politics. Just as the best-organized autocrats claim to represent "true" democracy, so they often claim legitimacy as guardians of a revolution against oppression and backwardness. In chapter 5 we rejected as manipulative persuasion all uses of *democracy* that do not refer to authority derived from free competition for people's votes. It is impossible, though, to be nearly so specific about what *revolution* does, much less should, mean.

Problems in Defining Revolution

Everyone agrees that a **revolution** is some kind of sudden, out-of-the-ordinary political change, but beyond that point disagreement and special pleading set in. The term was first used in a modern sense to refer to the American and French revolutions in the eighteenth century. Defenders of those very different political developments identified them with the progressive onward march of human enlightenment, humanitarianism, and, above all, liberty.[1]

The Progressive Bias

The concept of historical progress through revolution was taken over and transformed into a supposedly scientific forecast by Marx and his followers, as chapter 8 explained. Although Marxist theory failed scientifically, Lenin and the Bolsheviks claimed that their successful seizure of total power in Russia somehow validated Marx's prophecy. In particular, they insisted that their revolution was inevitable, historically progressive, and irreversible.

Popularized versions of the modern "progressive" and Marxist-Leninist interpretations of revolution have helped produce, over time, a vague but influential **progressive bias.** It is a tendency to interpret every new revolution, at least initially, as the inevitable response of oppressed masses to intolerable exploitation and tyranny. To be **counterrevolutionary,** then, is to be against the masses and historically irrelevant—trying to "turn back the clock" of progress.

It is very important to be aware of this attitude toward *revolution:* "any word that grants automatic legitimacy and at the same time is capable of supporting any meaning becomes a source of great power."[2] It is just as important, though, to recognize that this sense of *revolution* as identical with *progress* is useless for interpreting the phenomena associated with particular revolutions. We are very skeptical of the idea that there is any knowable direction to history; the poor predictive record of Marxist theory certainly does not persuade us otherwise. It should be obvious from our discussion of totalitarian regimes that revolutions do not necessarily lead to progressive increases in welfare, justice, and freedom.

Revolution and Coups d'État

For political analysis, it is most useful to approach revolution as a type of political conflict in which the power to govern is directly at issue. More precisely, *revolution* most often refers to one or more of these developments: first; the downfall of a government, either because it is overthrown by force or because its authority and capacity to command effective coercion have collapsed; second, the emergence of a new government from an all-out struggle for power; third, attempts by leaders of the new regime to bring about sweeping changes in society.

As a rule, military overthrow of a civilian government is not called a revolution. That kind of development is a **coup d'état,** which literally means a "stroke of state." Originally it was used to label an illegal seizure or extension of ruling power by an official already in a position of authority. For example, Louis Napoleon, who had been elected president of the French Second Republic in 1848, suddenly proclaimed himself emperor of France in 1851 and mobilized enough military and political support to make his coup attempt a success.

Coup has come to be applied very loosely to any coercive and illegal seizure of governmental power, whether by governmental insiders or by revolutionary outsiders. In this sense, revolutions often feature one or more coups (for example, the Bolsheviks' overthrow of the Russian government on November 7–8, 1917), although by itself a coup does not make a revolution. Sometimes regimes originating in military coups, as in Egypt, Syria, and Iraq in recent decades, call themselves revolutionary. Their ability to prevent an all-out struggle for power among diverse groups distinguishes their situation from political circumstances most often called revolutions.

Political, Social, and "Great" Revolutions

A useful distinction made in many analyses of revolution differentiates between political and social revolutions. A **political revolution** could more appropriately be described as governmental; its leaders aim almost exclusively at destroying the existing government and creating a new and supposedly more legitimate one in its place. One of the clearest examples was the American Revolution (1775–1783). After a decade of protests against taxation and other colonial policies of the British government, important political elites in the colonies declared their independence of British control. They also mobilized sufficient military force to defeat the effort by the London government to put down their rebellion.

As the colonists' Declaration of Independence made clear, their main objective was to create and control their own system of government. They had no desire to change such features of society as the property and legal systems, religious institutions, or education. Most white Americans had been content with their political and social systems until the British government began imposing new taxes and regulations on them in the 1760s. The revolution can be seen as mainly an effort to reestablish on a permanent basis the representative self-government that most of the colonies had enjoyed in practice for more than a century.

Furthermore, most Americans believed in a limited role for government—essentially to protect against external attack and internal disorder, guarding the rights to life, liberty, and property of individual citizens. A near-absence of hereditary rank and privilege was combined in America with a high degree of economic opportunity in a rapidly expanding society. These conditions made it seem natural to most Americans that individual initiative and choice could and should determine the direction and character of society.

A **social revolution** includes the political aims of destroying an old government and replacing it with a new regime, but its leaders also attempt to make significant changes in society. They may seek to transform the social status system, class structure, economic system, religious institutions and practices, educational and even family systems. Just as the American Revolution was the landmark political revolution, so the French Revolution, which soon followed, became the first modern social revolution. It developed into an attack not only on royal government but on hereditary economic privilege and social status; virtually all kinds of traditional rights, privileges, and legal procedures; and traditional church institutions and doctrines. It featured peasant uprisings and active urban crowds, some of whom demanded revolutionary redistribution of land and wealth to the lower orders of society—with little success.

Traditionally, certain revolutions tend to be singled out by historians and analysts as **great revolutions**. This term does not refer to their moral character but to the degree to which societies were affected, the scope and intensity of upheaval and conflict, the extreme character of revolutionary and antirevolutionary tactics, and their long-term historical effects. By consensus, the French and Russian revolutions always appear on any list of great revolutions, and we would add the Chinese Revolution. It involved decades of violent political conflict within the most populous country in the world and produced enormous changes in its society. In addition, it demonstrated that prolonged guerrilla warfare could help a revolutionary movement finally gain power.

The American Revolution was not great in the same sense as the French, Russian, and Chinese, but its historic impact was very significant. It was the first successful modern war of national liberation against a European colonial power, and its rhetoric and example had an immediate impact on the political situation in France. What appeared to be a distinctive people asserting and successfully defending their "natural rights" encouraged many Frenchmen to believe that they could do the same: "it broke the eighteenth-century code of custom at a stroke."[3]

Whatever the difficulties of defining and categorizing revolutions, they are obviously one of the most important phenomena in modern politics. We need to begin trying to learn and think seriously about why revolutions occur, what kinds of developments and events tend to typify at least some of them, and the nature of the changes that revolutions bring about.

Why Revolutions?

It is impossible to give a clear, satisfactory, completely adequate answer to the important question of why revolutions occur. "Unfortunately, there is no simple law of revolution under which we can subsume particular instances with their set of appropriate initial conditions, and accordingly explain past or predict future revolutions."[4] Even when we try to understand particular revolutions, we discover that historians are still arguing over the causes, courses, and consequences of every single one of them.

Yet there are some important similarities among many revolutions, and certain kinds of social and political conditions seem more likely to give rise to them than others. In addition, numerous revolutions go through similar phases of development, and at least with hindsight it becomes possible to gain some perspective on why particular revolutions turned out as they did. On this subject, though, we need to be very cautious and tentative about most generalizations, and especially about attempts to predict where revolutions are likely to occur in the future.

Massive historical evidence clearly does refute the simplistic assumption that extreme oppressiveness and mass suffering are the main causes of revolutions. If this were true, revolutions would tend to occur in countries with the most tyrannical governments or in those with the highest levels of desperate, life-threatening poverty. That is clearly not the case.

In the late eighteenth century, for example, the common people were both much poorer and more brutally exploited and oppressed in Russia than in France, but revolution broke out in France. Perhaps there has never been a more oppressive regime than that of Stalinist Russia, but revolution there was not even a remote possibility. Compared with most Latin American countries, Cuba in the late 1950s was one of the more prosperous and middle-class societies, yet it underwent a drastic revolution.

None of this means that oppression, poverty, and suffering have nothing to do with revolutions, but the relationships are much more complex, indirect, and variable than they appear in the popular stereotype of a revolutionary situation. One way of trying to understand them is to emphasize people's feelings of **relative deprivation.** Put simply, this involves a belief that they are getting fewer rewards—whether income, power, or status—than they deserve when compared with other people. Poor and hardworking peasants in prerevolutionary France bitterly resented paying taxes from their meager incomes while leisured, wealthy aristocrats successfully resisted almost all taxation. Prior to 1917, many Russian intellectuals believed that their modern knowledge and concern for the masses entitled them to exercise ruling power. They felt bitter antagonism toward the traditional, "backward," and "superstitious" tsarist autocracy.

If people feel sufficiently deprived they become increasingly frustrated and prone to lash out aggressively against whomever they blame for cheating and exploiting them. Under some circumstances, the result can be violent rebellion that turns into full-scale revolution.

The trouble with relative deprivation as an explanation for revolutions is that many people feel it very strongly in every society. We have no way of knowing whether there is more of it in societies that undergo a revolution than in those where none occurs. People have a variety of ways of coping with feelings of relative deprivation and frustration. In most of human history they have accepted their unhappy condition as the will of God or as blind fate—for whatever reason, as simply unchangeable. By itself, relative-deprivation theory tells us nothing about when and why people sometimes express their resentments and aspirations in the kinds of extraordinary political actions that make for revolution.

Background Causes

As Jean Baechler suggests in the quotation that heads this chapter, revolutions involve above all a struggle for effective power, and our analysis will focus mainly on their political dimension. To provide a degree of historical context, though, we will briefly discuss some pertinent intellectual and social changes that have occurred in the West and spread to the rest of the world during the past few centuries.

Secularization is an important trend related to the origins and progress of modern natural science since the seventeenth century. In simple terms, it refers to loss of belief that the world is a divinely established order that people must simply accept as they pass through it on the way to an eternal afterlife. Instead, many intellectuals in the seventeenth and eighteenth centuries came to believe that the world operates exclusively according to natural laws. Human beings can discover and understand them and use their knowledge to improve the human condition—through medicine, technology, and, possibly, the systematic, rational reconstruction of society.

We have already noted in chapter 5 how the secularization of ideas helped lead to the demise of divine-right monarchy. To think of society not as produced, endorsed, and sustained by divine decree but as the product of human actions and interests suggests the possibility of deliberately redesigning and remaking it. New forms of government, of property systems, of all kinds of social relationships become thinkable once the crust of hallowed custom is broken.

Secularization was only one component of a quickening process of change in Western societies in the postmedieval era. Exploration, colonization, the commercialization of agriculture in England, and the spread of commercial banking all contributed to long-term economic growth and development, especially in Holland and England. The invention of mechanical printing and its spread from the sixteenth century onward brought the emergence of the modern **intellectual class.** This is a loose and variously defined term that usually includes writers, artists, journalists, professors, scientists, some members of professions such as law and medicine, and political publicists and ideologists.

Intellectuals specialize in the power of persuasion, and they have played a critically important part in every modern revolution. By no means are all intellectuals revolutionary; most are not, and some are self-consciously conservative and antirevolutionary. Intellectuals, though, not only reflect social change; they help to point it out and interpret it. Some have done so by promoting the idea that change can and should take the form of radical social engineering.

A frequently neglected background factor that has often contributed to the onset of revolution is rivalry between states.[5] Throughout the eighteenth century, for example, France competed with Britain for military and colonial success. The French had little to show for their efforts until they gave decisive military aid to the rebellious Americans and helped deal the British a severe defeat. The French economy was much less commercialized and productive than the British, and the expense of the American war created financial problems for the French government that led it unwittingly to provoke a revolution in France.

The terrible human and financial costs of wars also contributed greatly to the downfall of both the tsarist government in Russia and the Nationalist government in China. In general, lagging behind rival states militarily and economically can produce or reveal potentially fatal weaknesses in a government and make it a candidate for drastic transformation.

Conditions Favoring Revolution

Ineffective government   The character, competence, and capacities of the existing government have a great deal to do with whether it is vulnerable to revolutionary overthrow. Oppressiveness alone is not likely to provoke the downfall of a government. Inability to cope with serious economic problems can prove much more threatening to its continued existence. Attempts to impose taxes for badly needed revenues helped trigger antiroyalist revolutions in seventeenth-century England (the Civil War) and in eighteenth-century America and France. The governments involved had not been strong enough previously to enforce taxation on certain elements of the population, and their attempts to do so provoked reactions that fatally demonstrated their weakness.

Desperate to raise money for its war debts, the French government of Louis XVI decided to convene the first meeting in 175 years of a semiparliamentary institution, the Estates-General. Leading up to that event were numerous local meetings and the framing of many petitions of grievances of class against class and of all against the government.

Peasants were outraged that landed aristocrats were enforcing ancient feudal rights and claims, involving crop payments, exclusive hunting rights, and insecurity for peasants' property. The harvest in 1788 was very poor; bread prices reached a record high in the spring of 1789, and urban workers and petty merchants protested and rioted. Hereditary nobles resented the monarchy's raising money by selling aristocratic positions and titles, and members of the growing business class protested the nobles' ability to use the courts to evade or escape almost all taxation. Fueled by the multitude of conflicting grievances, the Estates-General turned into an engine for revolution instead of the consultative taxing body that the royal government had intended.

Much more recently, a violent and protracted revolution broke out in Iran. The shah's monarchy, which was to collapse in 1979, had presided over a massive national development program and a rapid increase in oil revenues. Demand for consumer goods outran supply, and inflation shot up. Trying to hold down prices, the government alienated much of the business community by fining and jailing some shopkeepers and traders.

A sudden austerity program had drastic effects on much of the population; middle-class families accustomed to rising incomes suddenly found themselves unable to buy a house or even a car. Merchants' sales fell off rapidly, and government workers on fixed salaries felt resentful and betrayed. "The pressure of frustrated aspirations triggered the political crises that followed."[6]

■ The J-Curve

The outbreak of the Iranian Revolution—as well as the French Revolution two centuries earlier—seems to exemplify the **J-curve** phenomenon. This means that a revolution is likely to result from a sudden sharp decline in economic conditions after an extended period of improvement has continuously raised expectations. In terms of the diagram in figure 12-1, people's "actual need satisfaction" suddenly falls far short of their "expected need satisfaction" based on past experience. (The J in the curved lower line is upside down.) This is one important form of relative deprivation that gives rise to intense and potentially explosive frustrations.

The J-curve phenomenon is real and significant, but it is far from an adequate explanation of the onset of revolutions. In some revolutionary situations—the Chinese, for example—it was absent. Also, a J-curve pattern sometimes doesn't even produce violent opposition, much less a revolution. In the 1930s the United States experienced massive unemployment after the steadily rising prosperity of the twenties, but there was no very serious radical challenge to the existing government.

As we pointed out in chapter 2, the U.S. government rode out the Great Depression because of the enormous degree of legitimacy bestowed upon it by most of the American people. A long-term erosion of authority makes a government extremely vulnerable when it proves unable to cope with economic or other serious problems. One of the major symptoms of and contributors to that erosion is what historian Crane Brinton called **"the desertion of the intellectuals."**[7] If many writers, scholars, journalists, and other would-be political persuaders become increasingly alienated from existing governmental and social structures, they will relentlessly attack the regime's basic claims to authority. This pattern has appeared in many societies during the past two centuries, but the classic modern example remains eighteenth-century France.

Intellectuals' influences: The French example Most French writers of the Enlightenment epoch were bitterly opposed to the supernaturalist doctrines, social role, and privileges of the Catholic Church. The Church was a major landowner; it was supported by a compulsory tithe, or tax, of ten percent; officially it was intolerant of all other religious groups and of "blasphemous" criticisms. Most intellectuals also despised the inherited position and privileges of the nobility as impossible to justify rationally

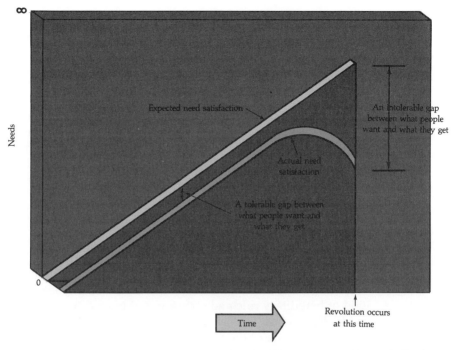

Figure 12-1 The J-Curve and revolution (Source: James C. Davies, "The J-Curve of Rising and Declining Satisfactions as a Cause of Some Great Revolutions and a Contained Rebellion," in *Violence in America: Historical and Comparative Perspectives*, ed. Hugh Davis Graham and Ted Robert Gurr [New York: New American Library, 1969], pp. 671–709.)

and therefore illegitimate. Thousands of articles, pamphlets, and books hammered away at these critical themes for decades before 1789, despite sporadic and largely ineffective censorship.

Perhaps as influential as head-on attacks were witty, satirical works such as the fictions of Voltaire (born François-Marie Arouet, 1694–1778), the unofficial leader of the French Enlightenment. In his famous fable *Candide* (1758), Voltaire depicts priests and officials of the Church as tyrannical, lustful, superstitious hypocrites determined to protect their power and privileges by burning at the stake loosely defined categories of "heretics." A titled aristocrat goes to absurd lengths to prevent marriage between his sister and the naive and generous hero whose character and good deeds count for nothing in the absence of noble birth.

In the long run, the most influential political ideas to appear in eighteenth-century France were proclaimed by a self-educated, self-exiled citizen of Geneva, Jean-Jacques Rousseau (1712–1778). He outraged rationalists such as Voltaire by insisting that the "natural" emotions rather than reason should be the supreme measure of human truth. Yet Rousseau's ideas undercut the existing social-political order in a much more radical and uncompromising way than did Voltaire's.

In his *Discourse on the Origin and Foundation of Inequality among Mankind* (1755), Rousseau declared that social, economic, and political inequality were the main causes of conflict and suffering. Societies in primitive times had been small, egalitarian, harmonious, and happy. The fatal establishment of private property in land had led to slavery, warfare, social disorder, and finally, governments that protected the rich minority against the poor majority. The so-called progress of civilization mainly represents the development of new techniques for exploiting the powerless mass of mankind and of ideas that rationalize or divert attention from their unjust suffering.

Inequality of rights and extremes of wealth and poverty, Rousseau declared, have no basis in nature. Instead they spring from a decadent and corrupting social order that has nearly stifled the naturally compassionate voice of human conscience. Using the emotionally charged rhetoric of which he was a master, Rousseau concludes his discourse with blunt rejection of hereditary rule and status and of large economic inequalities: "It is evidently against the law of nature that children should command old men, and fools lead the wise, and that a handful should gorge themselves with superfluities, while the starving masses lack the barest necessities of life."[8]

Root-and-branch criticisms of the established order appealed not merely to intellectuals of nonaristocratic origin but to numerous members of such privileged groups as the nobility and clergy. Many aristocratic French ladies held *salons* (social gatherings), in which celebrated authors and critics would wittily or passionately denounce the ideas and institutions that sustained the nobility's privileges. Some of the most radical philosophical and political intellectuals were themselves aristocrats or clerics.

Events in France were to illustrate the shrewdness of a remark made more than two thousand years earlier by the first great Western political theorist, Plato: "Is it not a simple fact that in any form of government revolution always starts from the outbreak of internal dissension in the ruling class? The constitution cannot be upset so long as that class is of one mind, however small it may be."[9]

None of this discussion implies that critical intellectuals' writings were *the* cause of the French Revolution. The French political environment in the eighteenth century contributed enormously to the enthusiastic reception of their ideas. The great nineteenth-century French historian and political theorist Alexis de Tocqueville (1805–1859) attempted to explain why.

Tocqueville emphasized that for many decades before the Revolution the royal government had tried with increasing success to centralize administrative control and direction of French society in its hands. One result was the weakening or destruction of traditional local and provincial governments, greatly narrowing the range of participants in public affairs. Even most aristocrats had no governmental role, as they emphatically did in the British parliamentary and local governments of the time. Excluded from actual politics, both the intellectuals and the rest of the literate population were attracted to unrelenting criticism of the existing order. Without practical experience as a basis for judgment, they readily endorsed attractive-sounding schemes for social transformation as sure cures for all political and social ills.

Americans in the eighteenth century used a similar "Enlightenment" political vocabulary, emphasizing universal natural rights and rational laws of nature. However, the generations-long experience of colonial self-government led American revolutionary leaders to favor practical solutions to specific problems rather than sweeping plans for total social change.[10]

Multiple enemies of the status quo: The Iranian example Critical attacks tend to be most effective in a society already torn by severe antagonisms among social groups, especially when mutually hostile groups begin attacking the government as the chief source of all problems and discontents. A recent dramatic example is provided by Iran in the years leading up to the 1979 revolution.

The shah had become increasingly autocratic since the early 1960s, packing parliament with his supporters and suppressing independent political parties. His security police had become more active and brutal in their methods of protecting the regime. These techniques increasingly alienated middle-class intellectuals and professionals. Under pressure from the U.S. government, the shah implemented some new legal protections for defendants and eased press controls in 1977. As a result, secular, modernized professional groups and parties began protesting, organizing, and meeting to demand sweeping political changes.

Very soon, however, these efforts were dwarfed by massive demonstrations and rallies led by the **militant Islamic clergy.** They were inspired and led by the exiled Ayatollah Khomeini, who had been an active enemy of the shah's regime since 1962. The activist clergy denounced the shah as the great secularizer and called for replacing his regime with a truly Islamic system of government. Groups with radically conflicting purposes—some desiring the further advancement of modern secular education and reforms and others seeking to halt and reverse such modernistic Western "heresies" as voting rights for women—combined in an assault on the shah's regime.[11]

Revolutionary nationalism The direction taken by the Iranian revolution illustrates another feature of many revolutionary situations: **revolu-**

tionary nationalism based on hatred of foreigners accused of interfering in the political and social life of the nation. United States military trainers and advisers were exempt from Iranian laws. U.S. corporations had assumed a prominent and visible role in the shah's drive for economic development, and American popular culture was gaining a considerable following among Iranian youth.

In response, Khomeini and his followers portrayed the United States as the "Great Satan" supporting the oppressive rule of the shah and, in collaboration with the Israeli "gang of Jews," spearheading a Western plot to destroy Islam.[12] Appeals to throw off the yoke of alien powers characterize all wars of national liberation, some of which are led and dominated by revolutionary movements—for example, in Algeria and Vietnam in the post–World War II period.

Revolutionary Detonators

What kinds of events or circumstances can become short-run causes of a revolutionary explosion? Specific answers to that question have differed from one revolution to another and include strikes, mass protests, massacres, coups, and armed uprisings. Whatever the specific occurrences, however, they trigger a revolution because they disclose or bring about a lessening or loss of the **government's capacity to coerce** its opponents: "History shows that, in the last resort, success or failure hinges on the attitude which those armed forces of the *status quo* government will take toward an insurrection . . . whatever government or party has the full allegiance of a country's armed forces is to all intents and purposes politically impregnable."[13]

Revolutionary outbreaks in Russia Unsuccessful warfare has helped bring about the revolutionary collapse of certain governments. The contrast between two revolutionary years in twentieth-century Russia points up the critical importance of military force. In 1905 the tsarist government showed unexpected weakness by losing a brief Far Eastern war that it had confidently entered against Japan. Many groups opposed to the regime joined in popular demonstrations and uprisings, and the tsar made a number of political concessions. The revolution was halted and to a degree reversed, though, when the government brought back enough loyal troops from the Far East to suppress and intimidate its opponents.

During the First World War, Russian armed forces had suffered nearly two million deaths by 1917 and were very much on the defensive against Germany and Austria. The longing for peace was widespread among the troops, and those stationed inside Russia were reluctant to go to the front. Many troops were garrisoned in and near Petrograd, the capital, which was also the home of the largest concentration of industrial workers in the country.

When serious food shortages led to larger and larger strikes and street protests in late February (by the old-style Russian calendar), the police fired on militant demonstrators and were in turn attacked. But soldiers proved very reluctant to take action against the demonstrators. When ordered to do so on February 27, many of them mutinied, shot their officers, and joined the striking workers in rioting and anarchy. Even troops at the tsar's residence participated in the mutiny. With the collapse of its coercive capabilities, the royal government was finished; on March 2 Tsar Nicholas II abdicated.[14]

Collapse of official coercion in Iran Even in the absence of warfare, popular strikes and demonstrations can sometimes precipitate a revolution. That outcome seems most likely when a government uses enough violence to increase hatred toward it but not enough to crush its enemies. In January 1978, Islamic seminary students in the Iranian holy city of Qom protested against a government newspaper attack on the Ayatollah Khomeini. Their confrontation with police resulted in a number of deaths. This event sparked a series of public mourning ceremonies, funeral processions, and riots over the next year. They amounted to a nearly continuous round of provocative protests, deaths inflicted by the authorities, renewed demonstrations commemorating the "martyrs," repression with fatalities, and so on.

In response to the protests, the shah offered political concessions, but his most determined opponents, the radical Islamic clergy, saw these offers as a sign of weakness. A massive three-day rally in Teheran in early September 1978 ended with a declaration of martial law and many deaths when troops opened fire in a working-class district. At that point the only hope for the government's survival was ruthless repression. The shah did not follow that course but, ill with terminal cancer, left the country on January 16, 1979, after appointing a former opposition politician as prime minister.

Without the shah's leadership the military commanders proved indecisive in coping with massive demonstrations—as many as a million people at one time in the streets of Teheran. The demonstrators demanded that the Ayatollah Khomeini be allowed to come back from exile and replace the shah's regime with a new Islamic government. He did return on February 1, and some air force units began siding with the Khomeini forces; the top military officers announced their neutrality in the domestic power struggle on February 9. The royal government totally collapsed two days later, and Khomeini announced the establishment of a new Islamic state.[15]

The coercive capacities of governments do not always disappear so suddenly as in Russia and Iran. No revolution is possible, though, so long as the government's armed forces are larger, more professional, and better equipped than the opposition and are willing to fight off challengers for sovereign power.

Potential revolution in Poland Events in Poland in 1980–1981 demonstrate the absolutely critical importance of coercive capacity in determining whether a revolutionary situation will develop into a revolution. The communist government of Poland had presided over a string of failed economic policies. Corruption and privilege had helped earn for it the contempt of most of the population, as did the Poles' resentment against it as a Russian puppet regime. Most intellectuals had long been alienated from the government and had managed to publish or circulate numerous critical works. Some of them had also participated in the activities of "flying universities"—unofficial lecture and discussion sessions that moved from place to place. Shrewd political intellectuals also served as advisers to the leaders of Solidarity, the workers' federation born out of massive strikes in August 1980.

The government's negotiating with striking workers and signing an agreement recognizing their right to an independent union seemed to show its weakness and vulnerability. Over the following months, large protest demonstrations often occurred as Solidarity denounced violations of earlier agreements. Despite its leaders' claims that it did not seek governmental power, Solidarity quickly became in fact an alternative organization to the communist party and the government that it controlled. In addition, the overwhelming majority of Polish workers became members of Solidarity. If ever a society appeared ripe for revolution, it was Poland, in light of nearly all the potential causes of revolutionary political change discussed in this chapter.

One essential ingredient of the revolutionary recipe was missing, however: the collapse of the government's coercive capabilities. On December 13, 1981, the head of government suddenly declared martial law; most Solidarity leaders were arrested and the organization outlawed. The regime had at its command large contingents of specially trained and heavily armed **security forces.** Its members were carefully selected, often from poor rural backgrounds, and kept isolated from society most of the time. They were well fed, housed, and given excellent medical treatment, thoroughly indoctrinated and brutalized. These forces had put down workers' protests earlier in 1968 and 1970 and proved reliable once more.

Unlike the shah's government in Iran, the communist party leaders in Poland did not hesitate to use force to prevent a revolution against them. In addition, they were strongly backed—no doubt even prodded to act— by their enormously more powerful Soviet neighbor. In this critical sense the international environment strongly disfavored a Polish revolution, as we pointed out in chapter 9. The erosion, even the collapse, of a regime's authority, then, can push it toward destruction, but it goes over the edge only if and when its coercive capacity disappears.[16]

Organizing for Revolution

Among the causes of revolutions, what is the role of deliberate planning and organization? One leading interpretation stresses almost exclusively the structural weaknesses of societies and the gradually developing incapacity of governments to cope with serious problems: "As far as the causes of historical social revolutions go, Wendell Phillips was quite correct when he once declared: 'Revolutions are not made; they come.'"[17]

The opposite view emphasizes conspiratorial organizations as the only significant cause of revolutionary upheaval. This extreme interpretation seldom if ever seems substantiated by adequate evidence and has virtually no support among academic students of revolution. But in our judgment, to focus exclusively on problems in social and governmental structures, as important as they are, plays down too much the significance of ideology and, in many circumstances, the efforts of revolutionary organizations.

The Leninist example The first—or "February"—revolution in Russia in 1917 *did* just "come," but there was nothing spontaneous about the second—"October"—revolution that year. It was launched by a deliberately planned Bolshevik coup against the provisional government. Weaknesses in that government and its inability to solve massive problems contributed crucially to the Bolsheviks' success. However, their long-established discipline and military-type organization gave them a decided advantage in an all-out struggle for power. No Bolsheviks, no "total" social revolution in Russia.

The eventual success of an originally tiny revolutionary party in winning supreme power over a huge and complex society has inspired dozens of more or less imitative movements since 1917. They have by no means been slavish copiers; important revisions in strategy and tactics were introduced, for example, in China and Cuba. Nor do "Leninist" movements have a sure-fire recipe for making a revolution; most of them have failed to win power.

By definition, a revolutionary movement can succeed only under favorable social and political conditions. We usually can't identify those conditions very precisely, however, until a revolution has actually occurred. As usual, hindsight is clearest. It may also be that in every case where a Leninist party has won power, structural weaknesses in the old government and society would have produced a revolution even in the absence of that party. But we can never know that, and in many cases it seems quite probable that there might well have been no revolution, or at least that it might have followed a different course.

Intellectuals as revolutionaries Revolutionary intellectuals—nationalist, socialist, anarchist—multiplied in nineteenth-century Europe, establishing study groups and conspiratorial societies. Although they played active parts in certain revolutionary situations, such as the Paris Commune of 1871, they had little success in producing political revolts. Most of the leading revolutionary ideologists of that era, including Mazzini and Marx, assumed that mass uprisings will occur when society is ripe for them. Only when social conditions have developed in the proper way will the masses respond to calls for revolutionary action.

By the latter part of the century it was clear that the masses were seldom inclined to rise up spontaneously, even when theorists predicted that they should. To deal with that problem, revolutionary intellectuals produced several versions of **"directed" revolutionary activism;** as a means of winning power, Leninism has been the most successful variety.[18]

Lenin's concept of the revolutionary party was explained in chapter 8. In the present context we would suggest that it appealed strongly to revolutionary intellectuals in many parts of the world, and not only because of the Bolsheviks' political success. It also provided a legitimacy claim for a self-selected intellectual elite—those who believed that they were best qualified to interpret and apply an infallible "scientific" doctrine.

Marxism-Leninism was simply the most successful version of modern revolutionary ideology, which, in all its forms, shows a common tendency: "Ideology is the activity especially of intellectuals, and what it provides them is the equivalent of the role of priests and prophets in traditional religions. It offers a redemptive sketch of history in which they, the intellectuals, will supplant the traditional elites, and become the new governing elite."[19]

It is not really surprising, then, that the leaders of Marxist-Leninist revolutionary movements are seldom if ever proletarians or peasants. Nearly always they come from middle-to-upper-class backgrounds and have much more experience of formal, Western-type secular education than do most young people in their societies. Lenin and Castro, for example, were both university law graduates and Mao Zedong a university librarian.

A more recent, dramatic, but not untypical example is provided by the Cambodian Communists who ran the Khmer Rouge regime from 1975 to 1979. Of the half-dozen most powerful inner-party leaders, three earned Ph.D. degrees at the University of Paris, and all came from landowning or civil servant families.[20] Starting in their student years, they worked and organized for about a quarter of a century to gain supreme power for their revolutionary movement. They finally did so when favored by complex political circumstances, but their own efforts were important also. Their longstanding ideological commitments and plans had everything to do with the drastic programs that they imposed upon an overwhelmingly peasant and traditional society.

The peasant-support strategy Intellectual-led revolutionary parties, even if thoroughly Leninist in organizational structure and techniques, can never win power on their own. To do so they must develop an effective strategy of cooperation with other political and social groups. In some circumstances that means seeking support mainly among peasants. This important strategy was invented by Chinese Communist leaders after they were driven out of urban bases by their former coalition partner, Chiang Kai-shek's Nationalists, in the late 1920s.

The Communists found refuge in a wild and mountainous region and, when Nationalist forces threatened, undertook an arduous "Long March" of thousands of miles to an even more remote region in northern China. Although the Nationalists controlled the government, effective coercive power in many parts of the country was wielded by war lords who commanded their own armies. The Communists resorted to guerrilla warfare—fighting in small mobile units, specializing in surprise attacks, always retreating before superior forces. At the same time they mobilized support among landless or land-poor peasants by attacking landlords, redistributing some land in regions they could control, and setting up ideological training and recruitment programs.

The Japanese invaded Manchuria in northeastern China in 1931 and launched an all-out war against China in 1937. The Nationalist government was never strong enough to fight a two-front war against both the Communists and the Japanese. The Communists gained many supporters by claiming that their first priority was defense of the homeland against the foreign invader.

By the time the Japanese surrendered in 1945, the Communists controlled enough territory and population to move from guerrilla to conventional warfare. Their **peasant-support strategy** continued to give them a crucial advantage over the Nationalists, whose leaders fled to Taiwan after their final defeat in 1949.

Mao Zedong's strategy of turning the peasant population into a friendly "sea" in which revolutionary guerrillas could safely "swim" was exploited successfully elsewhere, most notably in North Vietnam and Cambodia. It failed, though, in other agrarian societies such as Malaya, the Philippines (in the 1950s), Bolivia, Venezuela, and Guatemala. In the 1980s guerrilla Leninism (or "Maoism") was still the primary strategy of some active revolutionary movements, such as those in Peru and the Philippines.

A brief look at the most recent effort by Philippines revolutionaries to emulate Mao Zedong's success should give a more specific idea of the plan-

One of many efforts to persuade communist NPA guerillas to cease hostilities after the democratic revolution in the Philippines in 1986. Communist leaders refused, instead continuing their efforts to overthrow the government with revolutionary armed force and gain absolute power.

ning and tactics typical of guerrilla Leninism. We refer to the **New People's Army** (NPA), the military wing of the Communist Party of the Philippines. Unsurprisingly, the leaders of this group come from the urban, educated middle class. They have attracted peasant recruits mainly by promising them land and, until the collapse of the Marcos regime in 1986, attacking the government for corruption and abuse of power. Recruits are trained and indoctrinated with Marxist-Leninist ideology. They are instructed to kill informers, government officials, anti-Communists, and "criminals" convicted in revolutionary "people's courts" held in areas controlled by the guerrillas. According to a long-time Asia correspondent for *Time*, intimidation through terror plays an important part in the NPA's control of many villages.[21]

Land expropriated from government forests or simply seized from owners incapable of resisting is given to poorer peasants to back up the guerrillas' promise that has most appeal in the countryside. One NPA commander, who had apparently progressed much further in his ideological training than the rank and file, explained that all peasants would receive land after the revolution but would not be allowed to sell it to each other or leave it to their children. As the people acquired a deeper idea of communism, many would freely surrender their land to the government, and eventually it would all be collectivized. Only upper party members were told of these plans for the ultimate ownership and control of land.²² These kinds of efforts to win peasant support are standard Leninist-Maoist tactics. They reflect the critical importance for such movements of manipulative persuasion designed to camouflage their leaders' ultimate objectives.

The united-front strategy The coalitional or **united-front** technique for a totalitarian takeover was discussed briefly in chapter 8, but it deserves reemphasis as a frequently successful form of revolutionary planning. In Cambodia, for instance, a military coup overthrew the long-time government of Prince Sihanouk in 1970. The prince, who had a large following among peasants, found refuge in China and soon announced the creation of a government in exile. It included several Cambodian Communist Party leaders in such key positions as ministers of defense, interior, and information.

They encouraged the prince and his advisers to remain in China while communist guerrillas, with North Vietnamese military help, brought additional Cambodian territory under their control. Prince Sihanouk's broadcasts and the peasants' great respect for him as the embodiment of religious and political tradition persuaded many peasants to support the antigovernment coalition.

As its areas of control expanded, the communist faction steadily undermined Prince Sihanouk's administrative authority. By 1974 they had purged the last traces of his influence from the armed movement that took control of the entire country when the military government collapsed in April 1975. Only then did the Khmer Rouge fully reveal their total hostility to Khmer traditions and their ideological determination to mold a new, revolutionary Cambodia. They proceeded to eliminate at least a quarter of the Khmer people in the process.²³

It is not only peasants and princes who can become critically important—though temporary—revolutionary coalition partners of a Leninist party. A study of why two Latin American guerrilla movements, Castro's forces in Cuba and the Sandinistas in Nicaragua, succeeded in gaining power while all others have failed concludes that the ability to form a broad **negative coalition** made the difference. Peasants were a minor component of these coalitions; decisive support came from the urban middle and professional classes. Narrowly based, highly personalized, and cynically corrupt dictatorships had alienated increasing numbers of the educated and middle-class elements of the population. Their antiregime hostility intensified when Batista in Cuba and Somoza in Nicaragua responded with increased brutality to the guerrillas challenging their regimes. Without broad middle-class coalitional support for the overthrow of these rulers, the small guerrilla movements could not possibly have succeeded on their own.²⁴

The question remains, though, why such coalitions were possible, given the radically different aims of revolutionary guerrillas and mostly middle-class business and professional people. In Cuba those differences were not apparent before the revolution. Castro came to power in 1959 promising to restore the 1940 democratic constitution and hold free elections in the near future.

It became clear only in 1986, through interviews granted by Castro and a number of his long-time collaborators, that the leader of the Cuban revolution had successfully used wholesale manipulative persuasion from the very beginning of his revolutionary career. Well before 1959 he had planned to create a Marxist-Leninist regime in Cuba but publicly denied it in order to gain critical support and avert U.S. intervention. As soon as his small guerrilla movement took power he established a broad-based coalitional government in public and a secret communist parallel government that manipulated events from behind the scenes and eventually emerged as *the* government.[25]

In Nicaragua, the Sandinistas' Marxism-Leninism was no secret, but a prerevolution agreement was drawn up between them and other anti-Somoza parties guaranteeing political and economic pluralism. It was also endorsed by the hierarchy of the Catholic Church, which had played a significant role in undercutting Somoza's support. In addition, the Sandinistas and their coalition partners joined in a letter to the Organization of American States (OAS) promising to hold democratic elections soon after taking power.

As soon as Somoza fled the country, a coalition government was established. It soon became clear, though, that the Sandinista National Directorate actually controlled all decisions of the government, and the prominent non-Sandinista political figures resigned in disillusionment. Within a few years some of them had become supporters of anti-Sandinista guerrilla forces, and Church leaders were criticizing the Sandinista regime for moving toward Marxist-Leninist monopoly rule.[26]

In trying to create or, as in Cuba, to take advantage of revolutionary situations, Marxist-Leninist groups have been favored by two of their characteristic features: an operationally flexible but totally concentrated focus on winning and holding absolute power and a highly disciplined, top-down command structure that makes the party a formidable **organizational weapon** in the revolutionary struggle for power. When a Leninist party tactically supports a coalition with other parties, it is "in the same way, as Lenin once said, 'as the rope supports a hanged man.'"[27]

Foreign assistance The causal effectiveness of an organized revolutionary movement can be increased by its ability to attract foreign support. The most important example is the long-established policy of the Soviet Union to provide military aid, tactical and political training, and interna-

"I don't have much hope for this broad-based coalition."

tional propaganda support for self-identified Marxist-Leninist revolutionary groups. Directly or indirectly, the Soviets have aided such movements in many countries, from China in the 1920s to El Salvador in the 1980s. As we suggested in chapters 9 and 11, this policy seems designed in part to bolster the ideological legitimacy claim of Soviet leaders that they represent the "inevitable wave of the future." Quite obviously it is also a major technique for undercutting the influence of the United States, the Soviets' main rival for international power.

In concluding this discussion of the causes of revolutions, summarized in table 12-1, we would emphasize that a revolution can't simply be whipped up on demand by a Marxist-Leninist or any other kind of antigovernment party, even with the support of a foreign superpower. But it does appear to us that in some favorable circumstances strategic and tactical planning, coupled with effectively disciplined organization, can function as an important causal force. It can sometimes impose direction on the confusing morass of trends, developments, and unexpected events that give rise to every revolution.

Summary

Revolution has become a magic word in modern politics, even though there is little agreement on precisely how and when it ought to be used. Over the course of two centuries it has come to be virtually identified with

Table 12-1 Possible causes of revolutions

	Examples	*Significance*
Background Factors	Secularization, rise of intellectual class	Decrease sanctity of status quo, undercuts traditional legitimacy
Favoring Conditions	Splits among elites	Weaken government's decisiveness
	Severe financial problems, sudden economic downturn, diverse groups opposing government	Increase feelings of relative deprivation—frustration, resentment, generalized political negativism
	Revolutionary nationalism	Identifies government with hated foreigners
	Organized revolutionary groups	Can weaken government and focus strongest opposition
Short-Term Causes—"Detonators"	Lost or dragged-out costly wars, mass strikes, demonstrations, revolts, mutinies	Escalate hatred of government, can reveal its inability to coerce opponents
	Negative, antiregime coalitions	Can tip balance against shaky government

"progress," despite the fact that experience casts doubt on their connection.

We seek to analyze revolution as a type of severe political conflict that usually has broad and long-lasting effects on government and society. With some notable exceptions, military takeovers of governments are not revolutions; most coups d'état bring suppression of conflict and little long-term political and social change.

A distinction is commonly made between political and social revolutions. Political revolutions change only the form of government and the locus of official decision making, as did the American Revolution's ending of British rule in the colonies. Social revolutions change governments too, but they also involve attempts to transform other features of society such as religion, social status, education, and the economy. The French Revolution was the first modern social revolution, and it has provided an example that most later revolutionaries have tried to follow or improve upon.

There is no generally accepted theory of the causes of revolutions. Contrary to a popular impression, revolutions seldom occur in the poorest and most tyrannically ruled societies. Widespread, intense feelings of being unjustly deprived—swindled and exploited—may well contribute to revolutionary outbreaks. Many people feel that way in every society, though, and revolutions are relatively rare.

Certain developments that began in the West in the early modern era contributed to intellectual, social, and political environments favorable to the emergence of revolutionary ideas and movements. Secularization of thought and society, promoted by the decline of traditional religion and the rise of modern science, encouraged the belief that the social order is created by human activity rather than divine decree. Some thinkers argued that society, like nature, should be investigated scientifically and the resulting knowledge used to construct a just and rational sociopolitical system.

Attacks on traditional institutions as "irrational," coupled with plans for sweeping reforms, appealed to elements of the new intellectual class. Its growth was promoted by the invention of mechanical printing, more rapid economic change, and increasing demands for useful knowledge. Critical and revolutionary intellectuals attempted, with some success, to gain power through political persuasion.

The international environment has often served as another important background cause of revolution. Lagging behind rival states can lead to severe pressures on a government for economic and political changes, which, if resisted or bungled, can set the stage for revolutionary upheaval.

Conditions that can contribute more directly to the outbreak of revolution are headed by a government's inabililty to cope with serious problems that inspire considerable discontent and opposition. Unresolved financial and economic problems can be especially dangerous to stability. When a period of steady improvement is interrupted by a sudden sharp downturn, people suffering its painful effects may become frustrated and angry enough to attack the government as the supposed source of their misery. They are not as likely to do so, however, if they believe strongly in its legitimacy.

Critical intellectuals have done much to undercut the authority of governments and social systems in the modern world. In eighteenth-century France, the leading example, Enlightenment thinkers subjected traditional institutions to both indignant and satirical attacks. Irrational, unjust, grossly and indefensibly unequal—these were charges effectively leveled by brilliant writers such as Voltaire and Rousseau against church, aristocracy, and government. Ideas with revolutionary implications had a greater impact in France than in England or America, probably because literate Frenchmen had long been denied practical governing experience by the centralized monarchy.

An established government is especially endangered when groups with intense but contradictory grievances join in a negative coalition seeking to destroy it. In late-1970s Iran, for example, both secular and antisecular groups coalesced in a powerful movement of protest and outrage against the shah's authoritarian government. This antiregime coalition of incompatibles was also held together—temporarily—by nationalist hostility toward U.S. influence in Iran.

A variety of specific occurrences have set different revolutions in motion; in some way each triggering event demonstrates that the government has lost its capacity to put down rebellion with force. Events in Russia in 1905 and 1917 and in Iran in 1978–1979 show that governments unable to coerce their enemies will fall. In contrast, Polish events in 1980–1981 demonstrate that governments still able to wield effective coercion can survive, however vulnerable to revolution they may otherwise appear.

Finally, an important causal force in some revolutions has been the activities of organized revolutionary groups and parties. When the masses failed to rise up spontaneously in nineteenth-century Europe, some revolutionary theorists proposed the necessity of "guided revolution." The first revolutionary leader to practice it effectively was V. I. Lenin in the Bolshevik seizure of power in Russia. His success has inspired numerous revolutionary intellectuals throughout the world. Some, such as Mao Zedong and Castro, have modified Leninist strategy, but all have followed Lenin in creating tight-knit organizations of professional revolutionaries and in refusing to settle for less than total power.

Leninist groups, as in China and Cambodia, have often gained vital support from peasants by promising them land, never intending to honor that pledge once the revolutionary party has won power. In some cases, as in Cuba and Nicaragua, revolutionary parties have entered into negative coalitions with other groups and parties. After this strategy succeeds in destroying the old regime, the Leninist group moves step by step to exclude its coalition partners from any share in governmental power. In numerous cases the Soviet Union has provided important military, political, and security-police assistance to Marxist-Leninist movements and regimes.

Revolutionary Leninist parties can never create revolutions on their own, and most of them fail to win power. However, their influence in a number of revolutionary situations has been very significant and in some cases decisive.

Review List of Key Terms

revolution
progressive bias
counterrevolutionary
coup d'état
political revolution
social revolution
great revolutions
relative deprivation
secularization
intellectual class
J-curve
"the desertion of the intellectuals"
dissension in the ruling class
militant Islamic clergy
revolutionary nationalism
government's capacity to coerce
security forces
revolutionary intellectuals
"directed" revolutionary activism
peasant-support strategy
New People's Army
united front
negative coalition
organizational weapon

Notes

1. See Hannah Arendt, *On Revolution* (New York: Viking Press, 1963), esp. pp. 13–52.
2. Charles Krauthammer, "Grenada and the End of Revolution," *New Republic*, January 30, 1984, p. 18.
3. H. G. Nicholas, "The American Revolu-

tion," in *Revolutionary Theory and Political Reality*, ed. Noel O'Sullivan (New York: St. Martin's Press, 1983), p. 55.
4. Mark N. Hagopian, *The Phenomenon of Revolution* (New York: Harper & Row, 1974), p. 123.
5. Emphasizing this point is a real strength of Theda Skocpol, *States and Social Revolutions: A Comparative Analysis of France, Russia, and China* (Cambridge: Cambridge University Press, 1979), esp. pp. 19–24.
6. Shaul Bakhash, *The Reign of the Ayatollahs: Iran and the Islamic Revolution* (New York: Basic Books, 1984), p. 13.
7. Crane Brinton, *The Anatomy of Revolution*, rev. ed. (New York: Vintage Books, 1957), pp. 41–52.
8. Jean-Jacques Rousseau, "Discourse on the Origin and Foundation of Inequality among Mankind," in *The Social Contract and Discourse on the Origin of Inequality*, ed. Lester G. Crocker (New York: Pocket Books, 1967), p. 246.
9. *The Republic of Plato*, trans. Francis MacDonald Cornford (New York: Oxford University Press, 1945), p. 268.
10. Alexis de Tocqueville, *The Old Regime and the French Revolution*, trans. Stuart Gilbert (Garden City, N. Y.: Doubleday Anchor Books, 1955), pp. 138–148.
11. Bakhash, *The Reign of the Ayatollahs*, pp. 14–16, 20–24.
12. Ibid., pp. 33–38.
13. Katharine C. Chorley, *Armies and the Art of Revolution* (London: Faber and Faber, 1943), pp. 11, 16.
14. Leonard Schapiro, *The Russian Revolutions of 1917: The Origins of Modern Communism* (New York: Basic Books, 1984), pp. 15, 35–53.
15. Bakhash, *The Reign of the Ayatollahs*, pp. 14–18.
16. See Timothy Garton Ash, *The Polish Revolution: Solidarity* (New York: Scribner's, 1983), esp. chap. 10, "What Revolution?"
17. Skocpol, *States and Social Revolutions*, p. 17.
18. See Noel O'Sullivan, "An Introductory Essay: Revolution and Modernity," in *Revolutionary Theory and Political Reality*, ed. Noel O'Sullivan (New York: St. Martin's Press, 1983), pp. 3–22.
19. Lewis S. Feuer, *Ideology and the Ideologists* (New York: Harper & Row, 1975), p. 169.
20. Craig Etcheson, *The Rise and Demise of Democratic Kampuchea* (Boulder, Colo.: Westview, 1984), pp. 48–49.
21. Ross H. Munro, "The New Khmer Rouge," *Commentary*, December 1985, pp. 19–38.
22. John Whitehall, "Options in the Philippines, Part II," *Freedom at Issue*, May/June 1985, pp. 19–22.
23. Etcheson, *Democratic Kampuchea*, pp. 129–133.
24. Robert H. Dix, "Why Revolutions Succeed and Fail," *Polity* 16 (Spring 1984): 423–446.
25. Tad Szulc, "Fidel Castro's Years as a Secret Communist," *New York Times Magazine*, October 19, 1986, p. 47 ff. For a fuller account, see Szulc's *Fidel: A Critical Portrait* (New York: Morrow, 1986).
26. For a detailed and dispassionate account of the Nicaraguan revolution through 1985, of Sandinista Marxism-Leninism, and of the complex political maneuvering briefly summarized here, see Shirley Christian, *Nicaragua: Revolution in the Family* (New York: Random House Vintage Books, 1986).
27. Philip Selznick, *The Organizational Weapon: A Study of Bolshevik Strategy and Tactics* (Glencoe, Ill.: Free Press, 1960) p. 144.

Thirteen

Revolution: Sequences and Consequences

The task of the intelligentsia is to make special leaders from among the intelligentsia unnecessary.
V. I. Lenin, What the "Friends of the People" Are

But are we still living in a rebellious world? Has not rebellion become, on the contrary, the excuse of a new variety of tyrant?
Albert Camus, The Rebel

The intense struggle for power that marks a revolution does not end once the old government has collapsed or been destroyed. What kind of new government will emerge, who will control it, and what it will attempt to accomplish are crucial questions that remain unanswered at the dawn of revolutionary triumph. They are seldom decided without intensified conflict—not only with enemies of the revolution but also among its supporters. Official and unofficial terror, civil war, and international warfare often occur in revolutionary situations. The political stakes are high, and both domestic and foreign political actors may feel severely threatened or take opportunities to make political gains.

Sequences of Revolutionary Developments

There is no single typical pattern of development into which every revolution comfortably fits. Historian Crane Brinton's is the best-known effort to suggest a common pattern, but he applies it to only four revolutions: the English Civil War of the seventeenth century and the American, French, and Russian revolutions.[1]

Brinton and most other comparative analysts of revolutions tend to take their basic pattern from the French Revolution of the late eighteenth century. That approach can point up some significant parallels, but it also has severe limitations. Out discussion will bae organized roughly within the three-part French pattern: **rule of the moderates,** radical rule, and reaction against radicalism. However, we will treat revolutions that depart from it just as seriously as this classic sequence.

Rule of the Moderates, or Coalition Government

Who runs the government in the initial phase of revolutionary success depends very much upon how and by whose efforts the old government met its downfall. If it was overthrown in a protracted armed struggle led by a Marxist-Leninist movement, moderates never rule. The organized revolutionary movement controls all policy making and sets out at once to transform economy, society, and culture according to its ideological designs, as we saw in China in 1949, North Vietnam in 1954, and Cambodia in 1975.

Where Marxist-Leninist forces have not won entirely on their own but are the best-armed and best-organized elements of a broad negative coalition, they attempt from the start to gain actual control of the new government. More or less gradually, they undercut and finally squeeze out other parties that the Communists no longer need to provide an appearance of broadly based support for the new regime. Under these conditions also, as in the Cuban and Nicaraguan revolutions, there is no period in which moderates actually rule.

The Great French Revolution did begin with a moderate phase, and so have other revolutions such as the French Revolution of 1848, the Russian Revolution, the Portuguese Revolution of 1974, and the Iranian Revolution of 1979. In notable instances the moderates have lost out in the continuing power struggle, but occasionally they have defeated more radical challengers and won long-term control of postrevolutionary governments. We will consider some factors that contribute to the political success or failure of moderate forces.

By *moderates* we mean people opposed to the old government who want to replace it with a new regime open to control by new political forces. However, they do not want to use governmental power to bring about drastic social and economic changes. They may sponsor, for example, certain changes in the laws of property but are determined to retain the basic system of private ownership. Typically, they favor individual rights and liberties as an essential improvement on the old autocratic regime and aim at creating a limited, genuinely constitutional government.

Newly expanded political freedom opens up opportunities for political persuasion and organization not only for moderates and their supporters but for critics and opponents of moderation. Radicals usually claim to be more attuned to the true "spirit" of the revolution and more vigilant in protecting it than are the moderate officeholders.

The rule of moderate revolutionaries is most endangered by the emergence of **multiple sovereignty**.[2] This term refers to circumstances in which a government's authority is strongly contested by other groups claiming revolutionary legitimacy and possibly trying to gain undisputed control of government for themselves. For example, the constitutional monarchists who dominated the French revolutionary government for about three years after 1789 found themselves competing with other power centers. These rivals to the government included a sizeable organization of republican deputies and their supporters (popularly known as the **Jacobins**), the government of the Paris Commune influenced by the Jacobins, street crowds, and even more radical political orators and groups.

Russia, 1917 The most fateful instance of multiple sovereignty in a twentieth-century revolution developed in Russia immediately after the collapse of the tsarist regime in the "February Revolution" of 1917. At that time a **provisional government** emerged from an unofficial meeting of the parliament, which elected a committee of leaders of center-to-left parties. On the same day a provisional executive committee of the **Petrograd Soviet**—a spontaneously formed council—was constituted. It claimed to represent directly the workers of the capital city.

The soviet was dominated by socialists, initially the democratically oriented Mensheviks, but the Bolsheviks worked constantly and with much success to gain control of this popular council. The revolutionary authority of the soviet was established immediately when it entered into an agreement with the unofficial parliamentary committee to create the provisional government. This coalition government was supposed to rule as a caretaker until a constituent assembly could be elected and draw up a new constitution.

Two days after its creation, the Petrograd Soviet expanded its membership to include soldiers' deputies. Other soviets sprang up quickly both in cities and in the countryside, where land-hungry peasants controlled them.

The tumultuous public meetings and substantial working-class membership of the Petrograd Soviet seemed to give it a claim to revolutionary legitimacy at least as strong as the provisional government's. That governing body had not been officially elected or even chosen by the whole membership of the old and powerless parliament. Lenin brilliantly exploited the power and authority of the soviets, both to undercut the effectiveness of military command and to attach military and militia forces to soviet organs controlled by the Bolsheviks. Their successful "October" coup was conducted, in fact, in the name of the Military Revolutionary Committee of the Petrograd Soviet, giving it some cover of legitimacy.[3]

Iran, 1979–1981 After the fall of the royal government in Iran in 1979, there was an extreme fragmentation of power and a multisided battle for sovereign control. The first two heads of government—the prime minister of the interim revolutionary government and the first elected president of the new Islamic Republic—were relatively moderate. They were challenged from the start by the radical Islamic clergy and were able to hold office for only nine months and one year, respectively.

Militant clergy, inspired from exile by the Ayatollah Khomeini, had played a major part in organizing the series of protests and demonstrations that led to the revolution. Once it had triumphed, they immediately orga-

The Ayatollah Khomeini and the traditional garb that he requires women to wear in public symbolize the fanatically antimodern and anti-Western ideology and spirit of the Iranian revolution.

nized revolutionary committees centered on the mosques and revolutionary tribunals to put on trial and execute officials of the shah's regime. Within a few months Khomeini endorsed the creation of a **revolutionary guard,** providing the radical clergy with armed forces to counter both the official army and the paramilitary forces created by leftist parties.

The militant clergy (who did not include all Islamic clerics in Iran) were strongly hostile toward all modern, Western, secular ideas and cultural influences. The moderate leaders of the new revolutionary government were devout Muslims and had long opposed the shah. They had attended French universities, however, and were supported mainly by the educated professional and middle-class minority of Iranians.

President Bani-Sadr was constantly attacked by the Islamic Republic Party, the parliamentary majority, as a "liberal" and "secularizer," and he compared them to the shah's secret police and fascists. They were strong enough in parliament to prevent his selecting the prime minister. They used the revolutionary committees and revolutionary guards to harass his appointees in key government agencies and to gain control of state-run radio and television facilities. When the parliament voted to impeach President Bani-Sadr in June 1981, the never very moderate initial phase of the Iranian revolution was ended.[4]

Portugal, 1974–1976 In the mid-1970s Portugal went through a revolution that was most untypical for the late twentieth century. The way to revolution was not paved by a leftist movement, and, after a suspenseful struggle, moderates won out over well-organized radical forces who seemed on the verge of triumph. Why was this unusual outcome possible?

The short answer is that effective power continued to reside in the **Armed Forces Movement** (MFA), which never became unified in support of the organized Left—the Portuguese Communist Party (PCP). The corporate-rule authoritarian regime that had controlled Portugal since 1931 was overthrown by a military coup on April 25, 1974. It was inspired mainly by lower-ranking officers' frustration with costly and unwinnable warfare that the Portuguese had been waging since 1961 in an effort to hang on to their African colonies. There was much political diversity in the MFA. It appointed a moderately conservative general as interim president, but some of its members were sympathetic to the radical aims of the PCP. The Communists had long been organized and operating in exile and underground.

One other party—the Socialists—predated the revolution, organizing in exile in 1973. They were committed as strongly to the creation of constitutional democracy in Portugal as to the enactment of socialist policies. New centrist and conservative parties organized quickly after the coup, but some of their leaders were suspect as collaborators with the old government. The PCP moved quickly to gain influence in the media, labor unions, local governments, and land reform associations. Late in 1974, officers considered sympathetic to the PCP became prime minister and head of the internal security force.

An unsuccessful coup attempt by the conservative president in March 1975 strengthened leftist forces within the government and the new military-dominated **Supreme Council of the Revolution** (SCR). A constituent assembly election had already been scheduled, and the government allowed it to proceed. On April 25, 1975, the Socialists won 38 percent of the vote, a conservative party 26 percent, and the PCP 18 percent. It was clear that an overwhelming majority wanted a democratic government and not a communist autocracy.

However, printers in a PCP-dominated union took over a socialist newspaper, and Communists also seized control of a Catholic radio station. MFA radicals proposed to create "popular councils" to override the political parties. In July, leaders of the socialist and conservative parties resigned from the coalition government, urging their followers to resist attempts by the PCP and their military sympathizers to nullify the election returns.

Anticommunist rioting and demonstrations multiplied, and moderates in the MFA forced the radical military politicians to resign their government posts. The PCP stirred up strikes and demonstrations in an effort to bring down the new moderate government. In late November the dismissal of a leftist military commander of the Lisbon district triggered a coup attempt by leftist paratroop units. It was put down by troops commanded by General Antonio Ramalho Eanes, a professional soldier and committed democrat. This was the decisive victory of the political moderates.[5]

A new constitution was implemented in 1976 and yet another in 1982, finally removing all governmental authority from the military. A civilian was elected president in 1986. In the Portuguese Revolution it was decisively important that the majority of MFA members, who commanded the effective power of coercion, were committed to establishing constitutional democracy.

The international environment, on balance, also favored a democratic outcome. Although the Soviet Union heavily subsidized the PCP, the West German Social Democrats provided financial and organizational aid to the Socialists, and the United States assisted all the noncommunist parties.[6] Portugal's membership in NATO, geographic position in Western Europe, and aspirations for membership in the European Economic Community all proved significant. They helped persuade a majority of military officers to oppose the establishment of a communist regime when faced with a decisive choice.

Rise and Rule of the Radicals

In some revolutions more radical forces succeed in their struggle for power with the moderates and gain control of the government, temporarily or permanently. *Radical* does not have the same ideological meaning in every revolution. In France the Jacobins sought a totally unified national republic and the permanent abolition of monarchy and hereditary status. They displaced moderate constitutional monarchists who would have been content with a government similar to eighteenth-century British parliamentarianism.

In 1917 the Bolsheviks stood for a vanguard dictatorship that would impose total socialism upon Russia, rather than the representative and competitive democracy favored by democratic liberals and socialists in the provisional government. In Iran the radicals who pushed aside moderate politicians in the early 1980s were dogmatically hostile to secularist Western culture. They were determined to create a new state guided solely by the sacred laws of Islam—as interpreted by the Ayatollah Khomeini and his clerical disciples.

Why do violence, terror, and warfare so frequently increase in revolutions after the downfall of the old government? In very general terms, as we have noted, it usually takes a broad negative coalition of groups to force the collapse of the old regime. These groups may have conflicting interests and seldom if ever agree about the shape of postrevolutionary government and society.

If the moderate government is indecisive and doesn't command effective coercion, revolutionary turmoil continues. Under those circumstances, the best-organized groups with the most politically adept and ruthless leaders usually win out, at least for a while, in the struggle for governmental power. Leaders of these groups claim to embody the true purposes and principles of the revolution and to be most determined to defend it against foreign and domestic enemies.

France: Jacobin rule   In France the threats to the revolutionary regime were quite serious. In October 1789, national guards and a city crowd forcibly brought King Louis XVI and Queen Marie Antoinette to Paris from their palace at Versailles. The king then turned against the revolution and looked for rescue to his fellow European monarchs. French aristocrats in exile were also trying to organize an antirevolutionary invasion. France declared war on Austria in April 1792, and Prussia joined Austria. French defeat seemed a real possibility until late in that year, and the revolutionary government had to build up effective armed forces in short order.

In addition to the foreign threat, there was resistance to the revolution at various times and places in the provinces, sometimes even all-out fighting by opposing armed forces. Much popular hostility had been inspired by the **Civil Constitution of the Clergy,** enacted by the moderate-controlled assembly in 1790. This measure aimed at reorganizing the Catholic Church after its property had been seized by the government to provide backing for new paper money. Providing for the election of parish priests and bishops by secular bodies, the Civil Constitution was totally unacceptable to the pope and to all orthodox Catholics. It also encouraged more radical antireligious forces who wanted to destroy traditional religion or replace it with a new civic cult that deified reason.

Typically, radical revolutionaries are highly intolerant of alternative belief systems. To radical deists and atheists in France, traditional Christianity stood for obscurantism and superstition and was totally incompatible with the rule of enlightened reason that the revolution would inaugurate. The Bolsheviks' ideological hostility to religion has been amply discussed, and it has set the tone for most Marxist-Leninist revolutions.

In Iran it was the radical religious forces who took the offensive, both against secular ideas and ideologies and against those whom they considered Islamic heretics. These included both Islamic socialist groups and members of the tiny, apolitical, and peaceful Baha'i sect, which broke off from Islam in the nineteenth century.

Fanatical intolerance is one means of expressing commitment to the supposed principles of the revolution that radical groups claim to embody. Ideological propaganda runs riot, including all-out assaults on the "opportunism" of the government and its alleged inability or even unwillingness to protect and advance the revolution.

In the cause of revolutionary defense and, not incidentally, to improve their power position, radical groups try to rally mass support to pressure the government. In France, spontaneous peasant revolts and forceful seizures of some noble estates had given the revolution a radical push from its beginning, leading quickly to the abolition of feudal dues and compulsory tithes. The main support for radical forces, though, came from the local government and political clubs in Paris. Crowds in the city streets and in the assembly became a force to be reckoned with and also to be manipulated.

With the revolutionary regime endangered by foreign armies in the summer of 1792, the radical republican forces received a decisive boost from Parisian officials, crowds, and national guards, joined by armed revolutionary groups arriving from the provinces. All demanded dethroning of the "traitorous" king and the creation of a republic. Invading the royal palace in Paris, revolutionary armed forces waged a bloody battle with the king's Swiss guards. This event discredited the moderate constitutional monarchists, and power shifted to the Jacobins, a diverse collection of cautious to fanatical republicans. Their rule of about two years was marked by deadly political infighting, ever more radical leadership, intensifying terror, mass mobilization for war, military success, and, finally, self-destruction.

In 1793 the king became the most prominent victim of the revolutionary guillotine, and a republic was proclaimed. To guard against real and imagined enemies, a secret police was created; informing on supposed "spies" and "saboteurs" was encouraged. Agents of the central government were sent out to whip the provinces into republican shape. A **revolutionary tribunal** was set up to try opponents of the government and dispatch them to the guillotine. Violent resistance, especially in the west of France, was put down by equally bloody and indiscriminate force.

The radical Jacobins proved unable to institutionalize their rule. They deeply believed in republican government and maintained their seat of power and legitimacy in the elected assembly (the **National Convention**), however frequently they tried to purge or intimidate its members. By 1794, republican armies had succeeded so well against both domestic and foreign enemies that the regime no longer seemed in danger. Complicated intriguing and infighting led to the political trials and executions of both ultraradical and more moderate Jacobin leaders by the Jacobin-controlled **Committee of Public Safety.**

These actions produced so much fear and hatred among other deputies that a majority of them turned against the most prominent leaders of the committee, whose main spokesman was Maximilien Robespierre. The Convention voted to arrest them, and they also became victims of official terror. The radical Jacobin leaders' allies in the government of Paris threatened a popular uprising to rescue them, but national guards loyal to the Convention dissolved that local governing body. For the first time in two years the elected assembly was freed from the threat of invasion by militant crowds.

Russia: Origins of Bolshevik rule The Bolsheviks' effective alliance with mass pressures—soldiers and workers in the streets of Petrograd demanding instant peace and bread, peasants seizing unprotected estates while the provisional government declared its inability to consider land reform—has been discussed in chapters 8 and 12. Going beyond a successful takeover of power, the Bolsheviks became the first radical revolutionary group to consolidate its rule on a long-term basis. They were able to survive in part because of steps Bolshevik leaders took to provide their movement and regime with effective armed protection.

Months before they seized power, the Bolsheviks had begun to arm thousands of factory workers as loyal **Red Guards;** they played a critical part in the takeover of the government in Petrograd. A few months after that event, the Bolsheviks began to create a new **Red Army,** increasing its size to 5.5 million by the early 1920s. They also repealed the "revolutionary" provision for the troops' election of officers that had helped undercut military discipline under the provisional government, and they restored the death penalty for desertion in battle. Several hundred thousand officers from the tsarist era were brought back as a military necessity, although some had to be motivated and controlled by threats to their families.[7] A system of strict political controls within the military gave Communist Party leaders the means, when combined with their new security police, to protect themselves against the fate of the radical Jacobins.

Iran: Rule of radical clergy After the radical Iranian clerical politicians impeached and ousted the relatively moderate elected president in 1981, they were still confronted by dangerous and desperate competitors for power. These were the organized forces of the left, mainly Islamic socialist groups. They had earlier competed with the **Islamic Republic Party** (IRP) for support among the urban poor, young people generally, and university students in particular. (The Iranian Communist Party—the Tudeh—consistently proclaimed its support for the Ayatollah Khomeini and did not participate in revolutionary violence.)

IRP-directed mobs shut down leftist newspapers in 1980 and engaged in violent and deadly attacks in universities, which were then closed for **Islamization.** Under severe threat, one of the Islamic socialist groups went underground. Its continued existence was dramatically demonstrated when, a few days after President Bani-Sadr's impeachment, a powerful bomb exploded at IRP headquarters, killing several top party and government leaders. The leftist terror campaign continued for a few months, with more assassinations and bloody street clashes but no mass demonstrations supporting the left, much less the popular uprising that Islamic socialist leaders hoped for.

In the Iranian revolution the radical left more than met its match in the militant clergy who controlled the IRP and the government. They proved to be as well organized and at least as ruthless and determined to defeat and destroy their mortal enemies as any revolutionary socialists have ever been. The IRP-led official terror used the revolutionary guards, revolutionary tribunals, and armed street gangs to suppress leftist demonstrations and organizations. For eighteen months, there were about fifty executions per day—not only leftists but Baha'is, royalists, some merchants, teenagers, alleged adulterers, and prostitutes. Blood flowed readily, much of it in public executions, with little pretense of genuine trials.

The terror seemed to succeed in suppressing all opposition, moderate and leftist, secular and religious. It reinforced the position of the Islamic radicals in the government and inspired campaigns for greater conformity. The proper kind of Islamic loyalties were required for admission to universities and army staff colleges. Fresh purges took place within the government bureaucracy, and thousands of teachers were dismissed. The Ayatollah Khomeini insisted on Islamizing the law codes; new legal punishments included amputation of a hand for theft and stoning to death for adultery.[8]

Radical control of the government was also reinforced by external warfare, as it had been in the French Revolution. Hoping to settle a longstanding border grievance in its favor, the Iraqi government attacked Iranian territory in September 1980. Chaos and military disorganization enabled the Iraqis to advance at first, but the Iranians rallied, and the war settled into a deadly stalemate. The Iranian army regained some prestige after its long association with the shah, and the revolutionary guards became a separate force of 150,000 armed men.

The IRP and the Ayatollah Khomeini used the war to identify themselves with the threatened homeland and the true cause of Islam. Iranian commanders marched fervent teenagers into mine fields to die as martyrs for the holy cause. These religious-military efforts strongly reinforced the drive for greater conformity within educational institutions, the bureaucracy, and public life generally.

Thermidor?

The French Revolution was tremendously exciting to participants and to foreign sympathizers and observers. "Bliss was it in that dawn to be alive," wrote the English poet Wordsworth of his sojourn in France in the early 1790s. Enthusiasts—and many conservatives also—had a sense that the world was being turned upside down, that a unique era in human history was beginning. Reflecting this attitude, the radical-controlled National Convention voted in 1793 to establish a brand new calendar to replace the ancient calendar believed to be tainted by superstition.

With the establishment of the republic the Year I began, but the new calendar never made it past Year VII. One of the new months was Thermidor; the arrest of Robespierre and his radical colleagues on the Committee of Public Safety took place on the 9th day of that month in the Year II (July 27, 1794). Ever since, **Thermidor** has meant the end of radical rule and of radicalizing trends in a revolution.

The original Thermidor brought a sharp decline in revolutionary terror, closing of the Jacobin Club, and the abolition of emergency wage and price controls. In 1795 yet another new French constitution was adopted, as moderate politicians regained control of the government. They were beset by enemies on every side, including royalists who attempted an insurrection, the Parisian poor who rioted against the scarcity and high price of food, and the first modern communist conspiratorial group.

All were put down with some difficulty and with increasing reliance of the civilian politicians on military officers who were continuing to win victories abroad. The impressive success of a young general named Napoleon Bonaparte, combined with the unpopularity of the government, led to Napoleon's famous coup of **18 Brumaire** (November 9, 1799). The general took power as First Consul of the Republic. Thermidor proved to be a step toward the demise of the republic and its replacement by Napoleon's authoritarian empire.

The precise meaning of *Thermidor* is disputed by revolutionaries, ideologists, and scholars, and whether it occurred in this or that revolution is a constant topic of controversy. Some light has been cast on this subject by political theorist Michael Walzer. He argues that revolutions are always led by ideologically inclined, intellectual-dominated vanguards, such as the radical Jacobins or the Bolsheviks. The fate of a revolution depends on the relations between that vanguard and the groups or classes in society that provide the main support for the revolution.

If those classes have substantial resources and organization, experience in handling their own affairs, and self-confidence, they will eventually rein in the ideological vanguard. They will not tolerate vanguard policies so extreme that they arouse substantial resistance and hostility, as did the French radicals' campaign against Christianity. In the English Civil War the Puritan clerics who yearned for a rigid theocracy were successfully resisted by gentlemen and landowners. These were men of substance who were represented in parliament and had backed it against King Charles.

In most twentieth-century revolutions the vanguard has claimed to represent and sought support for gaining power from poorly educated and unorganized social classes—first-generation industrial workers in Petrograd, masses of land-hungry peasants in Russia and China. These classes are much harder to organize and mobilize than middle classes, making it easier for the organized vanguard to dominate the political situation. "**The Terror** is the dictatorial imposition of vanguard ideology. So Thermidor marks the end of dictatorship, and its success or failure is determined by the 'changing political relations' of the vanguard and the class. If Thermidor fails, the Terror becomes permanent."[9]

Walzer argues, consistent with our interpretation of totalitarianism in chapters 8 and 9, that communist revolutions have produced long-term control of the vanguard over the toiling classes it claimed to represent. Mass terror may cease—or it may reappear, as in Stalin's purges—but coercive and ideological domination become institutionalized. Over time the revolutionary vanguard develops into a distinct ruling class, the Soviet nomenklatura and its equivalent in other communist states. The Bolsheviks were determined to avoid the Jacobins' fate, and vanguard self-protection has remained the first priority of all ruling communist parties. (For a summary of developmental stages typical of many revolutions, see table 13-1.)

Revolutionary Consequences

What are the longer-term effects of revolutions on politics, government, and society? The answer varies somewhat from country to country and from one historical period to another. Some generalizations are possible, though. For instance, political philosopher Hannah Arendt declared: "The aim of revolution was, and always has been, freedom."[10] She touches upon an important truth about revolutionary ideals and motives, but hers is not an adequate description. In addition, **freedom** is another of those ambiguous magic words of modern politics; it has very different meanings for various kinds of revolutionary ideologists, activists, and rulers.

Table 13-1 Some revolutionary stages

Stage	Possible Characteristics	Likely Outcomes
Rule of moderates	Seeks constitutional rule, not sweeping social change	New constitutional government
	Political freedom, multiple sovereignty, coalition government, disorder and competing demands	Overthrow by radicals if best-organized and most ruthless
Radical rule	Suppression of opponents—reign of terror	Executions, massacres, mass imprisonment, refugees
	Ideological militance	Religious and intellectual intolerance
	Governmentally decreed social changes	Radical party rules alone
Thermidor	Reaction against radicalism	End of terror, halt or reversal of social changes
	Moderates retake control—enforce "law and order"	Vulnerability to military takeover

Two Revolutionary Traditions

Constitutionalist revolutionism In common with many other scholars and theorists (including Hannah Arendt), we will distinguish between two major types of modern revolutionism. Features of both have often appeared in particular revolutions, but one or the other tends to predominate. First is the **constitutionalist revolutionary tradition,** in which freedom means protection of individuals against arbitrary and autocratic governmental power and their right to participate in representative self-government. Securing freedom in this sense has been the aim of all modern *political* revolutions.

Leading examples include the English Civil War and "Glorious Revolution" of the seventeenth century and the American Revolution. The American Declaration of Independence remains the classic official statement of the constitutionalist understanding of freedom. That kind of liberty was also the professed objective of most leaders of the French Revolution. Under pressure from external and internal enemies, though, the radical Jacobins emphasized militant, self-sacrificial revolutionary "virtue" over individual liberty.

Transformationist revolutionism The second modern revolutionary tradition, by far the more influential in the twentieth century, can be labeled **transformationist.** It calls for a total restructuring of society in order to liberate everyone from poverty and from all unequal political and social relationships. The most famous version is Marxism, but a half-century before *The Communist Manifesto* the first organized social transformationist revolutionary movement emerged from the ideological and political frenzy of the French Revolution. This was the **Conspiracy of Equals,** spearheaded by a young self-educated revolutionary intellectual from the provinces, François-Noël Babeuf.

Influenced by other ultraradical ideologists, Babeuf concluded that "Liberty, Equality, Fraternity" (the slogan of the revolution) could not be realized without economic equality. Had not Rousseau, to whose ambiguous principles the Jacobins often appealed, declared that the establishment of private property was the root cause of man's fall into servitude and social misery? The revolution would remain "unfinished" until it moved on to destroy the "aristocracy of riches." Then it could create "common happiness" through a condition of "perfect equality" in which all members of the community would be dedicated to the collective development of commerce, agriculture, and industry.

The necessary means to achieve this perfected condition was a total social revolution. Babeuf declared: "May everything return to chaos, and out of chaos may there emerge a new and regenerated world."[11] To make it happen, Babeuf and like-minded colleagues organized a short-lived movement combining public propaganda with secret recruitment of thousands of activists. The conspiracy was discovered, and Babeuf was arrested in May 1796 and convicted of treason. His execution made him the first important martyr in the transformationist revolutionary tradition.

The Conspiracy of Equals was not a serious contender for power, but its example and aspirations nurtured one of the most potent political myths of the modern age, **revolution as social salvation:** "The French Revolution is but the precursor of another revolution, far greater, far more solemn, which will be the last."[12]

The myth of the total transformation of society through revolution has also been fervently embraced by revolutionaries who were not concerned with economic equality. Hitler's racist "New Order" was as revolutionary an objective as the Khmer Rouge leaders' aim of transforming Cambodia overnight into an egalitarian socialist paradise.

Iranian Islamic radicals' desire to change a partly modernized society into a thoroughgoing theocracy (rule of God) strongly reflects a transformationist impulse. For the Ayatollah Khomeini and his clerical disciples, freedom appears to mean conformity to the divine will as interpreted by the clergy and especially requires "liberation" from all the wicked and corrupting influences of secularized Western culture.

Chapters 8 and 9 dealt extensively with Marxist-Leninist theory and practice, clearly indicating the transformationist character of that doctrine. What should be emphasized, though, is the fervent belief of its chief ideologists that the "inevitable" revolution will ultimately produce not merely new social structures but **a new human nature.** This is the postrevolutionary future as envisioned by Leon Trotsky, who led in organizing both the Bolshevik coup and the Red Army that guaranteed its long-term success:

> Man will become immeasurably stronger, wiser and subtler; his body will become more harmonized, his movements more rhythmic, his voice more musical. The forms of life will become dynamically dramatic. The average human type will rise to the heights of an Aristotle, a Goethe, or a Marx. And above this ridge new peaks will rise.[13]

Political Outcomes

For revolutions generally, the more prolonged and intense the struggle for power—among revolutionary groups, with antirevolutionary forces, against foreign states—the more likely it is that autocratic government will be the ultimate result. In 1790, well before much revolutionary violence had occurred, British parliamentarian and political theorist Edmund Burke issued a warning to French revolutionaries. He predicted that the breakdown of established authority would open the door to

> some popular general, who understands the art of conciliating the soldiery, and who possesses the true spirit of command. . . . Armies will obey him on his personal account. There is no other way of securing military obedience in this state of things. But the moment in which that event shall happen, the person who really commands the army is your master, . . . the master of your whole republic.[14]

Within a few turbulent years, the rise of Napoleon fulfilled Burke's prediction.

Prolonged revolutionary turmoil and repeated violent changes of rulers, as well as much bitter opposition to the revolution, prevented the development of effective new authority in 1790s France. Command of the armed forces provided the bold, dashing, and successful general with the capacity to seize power. His ability to restore social order attracted the support of a sizeable proportion of French people who were wearied by years of conflict and upheaval. Napoleon used his autocratic power to complete the revolutionaries' program of rationalizing and centralizing government in France. For example, under his direction the whole of French law was organized into a detailed written code.

Centralization increases the capacity of the revolutionary or postrevolutionary victors to mobilize people and resources to protect and enhance the power and domain of the new regime. One way of doing so is to turn military defense against foreign enemies into conquest and **imperial ex-**

pansion. That was the path taken both by Napoleon Bonaparte and by Stalin—victors in revolutionary power struggles for control of states that were already major powers in international politics.

Even though Napoleon was obviously an autocrat who had put an end to the French Republic, he still made use of prorevolutionary propaganda and its aura of "modern" and "enlightened" ideas. They helped him gain local support for the regimes he established where his troops were temporarily victorious. The Soviets' ideology is, of course, much more explicitly revolutionary, and groups and regimes claiming allegiance to it can often count on financial and military assistance, propaganda support, and expert advice. Furnishing such assistance contributes to the expansion of Soviet influence and provides new bases of operations for further expansionism.

When we try to discover the most likely political consequences of revolutions within the two modern traditions, very significant differences appear. Constitutionalist revolutions end with new or revised and effective constitutions as defined in chapter 4—institutionalized limits on governmental power over citizens, embodying a commitment to the rule of law, not to the arbitrary will of the rulers.

As we pointed out in chapter 5, revolutionary violence seldom gives rise to constitutionalist government, especially in its democratized form. Violent conflict within a society leaves a legacy of hostility and distrust unfavorable to a politics of mutual toleration. The American revolutionaries fought mainly against troops of the imperial overlord, not against fellow Americans. British democracy evolved peacefully out of a narrowly based parliament well over a century after that body had established its supremacy through civil warfare.

In contrast, the Weimar Republic emerged in Germany in 1919 after brief but bitter revolutionary conflict involving political groups across the right-to-left spectrum. It never overcame the distrust and hostility inspired by its birth and was readily toppled by the Nazis' semiparliamentary coup d'état. Historically, it is only when constitutionalist political groups and leaders predominate in a revolutionary situation that a genuinely constitutional government, however insecure, has had a chance to emerge from it.

In contrast:

> Revolutions that aim at a total transformation of society claim to act in the interests of the majority, but since the majority does not realize where its own best interests lie, it is left to a small avant-garde to make decisions for it. In consequence it is more likely that a society will emerge in which severe repression seems to be permanently built in.[15]

That is, the likely outcome is some kind of totalitarian rule. Centralized vanguard rule becomes permanent; far from dying out, the state attempts to regulate and control almost everything according to the arbitrary will of unchecked political elites.

Writing in 1974, political scientist Mark Hagopian pointed out that every twentieth-century revolution has resulted in more centralized and greatly expanded governmental power within a one-party system.[16] This is true not only of Marxist-Leninist revolutions but of the semisocialist Mexican Revolution that produced the party-rule authoritarian regime described in chapter 7.

Hagopian's generalization needs to be qualified now with at least one exception, and possibly two. About the time his book was published, the Portuguese Revolution broke out. Its political outcome hung in the balance for months, as partisans of the two revolutionary traditions competed for control. Only because the bulk of the military came down on the constitutionalist side did representative democracy rather than Marxist-Leninist totalitarianism finally win out. It is a very rare case among revolutions in the twentieth century.

In 1986 a political revolution occurred in the Philippines. The long-time rule of authoritarian president Ferdinand Marcos collapsed when his defense minister and armed forces commander deserted to the opposition, leaving him unable to rely on military force. Massive demonstrations in Manila had protested Marcos's apparent use of fraud to claim victory over Corazon Aquino in a presidential election. After Marcos left the country with U.S. encouragement and assistance, Mrs. Aquino assumed the presidency with very broad public support. She appointed a coalition cabinet and authorized the writing of a new democratic constitution.

Later in the year, serious dissension developed within her government. In addition, the long drawn-out battle against the guerrillas of the communist New People's Army was continuing, as were negotiations between its political leadership and the Aquino government. It was too soon to determine if the Philippine constitutionalist revolution would survive multiple threats to its survival.

Revolutions and Development

Do transformationist social revolutions succeed in developing economic and educational systems that make life better for most people than it would have been if the revolution had never occurred? Since we cannot compare what actually happened with what might have but didn't, we can never find a certain answer to this hotly debated question. Comparisons across different countries and of periods of time lead us, however, to be extremely skeptical about affirmative responses.

Peasants Consider, for example, the fate of peasants. First and foremost, they always want as much land as they can farm for their own families. They want to be as free as possible from control by overlords, landlords, and moneylenders. Peasant revolts against desperate and oppressive circumstances have occurred throughout history, but nearly always feudal, royal, or imperial armies have savagely suppressed them. When, in a prerevolutionary situation, government becomes too weak to put down disorder, peasants may spontaneously seize landlords' domains, burn their houses, even kill some noble families. Or, as in China, guerrilla leaders situated beyond the effective control of weak government may exploit peasant grievances to build a revolutionary organization and army.

In both France and Russia peasant self-help and violence served as social dynamite, contributing to turmoil that made it impossible to stop the momentum of revolutionary demands, actions, and reactions. In Russia, the provisional government persistently refused to deal with land reform until a new constitution had been drawn up, despite mass desertions by peasant soldiers. Failure to respond to peasant demands critically undermined that government's chances to rally popular opposition to the Bolsheviks' challenge. Lenin's pledge to redistribute land produced enough peasant support or neutrality to enable the Bolsheviks to win the bloody civil war of 1918–1921.

What has happened to peasants as a result of "great" revolutions that their efforts helped mightily to intensify and accelerate? It is estimated that in France about 10 percent of the land changed hands during the revolution as a result of confiscations from the Church and emigrating aristocrats, and about half of that was sold to peasant proprietors. Peasants had already owned about a third of the agricultural land before the revolution, and class differences within peasant communities changed little if any as a result of it.

There was no wholesale seizure and redistribution of land, since neither the peasant proprietors nor the revolutionary governments were hostile to private property. The revolution did bring about the cancellation of feudal dues imposed on peasants by landed aristocrats. It also ended the compulsory tithes to the Church, relieving the peasantry of a drain on their income amounting to approximately 10 percent. Much of the French peasantry probably experienced some marginal improvement in their economic situation as a result of the revolution.[17]

In the aftermath of the Russian and Chinese revolutions, though, the mass of peasants became the most numerous victims of transformationist regimes. Stalin's massively murderous collectivization drive took millions of innocent lives in the countryside. In China, as in Russia, the initial communist agricultural program involved forced redistribution of land to poorer peasants, a continuation of prerevolutionary strategy to solidify support for the regime. Less than a decade later Mao Zedong decreed the

"Great Leap Forward," a sudden communalization of all agricultural production. The result was economic chaos, a drastic fall in food production, and millions of deaths from famine. Although the regime retreated from this extreme policy, collectivized farming remained the basic policy despite peasants' desire to control their own land.

In the early 1980s the post-Mao leadership of the Communist Party decreed a new **responsibility system** in the countryside, allowing individual peasant families considerable control over their own production. After meeting a quota of food delivery to the state, the family could sell its produce on the open market. These economic incentives produced a remarkable upsurge in food production. It was not clear, however, if this policy would be a temporary retreat from centralized economic control or might lead to profound transformations in a transformationist regime. Party elites remained in firm and uncontested control of government and policy making from the capital to the village.

Industrialization and standards of living In the Soviet Union, Stalinist centralized planning and control did produce the rapid buildup of heavy industry. It has served as the basis for a highly militarized economy and society long after the end of the Second World War and decades after Stalin's death, and Soviet citizens' standard of living has improved over time. It seems reasonable to compare conditions in the Soviet Union with those in Japan, a formerly militaristic and imperial state that began economic modernization at roughly the same time as Russia. In terms of improvement in average standard of living, the Japanese mixed economy comes out far ahead.

Transformationist regimes do poorly with respect to economic development and standard of living in other comparisons between countries having similar histories and cultural backgrounds. Relevant examples include North Korea versus South Korea, East Germany versus West Germany, and mainland China versus Taiwan. In communist Cuba rationing of many basic consumer goods seems to be permanent, and the performance of the economy has consistently fallen short of the regime's own targets. Also, Cuba has developed a much more thoroughgoing economic, political, and military dependence on the Soviet Union than ever characterized its prerevolutionary relationship with the United States. The cumulative experience of many countries over the past several decades leads us to believe that centrally controlled "revolutionary" development programs are more likely to retard than promote the growth of the civilian economic sector and consumer welfare.

Education and culture Transformationist regimes devote enormous effort and resources to shaping education and culture, as we explained in our analysis of totalitarianism. Typically, one of the first proclaimed goals of such a regime in a largely peasant society is to wipe out illiteracy, and massive **literacy campaigns** are conducted with much fanfare.

At the same time that people are being taught to read, however, the regime is systematically restricting what they will be allowed to read. State control of publishing, detailed censorship, ideologically saturated schooling, enforcement of an official literary style, and persecution of "uncooperative" writers and artists limit drastically what people can learn with their new literacy. These practices strongly suggest that transformationist educational and cultural programs are designed mainly to reinforce the dominance of the vanguard ruling class, not to develop the intellectual and creative capacities of individual students and citizens.

Human costs Our analysis of revolution has focused primarily on what has actually occurred in revolutionary situations, on results rather than rhetoric. We may seem to have overlooked the heady excitement, high hopes, and ecstatic sense of release from bondage that characterize revolutions, especially in the immediate aftermath of the collapse or overthrow of the old regime. Any comprehensive treatment of revolutions would need to recognize the passionate hatred of tyranny and injustice, romantic idealism, heroic self-sacrifice, and determination to persevere in the face of great danger that are all part of the human drama of revolution. Whatever the motivations of revolutionary participants, though, every revolution involves an intense struggle for political power and it always has specific consequences.

In many revolutions, especially the "great" and most of all in the transformationist variety, one consequence is considerable loss of human lives. Partisans of all revolutions always claim that the deaths involved were unavoidable and, in some longer perspective, justified by the alleged progress promoted by the revolutionary regime. As the saying goes among revolutionary apologists, "You can't make an omelet without breaking eggs."

It is not only revolutionaries and their supporters and critics who disagree strongly about the costs and benefits of revolutions: "Probably no subject in the social sciences arouses such passionate disagreements as the study of revolution. Whether revolutions in general or specific revolutions are involved, moral and political values obtrude themselves at nearly all stages of analysis."[18] Take, for example, a stimulating, influential, and controversial comparative study of revolutions and development published in 1966. Political sociologist Barrington Moore argued that revolutionary violence contributed to the growth of democratic freedom in some countries, especially Britain (the Civil War) and France. He further contended that going without a revolution, as did Germany and Japan, helped lead to aggressive fascist regimes.[19]

In considering the **human costs of revolutions,** Moore attempts to draw

Transformationist revolutionary regimes always produce many victims, as in Cambodia under Khmer Rouge rule from 1975 to 1979. The killing was so widespread and hasty that human remains littered many places in the countryside.

up a balance sheet, offsetting the number of revolutionary victims with the supposed number of preventable deaths that would have occurred in the absence of revolution. By his estimate the Great Terror in the French Revolution killed about 40,000 people, most of them enemies of the revolution, and no more than had annually suffered preventable deaths under the old regime.

According to one critic, however, Moore's prorevolutionary bias leads him to limit artificially and unjustifiably his estimate of the total victims of violence stemming from the revolution: "In addition to the terror, French military casualties during the Revolution and the Empire are estimated at about 1,300,000 men, to which must be added those who died during famines which resulted from general disorder and military action."[20]

When it comes to twentieth-century transformationist revolutions, even Moore's belief that "no commitment to a free society can dispense with some conception of revolutionary coercion" does not lead him to produce a positive balance sheet for the pattern-setting regime: "The range and depth of Stalinist repression and terror were far too great to find explanation, let alone justification, through some conception of revolutionary necessity. . . . Altogether the communist defense requires an act of faith about the future that involves too great a surrender of critical rationality."[21] Since he wrote those words, the Khmer Rouge revolutionary holocaust in Cambodia, as well as post-Mao information about the human costs of transformationist policies in China, have powerfully reinforced his understated point.

To conclude, we suspect that contemporary prospects for constitutionalist revolutions are dim. The Portuguese Revolution was quite exceptional. Only the suddenness with which it occurred and the prodemocratic commitments of most of the important military commanders enabled it to escape the common fate of most twentieth-century revolutions. A similar swift and surprising collapse of the old regime and the new government's control of the armed forces also seemed critical for the 1986 political revolution in the Philippines.

Much more often than not in twentieth-century revolutionary situations, democratic political forces have been outbid, outorganized, and effectively undercut by ruthless and determined transformationist vanguards. These have ranged from Lenin's Bolsheviks to Hitler's Nazis to the Ayatollah Khomeini's militant clergy-politicians. The ultimate irony is that when such movements gain supreme power they replace the fallen autocracy (or feeble democracy) with a new and much more coercive autocracy.

Because the new regime is first and foremost effectively organized to suppress its enemies, real or imagined, it is considerably less vulnerable to revolutionary overthrow than was the prerevolutionary government. This strong capacity for self-protection strikes us as the most enduring political result of transformationist revolutions, however remote it may seem from the heroic romanticism of revolutionary ideology and rhetoric.

Summary

There is no single pattern according to which revolutions predictably unfold. Three roughly defined stages based on the course of the French Revolution are often referred to in the analyses of other revolutions.

First comes rule of the moderates. This phase never develops in revolutions led by Marxist-Leninist movements. If they initially come to power as part of a broad negative coalition against the old regime, their first priority is to exclude all moderates and everyone else but themselves from actual control of the new government. Moderate governments establish political liberty, which gives their radical opponents a chance to organize and propagandize against them.

Moderate rule is endangered by multiple sovereignty as one or more additional centers of power emerge and become the government's competitor for revolutionary authority. The Jacobin clubs in the French Revolution, the Petrograd Soviet in 1917 Russia, and the clerically controlled revolutionary organizations in Iran all exemplify unofficial claimants to revolutionary sovereignty that succeeded in breaking moderates' hold on governments. The Portuguese Revolution of the mid-1970s stands out as a rare exception to that pattern. Portuguese moderates finally won in a fierce stuggle with organized radicals because key military commanders favored and defended constitutional democracy and foreign democratic parties and governments aided the moderates.

The second stage of the French and some other revolutions was radical rule, accompanied by a reign of terror. Radical groups claim to be more devoted to the revolution than the moderates, more determined to defend it against foreign and domestic enemies and to push it toward its logical conclusion. Conditions of threat and turmoil can make it impossible for a moderate, indecisive, nonruthless government to establish effective control. Organized radicals can then rally sufficient popular support and mobilize enough coercive capability to push aside the moderates and gain full power.

The Jacobins in the French Revolution, the Bolsheviks in Russia, and the Islamic Republic Party in Iran exemplify organized radical revolutionary groups that outmaneuvered their moderate rivals. In each case radical leaders mobilized militant supporters and freely employed violence and terror against opponents before and after gaining control of the government and implementing their revolutionary programs. The Jacobins declared a republic and sent the king and queen to the guillotine; the Bolsheviks abolished private property; the IRP proclaimed an Islamic theocracy.

Jacobin rule was short-lived; political infighting and the residual power of the elected convention made it possible for the radicals' opponents to remove them from office—and from life. Later revolutionary radicals, such as the Bolsheviks, have worked very hard at protecting themselves against the radical Jacobins' fate.

The third phase of the French Revolution was Thermidor, the end of radicalism in power and a return to relative moderation. Political theorist Michael Walzer suggests that Thermidor occurs only when the main class supporting a revolution has considerable education and organization. Then it is capable of reining in the ideological extremists who dominate the vanguard leadership group. The middle classes who provided key support for the French Revolution had that capability and used it to halt the radical Jacobins' reign of terror. Peasants and workers in Russia and China gave vital support initially to the communist vanguards but were not able to halt or moderate their radical programs. Thermidor did not occur in those countries, and the vanguard became a new, highly coercive, and self-perpetuating ruling class.

Finally, what are the longer-term consequences of revolutions, their major effects on politics, government, and society? These effects vary considerably, depending on whether a revolution is mainly constitutionalist or transformationist. Constitutionalist revolutionaries seek effective constitutional government, limiting the power of official decision makers by subjecting them to enforceable legal and electoral controls. Transformationist revolutionaries aim at using concentrated governmental power to remold all of society and culture, and possibly human nature itself.

Politically and governmentally, there is a strong tendency for protracted revolutionary conflicts to end in centralized autocracy. Increasing dependence of the French revolutionary government on the armed forces made it vulnerable to overthrow by the strongest and boldest general, Napoleon Bonaparte. The longer a revolutionary power struggle continues, the more hostility and distrust develop, the shakier authority becomes, and the longer the odds against a constitutionalist political outcome.

Transformationist revolutionary movements—Nazis, Communists, Islamic radicals—all seek autocratic power from the start. If they achieve it, they do their best to keep and use it to impose their totalist programs upon society.

Where such movements have gained power with peasant support, they have used it to reorganize, regiment, and victimize the mass of peasants who wanted above all to work and control their own land. Economic development has focused mainly on heavy industry and military strength; improvement in consumer welfare lags far behind comparable societies not ruled by transformationist revolutionaries. Massive literacy, educational, and cultural programs aim primarily at ideological indoctrination and control of the populace.

The human costs of transformationist revolutions have been enormous, and there are no rational grounds for believing that they will ultimately pay off in societies of utopian peace and justice. In the twentieth century especially, transformationist movements in power have displayed a supreme talent for protecting themselves against the threat of renewed revolutionary destruction.

Review List of Key Terms

rule of the moderates
multiple sovereignty
Jacobins
provisional government
Petrograd Soviet
revolutionary guard
Armed Forces Movement
Supreme Council of the Revolution
Civil Constitution of the Clergy
revolutionary tribunal
National Convention
Committee of Public Safety
Red Guards
Red Army
Islamic Republic Party
Islamization
Thermidor
18 Brumaire
the Terror
freedom
constitutionalist revolutionary tradition
transformationist revolutionary tradition
Conspiracy of Equals
revolution as social salvation
a new human nature
imperial expansion
responsibility system
literacy campaigns
human costs of revolutions

Notes

1. Crane Brinton, *The Anatomy of Revolution*, rev. ed. (New York: Vintage Books, 1957).
2. See Charles Tilly, "Revolutions and Collective Violence," in *Handbook of Political Science*, vol. 3, *Macropolitical Theory*, ed. Fred I. Greenstein and Nelson W. Polsby (Reading,

Mass.: Addison-Wesley, 1975), pp. 483–555, for a description of *multiple sovereignty* as applying both to the prerevolutionary challenge to government and to competitors for power after the fall of the old government.

3. Leonard Schapiro, *The Russian Revolutions of 1917: The Origins of Modern Communism* (New York: Basic Books, 1984), pp. 45–55, 130–134.

4. Shaul Bakhash, *The Reign of the Ayatollahs: Iran and the Islamic Revolution* (New York: Basic Books, 1984), pp. 52–70, 92–165.

5. Rodney J. Morrison, *Portugal: Revolutionary Change in an Open Economy* (Boston: Auburn House, 1981), pp. 18–37.

6. Thomas C. Bruneau, "Patterns of Politics in Portugal since the April Revolution," in *Portugal since the Revolution: Economic and Political Perspectives*, ed. Jorge Braga de Macedo and Simon Serfaty (Boulder, Colo.: Westview, 1981), pp. 9–10.

7. Schapiro, *Russian Revolutions*, pp. 158, 173–174.

8. Bakhash, *Reign of the Ayatollahs*, pp. 121–124, 219–227.

9. Michael Walzer, "A Theory of Revolution," *Marxist Perspectives* 2 (Spring 1979): 31–37.

10. Hannah Arendt, *On Revolution* (New York: Viking, 1963), p. 2.

11. Quoted in James H. Billington, *Fire in the Minds of Men: Origins of the Revolutionary Faith* (New York: Basic Books, 1980), p. 75.

12. See ibid., pp. 71–78; the final quotation comes from the *Manifesto of Equals*, written for Babeuf's group by Sylvan Maréchal.

13. Leon Trotsky, *Literature and Revolution* (Ann Arbor: University of Michigan Press, 1960), p. 256.

14. Edmund Burke, *Reflections on the Revolution in France* (Indianapolis: Bobbs-Merrill, 1955), p. 258.

15. Walter Laqueur, "Revolution," in *International Encyclopedia of the Social Sciences*, vol. 13, ed. David L. Sills (New York: Macmillan and Free Press, 1968), p. 505.

16. Mark N. Hagopian, *The Phenomenon of Revolution* (New York: Harper & Row, 1974), pp. 305–306.

17. Theda Skocpol, *States and Revolutions: A Comparative Analysis of France, Russia, and China* (Cambridge: Cambridge University Press, 1979), pp. 126–127.

18. Hagopian, *The Phenomenon of Revolution*, p. 364.

19. Barrington Moore, Jr., *Social Origins of Dictatorship and Democracy: Lord and Peasant in the Making of the Modern World* (Boston: Beacon Press, 1966); see esp. pp. 484–508.

20. Stanley Rothman, "Barrington Moore and the Dialectics of Revolution: An Essay Review," *American Political Science Review* 64 (March 1970): 71.

21. Moore, *Social Origins*, p. 507.

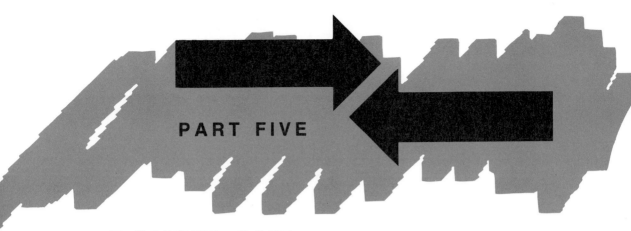

PART FIVE

POWER AND VALUES

FOURTEEN

Evaluating and Civilizing Political Power

For he that thinks absolute power purifies men's blood and corrects the baseness of human nature need read but the history of this or any other age to be convinced of the contrary.
John Locke, Second Treatise of Government

After his dismissal, Khrushchev said it was possible to get tired of anything: dinners, women, even vodka— but there was one thing of which one could never have enough, and that was power. Djilas, who knew this environment very well, called power the pleasure of pleasures.
Michael Voslensky, Nomenklatura: The Soviet Ruling Class

You can't build a utopia without terror, and before long, terror is all that's left.
E. V. Kohak, Requiem for Utopia

The past will not tell us what we ought to do, but it will what we ought to avoid.
José Ortega y Gasset, The Revolt of the Masses

These quotations, spanning the past three centuries, all reflect hard-earned wisdom. They also point to the major concerns of this final chapter, conclusions about political power and governmental systems that we think follow from our effort to analyze them.

This chapter is essentially **normative**—concerned with ethical evaluation—although we intend it to be clearly linked to the empirically grounded interpretation of politics in the preceding chapters. We will consider three questions: How should government and politics be evaluated? How can political power be civilized? What can we do about governments and the uses of power?

We stated in chapter 1 that our aim was not to persuade you to adopt a particular normative attitude toward politics but to promote realistic understanding of political phenomena. That remains our primary objective, but no one studies politics in the total absence of moral concerns and normative responses to ideas and events. Whether or not you agree with our approach to **political evaluation,** we hope it will stimulate you to think seriously and critically about your own moral standards and how they relate to the difficult and dangerous problems of political life.

How Should Government and Politics Be Evaluated?

Basic disagreement about applying normative standards to politics goes back at least to the first two great political philosophers in the Western tradition, Plato and his pupil Aristotle. In simplified terms, we can say that Plato's *Republic* approaches political evaluation using **absolute standards,** whereas Aristotle's *Politics* emphasizes **contextual standards.**

Absolute versus Contextual Standards

■ Platonic Idealism
Plato was a harsh critic of the democracy practiced in his native Athens, and he did much to give democratic government a bad reputation that

The unjust condemnation of Socrates both angered and inspired his greatest pupil, Plato, one of the most influential of political philosophers. Socrates receiving the fatal hemlock potion as he counsels his disciples is nobly portrayed by French artist Jacques-Louis David in this famous 1787 painting.

lasted for more than two thousand years. Why? At least initially, he was probably moved by tremendous anger and outrage at the fate of his revered teacher Socrates, a man of the noblest moral character who made enemies by his constant skeptical probing of his fellow Athenians' ideas and beliefs. In the year 399 B.C. Socrates was tried on charges of impiety and corrupting the young, then convicted and sentenced to death by a jury of several hundred ordinary citizens. For Plato, this stupid and vicious act showed the total inability of popular judgment to determine justice or make any decisions for the common good.

Understandably, he decided that wisdom and not the weight of numbers should govern the community. Experience and his own great intellectual gifts persuaded him that people are enormously unequal in their capacities for knowledge and wise judgment. Only genuine philosophers—who are brilliant, morally wise, and quite rare—can determine the meaning of justice both for individuals and for society. In the truly just social order, then, **philosopher kings** would have absolute power to rule according to their superior knowledge and moral insight. All other members of such a society would also be assigned social roles perfectly suited to their lesser natural talents and abilities.

Those who excel in courage would be trained as armed guardians of the community against attack and internal disorder. People of ordinary intellect and mundane interests would work at farming and crafts, supplying the physical necessities for society. The rare persons—male or female—in whom reason predominates would be rigorously educated from an early age as potential philosophers and rulers.

These all-wise autocrats would arrange and manage every aspect of life. They would forbid private property both for their own group and for the soldier-guardians, so that personal interests could not distract from their supreme duty of serving and protecting the public good. The ruling and military classes would not even have private families; they would therefore protect and cherish the entire society as their true family. The rulers would manipulate pairing off at annual mating festivals, assuring that the highest-quality men and women would serve most often as parents.

Children would be taken from their mothers at birth and reared communally. Parents supposedly wouldn't know their own children and so would treat all children with parental concern. The rulers would conscientiously move children up and down in the class system according to their inborn talents, should they differ significantly from their parents'.

The philosopher kings would thoroughly censor literature and the arts to screen out messages in conflict with their training and principles. They would indoctrinate all citizens with a "noble fiction": all are born as children of the same soil, but some have a bit of gold mingled with their souls, others silver, and the majority brass or iron. According to this **myth of the metals,** gold means aptitude for philosophic rule, silver for soldier-guardianship, and brass and iron for farming and craftsmanship. A society so ordered will embody perfect justice, as all persons receive the places to which nature entitles them.

Scholars have never agreed on whether Plato meant *The Republic* to be taken as a formula for actually creating the just society. He founded a philosophic academy in ancient Athens, not a revolutionary movement seeking total power for philosopher kings. It is possible, though, to interpret Plato as proposing absolute standards of justice that condemn as unjust and unworthy every actual human society.

To realize such "true" justice would require wrenching, fundamental changes in every political and social pattern and relationship. As a first step to constructing the just state, Plato proposes to exile from the city all inhabitants over the age of six. Otherwise it would be impossible to wipe the social slate clean of corrupt institutions and erroneous beliefs. In effect, all existing families would need to be ripped apart with no hope of ever reuniting.

A policy as radical in practice as Plato's imagined one was put into effect by the Khmer Rouge regime led by Pol Pot as soon as they captured the Cambodian capital of Phnom Penh in 1975. The new autocratic rulers immediately ordered the two million inhabitants to leave the city, marching under military guard—men, women, children, babies, the elderly, hospital patients, the handicapped, absolutely everyone—or be shot. People had few or no supplies, clothing, or protection against the elements, and tens of thousands were shot or clubbed to death when they collapsed from hunger and exhaustion.

Khmer Rouge leaders had long planned to create rural socialism and destroy the "decadent" cities as soon as they gained power; their earliest steps showed the depth of their commitment to this absolute goal. They were certainly not Platonic philosopher kings, but they did believe that the supposed correctness of their principles justified applying maximum coercion to the defenseless citizens of a corrupt society—for the people's own good, of course.

■ Aristotelian Practicality

Aristotle criticized Plato's proposals, mainly on practical grounds. For example, Aristotle pointed out that it would be extremely difficult to keep people ignorant about their biological parents and children because of physical resemblances between parents and offspring. He also argued that both children and property belonging to "everyone" will not receive the care and attention that people naturally devote to their personal possessions. Plato's proposals, Aristotle declares, so obviously contradict the lessons of experience that it would be folly to take them seriously.

Like Plato and all other great political theorists, however, Aristotle was very much concerned with political evaluation. He distinguished between an absolutely best political order and one that is the best realizable in most actual states. He devotes most attention to this **"practicable best" regime,** the "polity," which combines features of oligarchy (rule by the rich minority) and democracy (rule by the poor majority). As we noted in chapter 4, these are two of his unjust or "perverted" forms of government, since in each case the dominant group rules mainly in its own interests. Clearly, Aristotle considered it necessary and prudent to settle for much less than perfect justice in politics.

The polity is essentially controlled by a sizeable middle class, who are less inclined to rule arrogantly, oppressively, enviously, or violently than the rich or the poor. Above all, because of its broad and moderate social basis, the polity is much less likely than either oligarchy or democracy to give way to **tyranny,** the worst form of government. Tyrants monopolize ruling power, recognize no legal restraints, and aim above all to serve their personal interests.

For the most part, Aristotle's approach to political evaluation involves making judgments of better or worse about actual societies and institutions. His contextual standards grow out of wide knowledge and experience, the practices of governments and rulers, and estimates of the probability or improbability of accomplishing particular improvements within given circumstances. He is much less concerned with how perfect justice can be realized than with what degree of justice may be possible in specific political environments. He strongly insists that absolute *injustice* must be prevented, even urging tyrants to show some moderation and concern for the public interest if at all possible. For Aristotle, the lessons of experience always outweigh commitment to abstract ideals of political perfection.

In China, since Mao Zedong died in 1976, and especially after Deng Xiao-ping became the top leader in 1978, communist party elites have shown almost no interest in implementing the ideological goals of Marxism-Leninism. Instead they seem much more inclined to develop policies that will actually work to increase national production and economic strength. In accord with Aristotle's ancient wisdom that people care most about their own, individual peasants have been given much control over particular plots of land and benefit directly from hard work and successful crop growing. As we noted in chapter 13, agricultural production has shot up since this "responsibility system" was implemented in 1980. It is consistent with Aristotle's practical-minded approach to evaluating governments and policies to try to learn from mistakes and the relevant experience of others, producing improvements in society, if never a truly ideal condition.

Totalitarian regimes, including Maoist China, represent the most spectacular and largest-scale efforts anyone has ever undertaken to impose revolutionary visions of perfection upon actual human societies. It is impossible, we hope, for most people to empathize in any way with Hitler's murderously racist ideology, and at least in the West the Ayatollah Khomeini's theocratic Shi'a Islam has no appeal. The totalitarian ideology that has had broadest world appeal and the longest staying power is Marxism-Leninism.

In the past, especially, one of the most potent appeals of Marxism was its claim to represent the cause of human progress toward peace, harmony, material security, and perfect justice. The sight of gross poverty, of people living in slums and filth, afflicted by preventable diseases and growing up in illiteracy and despair, of long lines of shame-faced unemployed men at soup kitchens during the Great Depression—experiences like these have inspired strong feelings of anger, outrage, even hatred of the existing social system among numbers of morally sensitive people in the modern era.

For some of them it seemed natural and morally necessary to join a movement that aimed at ending these evils forever. After all, Marx had long ago declared: "The philosophers [such as Plato] have only *interpreted* the world, in various ways; the point, however, is to *change* it."[1] For people

In the early 1980s the Chinese communist government, apparently learning from its sad experience with dogmatic socialism, began introducing market principles into the economy. Production, especially in agriculture, began to increase rapidly, making it possible to provide new consumer incentives such as refrigerators.

who believed that the communist movement, led and sustained by the Soviet state, was the supreme historic agent of that great change, supporting and advancing its cause became an absolute moral duty. They came to

Table 14-1 Politically caused deaths in the twentieth century

Cause	Totals (in Millions)	Averages per 10,000 Population
Governments	119.4	349
Communist	95.2	477
Other totalitarian and extreme authoritarian	20.3	495
Other authoritarian	3.1	48
Democratic	.8	22
Wars	35.7	22
International	29.7	17
Civil	6.0	26

Adapted from R. J. Rummel, "War Isn't This Century's Biggest Killer," *The Wall Street Journal,* July 7, 1986.

see conventionally "immoral" means, such as lying, stealing, spying for a foreign power, or blowing up innocent bystanders, as moral acts serving the supreme moral end of total justice.

Marxism had begun as a doctrine of absolute ends disguised as a predictive theory of history. Marx fervently believed that a classless, completely harmonious, coercion-free, abundant, and richly creative society would emerge from the inevitable self-destruction of bourgeois capitalism. This was his vision of the truly just society that industrialism *should* make possible, the absolute standard by which he condemned all existing societies.

Marx did not envision or favor an organized minority's imposing its program upon an unwilling society. He did favor total state control and direction of the economy but believed that it would be implemented democratically by the will of the postrevolutionary proletarian majority. When the Marxian process failed to develop spontaneously, Lenin's commitment to Marxist ends didn't diminish. Instead he proposed, rationalized, and practiced elite direction and control, both of the revolutionary seizure of power and of the postrevolutionary transformationist regime. Those political means developed quickly into the overriding ends of Marxist-Leninist regimes—protecting and expanding the monopoly power of an ideologically defined elite, or nomenklatura.

Absolute Ends or Standards versus Experience

The political outcome of Marxism powerfully bolsters the contextualist criticism of efforts to judge and change societies according to total and absolute standards. Even more overwhelming support comes from a careful compiling of the results of twentieth-century governments' implementing the most terrible of power strategies—physical elimination. Study table 14-1 and figure 14-1 very carefully. They present the most important empirical data in this book.

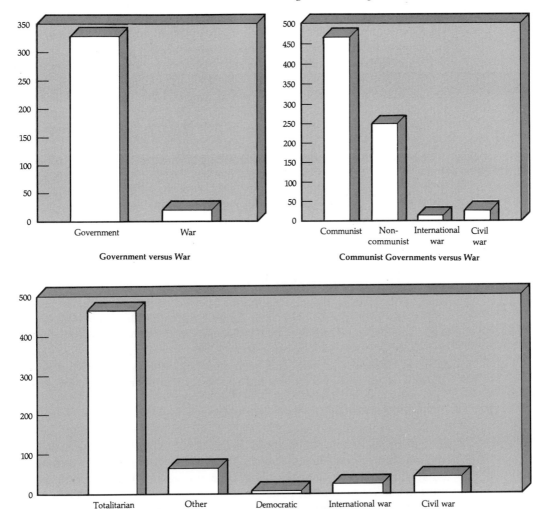

Figure 14-1 Politically caused deaths in the twentieth century: comparisons. Numbers are those killed per 10,000 population. (Adapted from R. J. Rummell, "Deadlier Than War: Non-Freedom" [Honolulu: Department of Political Science, University of Hawaii, 1986]).

Political scientist R. J. Rummel has laboriously pieced together the data on **politically caused deaths** from a great variety of sources that require careful evaluation. Governments responsible for mass murder don't ordinarily admit it, much less reveal the precise number of victims. His estimates err, if anything, on the very conservative side, especially with Stalin's Soviet Union and Mao's Communist China. Yet these stark numbers speak very powerfully about types of government and political experience in the twentieth century.

A few explanatory comments seem necessary to help you grasp the full meaning of these numbers. In the table's second category of governments, "other totalitarian and extreme authoritarian," 17 million of the 20.3 million deaths were caused by the German Nazi regime. At least 93 percent of the government-caused deaths in this century, then, have been produced by totalitarian systems.

The 800,000-plus victims of democratic governments require some explanation also. About 36,000 were civilians massacred by French forces during the post–World War II anticolonial struggle in Algeria, which ended with Algerian independence in 1962. Nearly all the victims were Arab Algerians who had no right to vote and therefore no political capacity for group self-protection within the French democratic system.

The rest of this category consists of approximately 795,000 victims who were not actually killed by democratic regimes. But the two main governments involved—the United States and Britain—willingly collaborated with the Soviets in the arrangements that led to these deaths. In accord with secret provisions of the **Yalta Agreement** signed by Stalin, Roosevelt, and Churchill near the end of the Second World War, the Western allies turned over to the Soviets more than 2,250,000 people. They were Soviet citizens, prisoners of war, and even Russian exiles who were not Soviet citizens, all of whom were located in Western zones of occupation at the end of the war.

Some high British and U.S. officials knew that nearly all the returnees would be executed or sent off to slave labor camps to die slowly. The potential victims had no doubt about their fate in Stalin's hands. Almost none of them wanted to return to the USSR, and "often whole families committed suicide to avoid it."[2] Officials in charge used manipulative persuasion and force to carry out this policy, and it did not become public knowledge until official records were opened in the 1970s. A deliberate violation of the democratic principle of freedom of information made possible this shameful collaboration with the most murderous of all totalitarian regimes. It could not even be justified on grounds of military expediency, since the war had ended. It is one of the most awful but still little-known blots on the twentieth-century records of the two oldest Western democracies.

Learning about this inexcusable action should not obscure for us, though, the obvious implication of Rummel's data: totalitarianism has been the overwhelmingly most deadly political phenomenon of our time, in fact in all of human history.

For the Marxist-Leninist variety, it is hard to imagine a greater contrast than the gulf between Marx's moral-humanitarian ends and the regimes whose rulers continue to invoke his authority. The deaths of those tens of millions of innocent victims—mostly ordinary peasants and workers—have utterly failed to produce noncoercive, egalitarian, harmonious societies.

A grim but fitting perspective on the twentieth century would view it as an enormous Frankensteinian political experiment. It has involved thoroughly and repeatedly testing the hypothesis that monstrous uses of power can lead to societies free of manipulation, coercion, domination, hierarchy, and executions. The evidence is in, and it is overwhelmingly negative.

In our judgment, it takes a wholly irrational faith in secular miracles to believe any longer in the "liberating" potential of Marxism-Leninism. Third World movements claiming that ideological label still manage to exploit, however, the same kinds of strong feelings of moral indignation against grinding poverty, gross material inequalities, and greedy authoritarian rulers that inspired some Europeans and Americans to identify with the Soviet cause in the 1930s and 1940s. Most people in Third World countries know very little about the historical record of communist regimes. Revolutionaries who do know are attracted by the Leninist legitimation of their desire to gain supreme power and use it to remold society.

Understandable and even commendable feelings of sympathy with efforts to change societies characterized by mass poverty, illiteracy, and oppressive, corrupt authoritarian regimes can lead to a political version of the selective perception described in chapter 3. It involves condemning the existing regime and condoning any efforts aimed at getting rid of it, while failing to think seriously about the contextualist question: In these particular circumstances, is it likely that a new regime will be better or worse than the old? If the new one would be controlled by Marxist-Leninists, the historical record strongly indicates that an affirmative answer could result only from ignorance or self-deception. For sympathizers with change, it may be psychologically easier not to pose the question at all, whatever the disastrous consequences for the societies in question.

How Can Political Power Be Civilized?

Our general formula for civilizing political power should certainly come as no surprise: the placing of effective restraints and popular controls on wielders of power, and especially on governments, normally the main controllers of power resources.

From the perspective of the cultural evolution of civilization and governments over thousands of years, as described in chapter 1, Marxist-Leninist totalitarianism can be seen as a great leap backward to self-proclaimed divine right. Historical progress functions as its great secular deity, commanding human sacrifice on a scale that would have stupefied the ancient

Aztecs. Regimes very different from these are necessary to sustain even a minimal degree of civilized decency.

In our judgment, ample experience has conclusively demonstrated that constitutional democracy is the present-day equivalent of Aristotle's "polity"—the **best realizable regime** within the context of sociopolitical reality. Societies with large populations, a great diversity of economic, religious, cultural, and ethnic interests, and a relatively large number of educated citizens can be governed least coercively and most flexibly by elected, truly accountable officials.

Most important of all, constitutional democracy provides the strongest guarantees against the emergence of Aristotle's *worst* form of government, tyranny. In his discussion of the normal techniques of tyrannical rule in ancient Greece, we can see the face of present-day autocracies. Aristotle declares that tyrants seek to suppress all possible critics and opponents, forbidding clubs and free education and "making every subject as much of a stranger as is possible to every other." They maintain strict surveillance of the people with secret police and networks of informers. They keep most of their subjects in a condition of material need, "partly to keep them so busy in earning a daily pittance that they have no time for plotting." Finally, tyrants are often "war-mongers, with the object of keeping their subjects constantly occupied and continually in need of a leader." In sum, tyrants usually try to "break the spirit of their subjects," "breed mutual distrust" among them, and "make their subjects incapable of action."[3]

What mainly distinguishes the worst of recent autocracies from ancient tyrannies is the scale and scope of modern destructiveness. As sociologist Peter Berger points out, premodern absolute rulers were usually limited by inefficiency and physical inability to exert continuous control over most people most of the time, especially in large kingdoms or empires. Extended kinship groups, churches or priesthoods, and other traditional institutions could also restrain royal autocrats to some degree.

With modern communications, transportation, and weapons, however, much more continuous and effective centralized control of large populations becomes possible. At the same time, traditional institutions in many societies have weakened considerably. The only way to impose restraints on the centralized modern state is to institutionalize them in the form of constitutional democracy: "*If democracy did not exist, one would have to invent it* . . . unless you want untrammeled tyranny, there is no alternative to democracy."[4]

The twentieth century has reinforced in spades Aristotle's evaluation of tyranny as the worst kind of regime. The mass murders authorized by rulers such as Hitler, Stalin, Pol Pot, and Ethiopia's Mengistu Haile Mariam dwarf the destructive feats of all ancient tyrants. Totalitarianism has produced not only the bloodiest but the most arrogant, pretentious, and mendacious tyrannies in history. Modern natural science, with its strict requirements of relevant empirical evidence and logical reasoning for claims to truth, represents perhaps the greatest intellectual achievement of human civilization. Totalitarian ideologues exploit the prestige of science but in practice deny both its critical methods and its findings that conflict with their ideological claims.

Rejecting both democratic and traditional legitimation, totalitarian rulers claim the authority of pseudoscience, whether racist social Darwinism or the ever-inaccurate but never-doubted inevitability of Marxist historical fortunetelling. To prevent public declarations of their intellectual nudity, these emperors of ideological nonsense must suppress not only the right to speak but, if possible, the capacity to think. **Intellectual regression** goes along with and helps rationalize their policies of mass killing and repression.

Regimes that seek first, foremost, and, if possible, forever to maximize and monopolize their dominant power over society must attract and employ those for whom coercive power is irresistibly attractive. O'Brien, torturer, interrogator, and voice of the ruling class in the novel *1984*, speaks the innermost thoughts, conscious or unconscious, of all dedicated totalitarians: "'Power is not a means; it is an end. One does not establish a dictatorship in order to safeguard a revolution; one makes the revolution in order to establish a dictatorship. . . . The object of power is power.'"[5]

It can be objected, correctly, that not every nondemocratic ruler or regime has been murderously oppressive. Recall the example of former President Senghor of Senegal, who voluntarily resigned his position and retired with honor. As a rare autocrat of political wisdom and integrity, however, he sponsored the establishment of a constitutional system legitimizing peaceful opposition and designed to evolve into effective democracy. Apparently he was well aware of the rarity of enlightened despotism and, wishing to leave his people the best possible political legacy, led in establishing the accountability of government to the governed. As a rule, that political arrangement provides much stronger protection against tyranny than does reliance upon the goodwill and wisdom of absolute rulers.

Flaws and Problems of Democracy

Realistic defenders of constitutional democracy must forthrightly recognize and confront its problems, however. It *is* imperfect and will always fall well short of ideal standards of justice and harmony. Competition among interest groups and parties for influence on public policy and control of government is inevitable and a vital element in the checks and balances that permeate a democratic system. However, this competition can sometimes breed cynicism and alienation from the political system on the part of many citizens who view it as nothing but a struggle for selfish advantage. Preserving some general sense of a common good or purpose is never easy when all leaders and institutions are open to criticism and attack. Leaders of democratic governments and parties have an important responsibility to rise above self-interested rivalry when vital national interests are at stake.

If political groups and parties push their interests and programs with total stubbornness, factional conflict carries the threat of democratic suicide. Violence and disorder can result, in many cases providing an excuse for the military to take over and restore "law and order." Even worse, a Hitler or a Mussolini can pose as a "strong man" who can put an end to political squabbling, fighting, and futility. Democracy works best and is most secure when all major parties are as genuinely attached to the democratic rules of the political game as they are to the interests and principles that they represent.

Charges of hypocrisy and fraud are often directed against constitutional democracy. A common criticism holds that democratic equality is purely legal and formal, while in fact wealthy interests use their resources to gain disproportionate influence over the government. Campaign contributions, financial favors, bribes, monied interests' domination of the media—all work to tilt public policy toward protecting, perpetuating, and expanding inequalities of condition.

There is some truth in this charge, but it greatly downplays the organized efforts of nonbusiness groups such as labor unions, farm organizations, environmentalists, and consumer groups. Business interests may win most of their public policy battles but by no means all of them. There would be no welfare state and possibly no health and safety and environmental regulation if they did. On this point also, simple contextual comparisons can put the criticism into perspective. In autocratic states groups opposed to the dominant interests in society—in some cases the authoritarian ruler or oligarchy, in others an entrenched nomenklatura class—are not even permitted to criticize them publicly, much less defeat them at the polls or in free legislative votes.

Democratic governments must, of course, respond to the distress of those who are unable to support themselves, whether temporarily or permanently. Which kinds of policies are most likely to help various categories of people is an endless and legitimate topic of debate within every democratic country. In practical terms, effective assistance to those unable to help themselves is what most voters expect and want, not some concerted effort to establish uniformity of material condition for all citizens.

What about the problem of corruption? The military officers who overthrew democracy in Nigeria in 1983 claimed that the civilian politicians had accepted bribes and payoffs and had diverted enormous wealth to their own bank accounts. The military rulers promised to end corruption. Almost every new autocrat makes that promise, but none has ever succeeded. There has probably never been any government totally free of at least borderline corruption.

By **corruption** we generally mean the use of public office for personal gain beyond the stated salary and perquisites of the office. It is the exploitation of public political power for extralegal material advantage. Democracies have often featured abundant corruption, as did the short-lived Nigerian democratic government from 1979 till 1983 and the government of the United States in the latter decades of the nineteenth century.

Again, comparisons are in order. Autocracies are far more likely to exploit unchecked power for rulers' personal gain on a mammoth and continuing basis than are constitutional democracies in which enough voters care about corruption to remove corrupt office holders. Recent kleptocracies in Zaire, the Philippines, and Haiti provide a reminder of that reality. So does the Soviet nomenklatura class, who use their monopoly of political power to assure themselves material advantages on a level undreamed of by ordinary citizens.

Note that our discussion of some weaknesses and problems of democracies points up only their *relative* advantages over authoritarian and totalitarian states. Group selfishness, nasty and devious political tactics, favoritism and evasion of the law, hypocritical professions of virtue and concern for the helpless, ethnic prejudice, class arrogance, and contempt for large bodies of citizens are all found in every democratic state. Claiming relative superiority for democratic government does not imply an endorsement of complacency toward these tactics and attitudes or toward the need to deal with important public concerns.

That claim rests on the firm conviction that total agreement and harmony or any other kind of perfection are not to be found in any sizeable community of human beings. To expect otherwise is **utopian**—a word that literally means "nowhere" and for that reason remains the correct label for promises of social perfection. The great social scientist Max Weber wisely remarked: "Politics is a strong and slow boring of hard boards. It takes both passion and perspective."[6] A contextualist perspective enables us to see that the gap between principles and practice is infinitely greater in totalitarian communist regimes than in the most ragtag and freewheeling democratic system.

Human Nature and the Permanent Problems of Power

We come back to first things: political power in the context of human nature and the origins of the state, as outlined in chapter 1. The argument is often made that viewing human beings as naturally competitive power seekers implies approval of all-out economic and political struggle as natural, inevitable, and even beneficial for society and humanity. That is nonsense. We agree, rather, with West German political scientist Karl Dietrich Bracher: "Power, like fear, is one of the basic motivations of all politics. . . . That is why a political anthropology which acknowledges power and fear to be 'natural' basic motivations, while freedom and justice are their **civi-**

lizing regulators, must assign supreme importance to the legal enactment and safeguarding of just these humane regulators."[7]

We do not endorse either laissez faire capitalism or a social Darwinist struggle among imperial states. Political freedom and civil liberties and the enforceable rule of laws based on democratic consent are essential regulators of power seeking if civilization is to survive and flourish under modern conditions. Those regulators, of course, are impossible without government, which originated and has flourished through history as, in large measure, an agency of domination. Yet too little government makes for Hobbes's "war of all against all," whereas too much accentuates or creates new structures of domination.

To recognize and genuinely accept that conflicts of interests and beliefs are inescapably built into human nature and the human social condition represents a giant step toward political maturity. This perspective implies that no group can ever get absolutely everything its own way and that dedicated efforts to do so will produce great misery and the continuous exploitation of concentrated but insecure coercive power. It further implies that a conflict-free, permanently harmonious and classless society is an adolescent myth that belongs on the same museum shelf as symbols of astrology and witchcraft. The leader of Polish Solidarity put it simply but clearly: "The road to a brighter future for the world leads through honest reconciliation of conflicting interests and not through hatred and bloodshed. To follow that road means to enhance the moral power of the all-embracing idea of human solidarity."[8]

Constitutional democracy, then, as the promoter of compromise and reconciliation, is the appropriate government for consenting adults. It may also provide the best hope for a stable and enduring world peace. Political scientist R. J. Rummel has calculated that since 1816 not a single war has been fought between democratic states, whereas 152 have occurred between democracies and autocracies and 194 between autocracies. He suggests two reasons that democratic institutions tend to promote nonbelligerency: first, political freedom brings popular pressures on government leaders to avoid the pain and sacrifice of war in the absence of obvious threats; second, the constant democratic necessity to find compromise policies tends to dampen the scope and influence of single-minded groups determined to get their way with another state, even at the cost of war.[9]

However, enabling constitutional democracy to replace existing autocracies is not simply a matter of effective rational persuasion. Nor can anyone seriously propose a militant armed crusade to make the world at long last safe for democracy. The most powerful autocrats today, led by the Soviet regime, have sharp and dangerous nuclear teeth; it is unsafe to assume that these weapons would not be used to counter imprudent threats to their political survival.

We do believe that the persistence of totalitarian tyranny is the gravest ongoing threat to world peace and order. Soviet Marxism-Leninism remains in principle a militantly intolerant political creed; it declares that its capitalist, bourgeois democratic rivals are doomed by history. Soviet leaders and their protegés in other countries work persistently to make that nineteenth-century prophecy come true. They are also prudent enough, though, to recognize the likely suicidal consequences of all-out war against the United States and its allies.

If nuclear deterrence can continue to work for several more decades, the lessons of twentieth-century political and economic experience may tend to favor the spread of democracy. Most authoritarian regimes seem less and less able to generate legitimacy or enthusiastic support. Only fanatical or power-hungry revolutionaries and their naive or self-deceived sympathizers any longer look to Marxist-Leninist states as models for humane politics and economic welfare. Repeated experiences of murderous and mind-numbing totalitarian rule have demonstrated that constitutional democracy is now the only practicable means of civilizing the always dangerous but indispensable concentration of power called government.

What Can We Do about Governments and Power?

Unlike Marxist-Leninists, we do not claim to know the political future and doubt that its shape can now be known or is in any significant sense inevitable. It depends on circumstances, political actors' knowledge and ignorance, and, to a real but unknowable extent, deliberate choices guided by values and beliefs about political causes and effects.

But what can you do as a voter, in rarer cases a political activist, and in the rarest instances a government official? The best use of your time and opportunities as a student is to try to learn to think as clearly and realistically about politics as you possibly can. This means finding a variety of sources for political news, interpretation, and analysis and doing the best you can to discover which ones tend to be most reliable. It also means truly grasping that moral feelings about politics, however altruistic and humane, provide no automatic knowledge or insight into political reality. Even further, if followed uncritically, they can distort your understanding and increase your vulnerability to manipulative persuasion.

You will inevitably develop and apply your own normative standards—self-consciously and critically or automatically and uncritically—to governments, leaders, and policies as you mature and enter upon adult responsibilities. To help stimulate that process, we conclude by suggesting four rules for evaluating fundamental political choices. They grow out of our desire to minimize the destructive uses and consequences of political power and our understanding of politics in the twentieth century.

1. Above all, try to avoid or prevent the worst—totalitarian tyranny. Knowledge and stubborn avoidance of self-deception can be enormously important means to this end. Writing about Cuba a year after Castro came to power, former political prisoner Armando Valladares observes:

> The great majority of the Cuban people didn't know much about Communism. They weren't really politically aware, and it was difficult for them to believe the bad things people were saying about Marxism. . . .
> Within the ranks of the revolutionaries who had fought against Batista, there were thousands of people who would not allow themselves to think that Castro was a Communist. They admitted that it was true that Communists were gradually moving into certain areas, that dreadful things were happening, but it was all behind Fidel's back. When he found out about it, he'd put a stop to it. How naive they were![10]

2. Never believe and, if possible, prevent the rise to power of anyone who claims the right to dominate and kill as necessary means to end domination and killing forever.

3. If a real and unavoidable policy choice lies between evils, don't let your moral distaste blind you to the necessity of choosing. It is almost always better to side with **the lesser evil;** the differences are likely to be greatly magnified in the longer run.

4. Assume the inevitability and permanence of political conflict, and try to contain, channel, and civilize its expressions and effects.

We would be not surprised but pleased if, after reading this book, you consider these rules to be trite and even self-evident. But if you think about them in the context of what you have now learned, you will soon realize that failure or inability to follow them has cost tens of millions of innocent lives in this bloodiest of all centuries. There is no guarantee that they can be readily complied with in much of the world, even today. We agree that, in the light of massive relevant experience, these guidelines *should* seem self-evident—yet they remain terribly insecure.

As with liberty, so with imperfect but effective and minimally destructive government: the price is educated and eternal vigilance.

Summary

Although the main purpose of this book has been to promote realistic understanding of politics, all political analysis is necessarily influenced by moral concerns. Also, the way we understand politics strongly affects our beliefs about the place of moral judgment in politics.

We consider first how government and politics should be evaluated. In broad terms, two major enduring ways of applying moral norms to politics are represented by Plato's *Republic* and Aristotle's *Politics*. Both of these ancient Greek philosophers were concerned with the ethical value of political systems. Plato's perspective emphasized absolute standards, proposing the best, totally just state as a standard for condemning all existing states. Aristotle outlined a best state also but devoted more attention to the best realizable regime, a middle-class-dominated polity that combines features of two unjust systems, democracy and oligarchy.

Plato's ideal was an autocracy ruled by supremely rational philosopher kings. They would place everyone in the social class and occupation for which he or she was best suited by innate abilities and temperament. Marriage, child rearing, property—all would be communal and controlled by wise rulers concerned only for the common good.

Aristotle rejected Plato's scheme as impractical and contrary to human experience. He emphasized rather a contextual-standards approach to political evaluation—judging regimes and institutions as better or worse within specific social circumstances. Although Aristotle classified tyranny as the most unjust regime, he advised tyrants to rule with some moderation and concern for the public interest. Even the worst regimes need not all be equally evil. In general, Aristotle's normative judgments were thoroughly grounded in broad political knowledge and observation.

As a rule, the contextualist, practical-minded approach to political evaluation is more realistic and humane in its results than the alternative. Efforts to impose absolute standards of justice or perfection upon entire societies have a strong tendency to increase conflict, coercion, and suffering. The best example is supplied by Marxist-Leninist regimes, in which a supposedly perfect political end justifies terrible means, which never produce the promised perfection.

The most sensible way to evaluate regimes is to analyze them within the context of relevant political experience, past and present, as well as basic beliefs about human nature and societies. What kind of political fate has history made possible or probable for a particular country? How does its government compare with governments of similar societies? Does totally condemning it imply a perfectionist or a skeptical view of human virtue and good intentions? These and similar questions—not simply whether the system in question is "unfair" or "corrupt"—need to be confronted in order to make realistic judgments of better or worse.

Applying the test of experience, we highlight a recent compilation of total deaths caused by governments and by wars in the twentieth century. Governments have killed more than three times as many people as have died in wars, and totalitarian regimes were responsible for at least 93 percent of government-caused deaths. The gulf between Marx's original humane and civilized political ends and the practices of Marxist-Leninist regimes is stark and unbridgeable. Intense moral outrage against noncommunist regimes and societies needs to be educated and tempered by an unblinkered awareness of the practical results of political Marxism.

Second, we consider relations between political power and civilization, with Marxist-Leninist regimes seen as a regression to rule based on divine right (in a secular guise) and human sacrifice. They also exploit the prestige of modern science by claiming pseudoscientific legitimacy while suppressing and corrupting the life of the intellect.

In practical terms, constitutional democracy is the present-day equivalent of Aristotle's best realizable regime. As a rule, large and diverse populations can be most effectively and least coercively governed by regimes featuring free participation and political choice. Above all, constitutional democracy protects best against the emergence of the worst kinds of tyranny. Modern weapons, communications, transportation, and organizational techniques make possible a kind of thoroughgoing despotism not possible in earlier times. Only regularized, enforceable limits upon government imposed by democratic liberty and accountability can prevent untrammeled tyranny and its horrendous assault on civilized decency.

Democratic regimes are inevitably imperfect and plagued by more or less serious problems. Factional conflict can breed corruption, cynicism, and alienation from the political system. If carried to violent lengths, it can lead to the suicide of democracy.

Substantial inequalities and corruption persist in every democracy. However, the use of political power to create and protect privilege is much more prominent in autocratic regimes, and their corruption is usually more pervasive and harder to attack than in democracies. Democratic citizens have no cause for complacency, but in comparative terms, there can be no serious doubt that constitutional democracy works better than autocracy for more people most of the time. This judgment is especially strong when comparison focuses on the harsher and more painful forms of political power.

From our perspective, constitutional democracy provides the only hope for taming and civilizing political power under present-day circumstances. Compromise and accommodation of conflicting interests is the central emphasis of democratic government and the mark of its realism and maturity. Autocracies seem to have increasing difficulty in sustaining much authority, but illegitimacy alone does not bring political decline and fall. No one can reliably predict our political future.

Finally, what can we do about governments and power in that future? It will be influenced by choices, as made by political leaders, analysts, and citizens. At the very least we should do our best to discover how to learn about political realities and how to think clearly about complex and emotion-laden situations and issues.

We conclude by suggesting four normative rules for political choice, derived from experience: to prevent the worst—totalitarian tyranny; to resist anyone who claims a right to dominate and kill in order to create permanent peace and harmony; to opt firmly for the lesser evil; and never to assume that political conflict is abnormal and can be abolished. For civilized life and human liberty to have a future, conflict must be channeled and limited—and accepted as our enduring political condition.

Review List of Key Terms

normative
political evaluation
absolute standards
contextual standards
philosopher kings
myth of the metals

the "practicable best" regime
tyranny
politically caused deaths

Yalta Agreement
best realizable regime
intellectual regression
corruption

utopian
civilizing regulators
the lesser evil

Notes

1. Karl Marx, "Theses on Feuerbach," in *Marx and Engels: Basic Writings on Politics and Philosophy*, ed. Lewis Feuer (Garden City, N. Y.: Doubleday Anchor Books, 1959), p. 243.
2. R. J. Rummel, "Deadlier Than War: Non-Freedom" (Honolulu: Department of Political Science, University of Hawaii, 1986), p. 8.
3. Ernest Barker, ed. and trans., *The Politics of Aristotle* (New York: Oxford University Press, 1958), pp. 244–246.
4. Peter L. Berger, "Democracy for Everyone?" *Commentary*, September 1983, p. 34. (Italics in original.)
5. George Orwell, *1984* (Harmondsworth, Middlesex: Penguin Books, 1954), pp. 211–212.
6. Max Weber, "Politics as a Vocation," in *From Max Weber; Essays in Sociology*, ed. Hans Gerth and C. Wright Mills (New York: Oxford University Press, 1946), p. 128.
7. Karl Dietrich Bracher, *The Age of Ideologies: A History of Political Thought in the Twentieth Century* (New York: St. Martin's Press, 1984), p. 229.
8. Lech Walesa, Nobel Peace Prize acceptance speech, December 10, 1983.
9. R. J. Rummel, "On Fostering a Just Peace," *International Journal on World Peace* 1 (1) (Autumn 1984): 4–15.
10. Armando Valladares, *Against All Hope: The Prison Memoirs* (New York: Knopf, 1986), p. 5.

Glossary

administrative discretion The capacity and need of bureaucratic officials to decide precisely what a generally worded law will mean when applied to specific categories of individuals or circumstances—can translate into significant policy-making power.

anarchy A condition without government, as in international relations, where no governmental authority exists above the level of each sovereign state.

autarky Condition or policy of trying to make a country economically self-sufficient, not at all dependent on trading or any other foreign economic ties.

authoritarianism Refers to autocratic government that seeks mainly to prevent and suppress political opposition but does not attempt to shape and control most spheres of social life, such as education, religion, economic relationships, and arts and literature.

authority Legitimate power, the right to give commands that people believe they have a moral obligation to obey: a basic category of political power.

autocracy Literally, "self-authorized rule." Any political system in which rulers are not subject to enforceable legal rules or limited by other governmental institutions, free elections, or freely expressed public opinion. Two main contemporary subtypes are authoritarian and totalitarian regimes.

balance of power Refers to a condition of equilibrium among states or alliances, a rough equality of internationally relevant power that governments of affected states generally accept. Also used to label policy of trying to create or maintain such an equilibrium.

basic political conventions Long-established and highly respected traditions and customs concerning the conduct of government and politics. In Britain they form the core of the mostly unwritten but effective constitution.

basic political rights For democracy to function, these rights must be assured to all citizens: freedom from arbitrary arrest and punishment, freedom of public expression, freedoms of association and assembly, freedom to participate in fairly conducted competitive elections.

bicameral Refers to a legislative body made up of two separate houses. A single-house legislative body is *unicameral*.

bipolarity A balance-of-power situation in which two opposing states are so much more powerful than their allies or any other states that the two states' competition polarizes, structures, and dominates the international scene: U.S.–USSR relations since the Second World War the prime example.

bureaucracy Agencies and departments of government, mainly in the executive establishment, with fulltime employees organized functionally and in hierarchies. Responsible for implementing virtually all policies of government.

Central Committee A Soviet Communist Party body of about 500 members, mainly representing higher levels of party and government officialdom. It supposedly elects a committee, the Politburo, to conduct daily Central Committee business between its twice-yearly meetings. In fact the Politburo determines all appointments to the Central Committee and decides when that body will meet, whom it will elect to the Politburo, and what it will do.

charismatic authority People's submitting to a leader because they believe that he or she has extraordinary personal qualities that command their obedience, such as magical gifts, access to divine or ultimate truth, or heroic military abilities.

chiefdom Most primitive form of multicommunity political system. The society is organized by kinship groups (lineages), but some are more prestigious and powerful than others. Chief's position is hereditary within the highest-ranking lineage; rule sanctioned and reinforced by religious beliefs, rituals, and an organized priesthood.

clientelism A political leader's maintaining a group of followers and helpers by using his political power to give them rewards such as jobs, contracts, and money, ensuring their financial and political support for the leader's position and purposes. A political patronage system.

coalition government Control of the executive (prime ministership, cabinet positions, and ministries) within a parliamentary system by two or more distinct parties working together, dividing up leadership positions, and cooperatively running the government.

coalitions Groups whose members cooperate with one another to realize common political objectives.

coercion The use or threat of severe sanctions by power wielders against those whose actions they seek to control: a basic category of political power.

collective security Concept of preserving peace by enforcing sanctions against states declared lawbreaking aggressors by an international organization such as the League of Nations or the United Nations.

compulsory participation Totalitarian governments' use of social, educational, and economic sanctions and inducements to force nearly everyone to engage in political activities designed to signify support and endorsement of the regime and its policies.

confederacy A loose-knit cooperative alliance among essentially independent political units whose major purpose, as a rule, is effective common defense. The minimal common government deals only with the unit governments and not with individual citizens.

constitutional democracy A government in which freely expressed public opinion and free elections provide both the foundations of governmental authority and the basic institutionalized restraints on the exercise of governmental power: one of the three basic types of contemporary governments.

constitutionalism A determinate, stable legal order that prevents the arbitrary exercise of governmental power and subjects both governors and governed to the same laws.

constructive vote of no-confidence Restrictive procedure for parliamentary removal of a federal chancellor in West Germany. Can be done only if lower house (Bundestag) elects a new chancellor by an absolute majority vote of its membership.

cooperation As a strategy of political competition, involves individuals or groups working together in order to increase their power as a means of reaching common goals.

corporate-rule authoritarianism Autocratic government controlled by an oligarchic coalition consisting of certain top military officers, high-ranking bureaucrats, technocrats, and representatives of some important economic and political groups.

corruption The use of public office for personal gain beyond the stated salary and perquisites of the office; exploiting public political power for extralegal material advantage.

counterrevolutionary Literally means antirevolutionary but often used to imply hostility to progress and reactionary desire to "turn back the clock" of allegedly inevitable historical change.

coup d'état Literally means "stroke of state." Originally referred to illegal seizure or extension of power by an officeholder. Now includes any forceful overthrow of an existing government, whether by members of its own military forces or by armed revolutionaries.

defensive modernization Government-guided efforts to industrialize a country very rapidly in order to create sufficient economic and military capacity to resist encroachments by already modernized states: Japan the outstanding example in the late nineteenth century.

delegitimation Attempts by proponents of an ideology to discredit regimes, policies, and ideas legitimized by competing ideologies.

democracy Literally, "rule by the people." In ancient and medieval times, referred to control of government by assembly of all citizens—direct democracy. In the modern world means constitutional, representative government in which top decision makers are elected in open and competitive elections, with almost all adults entitled to vote. Requires effective protection of basic political rights and liberties and effective restraints on government officials.

democratic centralism Leninist concept of communist party organization. In theory, elections and criticisms from lower ranks of party decide party leadership and policies. Actually, all nominations and elections are controlled from the top within the party structure, and all lower officials and members are expected to accept without question all their superiors' decisions. In practice a highly autocratic and centralized structure, not in the least democratic.

dictatorship In ancient Rome, temporary one-man rule aimed at dealing with a severe threat to the state. In the twentieth century a regime of unchallenged power and privilege headed by one leader or by a small group who maintain a police state.

diplomacy Carried on by official representatives of sovereign states, exchanging views with each other about their governments' intentions and policies of mutual interest; can also involve negotiations aimed at reaching formal agreement between governments.

direct democracy Government in which all citizens are entitled to participate in the supreme lawmaking assembly. Executive and judicial functions may also be conducted, at least in part, by ordinary citizens: ancient Athens and New England town meetings two of the best-known examples.

domination As a political strategy, refers to gaining and keeping positions of superior power and privilege by coercive means, mainly armed force and intimidation.

economic statecraft Efforts by a government to influence actions of another state by economic means: may involve inducements such as aid or changes in trade policy, or coercion, such as embargo, boycott, or other sanctions.

elimination As a political strategy, involves getting rid of competitors or supposed threats, temporarily or permanently, legitimately or illegally, nonviolently or violently—sometimes murderously.

ethnic group A basic category of human social groups; characterized by unity of race and culture.

ethnonationalism The claim that an ethnic group is and ought to be recognized as a distinct nation, entitled to political self-determination.

executive The most active and indispensable component of government, in charge of basic external and internal security functions and usually predominant in policy formulation and execution. May be headed by a single leader (monarch, prime minister, president, dictator) or a small group (cabinet, junta, politburo).

extended republic James Madison's term for describing popular, constitutional government in a large and populous country. He argued (in *The Federalist*) that its great number and variety of interests would check and control each other and prevent tyrannical rule by a majority faction.

federalism Refers to territorial organization of governmental authority: divided between a central government and a number of regional governments, so that government at each level has some activities on which it makes final decisions.

fundamental trust Belief by political groups within a democracy that their opponents can be trusted with control of government and will not use it in ways the minority cannot tolerate or to destroy the democratic process and entrench themselves illegitimately in power.

general secretary Top official of the Communist Party of the Soviet Union. Chairs the Central Committee, the Politburo, and the Secretariat. Most powerful single political leader in the USSR, though Stalin the only general secretary with nearly total dictatorial power. Post-Stalin general secretaries have been "first among equals" within an oligarchy of top leaders who make all major decisions and keep the general secretary from acquiring Stalin-like personal power that might be used against them.

governing Using power to handle conflicts within a society and to cope with problems common to the entire society.

government In general, any set of political roles, or offices, whose occupants assume the principal responsibility for governing within a given social grouping. *Public* government is any government that successfully upholds a claim to the exclusive regulation of the legitimate use of physical force in enforcing its rules within a given territorial area.

great powers States that far surpass most others in the resources—especially military capability—that make for effective power in international politics and that frequently use that power to pursue their national interests.

ideological power elite Refers to autocratic, oligarchic rulers of totalitarian, especially communist, political systems. Communist rulers' claim to authority based on ideological assertion that their party represents true historic interests of working class and, eventually, of the whole people in an allegedly classless society. Ideological indoctrination and exclusiveness strongly emphasized, and content of ideology always rationalizes and legitimizes power and policies of elites who monopolize the right to be its authoritative interpreters.

ideology Ideas and beliefs as applied to politics. Two main overlapping types: rationalization ideology (ideas intended to justify or legitimize anyone's material or power interests) and worldview ideology (set of ideas designed to interpret society and politics, justify a particular kind of political and social order, and encourage action on their behalf).

indoctrinational persuasion Efforts to shape people's beliefs, attitudes, and biases, usually over an extended period of time, so that they will respond as the indoctrinators desire to political events, messages, and symbols.

inducements Rewards promised and bestowed in order to control or at least influence the recipient's actions: a basic category of political power.

institutionalized totalitarianism A totalitarian system that has survived for more than a generation. Depends less on ideological fervor, mass terror, and a supreme leader than in its earlier revolutionizing phase. Based mainly on a pervasive, all-controlling, autocratically organized official party. Ruling elites direct indoctrinational efforts and control security forces that enable them to exercise institutionally unchecked power over the entire society: USSR the prime example.

intellectual class An important component of modern, increasingly secularized societies. People who specialize in producing and spreading ideas: writers, artists, journalists, academics, scientists, some lawyers and other professionals, political publicists and ideologists. Specialize in the power of persuasion. Critical role in all revolutions.

interest groups Organized groups whose leaders and members attempt to influence policies and actions of government in favor of their distinctive interests, whether economic, religious, political, ideological, or cultural.

international law A body of norms and rules that supposedly regulate the conduct of sovereign states in international relations. Derives mainly from long-established diplomatic practices, customs, and treaties. Primitive law in that there are no effective mechanisms for enforcement beyond the right reserved by each state to retaliate for what its government considers illegal injuries.

J-curve Diagrammatic representation of sharp and unexpected decline in economic conditions after a period of steady improvement, so that people's actual rewards suddenly fall well short of what they expect to receive. Can sometimes produce enough frustration and resentment aimed at government to help bring on a revolution.

kleptocracy Rule by thieves: label sometimes applied to authoritarian regimes in which corruption reaches extraordinary levels and enormous amounts in public funds are siphoned off by top officials for their own enrichment.

law of nature In John Locke's version, basic morally binding rules decreed by God but discoverable by natural human reason. Decrees that no one shall violate any person's inalienable rights to life, liberty, and property.

legal authority Rule based on acceptance of publicly articulated laws and regulations issued by duly authorized public officials.

legitimation A central function of ideology: to define a political system, regime, or government as morally entitled to claim and exercise authority and receive willing obedience.

majoritarian parliamentary system Type of democratic government in which a single party normally has a majority in parliament and supports the executive (prime minister and cabinet) as a disciplined voting bloc.

majority rule Basic principle of democratic procedure; ordinarily means that majority view prevails in elections and within legislative bodies. May be modified for constitutional amendments and for protection of vital group interests by, for example, requiring extraordinary or regional majorities to approve changes.

manipulative persuasion Using lies and deception, distorting and withholding relevant information as means of influencing people's beliefs and actions.

Marxism-Leninism Official ideology of the Soviet Union and of other communist states and movements. Combines Marx's emphasis on alleged scientific knowledge of the "inevitable" direction of historical development with Lenin's "vanguard" revolutionary party that claims a monopoly of ideological truth and seeks to establish and maintain its total control over society.

merit system Employing civil servants on the basis of specific training and competence demonstrated through competitive examinations. Employment rights and tenure guaranteed to protect against firing or manipulation of civil servants for partisan purposes. Career bureaucrats assumed to be able and willing to serve impartially whatever group or party assumes control of government.

modernization In economic terms, refers to development of money-based exchange system, sizeable industrial sector, specialization of jobs and functions, and proliferation of specialized organizations. Politically, has less definite meaning. Often refers to basing authority on a nontraditional claim to legitimacy, developing a specialized modern-type bureaucracy, creating effective mass parties, and establishing a system of relatively peaceful and orderly leadership succession.

national self-determination Right of any nation to have its own distinctive government in its own state free of interference by other nations or sovereign states; enshrined in United Nations Charter as principle of "equal rights and self-determination of peoples."

nationalism As a doctrine, holds that humanity is naturally divided into nations that are known by characteristics such as race, language, religion, and common traditions, and that only national self-government is legitimate. More generally and ambiguously, nationalism involves a belief that distinct cultures deserve some kind of political recognition.

nomenklatura Refers to positions of most power and influence, plus all others with highest prestige and most desirable rewards, in Soviet Union and, by analogy, in other communist systems. Access to these positions carefully controlled by Communist Party elites; political loyalty and reliability absolute requirements for filling them. Inducements of higher standard of living, foreign travel, access to accurate news, and ability to exercise power produce enough cooperation among decision-making and privileged elites to sustain their autocratic political system.

normative Concerning evaluative statements and judgments; in a political context usually refers to moral evaluations of regimes, institutions, people, policies, and actions.

offices Governmental positions filled by different people at different times.

oligarchy Rule by the few. To the ancient Greeks, term also implied that the few were wealthy; in effect, oligarchy meant plutocracy. Does not necessarily have that connotation today—only rule by a restricted group not accountable to the ruled.

organizations Coalitional groups that have an ongoing existence; usually structured as a formal hierarchy with multiple levels of authority; feature division of labor and responsibilities among personnel and operate according to relatively stable rules and procedures.

orientation A sense of understanding history and society, plus an ability to recognize cues about what one should pay attention to or ignore—provided by a worldview ideology to those who believe in it.

parliamentary government Democratic system that features "fusion" rather than "separation" of executive and legislative institutions and powers. Prime minister and cabinet elected by parliament, usually from among its members, and may be dismissed from office by parliamentary vote.

Party Congress Supposedly the supreme authority within the Communist Party of the Soviet Union. Made up of party delegates from throughout the country; usually meets every five years. In fact its delegates are all selected by higher party officials, not by ordinary members. Delegates applaud and praise the general secretary and other high party officials and vote unanimously to adopt programs decided upon by the party's autocratic elite.

party discipline Members of same party within a legislative body voting identically and in accord with official party or leadership positions on particular issues and measures. Usually most effective when party leaders can politically penalize members who deviate from party positions in legislative voting.

party-rule authoritarianism Apparently democratic but actually autocratic government based on a party whose leaders make certain that it wins every significant election. Regime combines patronage, institutionalized succession procedures, propaganda, coercion, and policy benefits to maintain complete dominance over all other parties and over political system as a whole. Main examples Mexico and Taiwan.

people's democracies Label that rulers of communist regimes usually attach to their governments (sometimes "people's republic" or "democratic republic"). Reflects claim that regimes have abolished social class differences, which supposedly distort Western-style democracy into rule by the wealthy, or the "bourgeoisie." Leaders of the "vanguard" communist party in a "people's democracy" claim to represent the true interests of the whole people. In reality, party elites are totally autocratic, accountable only to themselves. Elections not free and competitive, as required for political democracy.

personal politics People's seeking and using power to advance their self-defined interests within family, workplace, and other nonofficial social settings.

personal-rule authoritarianism Autocracy without long-established, secure institutions to legitimize and reliably implement decisions of top ruler. In their absence, ruler's personal desires, abilities, and luck are extremely important in determining direction and accomplishments of government. Ruler's position similar to monarch's but not backed by tradition or hereditary principle.

persuasion Influencing someone's actions by means of argument or information: a basic category of political power.

Politburo In theory, executive committee of the Central Committee of the Communist Party of the Soviet Union. Usually has about a dozen full members and a half-dozen nonvoting or "candidate" members. In reality, autocratic and supreme decision-making and policy-deciding body in Soviet political system. Determines its own membership and controls appointment process for all subordinate party bodies; chaired by general secretary of the party.

political lag Failure of a state's political institutions and organizations to change and adapt as rapidly as necessary to prevent social and economic changes from leading to frustration, disorder, and violence.

political parties In democratic systems, groups that present candidates and programs to voters, seeking to win office through elections and gain control over machinery of government. When out of office, usually present persistent and more or less organized opposition to policies of party or coalition in power.

political revolution Aims almost exclusively at destroying existing regime and creating new and supposedly more legitimate government to replace it.

political science The disciplined, scholarly study of ideas, behavior, institutions, and policies related to public politics and government.

politics Efforts, both successful and unsuccessful, by some people to gain and exercise power over others.

power The capacity of some persons to produce intended and foreseen effects on others.

presidential government Democratic system in which the chief executive officer is constitutionally and electorally separated from the legislative body.

proportional representation A democratic parliamentary election system with multimember districts; in a few cases the whole country is the only voting district. Seats in parliament are allocated to parties according to their proportion of the popular vote within each district. Systems differ in detail, but they are designed to enable each party to obtain approximately the same percentage of seats in parliament as its percentage of the countrywide popular vote.

public politics Power-related efforts to influence, regulate, or control activities and policies that concern the larger community beyond the domestic sphere.

rational persuasion Efforts to influence someone's beliefs or actions by means of information and advice that the persuader believes to be correct and in the best interests of the subject.

rationalization ideology All ideas that are intended to justify or rationalize anyone's material or power interests.

rationalized repression Strategy of institutionalized totalitarian regimes, especially the Soviet Union, aimed at preventing dissent or opposition. Much more limited use of arrest, imprisonment, and execution than characterizes indiscriminate mass-elimination programs such as Stalin's. Focuses mainly on actual deviants from official ideology and autocratic system; effort to make punishment certain and unpleasant enough to deter many other potential dissidents. Confinement and brutal treatment of some dissenters in mental hospitals a favored form of punishment.

referendum Deciding on a policy or constitutional issue by means of a popular vote.

relative deprivation Belief that one is getting fewer rewards or less recognition than deserved in comparison with certain other persons or groups. Can lead to frustration and resentment, which are sometimes expressed politically and may become a significant factor in revolutionary situations.

representation In modern constitutional democracies, refers to people's selecting and dismissing their governers through competitive elections rather than conducting the business of government themselves, as in direct democracy.

representational parliamentary system Type of democratic government based on proportional-representation electoral system. No single party ever wins a majority in parliament, and the executive is always controlled by a coalition of two of more distinct parties.

revisionist states States whose governments seek substantial, sometimes drastic, improvement in their power position relative to other sovereign states.

revolution An ambiguous word that refers to some kind of sudden and significant change in government accomplished by extralegal or illegal means. Usually denotes one or more of these developments: sudden downfall or overthrow of a government; emergence of a new government from an all-out struggle for ruling power; efforts by leaders of the new regime to bring about great changes in society.

revolutionizing phase of totalitarianism Refers to first period of time after a totalitarian movement has gained supreme power in a state. Actual and potential opponents ruthlessly eliminated, far-reaching steps taken to destroy old social order and to begin to implement ideology of total transformation. Apparatus of totalitarian party rapidly expands as its control extends to every sector of society. A supreme leader, such as Hitler, Stalin, Mao, or Castro, usually serves as main focus of ideological direction and inspiration and is likely to acquire dictatorial power over party itself.

Secretariat Peak of administrative structure of Central Committee of Communist Party of the Soviet Union. A committee of about ten party secretaries, each of whom heads a department of the enormous party bureaucracy. Chaired by general secretary of the party.

secularization Loss of belief that the world is a divinely established order that people must simply accept on religious grounds. Tends to be replaced by belief that the world is knowable through systematic investigation and rational thought, which can lead to improvements in the human condition. More broadly, a lessening of the impact of religious beliefs and institutions on society and politics.

selective perception Tendency to notice and pay serious attention only to certain kinds of observations and experiences—usually those that confirm what we already believe.

self-help Right reserved by every sovereign state to retaliate against what its government regards as breaches of international law, using either nonviolent or forceful sanctions.

single-member-district-plurality system Method of selecting legislative body in which each member is selected from a distinct geographical area. Candidate who wins most votes in district, even if not a majority, wins the seat. Tends to favor large and well-established parties, since smaller parties have little chance to come in first in any districts.

social programs Large and growing category of governmental policies in twentieth century: major types include social insurance, welfare payments, health and nutrition programs. Designed to cope with problems of economic security in highly interdependent and urbanized industrial societies.

social revolution Goes beyond destroying old government and replacing it with a new one. Leaders attempt to use power of government to transform such aspects of society as class structure, status system, religious institutions, property and economic systems, cultural life, and sometimes even family system.

sovereignty Concept first formulated by French political theorist Jean Bodin in the sixteenth century. Holds that a government must have supreme authority over all its subjects and that every full-fledged state is legally independent of the authority of all other states.

sphere of influence Originally referred to claims to specific areas of commercial and governmental jurisdiction by specific European colonial powers in imperial China. More broadly, now connotes region in which a great power is generally understood to have more than usual interest in retaining influence over other states at a level much superior to that of other great powers, especially its rivals.

spoils system Filling all kinds of government jobs with supporters of the party that has come to power by winning an election. Typical of Jacksonian democracy in the nineteenth-century United States. A democratic variety of the patronage system, which staffs officialdom with supporters of the government in power.

state In terms of cultural evolution, the first political systems with centralized governments able to collect taxes, draft men for work or war, and decree and enforce laws. In current terms, a political system with people, territory, government, and sovereignty.

state of nature For Thomas Hobbes (1588–1679), a condition in which no effective government exists to enforce law and order. Competition for power and its benefits is unrestricted, producing a state of virtual war in which everyone's life is "solitary, poor, nasty, brutish, and short."

state system Shorthand term referring to nothing more than the coexistence of independent states on the international political scene.

statecraft Methods used by governments in attempts to bring their power to bear upon other states, including international propaganda, diplomatic negotiations, economic inducements and sanctions, and use or threat of military force.

status quo states States whose governments support and desire to preserve the existing distribution of power among the states with which they are likely to interact.

survey research The systematic gathering and analysis of data based on questionnaire responses from a particular type of population—for example, eligible voters.

Thermidor Name of a month in new revolutionary calendar adopted in France in 1793. Radical Jacobin government removed from office on 9 Thermidor, the Year II (July 27, 1794). Term now usually refers to the end of rule by radicals and of most radical tendencies in a revolution.

toleration As a political strategy, involves accepting right of one's competitors to exist and to seek power within a framework of general rules that permit only peaceful methods of competition.

totalitarianism Twentieth-century type of autocratic regime in which ruling elite claims legitimacy on basis of an ideology of total social transformation that promises a previously unrealized ideal condition of mankind. Regime organized around a single legal party that penetrates and controls all sectors of society; utilizes large and active security police to prevent opposition or deviation from official norms. Regime monopolizes mass communications and controls all weapons. It sponsors and directs all legal organizations, using them to mobilize mass support and to prevent unofficial efforts to associate for purposes not endorsed by autocratic rulers.

traditional authoritarianism Usually refers to hereditary monarchy in which monarch actually exercises supreme directive power. Authority based on some version of divine right and on belief in principle of hereditary succession.

traditional authority Rule based on long-established customs, norms, and habits of obedience that people ordinarily assume to be valid and unchanging.

tyranny In classical times, denoted a regime dominated by one man who rules in his own interests and not for good of whole community. In broader sense, usually implies harshly coercive autocratic rule in which concentrated governmental power is relentlessly exploited for personal gain by its elite controllers.

unitary system Refers to territorial organization of government: central government has full legal authority over all other levels of government (provincial, county, district, local) and can regulate, modify, create, or abolish other units as it sees fit. Complete centralization of legal authority within a state.

united front Refers to tactics often used by radical revolutionary, particularly communist, parties to gain power: entering into coalition with noncommunist groups opposed to existing government. If and when government is overthrown, coalition takes power. Radicals use their tight-knit, disciplined organization, manipulative persuasion, and ruthless determination to eliminate coalition partners from government and establish monopoly rule for their party.

utopian Literally means "nowhere." Used to label imaginary "perfect" societies—usually harmonious, peaceful, secure, and happy, with conflict abolished forever.

veto power UN Security Council rule that allows any permanent member state to defeat a substantive resolution by voting against it.

worldview ideology A set of ideas intended to interpret society and politics, justify a particular kind of politics and social order, and encourage action on their behalf.

zero-sum conflict Conflict in which one side's gain is necessarily the other side's loss. Since compromise is impossible, this kind of conflict tends to be intense and even violent.

INDEX

Absolute standards of evaluation, 354
Acheampong, Ignatius, 171
Adams, John, 31
Administrative discretion, 93
Afghanistan, 238, 278, 280
Africanization, 171
African nationalism, 72–74
Agrarian societies, 44
Ahidjo, Ahmadou, 170
Alawi Moslems, 174
Alexander II, Tsar, 46
Algerian War, 362
Allende, Salvador, 291
Alliances, 282, 292
Almond, Gabriel, 84
Alsace-Lorraine, 286
Amalrik, Andrei, 212
Amending process, constitutional, 122, 144
An American Dilemma, 60
American government and politics, 11
American Revolution, 110, 301, 302, 337
Anarchy, 18, 106
Anarchy, international, 254–256, 260–263, 284
Andropov, Yuri, 193
Anthropology, 12
Antonov-Ovseyenko, Anton, 230
Apartheid, 64
Appeasement, 29, 254, 288
Aquino, Corazon, 341
Arab–Israeli conflict, 174
Arab socialism, 173
Arap Moi, Daniel, 173
Arendt, Hannah, 336
Argentina, 99, 117, 177
Aristocracy, 95
Aristotle, 7, 15, 107, 155

Aristotle *(continued)*
  on political evaluation, 354, 357–358, 364
  on types of government, 95
Armed Forces Movement, Portuguese, 329
Art, Robert, 282
Articles of Confederation, 143
Arts, officially sponsored, 91
Assad, Hafez al-, 174, 175
Assassination, 46–47
Atheism, Soviet, 208
Athens, 28, 38
Augustine, Saint, 15, 16
Australia, 128, 250
Autarky, 276
Authoritarianism, 99–100, 163
  corporate-rule, 173–178
  Latin American, 175–178
  Middle Eastern, 173–175
  party-rule, 178–180
  personal-rule, 168–173
  problems of, 178
  reasons for, 159–163
  Spanish, 178
  traditional, 166–168
  types of, 163–180
Authority, 6, 33–38
  and ideology, 60
  international, 38
  legal, 36–37
  traditional, 36
Autocracy, 97–99
Aztecs, 90, 364

Ba'ath socialist party, 174
Babeuf, Francois-Noel, 338
Baechler, Jean, 298, 303
Baha'is, 334
Balance of power, 43
  bipolar, 287–293
  and federalism, 143

Balance of power *(continued)*
  international, 283–286
  social and political, 110
Balance of terror, 286
Baldwin, David, 278
Balkans, 67
Baltic states, 85
Bangladesh, 75
Bani-Sadr, Abol Hassan, 329
Basic political conventions, British, 119
Batista, Fulgencio, 194, 317
Belgium, 141
Bell, Coral, 292–293
Bell, Daniel, 5
Bellow, Saul, 52
Bengalis, 75
Berger, Peter, 364
Beria, Lavrenti, 207
Best realizable regime, 364
Biafra, 75
Bialer, Seweryn, 237, 258
Bicameral legislature, 144
Bipolar balance of power, 287–293
Bismarck, Otto von, 67
Bodin, Jean, 249
Bolsheviks, 63, 191, 300, 313, 327, 333, 336
  land policies of, 342
  seizure of power by, 196
Bourgeoisie, 200
Bracher, Karl Dietrich, 367–368
Brainwashing, 27
Brazil, 142, 156, 176–177
Brezhnev, Leonid, 193, 207
Brezhnev doctrine, 238, 262
Brinton, Crane, 306, 325
Britain, 65
British empire, 45
Brittan, Samuel, 147–148
Bryan, William Jennings, 33

Brzezinski, Zbigniew, 98, 188
Bundesrat, 144
Bureaucracy, 37, 92–95, 125
Bureaucratic authoritarianism, 176–177
Burke, Edmund, 34, 339

Calvin, John, 16
Cambodia, 47, 95, 190, 314–315, 356–357
  mass killings in, 230–231, 260
  revolution in, 317
Cameroon, 170, 172
Camp David Agreement, 41
Camus, Albert, 324
Canada, 138, 143
Candide, 307
Capitalism, 200–201
Capitalist democracy, 204
Capitalist encirclement, 205, 237, 290
Cardenas, Lazaro, 179
Carneiro, Robert, 19
Carter, Jimmy, 278
Carthage, 46
Castro, Fidel, 176, 291
  Marxism-Leninism of, 176
  rise to power of, 194
  use of manipulative persuasion by, 318
Catholic Church, 90, 331
  medieval, 107
  in Nicaragua, 318
  and Polish nationalism, 76
  in Spain, 114
Caudillismo, 175
Cavour, Camillo de, 67
Censorship, 344
Central Committee, Soviet, 224–225
Central Intelligence Agency, 198, 291
Centralization, governmental, 145, 308–309, 339
Chancellor, German, 135
Charismatic authority, 35–36
Charles I, King, 35, 108, 336
Checks and balances, 132
Cheka, 197–198
Chernenko, Konstantin, 193
Chernobyl, 212
Chiang Kai-shek, 315
Chiefdoms, 19, 44
Chile, 43, 105, 116, 291
China, 35, 105, 118, 156, 166, 194, 250, 286
Chinese Revolution, 302, 315
  moderating of, 358

Christian Democrats, German, 138
Churchill, Winston, 130, 136, 150, 274, 362
City-state, 96, 110
Civil Constitution of the Clergy, 331
Civilization:
  emergence of, 20
  Indian, 71
  threat of power to, 363–369
  Western, 71
Civil War:
  English, 113, 336, 337
  Nigerian, 75
  Pakistani, 75–76
  Spanish, 114
  U.S., 111
Class conflict, 200
Class consciousness, 201
Clientelism, 170, 174
Coalitional tactics, totalitarian, 195–197
Coalition government, 140, 325–330
Coalitions, 39, 325–330
Coalitions, revolutionary, 317–318
Coercion, 6, 27–28
  and democracy, 150
  Mexican, 180
  in organizations, 41
  threat of, 86
  totalitarian, 197–199
Coercive capacity, loss of, 310–313
Cold War, 188, 255
Collective security, 264, 266
Collectivism, 208
Collectivization, Soviet, 206, 230, 342
College of generals, Brazilian, 176
Colombia, 132
Colonialism, 72–73, 169
Committee of Public Safety, 333
Communism, 54, 59, 202, 287
Communist Manifesto, 200, 338
Communist party:
  Czech, 112
  French, 42
  Iranian, 334
  of Philippines, 315–317
  Portuguese, 329
  self-protection of, 333
  Soviet, 208, 222–226, 234
Communist regimes, changes in, 239

Comparative politics, 10
Compulsory participation, 212
Concert of Europe, 263–264
Concurrent powers, 144
Confederacy, 143
Conflict among communities, 116–117
Conflict of interests, 13, 30
Congo crisis, 266
Congress, U.S., 4, 31, 133
Congress of Vienna, 263
Congress Party, 149
Conquest, 85
Consent as majority rule, 121
Consent of the governed, 109
Conservatism, 56, 59, 63
Conservative Party, 122, 124, 136–137
Conspiracy of Equals, 338
Conspiracy theory, 313
Constituent Assembly:
  in Portugal, 329–330
  in Russia, 196
Constitution:
  Canadian, 144
  effective, 118–120
  Soviet, 208
  U.S., 63, 143
Constitutional amending process, U.S., 122, 144
Constitutional democracy, 97
  types of, 131–145
  in Western Europe, 111
Constitutionalism, 97
Constitutionalism, British, 107–109, 119
Constitutionalist revolutionism, 337
Constructive vote of no-confidence, 135
Contextual standards of evaluation, 354
Cooperation, 39–42
Corruption, 366–367
Costa Rica, 132
Counterrevolution, 300
Coups d'état, 168, 173–174, 300, 335
Courts, 87
Crick, Bernard, 100
Crimean War, 251
Crisis management, 292
Cromwell, Oliver, 108
Cuba, 118, 176, 194, 231, 303, 370
  dependence of, 343
  revolution in, 318
Cuban missile crisis, 277, 292

Cultural reinforcement, governmental, 90
Cultural Revolution, Chinese, 28, 192
Czechoslovakia, 45, 238

Dahl, Robert, 5, 6, 111, 112, 117, 118, 146
Dahomey, Kingdom of, 34
Darkness at Noon, 27
Decision-making uncertainty, 255
Declaration of Human Rights, universal, 260
Declaration of Independence, 58, 109, 301, 337
Declaration of the Rights of Man and the Citizen, 66
Decoupling of conflicts, 292–293
Defense-heavy industry complex, Soviet, 237
Defensive modernization, Japanese, 161, 252
De Gaulle, Charles, 133–134
Democracy:
  and Aristotle, 96
  Athenian, 106–107
  criticisms of, 146–148
  development of, 106–111
  direct, 106–107
  economic, 146
  elements of, 118–126
  foreign policy problems of, 288
  Lenin's contempt for, 204
  need for, 364
  and peace, 368
  popularity of, 105–106
  preconditions for, 111–118
  problems of, 145–148, 365–367
  and property, 114–115
  strengths of, 148–151
Democratic capitalism, 56, 147
Democratic centralism, 223
Democratic Party, 33, 124, 137
Democratic socialism, 56, 62–63
Deng Xiao-ping, 358
Desertion, 49
De-Stalinization, 198, 207
Deterrence, nuclear, 282–283, 291–293, 369
Dictatorship, 98
Dictatorship of the proletariat, 201, 238
Diouf, Abdou, 172
Diplomacy, 85, 277–278
Dissidents, Soviet, 232
Divine right rule, 29, 34–35, 304
Division of labor, political, 120

Dominant class, 54, 200
Domination, 43–45, 195–215
Due process of law, 108
Dyadkin, Iosif, 230

Eanes, General Antonio Ramalho, 330
East Germany, 105
Eco, Umberto, 186
Economic coercion, 199
Economic development:
  African, 172
  and democracy, 115–116
Economic management, governmental, 88–90
Economic modernization, 163
Economic sanctions, 178
Economic statecraft, 278–279
Economic structure, 54
Economists, 11
Education, public, 90–91
Egypt, 30, 34, 41, 174, 300
Eisenstadt, S. N., 96
Elections, Soviet, 228–229
Electoral college:
  Brazilian, 177
  U.S., 122
Elimination, 45–48
  physical, 46, 175, 360–363
  political, 45
  of states, 286
  totalitarian, 229–232
Emergency power, French constitutional, 134
Empirical evidence, 9
Enabling Act, German, 37, 196
Engels, Friedrich, 200
Enlightenment, 309
Equality:
  in Declaration of Independence, 109
  economic, 338
Equilibrium, 283–284
Espionage, 60
Estates-General, 305
Estonia, 286
Ethics, 7
Ethiopia, 165–167, 250
Ethnic conflict, 117
Ethnic groups, 65, 141
Ethnonationalism, 74–76
European Economic Community, 330
Evolution:
  biological, 17–18
  cultural, 18–22
  political, 112–113

Executive, 85–86, 91
Extended republic, 110

Factions, 110, 145–146
Falklands war, 177, 280
Farm Bureau Federation, 42
Fascism, 56, 190, 194
February Revolution, 311, 313, 327
Federal Bureau of Investigation, 88
Federalism, 142–145
The Federalist, 16, 63, 110
Fichte, Johann Gottlieb, 72
"Final Solution," 197
First World War, 43, 47, 67
Floating voters, 137
Foote, Michael, 137
Force, 7, 20, 28
Forces of production, 200
Foreign debt, 177
France:
  constitution of, 133–134
  as nation state, 65
  political distrust in, 113
Franco, Francisco, 43, 99, 113, 178
Franco-Prussian War, 286
Frederick the Great, 72
Free Democratic party, 138
Freedom, democratic, 148–149
Freedom, revolutionary, 336
Freedom of association, 44
Free riders, 41
French Revolution, 111, 301, 302, 325, 326, 331–333, 337, 338
  background of, 305–309
  and nationalism, 66
French-speaking Canadians, 65
Friedrich, Carl J., 98, 188
Fundamental trust, 112
Fusion of powers, 134, 135

Gallup Poll, 9
Gandhi, Indira, 47, 116, 149
Gandhi, Mahatma, 68
Garfield, James, 47
General Assembly, UN, 266
General secretary, Soviet, 225
German Democratic Republic, 105
Germany, 32, 67, 282, 330
  federalism in, 142
  Federal Republic of, 138
  and nationalism, 72
  unification of, 67
Germ warfare, 32
Gestapo, 197

Ghana, 169, 171
Glasnost, 229
Glorious Revolution, 108
Goldwater, Barry, 137
Gorbachev, Mikhail, 193, 213, 229, 234, 236, 259
Governing, 6
Governing class, 44
Government, 6, 22
  basic functions of, 84–92
  defined, 7
  and Locke, 109
  origins of, 15
  private, 7
  public, 7
  types of, 95–101
Great Council, 108
Great Depression, 37, 38, 358
Great Leap Forward, 343
Great powers, 257–260
Greece, 43
Gromyko, Andrei, 258
Guatemala, 291
Guerilla movements, 317
Guinea, 73
Gulf of Tonkin, 276

Hagopian, Mark, 341
Hague conferences, 251, 264
Haile Selassie, 165
Haiti, 250
Hama, 175
Hammarskjold, Dag, 266
Hapsburg Empire, 66
Hart, Armando, 208
Hawaii, 28
Heath, Edward, 126
Hegemonic party, 178
Helsinki Accords, 282
Henry VIII, King, 30
Hierarchy, 40
Hindi, 117
Historical inevitability, 239, 287
Hitler, Adolph, 29, 32, 33, 37, 85, 91, 95, 100, 140, 197, 364
  and "honorary Aryans," 58
  ideological commitments of, 59, 63
  and mass killings, 47, 229–230
  rise to power of, 195–196
Hitler–Stalin pact, 286
Hobbes, Thomas, 5, 6, 15, 16, 155, 159–160, 247, 269, 368
Hollander, Paul, 236
Homo sapiens sapiens, 46
House of Commons, 42, 108, 110
  elections to, 136–137
House of Lords, 110

Human rights, 59
Human nature, 15
  and power-seeking, 160, 365–367
  revolutionary changes in, 339
Hungarian rebellion, 105
Hungary, 45, 156, 238
Hunger strikes, 126
Hunter-gatherer societies, 7, 18, 106
Hussein, Saddam, 285

Ibos, 75
Ideological coexistence, 290
Ideological combat, 60
Ideological incompatibility, 287
Ideological power elite, 233–234
Ideological monopoly, totalitarian, 199–215
Ideology:
  comprehensive, 62–64
  critical, 62–63
  and interests, 56, 58
  and legitimation, 59
  limited, 62–63
  Marx's concept of, 54–55, 57
  nature of, 54–56
  and objectivity, 61–62
  and orientation, 59–60
  paternalistic, 170
  as personal conviction, 57–58
  and political action, 55
  and science, 61
  supportive, 62–64
  total, 193
Imperialism, 290, 339–340
  Lenin's concept of, 204
Independence of states, 284
India, 116, 138, 286
  and Bangladesh, 75
  democracy in, 118
  federalism in, 142
  partition of, 116
  state of emergency in, 149
Individual rights, democratic, 122
Indoctrination, 22
  in education, 90
  Soviet, 209–215
Inducement, 6, 29–31, 42
  and interest groups, 125
  in Soviet Union, 227–228
Industrialism, 200
Influence, 6
Infrastructure, 89
Intellectuals, 304
  and German nationalism, 72

Intellectuals *(continued)*
  and revolution, 306–309, 314–315
Interdependence, 253, 282
Interest groups, 124–126
International Court of Justice, 261
International law, 38, 251, 260–263
International organization, 263–269
International politics, 11
Intervention, U.S., 258
Intolerance, revolutionary, 332
Iran, 35, 60, 90, 100, 168, 250, 285, 291
Iranian hostage case, 261
Iranian revolution, 305–306, 311, 327–329, 333–335
Iran–Iraq war, 285, 334
Iraq, 60, 285, 300
Irish Republican Army, 126
Islam, 90
Islamic clergy, 311
Islamic fundamentalism, 175
Islamic republic, 35, 60, 163, 327
Islamic Republic Party (IRP), 329, 334
Islamic socialists, 334
Israel, 30, 41, 139, 140, 254
Italian nationalism, 66–67
Ivan the Terrible, Tsar, 30
Ivory Coast, 156, 172

Jacobins, 326, 332, 333, 335, 337
Jamaica, 118, 138
James II, King, 108
Japan, 4, 161, 250
J-curve, 306
Jefferson, Thomas, 90–91, 124
Jews:
  and Israel, 75
  murder of, 230
John, King, 108
Johnson, Lyndon B., 137, 276
Jones, Jim, 28
Juan Carlos, King, 113
Judicial review, 119
Julius Caesar, 46

Kamenev, Lev, 41
Kedourie, Elie, 64, 72
Kennedy, John F., 47, 133, 277
Kenya, 169, 172, 173
Kenyatta, Jomo, 169–170, 173
KGB, 198, 225
Khmer Rouge, 47, 48, 231, 314–315, 356–357

Khomeini, Ayatollah Ruhollah, 35, 37, 62, 71, 100, 190, 309–311, 327, 334
Khrushchev, Nikita, 45, 192–193, 198, 207, 213
Kinnock, Neil, 137
Kleptocracy, 171–172, 367
Knorr, Klaus, 278, 279
Koestler, Arthur, 27
Kohak, E. V., 353
Komsomol, 211
Konrad, George, 221
Korean War, 32, 265

Laissez-faire capitalism, 368
Land reform, 333
Language rights, Belgian, 122
Latin America, 176
Latvia, 286
Law, 86
Law, due process of, 108
Law and order, 16, 87
Law of nature, Locke's, 109
Law of the sea treaty, 263
Leader, totalitarian, 191
Leaders, communist, 105
Leadership succession, 164
  Soviet, 192
League of Nations, 250, 252, 264, 278
Lebanese civil war, 253
Legislative branch, 91
Legitimacy, 33–35, 37, 181
  and ideology, 60
  Soviet, 236–237
  of Third World governments, 163
Legitimacy problems:
  of authoritarianism, 180–181
  in Eastern Europe, 235
  Soviet, 289
  of totalitarianism, 232–240
Lenin, V. I., 318, 324, 327, 360
  ideas of, 202–205
  as revolutionary, 314
  rise to power of, 196
  shrine of, 192
Lenski, Gerhard, 14
Lesser evil, 370
Levy, Jack, 257
Liberalism, 56, 59
Liberal Party, 124, 136, 140
Liberia, 250
Libertarianism, 63
Liberty, 109, 301
Libya, 261
Lidice, 46
Limited government, 301

Lincoln, Abraham, 47
Linz, Juan, 181
Literacy campaigns, 344
Lithuania, 286
Locke, John, 109–110, 121, 148, 353
Louis XVI, King, 35, 66, 305, 331
Louisiana Territory, 30
Luther, Martin, 16

Machiavelli, Niccolò, 25
Madison, James, 15, 16, 83, 110, 145–146
Mafia, 291
Magna Charta, 108
Majoritarian parliamentary systems, 134–138
Majority rule, 121–123
Malenkov, G. M., 192
Malvinas Islands, 177
Mao Zedong, 191–192, 342–343, 358
  and mass killings, 230
  as revolutionary strategist, 315
Marcos, Ferdinand, 316, 341
Marie Antoinette, Queen, 331
Marshall Plan, 258
Marx, Karl, 54–55, 57, 200–202, 314, 338, 358
Marxism, 17, 62, 338, 360
Marxism-Leninism, 56, 158, 199–205, 287, 358–360
  appeals of, 358
  in Cuba, 318
  in Ethiopia, 167
  intolerance of, 369
  and revolution, 313–319, 341
  and science, 232–233
  Soviet, 207–209
  and state sovereignty, 253
  in Third World, 363
Mary, Queen, 108
Mass media, 33, 212
Master Race, 47
Mazzini, Guiseppe, 66–67, 72, 314
McGovern, George, 137
McKinley, William, 47
Melos, 28–29, 38, 46
Mengistu Haile Mariam, 167, 364
Mensheviks, 196, 327
Merit system, 93
Mexican Revolution, 341
Mexican war, 45
Mexico, 90, 178–180, 189
Middle class, 96
Middle East, 75
Middle Kingdom, 251

Military aid, Soviet, 239
Military force, 85–160
Military-industrial complex, 288
Military power, 237, 279–283
Military rule, 59, 105, 160, 168
Military takeover, 85
Milosz, Czeslaw, 186
Mitterand, Francois, 134, 138
Mixed economy, 147
Mobutu Sese Seko, 171–172
Moderates, rule of, 325–330
Modernization, 161
Molotov, V. M., 85
Monarchy, 95, 165–168
Monarchy, Spanish, 113
Moore, Barrington, 344–345
Morality, international, 38
Moslem Brotherhood, 175
Multinational corporations, 262
Multinational peacekeeping forces, 268–269
Multiple sovereignty, 326
Multipolarity, 287
Musil, Robert, 52
Mussolini, Benito, 100
  on fascism, 63
  on totalitarianism, 187
Myrdal, Gunnar, 60
Myth of the metals, 356

Napoleon, Emperor Louis, 67, 113, 300
Napoleon Bonaparte, 45, 66, 85, 335, 339
Nation, 64–65
National Assembly, 134, 139
National Convention, 333, 335
National Health Service, British, 125
Nationalism, 56, 64–76, 193–194
  in Africa, 72–74
  and decolonization, 71
  flexibility of, 71
  Mexican, 180
  non-Western, 71
  and Polish Catholicism, 76
  and power, 71–74
  revolutionary, 309–310
  and ruling elites, 72–73
  Scottish and Welsh, 75
  Soviet, 211, 237
  spread of, 67–71
Nationalist ideology, 66–67
National liberation, 72
National Liberation Front (NLF), 197
National liberation movements, 310

National security, 254–256
National self-determination, 71
National Socialism, 190, 194
Nation-states, 248–249, 252
Native Americans, 46
NATO, 290, 292, 330
Nazis, 45, 112
Neanderthal man, 46
Needler, Martin, 180
Negative coalition, 331
Nepotism, 174
Netherlands, 135, 140
New Economic Policy, 206
New People's Army, 316, 341
New Program of the Communist Party, 207, 236
New Zealand, 138, 250
Nicaragua, 47, 169, 233, 318
Nicholas II, Tsar, 88, 311
Nietzsche, Friedrich, 57
Nigeria, 75, 105, 116
Nisbet, Robert, 99
Nixon, Richard, 43, 122, 291
Nkrumah, Kwame, 169, 171
Nobel Prize, 91
Nomenklatura, 226–228, 240, 288–291, 336, 360
Normative evaluation, 354
North Vietnam, 286
Nuclear deterrence, 282–283, 291–293, 369
Nuremberg trials, 38
Nyerere, Julius, 159

October Revolution, 313
Offices, 7
Oligarchy, 173
Olson, Mancur, 147
Opposition, parliamentary, 119
Organizational weapon, 318
Organization of American States, 318
Organizations, 40
Original sin, 15
Orridge, A. W., 71, 72
Ortega, Humberto, 233
Ortega y Gasset, José, 353
Orwell, George, 190
Ottoman Empire, 250–251

Pakistan, 75–76, 116, 286
Palestine Liberation Organization, 253
Papacy, 252–253
Paris Commune, 314
Park Chung Hee, 47
Parliament, British, 109, 119
Parliamentary dismissal, 135

Parliamentary governments, 134–141
Party activists, 137–138
Party cohesion, 133
Party Congress, Soviet, 223, 224
Party discipline, 133, 136
Party of Revolutionary Institutions (PRI), 178–180
Patriotism, 65
Patronage, 171
Peaceful coexistence, 60, 209
Pearl Harbor, 4
Peasants:
  in French Revolution, 332
  in revolutions, 336, 342–343
Peasant-support strategy, 315–317
The Peloponnesian War, 28
People's democracies, 228
People's Republic, 105
Persian Empire, 107
Persuasion, 6, 31–33
  indoctrinational, 32, 64
  and interest groups, 125
  manipulative, 32
  rational, 31–32
Petrograd, 310
Petrograd Soviet, 327
Philippines, 116, 314–317, 346
Phillips, Wendell, 313
Philosopher kings, 355–356
Philosophy, 57
Pipes, Richard, 289
Plato, 86, 107, 308, 354–357
Pluralism, socioeconomic, 114–115
Poland, 32, 45, 61, 85, 90
  martial law in, 87
  partition of, 286
  potential revolution in, 312–313
  security forces in, 198–199
Polis, 8, 96
Polish United Workers Party, 61
Politburo, 45, 207, 223, 225, 234
Political Action Committees, 125
Political activists, beliefs of, 117
Political apathy, 237
Political evaluation, 354
Political lag, 161–163
Politically caused deaths, 360–363
Political machines, U.S., 170
Political modernization, 163–164
Political participation, Third World, 162
Political parties, 164
  British, 136

Political parties *(continued)*
  democratic, 123–124
Political prisoners, Soviet, 87, 232
Political revolution, 301
Political rights, basic, 118–119
Political roles, 7
Political science, 9–12
Political theory, 10
Political threat hypothesis, 143–144
Political warfare, 291
Politics:
  defined, 4
  personal, 4, 5
  public, 4, 5, 6, 18
Polity, 96, 357
Portugal, 99
Portuguese Revolution, 329–330, 341, 346
Pot, Pol, 48, 95, 190, 231, 356–357, 364
Poverty, 161–162
Powell, G. Bingham, 84
Power, 8, 9, 17
  advantages of, 256–257
  in bureaucracies, 93–95
  concepts of, 5–6
  defined, 6
  elements of, 256
  as an end, 365
  and ideology, 55
  imbalances of, 22
  international, 275–277
  as means, 9
  motivation for, 17
  as nomenklatura interest, 227
  in political theory, 15
  and politics, 4
  pursuit of, 12–22
  strategies of competing for, 39–48
  types of, 27–39
Power elite, 156
Power-seeking, totalitarian, 195–197
Presidency:
  Mexican, 178
  of U.S., 31
Presidential government, 131–135
Presidential succession, Mexican, 178
The Prince, 26
Private plots, Soviet, 229
Progressive bias, 299–300
Proletariat, 200–201
Propaganda, 277

Property, Lockean view of, 109
Property rights, 301
Proportionality, 261
Proportional representation, 138–140
Protection, governmental, 20, 84–86
Provisional government, Russian, 196, 327
Prussia, 67, 257
Psychic pressure, 27
Psychology, 12
Public interest groups, 58
Public opinion polls, 9, 150
Public ownership, 179–180
Public works, 89
Punishment, 87
Puritans, 336

Quebec nationalism, 65, 75

Racial discrimination:
   in federal systems, 145
   and voting, 150
Radical revolutionary rule, 330–335
Randolph, John, of Roanoke, 104
Ranke, Leopold, 257
Rationalization, 57
Rationalization ideology, 55
Reagan, Ronald, 133, 138, 148, 261, 278
Reason, cult of, 331
Red Guards, Bolshevik, 333
Referendums, 120–121
Relations of production, 200
Relative deprivation, 303
Representation, democratic, 120
Representational parliamentary systems, 138–141
Repression, rationalized, 232
The Republic, 86, 355–356
Republican party, 58
Republicans, Jeffersonian, 124
Responsibility system, Chinese, 343, 358
Revisionism, Marxist-Leninist, 64
Revisionist states, 284
Revolution:
   causes of, 302–319
   consequences of, 336–346
   constitutionalist, 337
   and development, 341–346
   and education, 343–344
   Ethiopian, 167
   foreign assistance in, 318–319
   human costs of, 344–346

Revolution *(continued)*
   and living standards, 343
   Marxist, 201
   Mexican, 178
   in Philippines, 341
   political outcomes of, 339–341
   problems of defining, 299–302
   prospects for, 346
   right of, 109
   role of planning in, 313–319
   role of spontaneity in, 313
   sequences of, 325–336
   as social transformation, 337–339
   and totalitarianism, 341
Revolutionary activism, 314
Revolutionary Command Council, 174
Revolutionary guard, Iranian, 328
Revolutionary tribunal, 332
Revolutionary vanguards, 335–336
Ribbentrop, Joachim von, 85
Riker, William, 143–144
Robespierre, Maximilien, 333, 335
Roman Republic, 107
Romans, 46
Roosevelt, Franklin D., 150, 362
Rousseau, Jean-Jacques, 307–308
Rule of law, 96, 97
Ruling class, 344
   divisions in, 308
   Mexican, 180
   Soviet, 226
Ruling elite, 44
Rumania, 238
Rummel, R. J., 361–362, 368
Russell, Bertrand, 3, 5
Russia, 35
Russian Revolution, 302, 333
Russian Social Democratic Workers' Party, 202
Russo-Japanese War, 252, 310

Sadat, Anwar al-, 41, 47, 174, 175
Saint-Just, Louis de, 66
Sakharov, Andrei, 199
Sanctions, 5, 6, 27
Sandinistas, 47, 318
Sartori, Giovanni, 98
Satellite states, 45
Saudi Arabia, 99, 168
Savoy, 67
Scarcity, 13, 14, 30

Science:
   and Marxism-Leninism, 232–233
   in totalitarian ideology, 100
Second economy, Soviet, 229
Secretariat, Soviet, 223
Secularization, 304
Security Council, UN, 38, 265, 266, 268
Security dilemma, 255–256
Security police, 88
   Polish, 312
   totalitarian, 197–199
Segregation, racial, 61
Selective perception, 53
Self-centered power seeking, 16
Self-deception, 54, 56
Self-defensive power seeking, 14
Self-government:
   in America, 109
   national, 65
Self-help, 249–250, 261
Self-interest, 14, 15
   and ideas, 53
   in state of nature, 109
Self-preservation, 16
Self-protection, governmental, 87–88
Senate, U.S., 144
Senegal, 172
Senghor, Leopold Sedar, 172, 365
Separation of powers, 132
Shah of Iran, 62, 165, 309, 311
Shay's Rebellion, 143
Shostakovich, Dmitri, 206
Sihanouk, Prince Norodom, 317
Sinai desert, 30, 268–269
Single-member-district-plurality system, 122, 136
Slavery, 15, 58
Smith, Anthony D. S., 64
Social Darwinism, 368
Social Democratic Party:
   British, 136
   Germany, 202
Socialism in one country, 205
Socialist realism, 212–213
Socialist Worker's Party, Spanish, 114
Social programs, 89
Social revolution, 301, 338
Social Revolutionary Party, 196
Sociology, 12
Socrates, 107, 355
Solidarity, 61, 238, 312, 368
Solzhenitsyn, Alexander, 91, 99
Somoza, Anastasio, 47, 317, 318

Somoza family, 169
Sophists, 33
South Africa, 64, 87
South Korea, 181
South Vietnam, 197, 286
Sovereignty, 22, 249, 262, 269
Sovereignty, popular, 66
Soviet foreign policy, 237–239
Soviets, revolutionary, 196
Soviet Union, 32, 45, 90, 116, 189
Spain, 99, 113
Spanish Inquisition, 90
Spanish Republic, 43
Sparta, 28
Sphere of influence, 258
Spoils system, 31, 92
Sri Lanka, 116
Stalin, Joseph, 42, 85, 91, 100, 276, 290, 336, 340, 362, 364
  and mass killings, 47, 198, 230
  regime of, 205–207
Stalinism, Cuban, 232
State, 4, 5, 44
  defined, 19, 22
  end of, 136, 202
  expansion of, 250–252
  origins of, 19–22
Statecraft, 275
State of emergency, Indian, 116
State of nature, 109, 160
State of the whole people, 209
States, equality of, 249
State's rights, 145
State system, 250
Status quo states, 284
Sumeria, 43
Sunni Moslems, 174
Superpowers, 258, 287
Supreme Council of the Revolution, Portuguese, 329
Supreme Soviet, 225
Survey research, 9
Switzerland, 121, 141
Syria, 174, 300
Szelenyi, Ivan, 221

Taiwan, 156, 178, 189
Tanzania, 156, 159, 169
Tennyson, Alfred Lord, 247
Terror:
  in French Revolution, 345
  in Iranian revolution, 334
  in Philippines, 316
  in revolutions, 336
Terrorism, 47
Thailand, 250

Thatcher, Margaret, 126, 138, 148, 177
Thermidor, 335–336
Third Republic, French, 113
Third World, 158, 193, 262
  and ethnonationalism, 75–76
  nationalism in, 74
Thirty Years War, 249
Thucydides, 28
Tibet, 286
Tocqueville, Alexis de, 308–309
Tokugawa shogun, 30
Toleration, 42–43
  as balance of power, 183
  nonpolitical, 170
  political, 111–112
  in Soviet Union, 228–229
Tories, 124
Totalitarianism:
  causes of, 193–195
  controversy over, 188–190
  defined, 187
  as domination, 195–215
  features of, 188
  human costs of, 231
  institutionalized, 192–193
  mendacity of, 364–365
  numbers killed by, 362
  phases of, 191–193
  revolutionizing, 191–192
Toure, Sekou, 73
Tracy, Antoine Destutt de, 54
Trade-union consciousness, 202
Transformationist revolutionism, 337–339
Treaties, 260–261
Treaty of Paris, 251
Treaty of Westphalia, 249
Trotsky, Leon, 41, 205, 339
Truman, Harry S., 31, 133, 288
Tsarist regime, end of, 196
Turkey, 116
Tyranny, 96, 357, 364
Tyranny of majority, 106

Unalienable rights, 109
Unequal treaties, 262
Unitary government, 142
United front strategy, 317–318
United Nations, 38, 43, 265–269
United Nations Charter, 71, 266
Uniting for Peace resolution, 265
UN peacekeeping forces, 266–268
Uruguay, 116
U.S.–Soviet relations, 275–276,

U. S.-Soviet relations *(continued)*
  286, 287–293
Utopianism, 17, 367

Valladares, Armando, 370
Van den Berghe, Pierre, 56
Vanguard class, 336, 344
Vanguard party, Leninist, 204
Vanguard rule, 341
Venezuela, 117, 132
Veto power, 265
Vietnam War, 256, 276–277, 288
Voltaire (Francois-Marie Arouet), 307
Voslensky, Michael, 226–227, 290, 353
Voting, restrictions on, 110–111
Voting Rights Act of 1965, 58, 111

Walesa, Lech, 36
Waltz, Kenneth, 253, 256–257
Walzer, Michael, 335–336
War, 19, 280–281
  causes of, 285
  and revolutions, 304–305
  and Russian Revolution, 310–311
  and totalitarianism, 194
  and types of governments, 368
Warsaw Treaty Organization, 292
Washington, George, 124
Wave of the future, 237
Weber, Max, 4, 35, 37, 93, 367
Weimar Republic, 37, 43, 95, 135, 140, 196, 340
Whigs, 124
William of Orange, 108
Will to power, 57
Wilson, Woodrow, 71, 264
Women, voting rights for, 111
Wordsworth, William, 335
Worldview ideology, 55, 62–64
Wrong, Dennis, 6, 9

Yalta Agreement, 362
Yemen, Southern, 26
Young, Crawford, 74
Young Octobrists, 211
Young Pioneers, 211
Yugoslavia, 156

Zaire, 171–172
Zambia, 171
Zero sum conflict, 115
Zinoviev, Gregory, 41

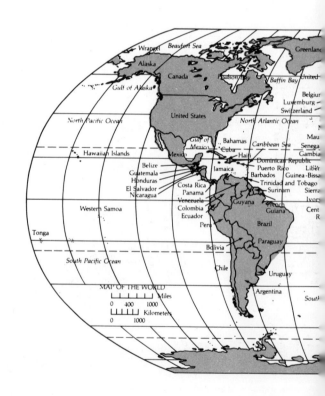